Lecture Notes in Computer Science   12312

More information about this series at http://www.springer.com/series/7407

Frederica Darema · Erik Blasch ·
Sai Ravela · Alex Aved (Eds.)

Dynamic Data Driven Applications Systems

Third International Conference, DDDAS 2020
Boston, MA, USA, October 2–4, 2020
Proceedings

 Springer

Editors
Frederica Darema 🆔
InfoSybiotic Systems Society
Bethesda, MD, USA

Erik Blasch 🆔
Air Force Office of Scientific Research
Arlington, VA, USA

Sai Ravela 🆔
Massachusetts Institute of Technology
Cambridge, MA, USA

Alex Aved 🆔
Air Force Research Laboratories
Rome, NY, USA

ISSN 0302-9743   ISSN 1611-3349 (electronic)
Lecture Notes in Computer Science
ISBN 978-3-030-61724-0   ISBN 978-3-030-61725-7 (eBook)
https://doi.org/10.1007/978-3-030-61725-7

LNCS Sublibrary: SL1 – Theoretical Computer Science and General Issues

This Springer imprint is published by the registered company Springer Nature Switzerland AG
The registered company address is: Gewerbestrasse 11, 6330 Cham, Switzerland

Preface

The Dynamic Data Driven Applications Systems (DDDAS 2020) conference showcases scientific research advances and technology capabilities stemming from the DDDAS paradigm, whereby instrumentation data are dynamically integrated into an executing application model, and in reverse, the executing model controls the instrumentation.

DDDAS/InfoSymbiotics[1] plays a key role in advancing capabilities in many application areas; driving innovation in a great many methodological areas ranging from *foundational methods* such as filtering, estimation, and uncertainty quantification to *applications approaches;* and coordinating system-level design, including representation models, network control, and sensor management. DDDAS incorporates comprehensive principle- and physics-based models, instrumentation (including sensing and actuation), planning and control methods, as well as theory involving models' convergence properties, uncertainty quantification, observation, and sampling. Over the last two decades, the DDDAS paradigm has shown the ability to engender new capabilities in aerospace, materials sciences, biosciences, geosciences and space sciences, resilient security, and cyber systems for critical infrastructures such as power-grids. The scope of application areas ranges from the nano-scale to the extra-terra-scale.

DDDAS permeates a great many areas: statistical estimation, machine learning, informative planning, decision support, network analysis, and big data. DDDAS also emphasizes foundational aspects in systems thinking with an overarching objective and the ability to judiciously structure, dynamically adapt, and optimally exploit resources. The DDDAS paradigm has influenced the extension of existing methods such as data assimilation and the digital twin, which have evolved to incorporate the adaptive aspects of DDDAS into their definitions. Other recent techniques such as generative adversarial networks (GANs) resemble the DDDAS paradigm by generating data from models and discriminating the information for enhanced system performance. For test and evaluation, DDDAS creates capabilities for lifetime assessment and optimization of the performance of components and systems. Also, a number of recent and emerging algorithms in machine learning, and other methods and approaches, such as informative sensing, informative estimation, informative planning, targeted observation, active learning, relevance feedback, recommender systems, stochastic modeling, reinforcement learning, and feature selection – applying and/or adopting the essence of the DDDAS paradigm, which includes high-dimensional simulation/modeling in order to facilitate data-driven exploitation and decision making dynamically, adaptively, and in real-time. Moreover, in addition to the homonymous DDDAS-based agencies sponsored initiatives and programs (which started in 2000), other initiatives such as

---

[1] InfoSymbiotic Systems or InfoSymbiotics are terms introduced to denote DDDAS.

cyber-physical systems (which started in 2006 by the embedded systems community) can benefit from the more comprehensive approaches of the DDDAS paradigm.

The DDDAS/InfoSymbiotics conference series is a forum that presents novel directions, reports innovative solutions, and documents advanced opportunities over a wide set of scientific and engineering application areas. A consequence of the growing interest, activities, and advances in DDDAS, the DDDAS2020 conference showcases 21 peer-reviewed plenary presentations, 14 peer-reviewed posters, 5 keynote presentations, and 3 panels from experts in academia, industry, and government sectors. The proceedings include the keynotes' overview papers, the panels' abstracts, and the accepted papers. All presentation slides are posted at the DDDAS website (www. 1dddas.org).

DDDAS 2020 follows from past DDDAS conferences and workshops, starting with the March 2000 National Science Foundation (NSF) DDDAS Workshop and subsequent DDDAS conferences, and DDDAS workshops in conjunction with conferences since 2003. Starting in 2018, efforts and results over the years are also discussed more extensively in a series of Springer handbooks on DDDAS.

We are thankful to all the contributors of this conference, including the keynote speakers and panelists, those who submitted abstracts and papers for their research work and authoring the papers included in these proceedings, and to the reviewers of the two-stage papers selection process.

August 2020   Frederica Darema
Erik Blasch
Alex Aved
Sai Ravela

The original version of the book was revised: The typo in the main title was corrected. The correction to the book is available at https://doi.org/10.1007/978-3-030-61725-7_44

Organization

General Chairs

Frederica Darena   SES Director; F/IEEE CS, USA
Erik Blasch   F/IEEE AESS, USA

Program Committee Chairs

Alex Aved   SM/IEEE, USA
Sai Ravela   Massachusetts Institute of Technology, USA

Program Committee

Robert Bohn	National Institute of Standards, USA
Newton Campbell	Science Applications International Corp., USA
Nurcin Celik	University of Miami, USA
Ewa Deelman	University of Southern California, USA
Salim Hariri	University of Arizona, USA
Thomas Henderson	The University of Utah, USA
Artem Korobenko	University of Calgary, Canada
Fotis Kopsaftopoulos	Rensselaer Polytechnic Institute, USA
Richard Linares	Massachusetts Institute of Technology, USA
Dimitri Metaxas	Rutgers University, USA
Jose Moreira	International Business Machines, USA
Chiwoo Park	Florida State University, USA
Sonia Sacks	Department of Energy, USA
Themistoklis Sapsis	Massachusetts Institute of Technology, USA
Amit Surana	UTRC/Raytheon, USA
Ludmilla Werbos	University of Memphis, USA

Contents

Keynotes

Predictive Digital Twins: Where Dynamic Data-Driven Learning Meets Physics-Based Modeling

Michael G. Kapteyn[1] and Karen E. Willcox[2]($\boxtimes$)

[1] Massachusetts Institute of Technology, Cambridge, MA 02139, USA
[2] University of Texas at Austin, Austin, TX 78712, USA
kwillcox@oden.utexas.edu

Abstract. A digital twin is an evolving virtual model that mirrors an individual physical asset throughout its lifecycle. An asset-specific model is a powerful tool to underpin intelligent automation and drive key decisions. The formulations and methods of dynamic data-driven application systems (DDDAS) have a key role to play in the tasks of inference, assimilation, prediction, control, and planning that enable the digital twin paradigm. Of particular importance is a tight feedback loop between models and data, which has long been a central concept in DDDAS. This keynote talk presents an approach to create, update, and deploy data-driven physics-based digital twins. We demonstrate the approach through the development of a structural digital twin for a custom-built unmanned aerial vehicle.

Keywords: Digital twin · DDDAS · Unmanned aerial vehicle

1 Key Elements of Our Mathematical Representation of a Digital Twin

A digital twin is an evolving virtual model that mirrors an individual physical asset throughout its lifecycle. An asset-specific model is a powerful tool to underpin intelligent automation and drive key decisions. The formulations and methods of dynamic data-driven application systems (DDDAS) have a key role to play in the tasks of inference, assimilation, prediction, control, and planning that enable the digital twin paradigm. Of particular importance is a tight feedback loop between models and data, which has long been a central concept in DDDAS. This keynote talk presents an approach to create, update, and deploy data-driven physics-based digital twins. We demonstrate the approach through the development of a structural digital twin for a custom-built unmanned aerial vehicle.

Key elements of our mathematical representation of a digital twin are:

State. We consider the evolution of the system over time. The physical asset refers to the physical component, system, or process for which we are providing decision support. We denote its state at time-step t by $S\_t \in S$, where S is the physical state

F. Darema et al. (Eds.): DDDAS 2020, LNCS 12312, pp. 3–7, 2020.
https://doi.org/10.1007/978-3-030-61725-7_1

space. In general, the asset state will be only partially and indirectly observable through observational data. The digital twin is a parametrized model or set of coupled models representing the physical asset, and evolving over time. The digital twin state comprises the parameters of these models, denoted at time-step t by $D\_t \in \mathcal{D}\_t$, where $\mathcal{D}\_t$ is the digital twin state space at time-step t. The digital twin state space may be adapted on the fly as new asset states are discovered or encountered. Due to model inadequacy, typically we have that $\mathcal{D}\_t \subset S$.

Observational data. The digital twin state is informed by observational data received from the physical asset. The observational data might include sensor data, physical inspection data, information from diagnostic or error reporting systems, etc. We also define a reference observation, generated using the digital twin to produce a prediction of the observational data.

Control. The control input defines actions that change the instantaneous state of the physical asset directly or change the operating conditions of the asset, thereby influencing the state evolution dynamics. Control inputs could also influence the observational data that is generated by an asset, either instantaneously (e.g., deciding to perform an inspection of the asset) or in the future (e.g., installing a new sensor). These control inputs could be issued autonomously by the digital twin or by a human operator. In the latter case, the role of the digital twin is to provide decision support. In this case the digital twin might still act as an interface to the physical asset, accepting a high-level directive from an operator and converting this into a valid control input before issuing it to the physical asset.

Reward. The reward quantifies preference of different states or trajectories of the asset-twin system, and could reflect a combination of performance, cost, uncertainty, tracking targets, etc.

With the state, observational data, control, and reward, we fully define the digital twin mathematical framework. However, the complexity of representing an entire physical asset remains a significant challenge. In particular, the physical asset state might require thousands or even millions of parameters to fully define it – parameters that will change during design, manufacture, and operation as the system is realized and then as it ages. Not only is the state of high dimension, it also embodies complex aspects of the asset across multiple spatial and temporal scales. Further, uncertainty plays a critical role in digital twin creation and decision-making. Uncertainty must be represented and tracked in all elements.

It thus remains a significant research challenge to translate this digital twin mathematical framework into robust, interpretable, scalable and efficient algorithms – algorithms that can handle the extreme high dimensionality and the level of complexity involved in building a digital twin of an entire aircraft. We do this by viewing the digital twin state through the lens of physics-based models. Physics-based models innately embed the concepts of time, space and causality. In doing so, they inherently define low-dimensional manifolds on which physical processes evolve, bringing structure to an otherwise intractable solution space of vast dimension.

Our use case builds a structural digital twin of an unmanned aerial vehicle (UAV). Monitoring the condition of critical engineering assets has for centuries been an important task for any engineering system whose condition changes over time due to environmental influences and/or operating wear and tear. Applications across land, sea, air, and space include vehicles (aircraft, engines, spacecraft, ships, etc.), civil infrastructure (bridges, buildings, railways, etc.), energy generation infrastructure (wind turbines, nuclear reactors, etc.), the nuclear stockpile, off-shore platforms, and many more. Historically, this monitoring has been manual, but the advent of pervasive in situ sensors and wireless communication technology enables DDDAS in all these applications—a new age of predictive maintenance, condition-based monitoring, and intelligent decision support, with the promise of saving money, time, and errors.

To illustrate our approach, we use the digital twin for dynamic in-flight decision-making to replan a safe mission in response to vehicle structural damage. The predictive digital twin is built from a library of component-based reduced-order models that are derived from high-fidelity finite element simulations of the vehicle in a range of pristine and damaged states. The digital twin is deployed and updated using interpretable machine learning. Specifically, we use optimal classification trees to train a scalable and interpretable data-driven classifier (Fig. 1). In operation, the classifier takes as input vehicle sensor data, and then infers which physics-based reduced models in the model library are the best candidates to compose an updated digital twin. Figure 2 shows snapshots of the approach at work, using strain measurements to dynamically update the estimate of the vehicle's structural health and then driving mission replanning.

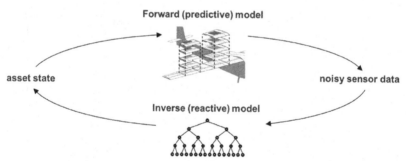

Fig. 1. We use a library of reduced-order models to generate training data to train an optimal classification tree. In operation, the classifier takes as input vehicle sensor data, and then infers which physics-based reduced models in the model library are the best candidates to compose an updated digital twin. The classifier also provides a foundation for adaptive sensing strategies.

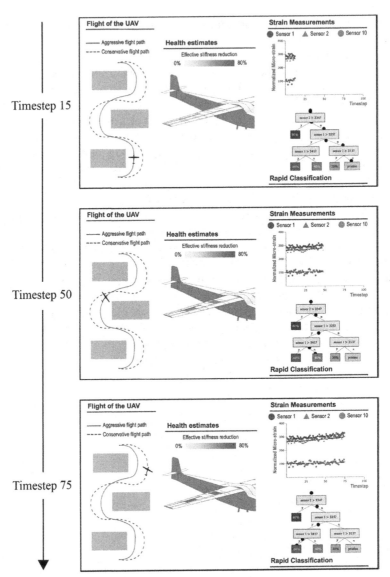

Fig. 2. In this scenario, the UAV undergoes damage to the wing and must dynamically replan its mission to take a less aggressive flight path (Kapteyn et al. 2020).

Acknowledgements. The authors gratefully acknowledge the support of AFOSR grant FA9550-16-1-0108 under the Dynamic Data Driven Application Systems Program and the SUTD-MIT International Design Center.

Reference

Kapteyn, M., Knezevic, D., Willcox, K.: Toward predictive digital twins via component-based reduced-order models and interpretable machine learning. In: Proceedings of 2020 AIAA SciTech Forum & Exhibition, Orlando, FL (2020)

Dynamic Data-Driven Application Systems for NASA's Science Mission Directorate

Michael S. Seablom$^{(\boxtimes)}$, Florence W. Tan, and Jacqueline J. LeMoigne

NASA Headquarters, Washington, DC 20546, USA
michael.s.seablom@nasa.gov

Abstract. NASA's Earth Science Technology Office (ESTO) is prioritizing a "New Observing Strategy" to help mitigate the risk, cost, size and development time of future Earth Science missions and their corresponding information systems and to increase the use of NASA's Earth Science data. The strategy consists of exploiting distributed spacecraft, constellations, and "sensor webs" to enable new observation measurements and information products. Although the overarching concept has been studied for nearly 20 years, the emergence of low-cost small spacecraft through commercial platforms and high quality, miniaturized science instruments makes possible domain-specific scientific investigations. When coupled with numerical prediction models, these types of spacecraft will enable new scientific investigations of phenomena that previously could not have been studied or would have been too expensive to study.

Keywords: Reference mission · Autonomous systems · Simulation

1 Introduction

In 2018, NASA's Science Mission Directorate (SMD) jointly hosted the Workshop on Autonomy for NASA Science Missions with Carnegie Mellon University to bring together scientists, NASA program managers, and experts in the field of autonomous systems. Its purpose was to increase awareness across NASA science disciplines of the growing capabilities of autonomous systems in industry and academia, and to stimulate thought on how these emerging technologies can contribute to more capable and more affordable science missions in the future. Eight teams were established to define design reference missions targeted for the period 2028–2033 for Astrophysics, Earth Science, Heliophysics, Mars, the Moon, Ocean Worlds, Small Bodies, and Venus. The teams were led by research experts in each area, and each team included a technologist in the field of autonomy. Following a two-day discussion, the teams presented their ideas for mission concepts that not only incorporated the current state-of-the-art in autonomy, but also attempted to anticipate the growth of such capabilities during the targeted period. With specific instructions for the participants to operate unconstrained from concerns over risk-averse management or limitations of budget, the teams were able to produce a set of fascinating mission concepts that could be delivered with realistic, concomitant

© Springer Nature Switzerland AG 2020
F. Darema et al. (Eds.): DDDAS 2020, LNCS 12312, pp. 8–11, 2020.
https://doi.org/10.1007/978-3-030-61725-7_2

technologies. For many of the design reference missions, key elements included the situational awareness, self-awareness, reasoning, and acting that can be delivered through coupled models and sensing systems, which is at the core of dynamic data-driven application systems (DDDAS). We will discuss some of these mission concepts and their relevance to NASA Science.

The suggested use of DDDAS for the Agency's science missions, however, predates the 2018 Autonomy Workshop. In 2002 NASA's Earth Science Technology Office (ESTO) convened a study [1] to identify key capabilities of an advanced Earth observation system that could significantly extend the skill of operational weather forecasts. The results of that study identified a uniquely-coupled "sensor web" observing system that would greatly enhance present-day Earth-observing capabilities of satellites, aircraft, and ground-based in situ observations. The sensor web was formally defined by ESTO to be "a coherent set of heterogeneous, loosely-coupled, distributed observing nodes interconnected by a communications fabric that can collectively behave as a single dynamically adaptive and reconfigurable observing system. Such an observing system would enable coordinated measurements from multiple vantage points and could be commanded either manually or through autonomous means, such as from a numerical model, allowing for adaptive targeting of rapidly evolving, transient, or variable meteorological features to improve the ability to monitor, understand, and predict their evolution. It would also enable measurements earmarked at critical regions of the atmosphere that are highly sensitive to data analysis errors, thus offering the potential for significant improvements in the predictive skill of numerical weather forecasts. ESTO recognized that implementation of an operational sensor web would not only involve technical cost and risk but also would require changes to the culture of how flight missions were designed and operated. For over a decade, ESTO funded a number of sensor web projects, including the development of a mission-planning simulator that would quantitatively assess the added value of coordinated observations. The simulator was designed to provide the capability to perform low-cost engineering and design trade studies using synthetic data generated by observing system simulation experiments (OSSEs). Another aspect of the investment strategy was to invest in prototype applications to implement key features of a sensor web, with the dual goals of developing a sensor web reference architecture as well as supporting useful science activities that would produce immediate benefit. The development of the simulator and the implementation of the prototypes both helped to build a foundation for the missions discussed at the Autonomy Workshop.

1.1 Sensor Web Simulator

The simulator was designed and built under ESTO funding from 2008–2010 and is described in detail by Talabac [1]. A hurricane use case was established to demonstrate the key functions of a sensor web that employed three future observing platforms: a tropospheric wind lidar, the operational GOES-R imager, and a next-generation ocean wind scatterometer (NGS). Adaptive targeting, necessary to collect data at specific regions of the atmosphere containing meteorological features of interest, was implemented by designing the spacecraft with the ability to repoint the wind lidar from its standard nadir position. The use case consisted of a two-week period with active tropical cyclone activity as depicted by an OSSE nature run. A vortex detection algorithm was applied to synthetic NGS data over regions in the Atlantic basin. An algorithm to compute surface vorticity was used to provide early detection of potential cyclogenesis, and a list of candidate targets within the NGS swath coverage area was created. The wind lidar was then tasked to target those regions, and the GOES-R imager was placed in rapid-scan "Mesoscale Imaging Mode" to produce high temporal resolution cloud motion vector winds (CMV) over the targets. The NGS data, winds from the lidar, and the CMV winds would then be assimilated to determine if an improved track forecast would result from the collection of the "best" possible data to capture development of a tropical cyclone. We will discuss the design of the simulator with its associated use case resulted in a number of lessons learned, including:

- In an operational mode, DDDAS implementations are limited by the ability of the initial guess and the predictability of the future state of the system. In this instance the hurricane intensity forecast was not very good, and resulted in undesirable feedbacks from subsequently poor data targeting.
- In a research mode, simulation of DDDAS implementations can help determine optimal observing strategies that can identify where more accurate predictions are needed.
- The diversity of the various applications (i.e., the very large software systems needed for prediction and data analysis, along with simulation of future instruments via OSSEs) increases the complexity of DDDAS and necessitates that each component be implemented as a separate service.

1.2 DDDAS Implemented for the Namibia Flood Pilot

A multi-phase ESTO investment that developed functional sensor web capabilities designed for direct societal benefit was the Sensor Web 3G (third generation of the architecture) led by Mandl [2]. The project developed a set of interconnected services to process data from Earth observing sensors and provide custom data products for science applications. The architecture consisted of interfaces compliant with Open Geospatial Consortium (OGC) standards, thereby providing scientists an easy-to-use environment to control ground and onboard sensors that allow creation, installation, and triggering of science processing algorithms seamlessly in order to process data in real time. The concept was implemented based on a flood disaster use case in which an algorithm was developed to identify floodwater extent based upon hyper-spectral imagery. The algorithm classified water in the imagery as either clear or murky, the latter assumed to be floodwater.

Following disastrous flooding in Namibia in 2009 the "Namibia Flood SensorWeb" project was established to integrate key remote sensing assets into a flood-monitoring, early warning decision support system. There were many lessons learned from the experiment, most notably the requirement for rapid turnaround of data products and the need for quality assurance during every step of the processing. We will discuss these and also how the project also demonstrated the value of customized data products, which were particularly useful for addressing the unique characteristics of Namibian flooding, as well as the successful implementation of sensor web capabilities for tasking satellite assets such as Earth Observing One (EO-1) and Radarsat to obtain timely delivery of hyper-spectral imagery and synthetic aperture radar data, respectively.

1.3 Ocean Worlds and DDDAS

Beyond the Earth, a key goal of SMD is to craft new missions to identify evidence of previous or extant life in other parts of our solar system. The discovery of evidence for large quantities of liquid water on several bodies in our solar system has led to "ocean worlds", or the icy moons of Jupiter and Saturn, becoming key astrobiology targets, for which many of our key science questions require in situ measurements both at the surface and in the liquid seas below. The challenges involved in implementing robotic subsurface missions on Ocean Worlds are immense, and advanced autonomy may be among the most demanding technology developments that will be required. Ocean Worlds present an environment that is uncertain, dynamic, and communication-constrained, which requires autonomy that is adaptive, reactive, and resilient. For example, the dynamic nature of plume ejecta on Enceladus or the harsh radiation of Europa prohibit human-in-the-loop control, especially during long-duration communication blackouts such as the two-week period during solar conjunction. Ocean World probes must be equipped to learn from their interactions with the environment, react to imminent hazards, and make real-time decisions to respond to anomalies. We will discuss one element of this mission concept, the Crevasse Explorer, which is designed to examine the plume material on the surface. Exploring crevasses and the nearby surfaces creates many challenges including resisting plume forces, dealing with the phase change of water, water vapor occluded imaging, constrained dynamic environments, liquid mobility, and others. The operations and scientific discovery will require deep autonomous capabilities to work in this environment.

Acknowledgments. The contribution of the Ocean Worlds design reference mission was made possible by the contributions of Rebecca Castano, Tom Cwik, and Bill McKinnon of the NASA Jet Propulsion Laboratory; by William Diamond and Pablo Sobron of the SETI Institute; by David Wettergreen of Carnegie Mellon University, David Smyth of Honeybee Robotics, Geranimo Vaillanueva of the NASA Goddard Space Flight Center, and Jonathan Weinberg of Ball Aerospace. The full text of this mission concept is available at https://science.nasa.gov under "Autonomy Workshop".

References

1. Talabac, S.J., et al.: End-to-end design and objective evaluation of sensor web modeling and data assimilation system architectures: phase II. In: Proceedings of the Earth Science Technology Forum. NASA's Earth Science Endeavors, Arlington (2010)
2. Mandl, D., et al.: Use of the earth observing one (EO-1) satellite for the Namibia sensorweb flood early warning pilot. IEEE J. Sel. Top. Appl. Earth Obs. Remote Sens. **6**(2), 298–308 (2013)

Revisiting the Top Ten Ways that DDDAS Can Save the World with an Update in the BioInfoSciences Area and on the Energy Bridge

Shiyan Wang(iD) and Sangtae Kim$^{(\boxtimes)}$(iD)

Davidson School of Chemical Engineering, Purdue University, West Lafayette, IN 47907, USA
kim55@purdue.edu

Abstract. Three years ago (DDDAS at the 2017 ASME Meeting) we looked at the speaker's top ten list of how DDDAS can save the world. Now as we adjust to life under the COVID-19 pandemic and a 2020 Conference in the virtual format, our world literally seeks rescue/saving. Under these circumstances, we revisit the top ten list and first consider briefly the dynamic data-driven aspects of the COVID-19 challenges from the speaker's experiences in the biotech/pharma industry and then move on to the more optimistic challenge of securing our energy future and life after the pandemic.

1 Introduction

In the 2014 and 2017 DDDAS conferences, the speaker (corresponding author) presented a top ten list of ways that DDDAS can save the world, and the list included biomedical and energy related themes. The biomedical themes are certainly timely given the current priority of overcoming COVID-19 and merit a few brief remarks in a presentation that is primarily focused on the energy land- scape. The challenge of suppressing transmission of a highly infectious virus and avoiding severe economic disruptions lies at the intersection of science and governmental policies. The dynamic stream of health data from an array of sources with associated uncertainties presents itself as a classic DDDAS problem for optimization of societal outcomes – overcoming the pandemic with minimal economic damage.

The main theme of the presentation is the remarkable transformation of the oil and gas (O&G) energy sector thanks to the shale revolution [1]. We consider the classical division of this sector as upstream, midstream and downstream segments and the past, present and future of DDDAS for each of these segments.

The applications of DDDAS in O&G have been regarded as one of the strategies to help advance the industry for the future energy. The concepts for Dynamic Data Driven Applications Systems (DDDAS) have developed for more than two decades starting with an initial NSF workshop in 2000 that brought together researchers in many disciplines [2]. The initial workshop aimed to instantiate systems-level opportunities by employing the power of modeling and hardware advances [2, 3].

© Springer Nature Switzerland AG 2020
F. Darema et al. (Eds.): DDDAS 2020, LNCS 12312, pp. 12–17, 2020.
https://doi.org/10.1007/978-3-030-61725-7_3

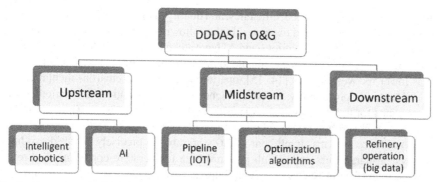

Fig. 1. Examples of DDDAS in all processes of O&G: upstream – well drilling (robotic solutions and artificial intelligence); midstream – pipeline transportation (internet of things framework) and optimization techniques for the pipeline managements; and downstream – refinery operations using big data.

The early development of DDDAS in O&G has shown progress and applications in oil exploration [4] and oilfield reservoir management [5–7]. For in- stance, the DDDAS were applied to oil well placement [8], where the dynamic data-driven steering of the reservoir optimization processes determined optimal well placement and config- uration. Additionally, the developed DDDAS-based detection and simulation system has improved oil spill simulation and provided decision-making information and tech- nical support for the remote sensing of the oil spills [9, 10]. For another application in the midstream process, DDDAS has integrated trajectory prediction and accelerated microscopic traffic simulation for monitoring transportation systems [11]. Therefore, the successful implementation of DDDAS depends on other hardware and software tech- nologies such as remote sensors and advanced algorithms (e.g. reservoir simulation [12] and optimization methods).

This extended abstract briefly discusses the current applications of DDDAS in the petroleum industry (scheme in Fig. 1). Note that this proceeding, by no means, covers all aspects of DDDAS in O&G industry, where we only show- case the existing practices combining with emerging technologies: upstream – well drilling (intelligent robotics and artificial intelligence); midstream – pipeline transportation (internet of things frame- work) and optimization techniques for the pipeline managements; and downstream – refinery operations (big data). Finally, we conclude to discuss the future directions towards the DDDAS in the O&G industry.

2 DDDAS Applications in Upstream, Midstream and Downstream

2.1 Upstream

Due to the huge daily expenses, oil well drilling is considered to be one of the most expensive operations in the exploration value chain [13]. Current intelligent drilling technologies are composed of many high-tech systems associated with DDDAS, such as intelligent robots, artificial intelligence (AI) and more. Incorporation of intelligent drilling aims to achieve the speed, efficiency, and quality of drilling while simultaneously reducing drilling accidents and expenses. In the following, we would like to summarize how technologies of robotic solutions and AI have advanced the well drilling operations.

First of all, robotic solution can handle increasing challenges for the O&G industry, such as lower recovery factors [14, 15], operations in extreme environ- mental conditions and business profitability. Robotics blend with new technical innovations especially designed for the industry such as intelligent drilling rigs and smart inspection. For instance, down-hole robots consist of miniature parts assemblies including sensors, actuator and guidance systems. Intelligent robot- s are able to precisely detect down-hole petro-physical parameters under high pressure high temperature conditions and relay them back to surface in real time, which helps determine the quality and quantity of hydrocarbons in the reservoir [16].

Secondly, the oil well drilling can be optimized by the application of AI with complex, non-linear and uncertain control parameters [13, 17]. In recent years, the development and upgrade of precise generic models and efficient data processing methods to prescribe a near-accurate impression of drilling operations when direct and real-time data are unavailable. Artificial intelligent tools are employed for the ease of operations and reduction of unnecessary expenses from selecting drill bit type all the way to the mapping of well trajectories [17].

2.2 Midstream

The midstream sector involves the transportation and storage of crude oil/refined petroleum-based products using pipelines, trucks and tanks [18]. Most of energy projects rely on pipelines because they can safely and efficiently transport the nation's energy products. Therefore, the development of the intelligent operations (e.g. internet of things - IOT) associated with DDDAS largely focuses on the pipeline system [19–21]. In this section, we first focus the pipeline technology developments with respect to the IOT modules. Next, a discussion of the current optimization methods for pipeline with configuration constraints.

An integrated IoT framework for an oil pipeline transportation system applies online monitoring and control to the entire oil pipeline transport system from the inlet to the delivery station [22, 23]. A smart IoT module collects pressure and flow rate data during oil transportation through pipelines by remote control [22]. It collects suitable real-time field data from oil stations and then the data are transmitted to both the cloud and field supervision center. Based on the analysis of received data, a feedback signal will control the valve to regulate both pressure and flow rate for any abnormality during oil transportation. The IoT framework also aims to detect or diagnose any catastrophic failure because of cracks, leakage, and/or blockage during the whole oil field transport system through the IoT module [22].

In addition to the IOT solutions in pipeline systems, there are necessary optimization methods during the pipeline planning activities. Optimization techniques are the tools that assist decision making and pipeline implementation [24]. For the midstream pipeline management, Nygreen and Haugen have surveyed the mathematical programming models in Norwegian petroleum field [25]. Bohannon [26] proposed a linear programming model for optimum drilling and facility expansion schedules for multi-reservoir pipeline systems. In another example, Neiro and Pinto [27] developed a complex multi-period mixed-integer-non-linear programming model for petroleum supply chain, including nodes representing refineries, terminals, and pipeline networks. Together, the extension of these methods can address more complex, highly dimensional pipeline problems in the near future.

2.3 Downstream

For the downstream of the refinery, we discuss the big data analytics applied in optimizing processes for maintaining the efficient energy consumption. For the refinery of the shale deposits, we will discuss recent efforts (i.e. CISTAR (NSF- ERC)) on bridging the transition to a sustainable energy future with fuels and chemicals from the stranded light hydrocarbons in shale O&G.

The big data analytics have a significant place in the petroleum downstream industry. Big data can be useful in prognostic foresight for the various areas of the refineries such as maintenance & repair, operations, finance, and life cycle management [28]. Prognostic analytics help refineries in short-term and long-term scheduling of maintenance and repairs along with staff planning and allocations. Additionally, within life cycle management, big data covers the remaining useful life which includes optimal exploitation and replacement [28].

For the supply chain from the shale deposits to the refinery [1], there is a significant technological gap in our current ability to efficiently and responsibly upgrade light hydrocarbon (LHC) reserves to chemicals and fuels, especially at the small scale typical of many shale O&G production sites. We note a recent transformative engineered system (i.e. CISTAR) which plans to convert LHC from shale resources to liquid chemicals and transportation fuels through smaller, modular, local, and highly networked processing plants [29]. This technology along DDDAS can be accomplished through new coupled reactions and separation processes that are both efficient and flexible [30, 31].

3 Conclusion

This extended abstract briefly discussed the current applications of DDDAS within the O&G industry. In today's petroleum industry, companies and corporations are looking for strategies of maximum operation efficiency and asset protection. The applications of DDDAS have offered significant opportunities in all processes of the petroleum industry. In the upstream sector, the intelligent robotics facilitate the well drilling. In the midstream, both IOT and optimization algorithms have been applied to the pipelines. Finally, the downstream applies big data to optimize the processes of refineries; for the shale O&G, the recent initiative (CISTAR) applies the DDDAS to the small modular/distributed units to efficiently upgrade the light hydrocarbon feedstock to more profitable products. The future applications of DDDAS in the O&G industry could gain traction by focusing on the operation efficiency, the environmental carbon footprint and many other practices.

Acknowledgement. We thank the CISTAR NSF-ERC team and Director Fabio Ribeiro for insightful discussions on the downstream shale revolution. We also thank Nathan Schultheiss for extensive discussions on the current state of the upstream and midstream O&G; this extended abstract is a summary version of a longer DDDAS O&G chapter.

References

1. Mason, C.F., Muehlenbachs, L.A., Olmstead, S.M.: The economics of shale gas development. Ann. Rev. Resour. Econ. **7**(1), 269–289 (2015)
2. Blasch, E., Ravela, S., Aved, A.: Handbook of Dynamic Data Driven Applications Systems. Springer, Cham (2018). https://doi.org/10.1007/978-3-319-95504-9
3. Darema, F.: New software architecture for complex applications development and runtime support. Int. J. High-Perform. Comput. (Special Issue on Programming Environments, Clusters, and Computational Grids for Scientific Computing) **14** (2000)
4. Smith, P.J.: Clean and secure energy from domestic oil shale and oil sands resources-quarterly progress report July 2011 to September 2011
5. Parashar, M., et al.: Application of grid-enabled technologies for solving optimization problems in data-driven reservoir studies. In: Bubak, M., van Albada, G.D., Sloot, P.M.A., Dongarra, J. (eds.) ICCS 2004. LNCS, vol. 3038, pp. 805–812. Springer, Heidelberg (2004). https://doi.org/10.1007/978-3-540-24688-6_104
6. Oden, J.T., et al.: Revolutionizing engineering science through simulation: A report of the national science foundation blue ribbon panel on simulation-based engineering science. National Science Foundation, Arlington, VA (2006)
7. Douglas, C.C.: An open framework for dynamic big-data-driven application systems (DDDAS) development. Proc. Comput. Sci. **29**, 1246–1255 (2014)
8. Parashar, M., et al.: Towards dynamic data-driven optimization of oil well placement. In: Sunderam, V.S., van Albada, G.D., Sloot, P.M.A., Dongarra, J.J. (eds.) ICCS 2005. LNCS, vol. 3515, pp. 656–663. Springer, Heidelberg (2005). https://doi.org/10.1007/11428848_85
9. Yan, J., Wang, L., Chen, L., Zhao, L., Huang, B.: A dynamic remote sensing data-driven approach for oil spill simulation in the sea. Remote Sens. **7**(6), 7105–7125 (2015)
10. Chen, X., Zhang, D., Wang, Y., Wang, L., Zomaya, A., Hu, S.: Offshore oil spill monitoring and detection: improving risk management for offshore petroleum cyber-physical systems. In: 2017 IEEE/ACM International Conference on Computer-Aided Design (ICCAD), pp. 841–846. IEEE (2017)
11. Pecher, P.K.: A DDDAS framework for managing online transportation systems. Ph.D. thesis, Georgia Institute of Technology (2018)
12. Wang, S., Ellett, K.M., Ardekani, A.M.: Assessing the utility of high-level CO2 storage and utilization resource estimates for CCS system modelling. Energy Proc. **114**, 4658–4665 (2017)
13. Bello, O., et al.: Application of artificial intelligence techniques in drilling system design and operations: a state of the art review and future research pathways. In: SPE Nigeria Annual International Conference and Exhibition. Society of Petroleum Engineers (2016)
14. Sandrea, I., Sandrea, R.: Recovery factors leave vast target for EOR technologies. Oil Gas J. **105**(41), 44–48 (2007)
15. Muggeridge, A., et al.: Recovery rates, enhanced oil recovery and technological limits. Philos. Trans. Roy. Soc. A: Math. Phy. Eng. Sci. **372**(2006), 20120320 (2014)
16. Shukla, A., Karki, H.: Application of robotics in offshore oil and gas industry a review part II. Robot. Auton. Syst. **75**, 508–524 (2016)
17. Agwu, O.E., Akpabio, J.U., Alabi, S.B., Dosunmu, A.: Artificial intelligence techniques and their applications in drilling fluid engineering: a review. J. Pet. Sci. Eng. **167**, 300–315 (2018)

18. Khan, W.Z., Aalsalem, M.Y., Khan, M.K., Hossain, Md.S., Atiquzzaman, M.: A reliable internet of things based architecture for oil and gas industry. In: 2017 19th International Conference on Advanced Communication Technology (ICACT), pp. 705–710. IEEE (2017)

19. Douglas, C.C., et al.: Advantages of multiscale detection of defective pills during manufacturing. In: Zhang, W., Chen, Z., Douglas, C.C., Tong, W. (eds.) HPCA 2009. LNCS, vol. 5938, pp. 8–16. Springer, Heidelberg (2010). https://doi.org/10.1007/978-3-642-11842-5_2

20. Li, C.-S., Darema, F., Chang, V.: Distributed behavior model orchestration in cognitive internet of things solution. Enterp. Inf. Syst. 12(4), 414–434 (2018)

21. Hu, X.: Dynamic data-driven simulation: connecting real-time data with simulation. In: Yilmaz, L. (ed.) Concepts and Methodologies for Modeling and Simulation. SFMA, pp. 67–84. Springer, Cham (2015). https://doi.org/10.1007/978-3-319-15096-3_4

22. Priyanka, E.B., Maheswari, C., Thangavel, S.: A smart-integrated IoT module for intelligent transportation in oil industry. Int. J. Numer. Model.: Electron. Netw. Devices Fields

23. Bonomi, F., Milito, R., Natarajan, P., Zhu, J.: Fog computing: a platform for internet of things and analytics. In: Bessis, N., Dobre, C. (eds.) Big Data and Internet of Things: A Roadmap for Smart Environments. SCI, vol. 546, pp. 169–186. Springer, Cham (2014). https://doi.org/10.1007/978-3-319-05029-4_7

24. Goldberg, D.E., Kuo, C.H.: Genetic algorithms in pipeline optimization. J. Comput. Civ. Eng. 1(2), 128–141 (1987)

25. Nygreen, B., Haugen, K.: Applied mathematical programming in norwegian petroleum field and pipeline development: some highlights from the last 30 years. In: Bjørndal, E., Bjørndal, M., Pardalos, P., Rönnqvist, M. (eds.) Energy, Natural Resources and Environmental Economics. ENERGY, pp. 59–69 (2010). Springer, Heidelberg. https://doi.org/10.1007/978-3-642-12067-1_4

26. Bohannon, J.M., et al.: A linear programming model for optimum development of multireservoir pipeline systems. J. Pet. Technol. 22(11), 1–429 (1970)

27. Neiro, S.M., Pinto, J.M.: A general modeling framework for the operational planning of petroleum supply chains. Comput. Chem. Eng. 28(6–7), 871–896 (2004)

28. Patel, H., Prajapati, D., Mahida, D., Shah, M.: Transforming petroleum downstream sector through big data: a holistic review. J. Pet. Explor. Prod. Technol. 10, 2601–2611 (2020). https://doi.org/10.1007/s13202-020-00889-2

29. Ramapriya, G.M., Tawarmalani, M., Agrawal, R.: Thermal coupling links to liquid-only transfer streams: an enumeration method for new FTC dividing wall columns. AIChE J. 62(4), 1200–1211 (2016)

30. Di Iorio, J.R., et al.: The dynamic nature of brønsted acid sites in cu–zeolites during no x selective catalytic reduction: quantification by gas-phase ammonia titration. Top. Catal. 58(7–9), 424–434 (2015). https://doi.org/10.1007/s11244-015-0387-8

31. Childers, D.J., Schweitzer, N.M., Shahari, S.M.K., Rioux, R.M., Miller, J.T., Meyer, R.J.: Modifying structure-sensitive reactions by addition of Zn to Pd. J. Catal. 318, 75–84 (2014)

Using Dynamic Data Driven Cyberinfrastructure for Next Generation Disaster Intelligence

Ilkay Altintas[1,2(✉)]

[1] San Diego Supercomputer Center, University of California, San Diego, La Jolla, CA, USA
ialtintas@ucsd.edu
[2] Halicioglu Data Science Institute, University of California, San Diego, La Jolla, CA, USA

Abstract. Wildland fires and related hazards are increasing globally. A common observation across these large events is that fire behavior is changing to be more destructive, making applied fire research more important and time critical. Significant improvements towards modeling of the extent and dynamics of evolving plethora of fire related environmental hazards, and their socio-economic and human impacts can be made through intelligent integration of modern data and computing technologies with techniques for data management, machine learning and fire modeling. However, there are still challenges and opportunities in integration of the scientific discoveries and data-driven methods for hazards with the advances in technology and computing in a way that provides and enables different modalities of sensing and computing. The WIFIRE cyberinfrastructure took the first steps to tackle this problem with a goal to create an integrated system, data and visualization services, and workflows for wildfire monitoring, simulation, and response. Today, WIFIRE provides an end-to-end management infrastructure from the data sensing and collection to artificial intelligence and modeling efforts using a continuum of computing methods that integrate edge, cloud, and high-performance computing. Through this cyberinfrastructure, the WIFIRE project provides data driven knowledge for a wide range of public and private sector users enabling scientific, municipal, and educational use. This paper (based on the keynote by the author) reviews some of our recent work on building this dynamic data driven cyberinfrastructure and impactful application solution architectures that showcase integration of a variety of existing technologies and collaborative expertise.

Keywords: Dynamic data-driven workflows · Wildfire modeling · Artificial intelligence · Knowledge management · Geospatial · Disaster management

1 Systems for AI-Integrated Dynamic Data-Driven Applications

From IoT to extreme scale computing connected by software defined networking, the data and computing ecosystem has never had more potential for real-time integration of AI with applications that can be steered using data. These data-driven applications include

© Springer Nature Switzerland AG 2020
F. Darema et al. (Eds.): DDDAS 2020, LNCS 12312, pp. 18–21, 2020.
https://doi.org/10.1007/978-3-030-61725-7_4

observations and social media data driven environmental and societal applications as well as closed loop simulations in many areas of science including material science, climate, high-energy, physics and chemistry. Although there are commonalities between these applications, most examples in this domain are built as a specialized integrated application involving many expertise driven components for data management, data analysis, machine learning, simulation, computing and workflow management. While some steps of such applications still require high capacity computing and data, the steps that depend on responsiveness to data, e.g., for data preparation and artificial intelligence (AI), often need to run on demand or continuously on specialized chips including GPUs, TPUs and FPGAs running in cloud or edge platforms. In addition, the growing data volumes from a variety of sources with various speeds and privacy requirements make it difficult or at times impossible to transport and integrated data centrally. Such specialized nature of these different steps due to challenges of portability, latency, privacy, data locality and performance optimization resulted in the need for new methods and research for dynamic data-driven application (DDDA) integration in the digital continuum.

Many research challenges and opportunities exist for collaborative team science, workflow composition and data management to realize the vision of streamlined, scalable, repeatable, responsible and explainable integration of AI in DDDA applications. These challenges and opportunities include intelligent infrastructure and systems with capabilities to enable dynamic scheduling and resource optimization, composable services that can run on intelligent systems, and automated workflow management software that can compose and steer dynamic applications that can adapt to changing conditions in a data-driven fashion while integrating many tools to explore, analyze and utilize data. This paper focuses on an example AI-integrated wildland fire application, describes some of the new systems that enabled these applications, and overviews a dynamic data driven workflow for AI-integrated fire modeling ensembles.

2 WIFIRE: Composable AI-Integrated Services for Dynamic Data Driven Workflows at the Digital Continuum

Wildfires hazards are growing due a number of factors. Modeling the dynamic and extent of the wildfire hazards is more important than ever with applications in wildfire mitigation, preparedness, response and recovery. Due to the changing behavior of wildfires, understanding the dynamics of the behavior of a fire while it is happening is an important area and a DDDA using real-time data. Cataloging, curating, sharing and discovering data and optimizing the integration of data sets for application-optimized modeling tools are potentially the biggest enablers for further progress in data-driven wildland fire science. A Moore Foundation Community Workshop in April 2019 [1] identified "a shared, integrated platform for diverse sources of data, intelligence and information" as the top requirement for a "Fire Immediate Response System". The NSF-funded WIFIRE project [2] (wifire.ucsd.edu) took the first steps to tackle this problem, successfully creating an integrated workflow-driven system for wildfire monitoring, simulation, and response. Today, WIFIRE provides an end-to-end management cyberinfrastructure (CI) with integrated data collection, knowledge management and modeling to enable scientific, municipal and educational use in partnerships with data providers, science communities, fire practitioners and government organizations to solve problems in wildland fire.

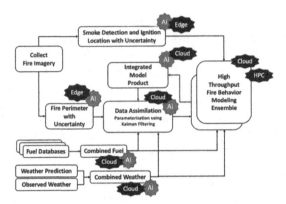

Fig. 1. A WIFIRE workflow for AI-integrated fire modeling in the digital continuum.

One of the important research directions for WIFIRE is dynamic data-driven fire modeling using real-time big data [3]. Fire modeling requires integration of data related to weather and landscape including topography and fuel characteristics. Depending on the fire modeling approach (empirical vs. physics-based), the data can come from field and remote observations, predictive models of weather and fuel, and operational systems providing a real-time view of the progression of an ongoing fire. When combined, these data sources enable learning about the dynamics of a fire incident and ability to adjust fire models based on these event-specific dynamics. WIFIRE's workflows [3–5] combine AI and other geospatial data management methods together with fire modeling ensembles in a real-time closed-loop fashion. The composed data services and the results of these workflows are made available to communities of used through a mapping platform called Firemap [6] (firemap.sdsc.edu).

Figure 1 shows a conceptual version of this workflow bringing together AI methods (e.g., [7]) to curate and prepare environmental data for fire modeling using a variety of modeling methods. The data include fire imagery (overhead aircraft and drones, ground-based cameras and satellites), fuel (at various resolutions) and weather (weather stations and model products). The steps indicated as AI convert data into insight with uncertainty that can then be used for model parameterization and adjustments using data assimilation techniques [3, 4]. The workflow represented in Fig. 1 is also a typical example where edge, cloud and high-performance supercomputing capabilities come together in an integrated AI-driven fire behavior modeling ensemble. Typically, the computing for the smoke and perimeter generation takes place in an environment built for big data and/or edge computing while the fire modeling and AI training needs to take place in a high-throughput or high-performance environment depending on the fire modeling codes that need to be executed. Currently, WIFIRE uses a combination of on-prem, edge (e.g., SAGE and CHASE-CI), cloud (e.g., Chameleon and AWS) and HPC (e.g., Comet and Expanse) environments. Figure 1 depicts this integrated workflow and various steps in relation to the type of underlying execution infrastructure required to run these applications.

3 Conclusions

The WIFIRE Cyberinfrastructure and associated AI, computing and data services demonstrate the possibility of generalized CI for closed-loop DDDA workflows. Although there are challenges is middleware, the evolving ecosystem of software and hardware environments enable intelligent integration of solutions in this area as well as smart resource optimization using AI.

Acknowledgements. The author thanks to and acknowledges the NSF grants (#1331615 for WIFIRE, #1730158 for CHASE-CI, #1935984 for SAGE AI on the Edge, #1928224 for Expanse), the WIFIRE team, and the support of various WIFIRE partners.

References

1. Fire Immediate Response System Workshop Report. Moore Foundation (2019). https://www.moore.org/docs/default-source/default-document-library/2019-firs-workshop-report.pdf
2. Altintas, I., et al.: Towards an integrated cyberinfrastructure for scalable data-driven monitoring, dynamic prediction and resilience of wildfires. In: Proceedings of the International Conference on Computational Science, ICCS 2015, pp. 1633–1642 (2015)
3. Srivas, T., de Callafon, R.A., Crawl, D., Altintas, I.: Data assimilation of wildfires with fuel adjustment factors in farsite using ensemble Kalman filtering. Proc. Comput. Sci. **108**, 1572–1581 (2017). International Conference on Computational Science, ICCS 2017, Zurich, Switzerland, 12–14 June 2017
4. Srivas, T., Artés, T., de Callafon, R.A., Altintas, I.: Wildfire spread prediction and assimilation for FARSITE using ensemble Kalman filtering. Proc. Comput. Sci. **80**, 897–908 (2016). International Conference on Computational Science 2016, ICCS 2016, San Diego, California, USA, 6–8 June 2016
5. Artés, T., Crawl, D., Cortes, A., Altintas, I.: Forest fire spread prediction system workflow: an experience using Kepler. In: Proceedings of the Third International Workshop on Advances in the Kepler Scientific Workflow System and Its Applications at the 16th International Conference on Computational Science, ICCS 2016 (2016)
6. Crawl, D., Block, J., Lin, K., Altintas, I.: Firemap: a dynamic data-driven predictive wildfire modeling and visualization environment. In: Proceedings of the Workshop on Urgent Computing (UC) at the 17th International Conference on Computational Sciences, ICCS 2017 (2017)
7. Nguyen, M.H., et al.: Land cover classification at the wildland urban interface using high-resolution satellite imagery and deep learning. In: 2018 IEEE International Conference on Big Data (Big Data), pp. 1632–1638 (2018)

Intelligent Contingency Management for Urban Air Mobility

Irene M. Gregory[1]([✉]), Newton H. Campbell[2], Natasha A. Neogi[1], Jon B. Holbrook[1], Jared A. Grauer[1], Barton J. Bacon[1], Patrick C. Murphy[1], Daniel D. Moerder[1], Benjamin M. Simmons[1], Michael J. Acheson[1], Thomas C. Britton[1], and Jacob W. Cook[1]

[1] NASA Langley Research Center, Hampton, VA 23681, USA
irene.m.gregory@nasa.gov
[2] NASA Goddard Space Flight Center, Greenbelt, MD 20771, USA

Abstract. The advent of third aviation revolution that is seeking to enable transportation where users have access to immediate and flexible air travel. The users dictate trip origin, destination and timing. One of the major components of this vision is urban air mobility (UAM) for the masses. UAM means a safe and efficient system for vehicles to move passengers and cargo within a city. In order to reach UAM's full market potential the vehicle will have to be autonomous. One of the primary challenges of autonomous flight is dealing with off-nominal events, both common and unforeseen; thus, intelligent contingency management (ICM) is one of the enabling technologies. In this context, the vehicle has to be aware of its internal state and external environment at all times, ascertain its capability and make decisions about mission completion or modification. All of these functions require data to model and assess the environment and then take actions based on these models. Necessarily, there is uncertainty associated with the data and the models generated from it. Since we are dealing with safety-critical systems, one of the main challenges of ICM is to generate sufficient data and to minimize its uncertainty to enable practical and safe decision making. We propose an overall architecture that incorporates deterministic and learning algorithm together to assess vehicle capabilities, project these into the future and make decision on mission management level. A layered approach allows for mature parts and technologies to be integrated into early highly automated vehicle before the final state of autonomy is reached.

Keywords: Autonomy · Contingency management · Data-driven modeling · Decision making

1 Introduction to Urban Air Mobility

The advent of third aviation revolution that is seeking to enable transportation where users have access to immediate and flexible air travel. The users dictate trip origin, destination and timing. One of the major components of this vision is urban air mobility (UAM) for the masses. UAM means a safe and efficient system for vehicles to move passengers and

F. Darema et al. (Eds.): DDDAS 2020, LNCS 12312, pp. 22–26, 2020.
https://doi.org/10.1007/978-3-030-61725-7_5

cargo within a city. UAM is not a new concept, currently there are helicopter services within large metropolitan areas that shuttle a small set of users between predefined set of destinations. The paradigm shift in this new incarnation of UAM is the democratization of the service (Fig. 1) [1]. Thus, at its core, UAM refers to the aerial movement of people, cargo and information, from one point in an urban landscape to another. UAM has the potential to reduce emergency response time, aid in combatting congestion in dense, urban cores characterized by impasses (e.g., bridges and tunnels), and improve the comfort and speed of travel. The adoption of electric vehicle technologies will likely set an industry standard, and will act to reduce emissions in metropolitan areas.

Fig. 1. Urban Air Mobility notional mission

UAM also has the potential to enable a suite of advanced aerial mobility missions in the surrounding metropolitan areas, such as suburban and rural communities. As the technologies of UAM mature, the ability to facility intra-city transportation for short takeoff and landing applications, as well as operations such as package delivery for medical transport, will act to unlock opportunities for social and economic engagement in all areas of the nation.

The ability to access the airspace above urban areas for commercial opportunities via small unmanned aerial systems (UAS) under the FAA's Part 107 has created an industry, which has been assessed to be worth $22 billion worldwide [2]. These operations are mostly limited to surveying and surveillance applications, such as agricultural, infrastructure inspection, journalism, film making and law enforcement. Initial cargo carrying operations, in rural areas, have just begun in the US, and are projected to become a dominant economic driver in urban and suburban areas. This UAS industry has catalyzed interest in passenger carrying UAM operations, and there has been many valuations of the market, which may be worth $15.2 billion USD by 2030 [3].

In this effort, we focus on a concept of operations that will involve passenger carrying vehicles operating in an urban environment. We consider an intermediate state of operations, that is defined by 100s of simultaneous operations; expanded networks including high-capacity UAM ports; many UTM inspired ATM [Aircraft Traffic Management] services available, simplified requirements for pilot certification; low-visibility operations." [4]. Note that this vision requires that several key assumptions be made, specifically regarding the increasing level of autonomous operation exhibited by the vehicle, as well as for UAM airspace management.

We assume the 'intermediate' UAM mission to be comprised of a vehicle, which takes off from a pre-prepared landing site (e.g., a UAM port), and travels to another pre-prepared landing site. There is appropriate communications, navigation and surveillance infrastructure available to enable multiple simultaneous operations at a UAM port (and to enable 100 simultaneous operations in the urban airspace). The vehicle has some level of human supervision, be it remote or in the cockpit. However, the supposition of a highly trained pilot may no longer be valid, and the role is that of an operator. The vehicle may encounter disturbances (e.g., weather events) and disruptions (e.g., restricted airspace) in the course of its journey, and may have to deal with contingencies (e.g., faults and failures) in an increasingly autonomous fashion.

We assume the 'intermediate' UAM mission to be comprised of a vehicle, which takes off from a pre-prepared landing site (e.g., a UAM port), and travels to another pre-prepared landing site. There is appropriate communications, navigation and surveillance infrastructure available to enable multiple simultaneous operations at a UAM port (and to enable 100 simultaneous operations in the urban airspace). The vehicle has some level of human supervision, be it remote or in the cockpit. However, the supposition of a highly trained pilot may no longer be valid, and the role is that of an operator. The vehicle may encounter disturbances (e.g., weather events) and disruptions (e.g., restricted airspace) in the course of its journey, and may have to deal with contingencies (e.g., faults and failures) in an increasingly autonomous fashion.

There are several challenges posed by UAM operations; these challenges can be broadly broken out into airspace-oriented challenges, vehicle-oriented challenges, community integration challenges and cross-cutting challenges. Airspace challenges include, but are not limited to, designing the airspace and operational procedures for UAM operations, including the design and operation of UAM ports and necessary supporting infrastructure, as well as disruption and fleet management, along with urban weather prediction. Vehicle challenges include safety, certification and noise qualities, as well as addressing issues such as increasing automation, manufacturing and supply chain issues, and maintenance. Community integration concerns are focused around public acceptance of the operations, their integration into a multi-modal transportation system and infrastructure (and the incorporation of smart cities technologies), as well as the local regulatory environment. Broad challenges such as the safety, certification, autonomy and infrastructure required for UAM operations cut across all stakeholders in the UAM ecosystem, and will require integrative solutions.

Two primary vehicle-oriented challenges center around the use of electric technologies, specifically for propulsion and control (e.g., electric vertical takeoff and landing vehicles (eVTOL)) and increasing levels of autonomy. The wide design space of these vehicles has led to multi-rotor paradigms, such as distributed electric propulsion. Currently, tools and technologies for the design, modelling, simulation, testing, verification and validation of these systems need to be developed. Specifically, the ability to certify these unconventional systems, some of which will require synthetic stability and control, and will operate in novel ways, is paramount to gaining access to the NAS. Additionally, with various sources [Boeing, Airbus] predicting a significant pilot shortage by 2030 for conventional commercial aircraft operations, with 400,000 to 750,000 additional pilots being needed, it is unclear where the trained pilots necessary to operate these vehicles will be found. Similarly, as these operations scale to the point where they will be profitable, it has been suggested that an increasingly autonomous operational paradigm will be required [5, 6].

2   Approach to Intelligent Contingency Management

We consider an architecture and associated functionality, see Fig. 2, that would allow the vehicle to safely achieve its mission, fly from pt. A to pt. B under all vehicle-allowable weather conditions, in a high-density airspace complex urban environment, and react appropriately to off-nominal situations and contingencies without direct human control. Currently contingency management is highly prescribed, rule-based approach. We are interested in exploring an intelligent contingency management that can appropriately handle unanticipated situations. This approach considers some emerging techniques machine learning and explores their integration into safety-critical systems and associated levels of safety assurance.

Fundamental to this architecture is a set of software components, each relying on a set of adaptive models that maintain a two-way interaction between model and system measurements. At the highest level, these components maintain models of the vehicle:

- Present Capability: Based on dynamic physical vehicle models and models of vehicle safety
- Future state: Based on reachability models and derivative data about Present Capability
- Mission Execution: Based on predictive vehicle flight models for decision making under uncertainty

Each component reflects the DDDAS paradigm, by using real-time data to enhance the vehicle's function in a manner congruent to its real-world context.

The collective state of the corresponding models for each component guide the incorporation of relevant data into the respective component during flight, as well as into the other system components. Furthermore, for computational feasibility, the level of fidelity for which data is analyzed and decision-making occurs is based on these models. Data flowing into a component improves the accuracy of its models and derivative analyses. Data flowing out to other components improve precision of predictions and control.

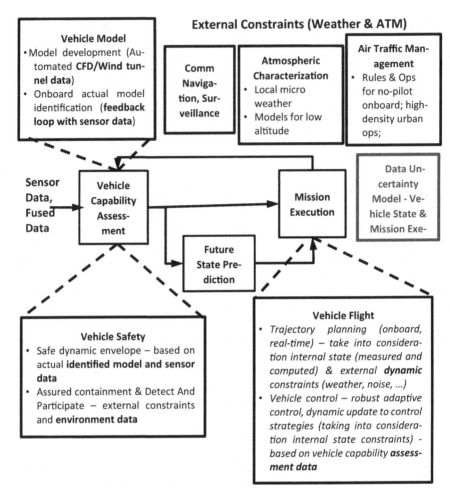

Fig. 2. Intelligent contingency management architecture

References

1. Gregory, I., Rizzi, S., Wincheski, R., Neogi, N., Siochi, E.: Self-aware vehicles for urban air mobility. In: AIAA Guidance, Navigation and Control Conference @ SciTech Forum, Kissimmee, FL (2018)
2. Deloitte ConOps Contract. https://www2.deloitte.com/us/en/pages/energy-and-resources/art icles/the-future-of-mobility-in-aerospace-and-defense.html
3. https://www.marketsandmarkets.com/Market-Reports/urban-air-mobility-market-251142 860.html
4. NASA Grand Challenge Industry Day Slides. https://www.nasa.gov/uamgc
5. McKinsey Study. https://www.nasa.gov/sites/default/files/atoms/files/uam-market-study-exe cutive-summary-v2.pdf
6. Booz Allen Hamilton Study. https://ntrs.nasa.gov/archive/nasa/casi.ntrs.nasa.gov/201900 01472.pdf

Plenary Presentations - Section 1: Digital Twins

A Dynamic Data Driven Applications Systems (DDDAS)-Based Digital Twin IoT Framework

Sarah Malik, Rakeen Rouf, Krzysztof Mazur, and Antonios Kontsos(✉)

Department of Mechanical Engineering and Mechanics, Theoretical and Applied Mechanics Group, Drexel University, Philadelphia, PA 19104, USA
ak866@drexel.edu

Abstract. One of the key elements of DDDAS is the ability to create a feedback control loop from the sensory system to the model to enable more accurate and fast data-driven analysis. When constructing such a framework, it is especially important to provide an efficient, filtered data stream to the model. To address this need, this investigation describes a DDDAS-based Digital Twin IoT Framework which comprises three layers, namely the Edge, Fog and Cloud. The Edge is composed of either commercial sensing data acquisition systems or by sensors without any commercial system being involved. The Edge layer is connected to the Fog which is a decentralized computing layer that consists of an in-house built Internet of Things (IoT) device. Within the Fog, real-time data is aggregated, parsed, filtered, and passed through a layer of user-defined algorithms. These algorithms can be either predefined or made using an interactive algorithm building application. The main goal of the algorithms used at the Fog, is to reduce the incoming data and classify it into known classes. This process allows a real-time data flow to the Cloud, as only important decision-making components of the data is propagated. The algorithms are trained in the Cloud layer using historic data to enable stronger confidence in Prognostics and Remaining Useful Life (RUL) calculations. The Cloud is also responsible for hosting a user interface (UI) to interact with the Edge and Fog Layers and the Digital Twin model. The UI enables users to start, stop, and modify their data acquisition and visualize their analytics in (near) real-time. In the proposed study, sensing data obtained through mechanical testing using a carbon composite will be leveraged for the framework. Diagnostics and Prognostics leveraging a probability framework will be conducted on the sensor data.

Keywords: Digital Twin · Internet of Things · Fog computing · Edge computing · Machine learning · Data processing · Diagnostics

1 Introduction

Both the material characteristics and the failure processes in the case of fiber reinforced composites (FRPs) are complex and highly variable depending on manufacturing, processing, geometrical and usage parameters which result in unique challenges when monitoring, simulating or predicting their failure [1]. In this context, diagnostics and

© Springer Nature Switzerland AG 2020
F. Darema et al. (Eds.): DDDAS 2020, LNCS 12312, pp. 29–36, 2020.
https://doi.org/10.1007/978-3-030-61725-7_6

prognostics methods vary in several ways related to the targeted length scale, the ability to relate local damage with global behavior and the potential to issue real time prognosis of incubated, incipient or evolving damage. Furthermore, there are significant differences between sensing methods that are used on actual composite structures for inspections and condition-based maintenance, and those that focus on material and mechanical behavior characterization which could only be applied at laboratory conditions [2–5]. Therefore, a wide range of descriptive and predictive tools have been developed with the objective of supporting multiple phases of composite material development and use [1–4, 6, 7].

What is understood currently is that prognostics must account for the stochastic and coupled, also often nonlinear, effects that govern the progressive failure process in composites [8]. Hence any data acquired from experimental testing of composites and is used to either fit prognostic parameters or perform statistical inference is typically subject to a high amount of variance. Consequently, monitoring of the progressive damage of composites is highly intricate and multiscale, making physics-based models either computationally expensive for live prediction or specialized to account for specific damage occurring between the micro and macroscale [8, 9]. This is especially true in the case that the convolution levels make it difficult to discriminate between noise and actual damage [10].

In this context, dynamic and data-driven predictions ultimately present a paradigm shift from reactive or time-based maintenance systems to condition-based maintenance (CBM). Specifically, CBM is a form of maintenance that takes real time system information to make maintenance-based decisions [4]. The goal of CBM is both to reduce the amount of unnecessary inspections and maintenance operations as well as to enhance system monitoring which in turn improves system reliability [6]. One of the formats for which CBM can be introduced to a system and or structure is health prognostics. The goal of health prognostics is to establish a metric of system health that can predict the RUL of the system. Such health prognostic frameworks consist of four distinct processes: data acquisition, health index (HI) development, health stage division and RUL predictions [4]. For a given system, sensor data is acquired and then processed to obtain the HI, at which point this HI will be the target of prediction for any chosen model. These models can be statistical, use artificial intelligence, physics-based models or be a hybrid of any of the above [4].

In terms of the construction of a HI, while multiple data-driven prognostics using sensors have been used for FRPs, the virtual HI produced generally have difficulty relating to hypothetical levels of damage [4]. This means that while the amount of damage in a FRP starts increasing it is difficult to account for the significance of certain damage modes as well as certain states of damage [1].

The objective of this investigation, therefore, targets the development of a data-driven modeling framework that can provide real time HI and RUL predictions for composite materials commonly used in aerospace-oriented applications. To achieve this goal the approach presented in this manuscript is based on: i) using sensing data including such obtained by mechanical testing and nondestructive evaluation (NDE), ii) leveraging an DDDAS-based Digital Twin IoT Framework enabling real-time usage of such datasets, iii) developing a data-preprocessing methods to create diagnostics information in the form of a HI capable to provide estimates of progressive failure, and iv) implementing a combined statistical/probabilistic approach based on a Hidden Markov Model (HMM) coupled to an Adaptive Neuro-Fuzzy Inference System (ANFIS) to provide RUL estimates.

2 Approach

2.1 DDDAS-Based Digital Twin IoT System Framework

The DDDAS-based Digital Twin IoT System framework is divided into three layers namely, the Edge, Fog, and Cloud (Fig. 1) to limit the information sent to the Cloud and to maintain a real-time flow. The onsite network hosts the Edge and Fog layers. Specifically, the Edge layer contains sensing which in this case includes the mechanical testing frame, and the Acoustic Emission (AE), Infrared Thermography (IRT), and Digital Image Correlation (DIC) monitoring systems, as well as processes that convert data into a .txt format so that could be used as inputs into the Fog layer. The Fog layer contains computing units that are parallelized for the specific tasks of filtering, classifying and aggregating data into the cloud. In addition, the data filtered data is visualized at the Fog layer to allow the user the capability of checking the full suite of features from the monitoring systems. Finally, the Cloud layer consolidates filtered data and uses NDE data classification as well as measured strain data to input into the HMM and ANFIS models for prediction of RUL. The data sent to the Cloud will be leveraged by the Digital Twin model to visualize the physical conditions of the components or environment.

Fig. 1. DDDAS-based Digital Twin IoT System Framework

In the implementation of this novel DDDAS-based Digital Twin IoT System Framework, the Edge nodes connect to the Fog layer over the Samba protocol. Samba is a free software re-implementation of the SMB networking protocol. In computer networking, Server Message Block (SMB) functions as an application-layer or presentation-layer network protocol. The SMB protocol is mainly used for providing shared access to files, printers, serial ports and miscellaneous communications between nodes on a network. The SMB protocol generally works with Windows platforms, however the re-implementation in the Samba protocol allows client-server connections between windows and Unix platforms. Thereby making a pathway over which files can be shared between the project's Edge layer and the Fog layer.

The Fog layer contains three Raspberry Pi's that are parallelized for specific tasks. Raspberry Pi 2 receives sensor data in the form of raw .txt files from the Edge layer. This data is then classified by a Support Vector Machine (SVM) model and filtered according to features identified in the diagnostic portion for further analysis setting aside features that do not provide analytical relevance. Raspberry Pi 1 provides a low-level diagnostic report based on the filtered data, while Raspberry Pi 3 transmits data into the Cloud. The Cloud consolidates filtered data and uses data classification as well as Cumulative Mahalanobis Squared Distance (CMSD) calculations to input into the HMM and ANFIS models for prediction of RUL. In this way the DDDAS-based Digital Twin IoT System Framework serves as a mechanism not only for reducing latency of prediction but also provides a network for converting data into information, storing this data and sharing across platforms.

2.2 DDDAS-Based Digital Twin IoT Computational Framework

In FRPs, damage can be evaluated based on discrete degradation states and their interactions. These states are computed, for example, in physics-based models to describe the progressively evolving damage. The overall goal, therefore, of any failure prediction model is to recognize such states and to examine transitions between them. To accomplish this goal, a DDDAS-based Digital Twin IoT Computational Framework was developed, a general overview of which is shown in Fig. 2 in relation to the system described earlier. Specifically, this prognostic model is a combination of a HMM and ANFIS models that ultimately provide the RUL estimates. The data exploration, diagnostic training, and prognostics training are all implemented offline at the Cloud to provide the model for the live case.

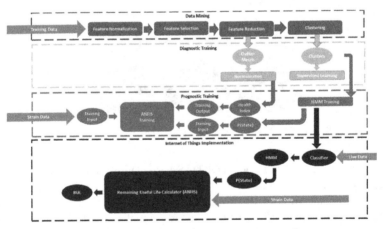

Fig. 2. DDDAS-based Digital Twin IoT Computational Framework

Specifically, the data exploration and diagnostic training results in a supervised classifier of incoming sensing data as well as an outlier metric, namely the Mahalanobis Squared Distance, to evaluate the full feature space of a given signal (Fig. 2). The CMSD has been shown by the authors that can be used to visualize damage evolution leveraging AE data [11, 12]. Taking the CMSDs for all tests and normalizing them creates an indicator which displays key points of extensive degradation and is used as the health index (HI) in this approach which will be used to train the ANFIS part of the model.

The HMM produces a probabilistic relationship between classifications of signals and several hidden states. This relationship is used to identify the current state of degradation as well as project the next set of potential (hidden) states. This is accomplished by describing relationships between the hidden states and signal classifications via a transition matrix and an emission matrix. Specifically, the transition matrix defines the probability that the system will either remain at a given state or transition to another one. The emission matrix gives the probability that given a certain observation, a system is at a given state. In this case, the observation used to identify a damage state within the emission matrix is classifications of signal.

To identify hidden states given a set of observations these are "decoded" using the Viterbi algorithm [13]. The Viterbi algorithm provides the ability to predict states given a known observation sequence. To forecast damage states a different calculation must be provided from traditional Markov chain theory. In a live case the HMM will be updated to the current state with the Viterbi algorithm for each incoming signal. Then the initial probability will be updated according to the most recent value. This provides the DDDAS-based Digital Twin IoT Computational Framework the ability to predict the sequence of damage states to failure.

Once an HMM can provide damage state probabilities and CMSD values are postprocessed into a HI, the following data combined with strain data and sensor data from DIC, can be used to train the ANFIS (Fig. 2). The steps to fuzzy reasoning start with input variables that are compared with membership functions to obtain membership values. The membership functions used in the following prognostic architecture are Gaussian bell membership functions with have the following form:

$$A_n(x) = \frac{1}{1 + \left| \frac{x-c}{a} \right|^{2b}} \tag{1}$$

where a and b define the width of the curve based on the maximum and minimum value of the input while c locates the center. The variables a, b and c of the membership function are tuned during training to capture the effect of the input on the output [14]. Combining the membership values by multiplication gives a firing strength of each rule. The membership values are also used to assess if-then rules that can trigger adaptive neural network regression the location of inputs within the membership functions define the activation of two different functions that have their own respective adaptive neurons. This gives the ANFIS architecture the ability to dynamically shift regression based on how the functions anticipate. Firing strengths are combined for a weighted average for ultimate outputs. The ANFIS architecture is then trained using a hybrid learning method which combines the backpropagation method and least squares estimation. Combining these two optimization techniques avoids common caveats of other methods which includes getting trapped in local minima and very slow training [14]. Moreover, this ANFIS architecture is trained using the damage state probabilities quantified by the HMM, as well as other experimental inputs that relate to the health index at any given point throughout monitoring. Finally, the forecasting of the HI and RUL occurs by forecasting the probability of HMM state until the HI reaches 0.

3 Results

A carbon fiber reinforced polymer composite (CFRP) was used in this manuscript (Hexply IM7/8552), consisted of a 16-ply layup of 8552 epoxy resin reinforced with unidirectional IM7 carbon fiber prepreg sheets both manufactured by Hexcel. Tensile tests using straight edge were conducted based on ASTM 3039 [15–18]. All specimens had a final nominal thickness of 5 mm, a width of 25 mm and a length of 250 mm in the loading direction. All specimens were loaded until failure using an MTS 370.10 Landmark servo-hydraulic load frame equipped with a 100kN load cell. For monotonic testing load was applied in displacement control at a rate of 2 mm/min based on ASTM 3039, while the specimens were monitored by AE at the Edge. Waveform files are then read by the Edge as voltage verus time .txt files.

The diagnostic training utilized the reduced feature space to perform the outlier analysis that ultimately produces a health index and the clustered results to train a SVM with a Gaussian kernel. Once the GMM clusters are analyzed to associate different classes with different damage types the clusters can then be used to train a SVM that can associate new damage signals with the clusters for live signal classification. The health index and classifications of signal from clustering provide diagnostic information related to damage from the experiment. The following input was trained under 10 Epochs to obtain 6 if-then rules and slightly outperformed the other variable set. The Epochs were increased to 50 to find that the model was repeatable and was not subject to a local minimum. The final target process for the ANFIS Model is identified by Fig. 4. According to Fig. 4 the goal of the architecture is to use strain data and weighted average probability of state to calculate the health index at each point within the RUL. The RUL in the following case is measured through strain to directly compare models, however the same approach can easily be applied for RUL in terms of time.

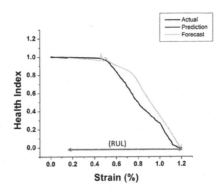

Fig. 4. Resulting Forecasting for One Test

The resulting predictions for straight edge specimen HIs are predicted post test. The results find that while ANFIS does suffer from certain instabilities directly associated with variation in damage states between specimens the overall accuracy described by mean squared error seen in Table 1. Such instabilities were self-corrected towards the end of the test and provided accurate RUL (when compared with the available mechanical test data). The table below provides the mean squared error between the predicted and forecasted sections.

Table 1. Mean Squared Error (MSE) for Straight Edge Test

Full MSE (%)	1.3720
Prediction MSE (%)	1.27E-03
Forecasting MSE (%)	1.407202
RUL Error (%)	1.3106

4 Conclusion

By leveraging the proposed DDDAS-based Digital Twin IoT Framework and data pre-processing methods that combine diagnostics and prognostics, RUL estimates were able to be found with acceptable errors. Future work includes using actual aircraft, naval or infrastructure components, as well as further real-time data collection and processing methods to strengthen the predictive and scalability aspects of the approach.

References

1. Beaumont, P.W., Soutis, C. (eds.): The Structural Integrity of Carbon Fiber Composites. Springer, Cham (2016). https://doi.org/10.1007/978-3-319-46120-5
2. Johnson, W.S., Hillberry, B.M., Johnson, H.B.: Probabilistic Aspects of Life Prediction. ASTM International, West Conshohocken (2004)
3. Hashemian, H.M.: State-of-the-art predictive maintenance techniques. IEEE Trans. Instrum. Meas. **60**(1), 226–236 (2010)
4. Sakib, N., Wuest, T.: Challenges and opportunities of condition-based predictive maintenance: a review. Procedia CIRP **78**, 267–272 (2018)
5. Hazeli, K., et al.: Three-dimensional effects of twinning in magnesium alloys. Scripta Mater. **100**, 9–12 (2015). https://doi.org/10.1016/j.scriptamat.2014.12.001
6. Lei, Y., Li, N., Guo, L., Li, N., Yan, T., Lin, J.: Machinery health prognostics: a systematic review from data acquisition to RUL prediction. Mech. Syst. Signal Process. **104**, 799–834 (2018)
7. Cuadra, J., Vanniamparambil, P.A., Hazeli, K., Bartoli, I., Kontsos, A.: Damage quantification in polymer composites using a hybrid NDT approach. Compos. Sci. Technol. **83**, 11–21 (2013)
8. Mesquita, F., Swolfs, Y., Lomov, S.V., Gorbatikh, L.: Ply fragmentation in unidirectional hybrid composites linked to stochastic fibre behaviour: a dual-scale model. Compos. Sci. Technol. **181**, 107702 (2019)

9. Mehrmashhadi, J., Chen, Z., Zhao, J., Bobaru, F.: A stochastically homogenized peridynamic model for intraply fracture in fiber-reinforced composites. Compos. Sci. Technol. **182**, 107770 (2019)

10. Ohtsu, M., Enoki, M., Mizutani, Y., Shigeishi, M.: Principles of the acoustic emission (AE) method and signal processing. Practical Acoustic Emission Testing, pp. 5–34. Springer, Tokyo (2016). https://doi.org/10.1007/978-4-431-55072-3_2

11. Aggarwal, Charu C.: Outlier analysis. Data Mining, pp. 237–263. Springer, Cham (2015). https://doi.org/10.1007/978-3-319-14142-8_8

12. McLachlan, G.J.: Mahalanobis distance. Resonance **4**(6), 20–26 (1999)

13. Rabiner, L.R., Juang, B.-H.: An introduction to hidden Markov models. IEEE ASSP Mag. **3**(1), 4–16 (1986)

14. Jang, J.-S.: ANFIS: adaptive-network-based fuzzy inference system. IEEE Trans. Syst. Man Cybern. **23**(3), 665–685 (1993)

15. Standard, A.: D3039/D3039M-00, Standard Test Method for Tensile Properties of Polymer Matrix Composite Materials. ASTM International, West Conshohocken (2000)

16. Marlett, K., Ng, Y., Tomblin, J.: Hexcel 8552 IM7 unidirectional prepreg 190 gsm & 35% RC qualification material property data report. FAA, FAA Special Project Number SP4614WI-Q (2011)

17. Stelzer, S., Brunner, A., Argüelles, A., Murphy, N., Pinter, G.: Mode I delamination fatigue crack growth in unidirectional fiber reinforced composites: development of a standardized test procedure. Compos. Sci. Technol. **72**(10), 1102–1107 (2012)

18. A. International: ASTM D5766/D5766M-07-Standard Test Method for Open Hole Tensile Strength of Polymer Matrix Composite Laminates, ASTM International, West Conshohocken (2007)

A Hardware Testbed for Dynamic Data-Driven Aerospace Digital Twins

Stefanie J. Salinger[1]([✉]), Michael G. Kapteyn[2]([✉]), Cory Kays[3]([✉]),
Jacob V. R. Pretorius[4]([✉]), and Karen E. Willcox[1]([✉])

[1] University of Texas at Austin, Austin, TX 78712, USA
stefaniesalinger@utexas.edu, kwillcox@oden.utexas.edu
[2] Massachusetts Institute of Technology, Cambridge, MA 02139, USA
mkapteyn@mit.edu
[3] CRG Inc., Miamisburg, OH 45342, USA
kaysca@crgrp.com
[4] The Jessara Group, Austin, TX 78704, USA
jacovrp@gmail.com

Abstract. This paper presents a hardware testbed that furthers the development of a dynamic data-driven application system (DDDAS). In particular, the focus of this testbed is on enabling a self-aware unmanned aerial vehicle (UAV). Self-awareness in this context refers to the ability of the vehicle to collect information about itself and use this information to alter the way it completes missions via on-board dynamic decision-making. Prior work has focused on developing computational methods that enable a digital twin of this vehicle, and demonstration of the resulting self-aware capability via simulation. This work presents a hardware testbed and associated experimental methodology for data collection, analysis, and demonstration of the self-aware UAV concept. The hardware testbed includes custom-built carbon fiber wings, the design of which have been validated via flight test. A sensor suite composed of wireless high frequency dynamic strain sensors has been developed and demonstrated using benchtop experiments. The proposed DDDAS architecture, which includes previously developed computational methods, has the potential to enable two-way coupling between estimation of the UAV structural state and dynamic mission replanning; capability that is critical for realizing the self-aware UAV concept.

Keywords: DDDAS · Digital twin · Self-aware unmanned vehicle

1 Introduction

This work presents a custom-built hardware testbed and experimental setup to support the development of a digital-twin-enabled self-aware unmanned aerial vehicle (UAV). A self-aware aerospace vehicle is one that can leverage online sensor data to dynamically gather information about its structural health, and

© Springer Nature Switzerland AG 2020
F. Darema et al. (Eds.): DDDAS 2020, LNCS 12312, pp. 37–45, 2020.
https://doi.org/10.1007/978-3-030-61725-7_7

respond intelligently by replanning its mission [12]. Dynamic Data-Driven Application Systems (DDDAS) concepts and algorithms provide an essential foundation for achieving the vision of a self-aware UAV [1]. A DDDAS is a system that has the ability to dynamically incorporate data into an executing application model, and in reverse, use the application model to dynamically steer the measurement process [2,4].

The digital twin paradigm embodies the concept of a DDDAS and has seen increasing attention in recent years [3,10], with promising aerospace applications in structural health monitoring and aircraft sustainment [5,8], simulation-based vehicle certification [5,13], and fleet management [5,11]. Inspired by these works, an approach has recently been proposed to enable the self-aware UAV concept by constructing a predictive digital twin of the vehicle [7]. The proposed digital twin is based on a high-fidelity component-based reduced-order structural model of the airframe. This model is capable of simulating the structural response of the airframe and characterizing the structural limits of the aircraft in a range of states. The digital twin is enabled by dynamically updating the structural state via online sensor data and using the updated structural model for rapid analysis and prediction. Adaptation of the digital twin is achieved by training interpretable machine learning classifiers offline and using these classifiers online to rapidly infer which structural state best explains the observed sensor data.

To date this approach has shown promising results in simulation. However, experimental investigations into the type of sensor-driven damage detection and characterization required to achieve this functionality have shown limited success. In particular, it has been shown that damage detection and characterization places high demand on sensing capability and robustness as well as computational efficiency of the data assimilation process, even for limited damage cases on simplified wing structures [9]. Thus, the need remains to validate the proposed digital-twin-enabled self-aware UAV concept experimentally. To this end, this work presents a hardware testbed and experimental setup for data collection and demonstration of the digital twin concept. Through experimentation with the hardware testbed, we aim to: 1) Develop a data acquisition architecture that produces high-quality data capable of enabling the self-aware capability 2) Identify challenges and limitations that might hinder the success of these computational methods when applied to experimental data; 3) Develop strategies for adapting and integrating the various computational methods to overcome these challenges; and 4) Successfully implement and validate these approaches on the testbed in order to demonstrate the effectiveness of the end-to-end DDDAS.

2   Hardware Testbed

This section describes the aircraft testbed system created to begin working through the integration challenges presented by the self-aware vehicle technology.

2.1 Overview

The testbed aircraft consists of a Telemaster aircraft kit (fuselage, landing gear, empennage), but outfitted with custom-designed and manufactured carbon fiber wings with custom sensors and avionics (Pixhawk autopilot, custom-built sensor boards, off-the-shelf power hardware). The fuselage-wing joint consists of a metal tube fitting so that different wings could be swapped onto the aircraft with minimal effort and in a rapid succession, such that multiple wings can be tested within a single flight test session. It was envisioned that this capability would enable several wings – from a pristine 'baseline' wing configuration through progressively more damaged wings – to be tested over the course of a single flight test, so that the same flight conditions and platform could be used to both collect sensor data and to test the DDDAS algorithms in real flight conditions.

2.2 Structural Design

The driving design requirement of the testbed aircraft was that the wing provide a structurally-similar response to a larger, more advanced Low-Cost Attritable Aircraft Technology (LCAAT) wing structure. Thus, even at the smaller scale, the preferred structural design of the wing used techniques similar to that of the larger LCAAT wing (albeit with reduced flight performance). The design criteria for the wings included: hollow carbon-fiber construction, 12-foot wingspan, plywood wing tip and root ribs, and inclusion of ailerons and flaps. The wing uses a constant 9% thick airfoil section representative of typical profiles at the mid-subsonic speed range (NACA 2309). The wing structure is split into 4 bays where the boundaries of each are designated by the plywood ribs. A split flaperon (carbon laid up over a foam core) is located in the outer two bays. The wing spar was sized for a maximum tip deflection in a 4G pull-up maneuver and the wing skins were sized for buckling in a 4G pull-up maneuver. Finally, the wing was designed to have access panels on the bottom skin so that any sensors,

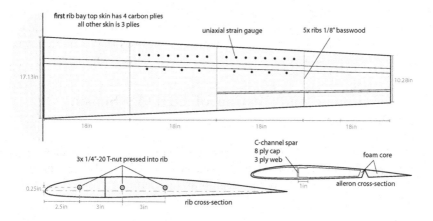

Fig. 1. Schematic of the designed and manufactured wing structure.

wiring, or other hardware could be placed or modified after the wing has been constructed and assembled. Figure 1 contains a schematic of the wing structure.

2.3   Flight Test: Validation and Initial Data Collection

Figure 2 shows the final manufactured aircraft during a series of flight tests.

Fig. 2. The custom-built self-aware UAV hardware testbed.

The first flight test conducted for the testbed aircraft consisted of a full system assembly and checkout at the field, as well as a maiden flight. The maiden flight of the testbed aircraft was primarily used to verify that all flight hardware functioned properly in-flight and to verify that the aircraft is fully controllable and flies as anticipated. Thus, a relatively benign flight path was flown – takeoff and climb to 300 ft AGL, fly general racetrack patterns with banks limited to 30° for up to 6 min of flight time, and a typical descent and landing. For this maiden flight the testbed aircraft was outfitted with a preliminary sensor suite consisting of twenty-four uniaxial strain gauges mounted on the top surface of the right wing, as shown in Fig. 1. However, analysis of this data showed that the measured strain had a low signal-to-noise ratio, and thus did not correlate well with z-acceleration (i.e. aircraft maneuver) data as one would expect. Finite element simulations of the wing during the design phase showed that differences in wing deflection caused by damage would be much smaller than any differences due to varying aircraft maneuvers. Thus, this result suggests that a more advanced sensing architecture is necessary in order to detect damage in-flight.

3   Development and Testing of DDDAS Sensing Architecture

The maiden flight of the testbed aircraft revealed that a more advanced sensing architecture is required to enable the self-aware UAV DDDAS. This section presents a recent effort to develop such an architecture.

3.1   Experimental Setup and Sensor Technology

A bench-top experimental setup was developed with the hardware testbed that enables controlled experiments and collection of realistic sensor data for the aircraft. In the bench-top setup, the wings are mounted upside-down to a wooden mount that mimics the fuselage. The opportunity also exists to mount the electric motor from the testbed onto this fuselage mount in order to excite vibrations in the wings that are characteristic of those expected in-flight. The experimental setup for these tests is shown in Fig. 3.

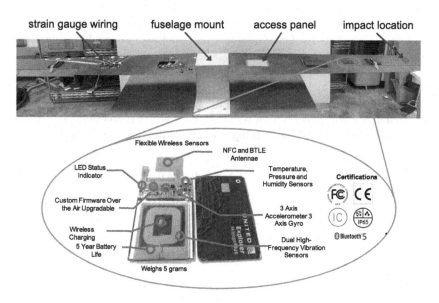

Fig. 3. Experimental setup and wireless sensor used for data collection in this research.

Based on the data collected during the validation test-flight, the decision was made to switch from the traditional uniaxial strain gauges mounted on the top surface of the right wing, to a set of dual high frequency dynamic strain sensors mounted on the bottom surface of the left wing. The primary motivation for this change was the improved signal-to-noise ratio. The wings on the testbed vehicle are relatively flexible, so the strains observed in-flight are typically dynamic with significant high frequency content. In this setting the dynamic strain gauges provide increased sensitivity, as well as reduced susceptibility to electromagnetic noise, and thus a higher signal-to-noise ratio.

The dynamic strain sensors used in this work are embedded in a set of wireless, self-adhering sensor suites, one of which is shown in detail in Fig. 3. In addition to the dynamic strain sensors, each wireless sensor includes temperature, pressure, and humidity sensors, as well as a 3-axis accelerometer and gyroscope. In addition, the sensors have a built-in analog-to-digital converter, bluetooth transmitter, and long-life battery. The wireless nature of the sensors provides additional benefits such as reduced weight, system complexity, and aerodynamic drag due to the absence of wires and other sensor hardware. Preliminary data for this work was collected using one of these wireless sensors, but the form factor and ease of installation would allow for many of these sensors to be used.

3.2 Proof-of-Concept Results

As shown in Fig. 3, there is a removable access panel, originally intended for modifications to sensing hardware. However, this component also allows the testbed to represent a scenario in which the access panel is unintentionally left open or entirely detached. Customizing this panel also allows for emulation of different structural states. For example, a flexible panel emulates a reduction in stiffness in the wing skin caused by damage or degradation. In preliminary data collection, both the thickness and elastic modulus of the panel were varied. In particular, the cases tested were carbon fiber panels of two different thicknesses, a PVC panel, a nylon panel, and a reference case with no access panel attached. The material properties of the varying panels are provided in Table 1.

Table 1. Material properties of different access panel cases.

Material	Thickness	Elastic modulus
Thick carbon fiber	1/16"	2400 ksi
Thin carbon fiber	1/32"	2400 ksi
PVC	1/16"	450 ksi
Nylon	1/16"	400 ksi

In the preliminary data collection, a small hammer is tapped at the impact location site (indicated in Fig. 3) to induce high frequency vibrations in the wing, and one of the wireless sensors collects data through the vibration sensor at a sampling frequency 5000 Hz. This hammer impact test is repeated using the different access panels described in Table 1.

The goal of these experiments is to process the sensor data from the hammer impact tests in order to extract features containing information about the structural response of the wing, and demonstrate how these features can be used to estimate the structural state of the wing, in this case represented by the access panel properties. Figure 4 shows the vibration sensor output for each case after filtering with 250 Hz high-pass filter (top). The high-pass filtered data shows that there is a variation of high frequency content between each access panel case. This can be more clearly seen in Fig. 4 (bottom), which shows the integrated high-pass filtered sensor output for two trials of each of the panel cases.

The integrated filter output shows a clear trend based on the access panel stiffness. As the stiffness of the panel is reduced, the integrated filter output

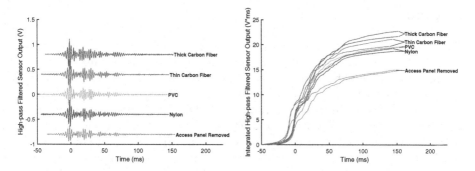

Fig. 4. Preliminary experimental results. Top: High-pass filtered vibration sensor output. Vertical offsets are added to better show the difference between cases. Bottom: Integrated high-pass filtered sensor data (two repeated trials for each case).

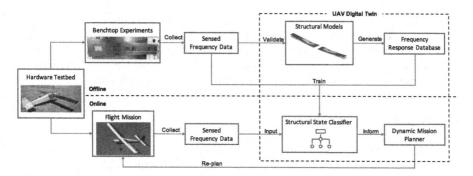

Fig. 5. Information model for the proposed DDDAS architecture.

decreases with respect to time. The two trials show a fair degree of consistency, however in future work more data will be collected to ensure consistency and provide a more complete dataset. These preliminary experiments demonstrate that the wireless sensors are capable of detecting differences in the structural response of the wing, even when the difference in the underlying structural state is small; in this case only the properties of the (relatively small) access panel are varied. In future, the data collected using these bench-top experiments will be integrated into the self-aware UAV DDDAS framework, which is summarized by the information model shown in Fig. 5. In this framework, the experimental data will be used in conjunction with structural models to train a classifier [6,7] in which features extracted from in-flight sensor data (in this case the amount of high-frequency content) can be used to estimate the structural state of the wing (in this case which access panel is attached to the wing). Online, this classifier can be used as part of a digital twin that enables condition-aware sensing and dynamic mission replanning, thus enabling the UAV to become self-aware.

4   Conclusion

This work presented a hardware testbed to support the development of a self-aware UAV. The hardware testbed aircraft system was successfully designed, manufactured, and flight-tested. A sensor architecture was developed that leverages wireless self-adhering dynamic strain sensors capable of measuring high frequency vibrations in the structural response of the wing. Bench-top experiments were conducted and the resulting data suggests that the degree of high-frequency content provides a useful feature for classifying the structural state of the wing. The development of a fully functional aircraft system capable of generating high quality experimental data serves as a key enabler towards validating and verifying the DDDAS approach for a fully self-aware aircraft system. Future work will involve leveraging the experimental testbed to further advance and demonstrate the DDDAS paradigm in the context of self-aware aircraft structures.

Acknowledgments. The authors thank Gray Riley and Alexander Vladimir Andersen of Aurora Flight Sciences for their contributions to the development of the testbed aircraft. This work was supported in part by AFOSR grant FA9550-16-1-0108 under the Dynamic Data-Driven Application Systems Program, the MIT-SUTD International Design Center, and a Cockrell School of Engineering graduate fellowship.

References

1. Allaire, D., Biros, G., Chambers, J., Ghattas, O., Kordonowy, D., Willcox, K.: Dynamic data driven methods for self-aware aerospace vehicles. Procedia Comput. Sci. **9**, 1206–1210 (2012)
2. Blasch, E., Ravela, S., Aved, A. (eds.): Handbook of Dynamic Data Driven Applications Systems. Springer, Cham (2018). https://doi.org/10.1007/978-3-319-95504-9
3. Boschert, S., Rosen, R.: Digital twin—the simulation aspect. In: Hehenberger, P., Bradley, D. (eds.) Mechatronic Futures. Challenges and Solutions for Mechatronic Systems and their Designers, pp. 59–74. Springer, Cham (2016). https://doi.org/10.1007/978-3-319-32156-1_5
4. Darema, F.: Dynamic data driven applications systems: a new paradigm for application simulations and measurements. In: Bubak, M., van Albada, G.D., Sloot, P.M.A., Dongarra, J. (eds.) ICCS 2004. LNCS, vol. 3038, pp. 662–669. Springer, Heidelberg (2004). https://doi.org/10.1007/978-3-540-24688-6_86
5. Glaessgen, E., Stargel, D.: The digital twin paradigm for future NASA and US air force vehicles. In: 53rd AIAA/ASME/ASCE/AHS/ASC Structures, Structural Dynamics and Materials Conference 20th AIAA/ASME/AHS Adaptive Structures Conference 14th AIAA, p. 1818 (2012)
6. Kapteyn, M., Knezevic, D., Huynh, D., Tran, M., Willcox, K.: Data-driven physics-based digital twins via a library of component-based reduced-order models. Int. J. Numer. Methods Eng. (2020)
7. Kapteyn, M.G., Knezevic, D.J., Willcox, K.: Toward predictive digital twins via component-based reduced-order models and interpretable machine learning. In: AIAA Scitech 2020 Forum, p. 0418 (2020)
8. Li, C., Mahadevan, S., Ling, Y., Choze, S., Wang, L.: Dynamic Bayesian network for aircraft wing health monitoring digital twin. AIAA J. **55**(3), 930–941 (2017)

9. Martins, B.L., Kosmatka, J.B.: Health monitoring of aerospace structures via dynamic strain measurements: an experimental demonstration. In: AIAA Scitech 2020 Forum, p. 0701 (2020)
10. Rasheed, A., San, O., Kvamsdal, T.: Digital twin: values, challenges and enablers from a modeling perspective. IEEE Access **8**, 21980–22012 (2020)
11. Reifsnider, K., Majumdar, P.: Multiphysics stimulated simulation digital twin methods for fleet management. In: 54th AIAA/ASME/ASCE/AHS/ASC Structures, Structural Dynamics, and Materials Conference, p. 1578 (2013)
12. Singh, V., Willcox, K.E.: Methodology for path planning with dynamic data-driven flight capability estimation. AIAA J. **55**, 2727–2738 (2017)
13. Tuegel, E.J., Ingraffea, A.R., Eason, T.G., Spottswood, S.M.: Reengineering aircraft structural life prediction using a digital twin. Int. J. Aerosp. Eng. (2011)

Plenary Presentations - Section 2: Environment Cognizant Adaptive-Planning Systems

A DDDAS Protocol for Real-Time Large-Scale UAS Flight Coordination

David Sacharny[ID], Thomas C. Henderson[(✉)][ID], and Ejay Guo[ID]

The University of Utah, Salt Lake City, UT 84112, USA
{sacharny,tch}@cs.utah.edu, ejay.guo@gmail.com,
http://www.cs.utah.edu/~tch

Abstract. NASA engineers have published a number of system requirements in an effort to enable dense operations of unmanned aircraft systems (UAS) in urban environments [7,8]. These requirements describe
a free-flight model, where operators are afforded the maximum flexibility to design individually optimal trajectories, with the caveat that
all operations must be strategically deconflicted prior to flight. Strategic
deconfliction reduces the probability of having to perform tactical decon-
flicton using onboard sensors and real-time algorithms to avoid conflicts.
Such approaches require a common protocol to guarantee that UAS do
not collide, but do not scale well. Thus, UAS Service Suppliers (USS)
must deconflict their planned trajectories pairwise prior to flight in order
to achieve strategic deconfliction. We propose a communication-based
protocol to coordinate airspace during flight. We present a dynamic distributed protocol for reactive conflict management that serves a similar
purpose, albeit functioning at a time-horizon in between strategic deconfliction and sensor-based conflict management. This DDDAS inspired
approach obviates the need for any centralized control by having each
UAS maintain a model of its environment, and exploiting sensing and
communication resources as dictated by the lane-based model.

Keywords: UAS traffic management · Tactical deconfliction · DDDAS

1 Introduction

In a seminal article describing the purpose and scope of dynamic data-driven
applications systems (DDDAS), Darema describes a motivating example where
injecting experimental data into a long-running computation (informing oil
exploration decisions) could be performed in an online manner to produce better
results [3]. An *online* program in the DDDAS paradigm accepts data whenever
it is available and could also inform the measurement process to improve system efficiency. The computational effort required to produce good decisions is
also a motivating factor for the development of a DDDAS approach to traffic
management described in this paper.

NASA and the FAA are making a concerted effort to develop an Unmanned
Aircraft System (UAS) Traffic Management (UTM) system to enable large-scale

© Springer Nature Switzerland AG 2020
F. Darema et al. (Eds.): DDDAS 2020, LNCS 12312, pp. 49–56, 2020.
https://doi.org/10.1007/978-3-030-61725-7_8

UAS exploitation in urban environments. The UTM is organized in terms of UAS operators who manage their flights through UAS Service Suppliers (USS). These service suppliers must declare the geographic region of their flights (in terms of 4D trajectories of space-time), and moreover, must strategically deconflict their flights pairwise with all other UAS flights in the region (we call this method *FAA-NASA Strategic Deconfliction* or FNSD). This can easily lead to quite complex path planning and coordination problems, and also requires USS to share data which would best be kept private. We have introduced a lane-based organizational structure for a UTM in which a set of lanes are defined (much like a ground road network), and then a USS simply reserves a sequence of lanes from takeoff site to destination site [5,11]. In that work, we demonstrated a lane reservation system that efficiently guarantees strategic deconfliction, however that only applies to flights that have yet to be active in the airspace. Active flights experience a more dynamic situation, where contingencies (possible future events, usually causing problems or making further plans necessary) can occur.

Contingencies are communicated to agents in an online fashion, either by tactical avoidance sensors such as radar and sonar, or as information from authorities and other agents. Both sources can result in undesirable system responses, for example cascading effects due to high-density operations [6] and unstable control response due to the structure of the information flow [4]. We describe here the Lane Strategic Deconfliction algorithm (called LSD), and show that it has very low complexity, and allows for quite acceptable lane stream properties. Overall, contingencies that lead to a violation of safe separation represent the most critical element to consider in the design of a large-scale traffic management system. Safe separation requires agents to plan collision-free paths, which in the most general case of multiple-agent planning is PSPACE-hard. Even the more narrow problem of tuning velocity profiles is NP-hard [1].

In this paper we consider a lane-based airspace model that enables the propagation of contingency information in a well-defined manner. UAS plan locally in real-time within lanes, broadcasting contingencies (as deceleration events) to neighboring lanes that are likely to be effected. Unlike car-following models [9], information from a contingency can reach multiple agents at the same, yet enabling agents to react in a similarly predictable way. The theoretical contribution of this paper provides an efficient real-time algorithm for strategic deconfliction and applies a solution in terms of ground-delay (delaying access to the airspace network) or air-delay. The experimental section of this paper demonstrates the ability to resolve conflicts within a simulated environment.

1.1   Lane-Based UTM

A central issue concerning the DDDAS paradigm is the choice of model, and how information is represented, distributed, and consumed. The lane-based airspace structure is a model for the configuration of UAS in space and time and contrasts with other proposed models, such as the grid-based structure proposed by NASA. For example, in a grid model UAS share position information (through a USS as a proxy) within cells of a grid, and it is incumbent on USS to determine whether changes to trajectories could impact operations in neighboring cells. In other words, the flow of information between cells is not explicit in the model and represents a major point of uncertainty in the system. This contrasts to the lane-based approach, where impacts of trajectory changes (the dynamic data in this system) within a lane propagate in a well-defined manner throughout the lane network. The lane-based approach imposes a clear downstream and upstream direction to the information flow because lanes form a graph structure that mirrors the possible paths by UAS. The representation of trajectories in the lane-based approach is simple, as described below, and limits the amount of information that must be shared between aircraft to ensure safe separation. Finally, utilities can be defined in a straightforward way for both the UTM and UAS; e.g., the distance between all flights is important for the UTM, while maintaining desired speed and distance to destination characterize the utility of a configuration for a UAS.

Given a set of ground launch and land sites, a set of one-way lanes is defined which provides a path from any launch to any land site. A lane is a directed 3D vector with its tail as the entry point to the lane and its head as the exit point. A flight path is a sequence of lanes starting with a vertical launch lane and ending with a vertical land lane. A crucial constraint on lanes is that every vertex (entry or exit point) has either in-degree 1 or out-degree 1; this allows the deconfliction of flights by considering lanes as opposed to nodes in the network.

In order for two UAS to be safe, they must at no time be closer than some minimal Euclidean distance, called d_S. We assume that lanes are defined so that no two lanes have points closer than d_S unless the two lanes share an endpoint. Figure 1 shows the simple lane layout used in the set of experiments described below. There are 51 lanes, along with 10 launch lanes and 10 land lanes.

1.2 Contingencies

Both approaches (FNSD and LSD) are subject to the problem of contingencies when a UAS flight departs from its nominal plan (e.g., slows down, goes off course, etc.). Due to the complexity of the UTM system, predicting the effects of contingencies is a major impediment to the wide-spread integration of UAS into the urban airspace. The currently published protocol for mitigating many contingencies requires the UAS to try to return directly to its launch site [2]. However, this trajectory may not be strategically deconflicted and requires obstacle detection and avoidance along the way.

The lane-based model, together with the coordination protocol proposed in this paper, offer methods to mitigate such a contingency and also provides techniques to analyze the possible outcomes of different contingencies. The well-defined structure of lanes suggest that only a restricted set of contingency trajectories need to be considered, those that follow the lane structure and those that do not. For example, addressing contingencies where UAS must exit a lane could include designating emergency side lanes where a UAS can wait, or dynamic landing lane creation to go to the nearest safe landing site. In the case that the UAS can still follow lanes, the simulations demonstrated in the experimental

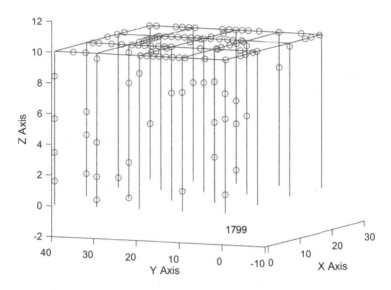

Fig. 1. Set of UAS on airways during discrete event simulation. Red dots represent UAS in Flight; blue lanes are launch lanes (Color figure online).

section of this paper offer a method to understand the possible outcomes. In [11] an analysis of the impact of lane density on the delay of a requested lane reservation was shown to be an instance of a process of random space filling, sometimes referred to as Renyi's parking problem [10]. The lane-based structure imposes constraints on the network that make this analysis possible and could inform what a safe operating density for the UTM should be.

The proposed real-time tactical deconfliction method described in this paper simply modifies UAS speeds throughout the network in such a way as to avoid conflict. This method effectively absorbs contingencies when the UAS agent is still capable of following lanes. In the event of a contingency where a UAS cannot still follow lanes, the impact is minimized because non-contingent operations remain within the lane structure.

2   Real-Time Tactical Deconfliction

Each lane has a set of neighboring lanes with which it shares an endpoint. A flight in a given lane is tactically deconflicted if there is no point in its trajectory along the lane such that it is within distance d_S of any flight in a neighboring lane. This can be efficiently checked using the Closest Point of Approach (CPA) algorithm as follows. Let two lanes, $\mathcal{L}_1$ and $\mathcal{L}_2$, be defined by vectors $\bar{S}_1$ and $\bar{S}_2$, where $\bar{S}_1 \equiv \overrightarrow{\bar{P}_1 \bar{P}_2}$ and $\bar{S}_2 \equiv \overrightarrow{\bar{Q}_1 \bar{Q}_2}$. The trajectories of flights f_1 and f_2 in lane $\mathcal{L}_1$ and $\mathcal{L}_2$, with velocities $\bar{v}$ and $\bar{w}$, are defined as $\bar{P}(t) = \bar{P}_1 + t\bar{v}$ and $\bar{Q}(t) = \bar{Q}_1 + t\bar{w}$. Since the velocities are $\bar{v} = \frac{s_1(\bar{P}_2 - \bar{P}_1)}{|\bar{P}_2 - \bar{P}_1|}$ and $\bar{w} = \frac{s_2(\bar{Q}_2 - \bar{Q}_1)}{|\bar{Q}_2 - \bar{Q}_1|}$, where s_1 and s_2 are the respective speeds of f_1 and f_2, then the time, t_{min}, when the two flights are closest in their trajectories is:

$$t_{min} = \frac{-(\bar{P}_1 - \bar{Q}_1) \cdot (\bar{v} - \bar{w})}{\mid \bar{v} - \bar{w} \mid^2}$$

If t_{min} is found for $t \in [t_{current}, t_{min\_TOA}]$, where t_{min_TOA} is the minimum time of arrival at the end of the lane for flights f_1 and f_2, then the minimum distance, d_{min}, between the flights across these intervals is just $\mid \bar{P}(t_{min}) - \bar{Q}(t_{min}) \mid$. If $d_{min} < d_S$, then a conflict exists between the two flights. Figure 2 illustrates the CPA method.

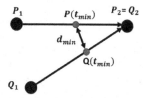

Fig. 2. CPA algorithm: two flights at closest points $P_{t_{min}}$ and $Q_{t_{min}}$.

If a flight, f_1, has a conflict with flight f_2, then the two flights can be deconflicted as follows:

Deconflict_Pair

while conflict(f_1, f_2)
 reduce speed, s_1, of f_1
 if $s_1 < s_{min}$
 then flight f_1 fails

This allows the definition of the Closest Point of Approach Deconfliction (CPAD) algorithm:

Algorithm 1: Closest Point of Approach
1 ∀ active flight, f
2 **if** f enters a new lane
3   **OR** a neighboring flight has slowed
4   **OR** f has reduced speed on its own
5 **then** call Deconflict_Pair for all flights in neighboring lanes
6 **if** f has reduced speed
7 **then** f broadcasts this information.

2.1 Approximate Global Deconfliction Using CPAD

Global tactical deconfliction is achieved by having each UAS run the CPAD algorithm. CPAD does not guarantee strategic deconfliction (i.e., that no two flights get within distance d_S across the entire set of current flight plans), however, it does guarantee that no two flights are ever within distance d_S of each other at any time. The benefits of this approach include that there is no centralized flight planning, no sharing of detailed flight info between USS, and robustness in the face of contingencies. The cost of the approach is that some flights may be forced to fail; however, this can be mitigated by choosing appropriate lane structure, controlling the number of flights, and eventually by dynamic flight route selection (currently the lane sequence is fixed). Certain communication requirements are imposed, however, the data shared between flights is essentially their telemetry data which the FAA-NASA UTM requires broadcasting anyway.

3   Experiments

A discrete event simulation is run which allows specification of the simulation time interval, $[0, t_{max}]$, and the number of flights, n_f. One unit distance corresponds to 50 ft, and one unit time corresponds to 10 s. Two maximum speeds are considered: 5 and 9, which correspond to about 17 and 30 mph, respectively. Each flight has randomly selected launch and land sites, as well as a random desired launch time. The desired speed is set to a max speed of 5 units distance per unit time. A fixed 3×4 grid of lanes at altitude 10 units are serviced by 10 launch lanes and 10 land lanes (see Fig. 1).

When a flight plan is created for a flight, it consists of a sequence of lanes and for each a specific Time of Departure (TOD: departs entry point to lane) and Time of Arrival (TOA: arrives exit point of lane). The next event is just the flight with the earliest TOA in its current lane, unless it has not yet launched in which case it is the current launch time. The launch times of the flights are uniformly distributed across the simulation time interval. Note that if a flight cannot launch at its desired launch time due to conflicts in the launch lane, then it is rescheduled to a later time (with fixed delay). Once an event is selected, all flights are advanced according to their respective speeds in their current lanes. Next, the flights are deconflicted.

We consider two aspects for study: (1) maximum simulated time (set to 100 and 200 units), and (2) maximum UAS speed (set to 5 and 9 units distance per unit time). These correspond to about 17 and 33 min, and 17 and 31 mph, respectively. The number of flights is chosen to equal the maximum time since this represents on average one launch per launch site every 50 s. Given a max time, UAS max speed, and number of flights, the simulation is run using the CPAD algorithm. Table 1 gives the data for five representative runs, as well as the means.

As can be seen, these results indicate that the CPAD algorithm works well in these scenarios with only one flight failure in all of the experiments (3000 flights overall). Moreover, the average speed is quite near the maximum allowed speed, and there are very few delays (68 out of 3000). The most critical parameter for algorithm performance is the maximum speed of the UAS. Other trends revealed in the data include that the longer the time period, the more flights complete their mission, and the fewer flights are delayed or in the air (on average).

Table 1. Delays and failures in experimental simulations

t_{max}	n_f	s_{max}	Wait	Fly	Done	Fail	Avg speed	Delays
100	100	5	1	18	81	0	4.98	2
			2	12	86	0	4.98	2
			0	15	85	0	4.99	1
			0	11	89	0	4.98	2
			1	18	81	0	4.96	4
	Means		0.8	14.8	84.4	0	4.98	2.2
100	100	9	0	11	89	0	8.98	1
			1	8	91	0	8.94	2
			0	12	88	0	8.99	0
			0	6	94	0	8.99	0
			0	11	88	1	8.98	0
	Means		0.2	9.6	90	0.2	8.98	0.6
200	200	5	0	14	186	0	4.96	6
			0	11	189	0	4.97	8
			0	17	183	0	4.98	6
			1	13	186	0	4.99	10
			0	6	194	0	4.96	9
	Means		0.2	12.2	187.6	0	4.97	8.6
200	200	9	0	7	193	0	8.96	4
			1	6	193	0	8.97	2
			0	8	192	0	8.97	4
			0	7	193	0	8.98	3
			0	4	196	0	8.97	2
	Means		0.2	6.4	193.4	0	8.97	3

4 Conclusions and Future Work

The lane-based approach provides a viable model for large-scale urban air traffic, and CPAD closes the symbiotic DDDAS feedback loop to update the model based on measurements and communication as required by the model. The results here lay the foundation for a further study into the role of DDDAS in large-scale unmanned traffic management. System designers must consider the impact of airspace structure on information flow as well as the accessibility of the network (as measured in delay in this paper). This paper demonstrates the importance of considering the structure of the descretization of the configuration space and how a real-time dynamic flight deconfliction algorithm can operate under strong assumptions about the space/time structure of the environment. Future issues to be explored include: (1) a broader set of experiments will be run to study the role of the number of lanes, the distribution of flights over lanes, etc., as well as a sensitivity analysis of the experimental parameters, (2) flights are assigned a complete sequence of lanes in this study, but we intend to explore the application of the software defined networking paradigm to dynamically select the lane sequence, (3) the structural properties of the airway network also play a role in facilitating flight deconfliction, and those parameters will be studied, (4) experiments will be conducted on realistic airways scenarios; e.g., the Utah Department of Transportation is exploring the use of the lane-based approach in Utah, where the airways are located above roadways, and (5) CPAD imposes communication requirements on the aircraft, and this aspect will also be studied in terms of the likelihood of failure to communicate correctly and its impact on deconfliction.

References

1. Alejo, D., Díaz-Báñez, J., Cobano, J., Pérez-Lantero, P., Ollero, A.: The velocity assignment problem for conflict resolution with multiple aerial vehicles sharing airspace. J. Intell. Rob. Syst. Theor. Appl. **69**(1–4), 331–346 (2013)
2. Baculi, J., Ippolito, C.: Onboard decision-making for nominal and contingency sUAS Flight. In: AIAA Scitech 2019 Forum. American Institute of Aeronautics and Astronautics Inc, AIAA (2019)
3. Darema, F.: Dynamic data driven applications systems: a new paradigm for application simulations and measurements. In: Bubak, M., van Albada, G.D., Sloot, P.M.A., Dongarra, J. (eds.) ICCS 2004. LNCS, vol. 3038, pp. 662–669. Springer, Heidelberg (2004). https://doi.org/10.1007/978-3-540-24688-6_86
4. Fax, J.A., Murray, R.M.: Information flow and cooperative control of vehicle formations. IEEE Trans. Autom. Control **49**(9), 1465–1476 (2004)
5. Henderson, T.C., Sacharny, D., Cline, M.: An efficient strategic deconfliction algorithm for lane-based large-scale UAV flight planning. Technical report. UUCS-19-005, University of Utah, Salt Lake City, UT, September 2019
6. Jardin, M.R.: Analytical relationships between conflict counts and air-traffic density. J. Guidance Control Dyn. **28**(6), 1150–1156 (2005)
7. Kopardekar, P., Rios, J., Prevot, T., Johnson, M., Jung, J., III, J.R.: Unmanned aircraft system traffic management (UTM) concept of operations. In: 16th AIAA Aviation Technology, Integration, and Operations Conference. AIAA Aviation), Washington, D.C., June 2016
8. NASA: Unmanned Aircraft Systems (UAS) Traffic Management (UTM) Concept of Operations, V2.0. Technical report, Federal Aviation Administration, Washington, D.C, March 2020
9. Newell, G.: A simplified car-following theory: a lower order model. Transp. Res. Part B Methodol. **36**(3), 195–205 (2002)
10. Réenyi, A.: On a one-dimensional problem concerning random space filling. Publ. Math. Inst. Hungar. Acad. Sci **3**, 109–127 (1958)
11. Sacharny, D., Henderson, T.: A lane-based approach for large-scale strategic conflict management for UAS service suppliers. In: IEEE International Conference on Unmanned Aerial Systems. Atlanta, GA, June 2019

Data-Driven State Awareness for Fly-by-Feel Aerial Vehicles via Adaptive Time Series and Gaussian Process Regression Models

Shabbir Ahmed, Ahmad Amer, Carlos A. Varela, and Fotis Kopsaftopoulos[✉]

Rensselaer Polytechnic Institute, Troy, NY 12180, USA
{ahmeds6,amera2,cvarela,kopsaf}@rpi.edu

Abstract. This work presents the investigation and critical assessment, within the framework of Dynamic Data Driven Applications Systems (DDDAS), of two probabilistic state awareness approaches for fly-by-feel aerial vehicles based on (i) stochastic adaptive time-dependent time series models and (ii) Bayesian learning via homoscedastic and heteroscedastic Gaussian process regression models (GPRMs). Stochastic time-dependent autoregressive (TAR) time series models with adaptive parameters are estimated via a recursive maximum likelihood (RML) scheme and used to represent the dynamic response of a self-sensing composite wing under varying flight states. Bayesian learning based on homoscedastic and heteroscedastic versions of GPRM is assessed via the ability to represent the nonlinear mapping between the flight state and the vibration signal energy of the wing. The experimental assessment is based on a prototype self-sensing UAV wing that is subjected to a series of wind tunnel experiments under multiple flight states.

1 Introduction

Future intelligent aerial vehicles will be able to "feel," "think," and "react" in real time based on high-resolution ubiquitous sensing leading to autonomous operation based on unprecedented self-awareness and self-diagnostic capabilities. But flight in complex dynamic environments requires unprecedented levels of sensing, awareness and diagnostic capabilities. Such capabilities can be enabled via the concept of "fly-by-feel" aerial vehicles, i.e., vehicles that can "feel," "think," and "react" inspired by avian flight. Such systems fall within the core of *Dynamic Data-Driven Application Systems (DDDAS)* concept as they have to dynamically incorporate real-time data into the modeling, learning and decision making application phases, and in reverse, steer the data measurement process based on the system's dynamic data integration and interpretation [3–5,8].

Towards the "fly-by-feel" concept, in this study two dynamic data-driven state awareness approaches based on stochastic time series models and Bayesian Gaussian process regression models (GPRMs) are presented and experimentally

© Springer Nature Switzerland AG 2020
F. Darema et al. (Eds.): DDDAS 2020, LNCS 12312, pp. 57–65, 2020.
https://doi.org/10.1007/978-3-030-61725-7_9

assessed on a prototype self-sensing composite wing subjected to a series of wind tunnel experiments under multiple flight states –defined by a pair of angle of attack (AoA) and airspeed [8,9]. Adaptive parametric time-dependent autoregressive (TAR) models are used to represent the time-varying dynamics of the wing as it undergoes different flight states. Model parameter estimation is based on a recursive maximum likelihood (RML) statistical scheme that allows the AR parameters to adapt with time in order to capture the non-stationary dynamic response of the wing [12,14]. In addition, non-parametric Bayesian learning via GPRMs [10,13] is used to "learn" the nonlinear relationship between sensor signal energy and the flight state, as defined by the AoA and airspeed (GPRM covariates). Both homoscedastic [1,13], i.e. model observations' noise is assumed constant throughout the input space, and heteroscedastic [10], i.e. considering input-dependent variance, GPRM versions are presented and critically assessed.

This study is a continuation of recent DDDAS work by the authors and co-workers [3,4,7,8], with the main novel contributions related to addressing the DDDAS fly-by-feel state awareness concept within (i) a non-stationary framework via adaptive time series models with unstructured time-dependent parameter evolution, and (ii) a Bayesian learning framework that represents the relationship between several flight-state inputs (covariates) and data-driven flight-state-sensitive features accounting for potential input-dependent noise variance.

2 Bayesian Learning via Gaussian Process Regression

Being kernel-based linear regression models, GPRMs allow for the modeling of complex, nonlinear relationships between observations (targets) and covariates (inputs), and the extraction of prediction confidence intervals (CIs) at a relatively small computational cost [13]. As a result, they have been widely used in many applications in the machine learning community [13] and recently in Structural Health Monitoring (SHM) applications [1,2]. However, the inherent and oftentimes unrealistic assumption of a fixed noise variance across the input space [13, Chapter 2, pp. 16] that governs standard (homoscedastic) GPRMs, makes them inappropriate in modeling many real-life processes. As such, heteroscedastic GPRMs have been proposed [6,10] that allow for input-dependent variance with the cost that the predictive density and marginal likelihood are no longer analytically tractable [10].

2.1 Homoscedastic Gaussian Process Regression

In this section, a concise overview of homoscedastic GPRMs will be provided. For a full treatment, the reader is directed to [13]. Given a training data set $\mathcal{D}$ containing n inputs-observation pairs $\{(\mathbf{x}_i \in \mathbb{R}^D, y_i \in \mathbb{R}, i = 1, 2, 3, \ldots, n\}$, a standard GPRM can be formulated as follows:

$$y = f(\mathbf{x}) + \epsilon, \quad f(\mathbf{x}) \sim \mathcal{GP}(m(\mathbf{x}), k(\mathbf{x}, \mathbf{x}')), \quad \epsilon \sim iid \, \mathcal{N}(0, \sigma_n^2) \tag{1}$$

where, in a Bayesian setting, a GP prior with mean $m(\mathbf{x})$ and covariance $k(\mathbf{x}, \mathbf{x}')$ is placed on the latent function $f(\mathbf{x})$, and an independent, identically-distributed (iid), zero-mean Gaussian prior with variance σ_n^2 is placed on the noise term ϵ. $\mathcal{N}(\cdot, \cdot)$ indicates normal distribution with the indicated mean and variance. The mean $m(\mathbf{x})$ may be set to zero and the squared exponential covariance function (kernel) is used for the latent function GP $k(\mathbf{x}, \mathbf{x}') = \sigma_0^2 \exp(-\frac{1}{2}(\mathbf{x} - \mathbf{x}')^T \Lambda^{-1}(\mathbf{x} - \mathbf{x}'))$. σ_0^2 is the output variance and Λ^{-1} designates the inverse of a diagonal matrix of the characteristic input length scales corresponding to each dimension (D, i.e each covariate) in the input data.

Training involves optimizing the hyperparameters ($\theta \equiv \sigma_0^2, \Lambda, \sigma_n^2$), which is typically done *via* Type II Maximum Likelihood [13, Chapter 5, pp. 109], whereas the marginal likelihood (evidence) of the training observations is maximized, or its negative log is minimized with respect to θ:

$$- \log p(\mathbf{y}|X, \theta) = -\frac{1}{2}\mathbf{y}^T (K_{XX} + \sigma_n^2 \mathbb{I})^{-1}\mathbf{y} - \frac{1}{2}\log|K_{XX} + \sigma_n^2 \mathbb{I}| - \frac{n}{2}\log 2\pi \quad (2)$$

Prediction can be achieved by assuming joint Gaussian distribution between the training observations $\mathbf{y}$, and a test observation (to be predicted) at the set of test inputs ($\mathbf{x}_*$) [13].

2.2   Heteroscedastic Gaussian Process Regression

One of the inherent drawbacks of homoscedastic GPRMs is the assumption of a fixed noise variance throughout the input space, which, in many real-life applications, is impractical. Thus, a number of extensions have been proposed to allow for the noise variance to vary with the input within a heteroscedastic GP (HGP) framework. In this work, we have implemented the variational inference that is based on variational Bayes and Gaussian approximation [10]:

$$y = f(\mathbf{x}) + \epsilon(\mathbf{x}), \quad \epsilon \sim \mathcal{N}(0, r(\mathbf{x})) \quad (3)$$

The added complexity of the heteroscedastic formulation results in not analytically tractable marginal likelihood and predictive distribution. One of the proposed approaches for their approximation was put forward by Lázaro-Gredilla and Titsias and is based on variational inference [10].

For training, the number of free variational heteroscedastic GPRM (VHG-PRM) parameters to be determined becomes $n + n(n + 1)/2$, which makes the training process computationally exhaustive. Thus, Lázaro-Gredilla and Titsias [10] proposed a reparametrization of μ and Σ at the maxima of the marginal variational bound. The predictive distribution for a new point in terms of the first two moments can be calculated analytically [10].

2.3   GPRM-based Flight Awareness Results

The demonstration and assessment of the methods presented is based on wind-tunnel experiments for a self-sensing composite UAV wing under varying AoA

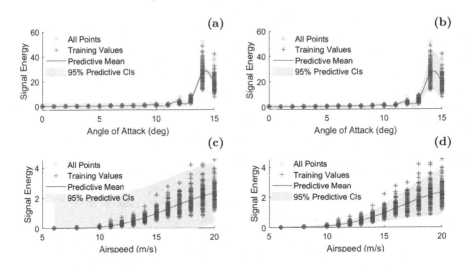

Fig. 1. Indicative GPRM results: (a) standard and (b) variational heteroscedastic (right) GPRMs representing the evolution of signal energy vs AoA (set airspeed of 15 m/s; top row); and (c) (d) airspeed (set AoA of 10 deg; bottom row).

Table 1. Performance of standard GPRMs and VHGPRMs based on validation data.

GPRM Input	Standard GPRMs	VHGPRMs
AoA – MSE[a]	5.7337	5.7624
AoA – NMSE[b]	0.0947	0.0952
AS – MSE	0.0822	0.0816
AS – NMSE	0.1124	0.1115

[a]Mean Square Error; [b]Normalized Mean Square Error [10].

(from 0 to 17°) and airspeed (0 m/s to 20 m/s); for details see [8,9]. Embedded piezoelectric sensors recorded stochastic vibration 90, 000-sample-long (90 s) signals (sampling frequency $f_s = 100$ Hz) for which the signal energy for varying time-windows was calculated (indicative results are currently presented for one-second-long windows). Model inputs (covariates) are represented via a flight state vector consisting of the AoA and airspeed values, and the signal energy is the output. For training, after an initial investigation in terms of model effectiveness versus computational cost, 1000 signal energy points were randomly selected under the considered flight states, and 486 and 183 test points were used for the AoA and airspeed, respectively. In the said format, the trained GPRMs are capable of predicting signal energy for a given flight state; however, the flight state can be identified via the trained GPRMs based on the predictive confidence intervals (CIs) at the test signal energies and the calculation of the probability that a point sampled from the predictive distribution of each set of flight states falls within the calculated CIs. The flight state that has the highest probability is determined as the actual state corresponding to the observed test signal energy. Figure 1 presents indicative GPRM results for the standard and VHGPRM cases for varying AoA (top row; Fig. 1a and b) and airspeed (bottom row; Fig. 1c and d). It can be readily observed that the VHGPRM predictive mean and variance can accurately represent the evolution of the signal energy along with the corresponding variance that varies with the input state. On the other hand, the standard GPRM, as expected, fails to capture the predictive variance, as evident by either too narrow or too broad CIs.

Figure 2 presents indicative results of the flight state prediction based on the standard and VHGPRM models. It can be observed that the VHGPRM provides more accurate predictions especially in the case of the airspeed for which the standard GPRM fails to capture the variance (see Fig. 1). Table 1 presents the comparison of the standard GPRM and VHGPRM performance.

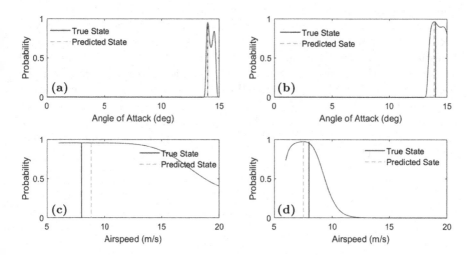

Fig. 2. Indicative flight state probabilities: (top) AoA predictions at an airspeed of 15 m/s for (a) standard and (b) VHGPRM models; (bottom) airspeed predictions at an AoA of 10° for (c) standard and (d) VHGPRM models.

3   Adaptive Modeling via Time-Dependent AR Models

The dynamic response of aerial vehicles is governed by non-stationary stochastic vibrations under varying operating and environmental states characterized by time-dependent (evolutionary) characteristics. From a physical standpoint, non-stationary behavior is due to time-dependent and/or inherently non-linear dynamics. Non-stationary models can be based on non-parametric or parametric representations [11,12,14]; for a review of non-stationary random vibration modeling and analysis see [12]. In this study, TAR models are used to represent stochastic time-varying vibration signals recorded from piezoelectric sensors embedded within the composite layup of the wing under the aforementioned flight states (for details see [7,9]). TAR models resemble their stationary AR counterparts allowing their parameters depend upon time and can *adapt* based on the time-dependent dynamics of the system [12]. A TAR(*na*) model, with *na* designating its AR order, is thus of the form:

$$y[t] + \sum_{i=1}^{na} a_i[t] \cdot y[t-i] = e[t] \quad \text{with} \quad e[t] \sim \text{iid}\,\mathcal{N}\left(0, \sigma_e^2[t]\right) \qquad (4)$$

with t designating discrete time, $y[t]$ the signal to be modeled, $e[t]$ an (unobservable) uncorrelated innovations sequence with zero mean and time-dependent variance $\sigma_e^2[t]$, and $a_i[t]$, the time-dependent AR model parameters. The TAR representation imposes no "structure" on the evolution of its parameters, which are thus "free" to change with time, and is thus directly parameterized in terms of time-dependent parameters $a_i[t]$ and innovations variance $\sigma_e^2[t]$.

Given a single, N-sample-long, non-stationary signal record $\{y[1], \ldots, y[N]\}$, TAR model identification involves selecting the corresponding model structure, and estimating the model parameters $a_i[t]$ and the innovations variance $\sigma_e^2[t]$ that "best" fit the available data. The TAR model is parameterized via the parameter vector $\theta[t] = [a_1[t] \ \ldots \ a_{na}[t]]$ to be estimated based on the recorded non-stationary signal. For a detailed review see [12]. In this work, parameter estimation is based on an exponentially weighted prediction error criterion and a recursive estimation scheme accomplished via the recursive maximum likelihood (RML) method [11,12].

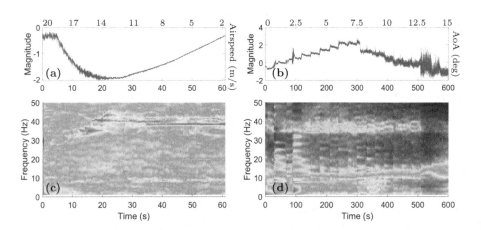

Fig. 3. Top: indicative non-stationary signals under continuously varying (a) airspeed and (b) AoA. Bottom: RML-TAR(40)$_{0.998}$-based time-dependent power spectral density estimates under continuously varying (a) airspeed and (b) AoA.

3.1 Adaptive TAR-Based Flight Awareness Results

The parametric identification via TAR models is based on $60,100$ (601 s) and $6,100$ (61 s) sample-long response signals (sampling frequency $f_s = 100$ Hz) under *continuously* varying AoA (from 0 to $15°$) and airspeed (decreasing from 20 m/s to 0 m/s), respectively, recorded via embedded piezoelectric sensors (see Fig. 3a and b). The model structure selection problem, i.e. determination of the model order and forgetting factor [12], is based on the successive estimation of TAR(na) models for orders $na = 2, \ldots, 50$ and forgetting factors $0.900, \ldots, 0.999$, with the best model selected based on the combined consideration of the Bayesian Information Criterion [12] and the comparison with the corresponding non-parametric power spectral density (PSD) estimates. This process resulted in RML-TAR(40)$_{0.998}$ models for representing the non-stationary dynamics due to time-dependent evolution of the AoA and airspeed of the wing.

Figure 3c and d presents indicative RML-TAR(40)$_{0.998}$-based time-dependent PSD estimates for continuously varying airspeed and AoA, respectively. Observe the time-dependent nature of the wing dynamics; in the case of varying airspeed (Fig. 3c) observe the separation of 9 Hz natural frequency at 20 s, as the two vibrational modes are decoupled as the airspeed decreases and the aeroelastic flutter diminishes. Figure 4(a–c) presents the first three RML-TAR(40)$_{0.998}$-based time-dependent AR parameters along with their estimated 95% CIs for a close-up time window of one second. Again, the time-dependent nature of the parameters is evident with the evolution of the flight state dynamics. In addi-

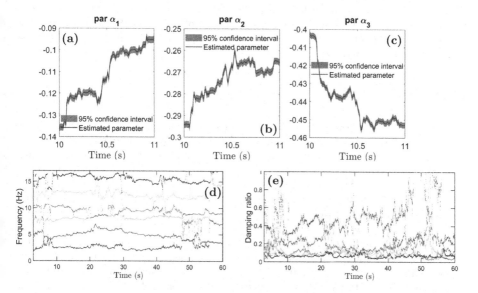

Fig. 4. Top (a–c): RML-TAR(40)$_{0.998}$-based time-dependent evolution of three indicative model parameters. Bottom (d–e): identified RML-TAR(40)$_{0.998}$-based time-dependent (d) natural frequencies and (e) damping rations in the [0 – 15] Hz range.

tion, observe the narrow confidence intervals of the model parameters that are based on the recursive estimation of the parameter covariance matrix. Figure 4d and e depicts RML-TAR(40)$_{0.998}$-based the time-dependent natural frequencies of the wing and their identified damping ratios within the frequency bandwidth of $[0-15]$ Hz. Again, observe the time-dependent nature of the identified modes based on the RML-TAR model and compare with Fig. 3.

4 Conclusions

The investigation and assessment of non-parametric Bayesian Gaussian process regression homoscedastic and variational heteroscedastic models, and adaptive time-dependent models for flight awareness, were presented based on experimental data collected from a UAV wing during wind tunnel experiments under varying flight states. The VHGPRMs outperformed their homoscedastic counterparts in terms of the predictive input-dependent variance estimation accuracy. Stochastic adaptive RML-TAR models were shown to be capable of identifying the time-dependent stochastic wing vibration dynamics under continuously varying AoA and airspeed by imposing no structure on the time evolution of their parameters. Ongoing work addresses the investigation of time-dependent stochastic models that impose structured stochastic (parameters are random variables allowed to change with time) and deterministic (parameters are projected on time-dependent functional subspaces) evolution on their parameters.

Acknowledgment. This work is supported by the U.S. Air Force Office of Scientific Research (AFOSR) grant "Formal Verification of Stochastic State Awareness for Dynamic Data-Driven Intelligent Aerospace Systems" (FA9550-19-1-0054) with Program Officer Dr. Erik Blasch.

References

1. Amer, A., Kopsaftopoulos, F.P.: Probabilistic damage quantification via the integration of non-parametric time-series and Gaussian process regression models. In: Proceedings of the 12th International Workshop on Structural Health Monitoring (IWSHM 2019), pp. 2384–2393, Palo Alto, CA, USA, September 2019. https://doi.org/10.12783/shm2019/32379
2. Avendaño-Valencia, L.D., Chatzi, E.N., Koo, K.Y., Brownjohn, J.M.: Gaussian process time-series models for structures under operational variability. Front. Built Environ. **3**, 69 (2017)
3. Blasch, E., Ashdown, J., Kopsaftopoulos, F., Varela, C., Newkirk, R.: Dynamic data driven analytics for multi-domain environments. In: Artificial Intelligence and Machine Learning for Multi-Domain Operations Applications, vol. 11006, p. 1100604. International Society for Optics and Photonics (2019)
4. Breese, S., Kopsaftopoulos, F., Varela, C.: Towards proving runtime properties of data-driven systems using safety envelopes. In: Proceedings of the 12th International Workshop on Structural Health Monitoring (IWSHM 2019), pp. 1748–1757, Palo Alto, CA, USA, September 2019. https://doi.org/10.12783/shm2019/32302

5. Darema, F.: Dynamic data driven applications systems: a new paradigm for application simulations and measurements. In: Bubak, M., van Albada, G.D., Sloot, P.M.A., Dongarra, J. (eds.) ICCS 2004. LNCS, vol. 3038, pp. 662–669. Springer, Heidelberg (2004). https://doi.org/10.1007/978-3-540-24688-6_86
6. Goldberg, P.W., Williams, C.K., Bishop, C.M.: Regression with input-dependent noise: a Gaussian process treatment. Adv. Neural Inf. Process. Syst. **10**, 1124–1136 (1998)
7. James, A., Kopsaftopoulos, F.: Data-driven stochastic identification of a UAV under varying flight and structural health states. In: Proceedings of the 12th International Workshop on Structural Health Monitoring (IWSHM 2019), pp. 1758–1767, Palo Alto, CA, USA, September 2019. https://doi.org/10.12783/shm2019/32303
8. Kopsaftopoulos, F., Chang, F.-K.: A dynamic data-driven stochastic state-awareness framework for the next generation of bio-inspired fly-by-feel aerospace vehicles. In: Blasch, E., Ravela, S., Aved, A. (eds.) Handbook of Dynamic Data Driven Applications Systems, pp. 697–721. Springer, Cham (2018). https://doi.org/10.1007/978-3-319-95504-9_31
9. Kopsaftopoulos, F., Nardari, R., Li, Y.H., Chang, F.K.: A stochastic global identification framework for aerospace structures operating under varying flight states. Mech. Syst. Signal Process. **98**, 425–447 (2018)
10. Lázaro-Gredilla, M., Titsias, M.K.: Variational heteroscedastic Gaussian process regression. In: Proceedings of the 28th International Conference on Machine Learning, pp. 841–848 (2011)
11. Ljung, L.: System identification. Wiley encyclopedia of electrical and electronics engineering, pp. 1–19 (1999)
12. Poulimenos, A., Fassois, S.: Parametric time-domain methods for non-stationary random vibration modelling and analysis – a critical survey and comparison. Mech. Syst. Signal Process. **20**(4), 763–816 (2006)
13. Rasmussen, C.E., Williams, C.K.I. (eds.): Gaussian Processes for Machine Learning. MIT Press, Cambridge (2006)
14. Sotiriou, D., Kopsaftopoulos, F., Fassois, S.: An adaptive time-series probabilistic framework for 4-D trajectory conformance monitoring. IEEE Trans. Intell. Transp. Syst. **17**(6), 1606–1616 (2016)

Integrated Planning, Decision-Making, and Weather Modeling for UAS Navigating Complex Weather

John J. Bird$^{(\boxtimes)}$, Katherine Glasheen$^{(\boxtimes)}$, and Eric W. Frew$^{(\boxtimes)}$

University of Colorado Boulder, Boulder, CO 80309, USA
{john.bird,katherine.glasheen,eric.frew}@colorado.edu

Abstract. Aircraft of all types, and especially small UAS, are significantly affected by atmospheric motion. Employing numerical weather models and trajectory planning algorithms that reason over model uncertainty can allow an aircraft to safely and efficiently traverse a complex, uncertain environment. However, even paths robust to a priori uncertainty may be inferior to trajectories planned using an environmental model refined using in situ observations. This work develops a dynamic data driven applications system (DDDAS) architecture that uses the aircraft as a sensor to the environmental state and updates a model of the wind field model through trajectory execution. A Monte Carlo Rapidly-Exploring Random Tree (MCRRT) algorithm plans a set of probabilistically safe paths and predicts the distribution of their cost. Decision-making at the tasking level directs aircraft on paths which are possibly suboptimal with respect to a single mission in order to sample the environment and update the model. This tasking reconfigures the observations gathered to target portions of the environment relevant to mission execution. Initial simulations show that this approach is able to reduce error in the modeled environment.

Keywords: Dynamic data driven applications systems · Flight planning · Wind field uncertainty · Online

1 Introduction

The atmospheric environment can significantly affect the performance of all aircraft, especially small uninhabited aircraft systems (sUAS) which frequently fly slowly in the turbulent lower atmosphere [1–3]. Flight planning algorithms which consider weather forecast predictions when simulating the aircraft dynamics can account for the expected effect of weather on a mission [4]; however, forecasting at the scale of sUAS missions is complicated by uncertain boundary conditions and subgrid-scale dynamics which affect resolved-scale motion. The mean error in high resolution wind forecasts is approximately 2.5 ms^{-1} [5, 6], more than 10% of the flight speed of many sUAS. This wind field error makes it likely that the a priori predicted cost of performing a flight plan has significant error. It is also possible that a trajectory which is optimal in the predicted wind field is suboptimal in the true environment.

© Springer Nature Switzerland AG 2020
F. Darema et al. (Eds.): DDDAS 2020, LNCS 12312, pp. 66–73, 2020.
https://doi.org/10.1007/978-3-030-61725-7_10

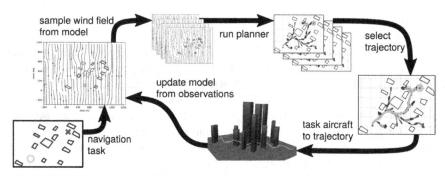

Fig. 1. The DDDAS paradigm applied to maintaining an environmental model which is used to plan and assign trajectories to small UAS navigating an urban environment.

One approach to managing this error is to use the uncertain forecast as an input in a probabilistic planner which penalizes the resulting cost distribution, resulting in high-confidence paths [7]. Another approach is to consider the uncertainty introduced by atmospheric disturbances in transitions between nearby states. The planning problem can then be viewed as a Markov Decision Process and dynamic programming can be used to find policies which efficiently reach a goal [8]. These methods can produce trajectories that are robust to uncertainty in the wind field but do not seek information about the environment which can be used to inform the path of subsequent missions.

The dynamic data driven applications system (DDDAS) paradigm [9, 10] provides a framework for updating data-driven models with online observations to inform decision making in subsequent missions. This framework has been applied to energy-aware trajectory optimization [11] and self-aware probabilistic trajectory planning [12] in systems that integrate observations into atmospheric and flight envelope models during flight. Despite updating data-driven models in near-real-time for informed path planning, these systems do not generate trajectories that improve model uncertainty. The DDDAS paradigm has been applied to gathering wind field information, but only in the case where the aircraft's sole objective is to explore the wind field [13].

This work introduces a DDDAS architecture for trajectory planning over atmospheric models to meet mission requirements while avoiding obstacles and gathering information to improve the atmospheric model (Fig. 1). Prior to each mission the atmospheric model is sampled. A probabilistic planner uses these samples to produce a candidate set of efficient trajectories which are safe with respect to random wind disturbances. A task assignment algorithm then assigns a trajectory from the candidate set to the aircraft. By sampling the model used for planning and the cost for task assignment the aircraft is tasked to visit regions where uncertainty produces variation in the trajectory and its cost. During a mission the wind can be inferred from the difference between inertial and air-relative velocity measured by the aircraft. These observations are assimilated by the atmospheric modeling system during trajectory execution to reduce uncertainty in the environmental state. The updated model is made available for subsequent mission planning, closing the DDDAS loop.

2 Probabilistic Planning

A key component of the system is a planner for the aircraft mission which provides multiple candidate trajectories and the distribution of cost predicted for each. The Monte Carlo Rapidly-Exploring Random Tree (MCRRT) takes a particle approach to planning, which allows the distribution of the vehicle states and cost to be estimated based on a data-driven environment model. The branching, randomly exploring nature of the MCRRT algorithm allows the trajectory quality to be refined as computational resources permit and identifies a number of trajectories which can be provided to the task assignment algorithm.

Figure 2 shows how the MCRRT algorithm operates. A random position is sampled in the problem space and the optimal parent belief state is chosen from the search tree based on a cost function.

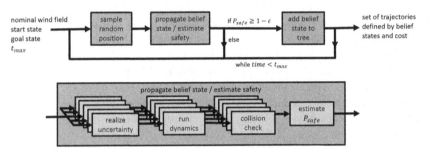

Fig. 2. The Monte Carlo RRT plans multiple candidate paths, returning vehicle belief states and cost estimates for each path.

The turbulent wind motion is sampled for each particle composing the parent belief state, and a closed loop dynamic simulation drives each particle toward the reference position. The closed loop model consists of a Dubin's aircraft model [14] modified to consider wind and a look-ahead path-following controller [15]. Each resulting trajectory is characterized by its state distribution and cost distribution.

Safety of the trajectory distribution is reasoned over probabilistically using the collision status of each particle's trajectory to estimate the probability of safety from the root of the search tree to each belief state. Belief states that cause the path to violate the safety chance constraint, $P_{safe} \geq 1 - \epsilon$, where ϵ is a user-defined threshold, are discarded. Belief states that satisfy the safety chance constraint are added to the search tree.

A path is found when the mean value of a belief state in the search tree is extended into the goal region. When the randomly sampled position falls in the goal region, the optimal parent is chosen from belief states that have not yet been extended towards the goal to increase the likelihood of diverse paths reaching the goal region. The planner is run for a fixed time t_{max}, and all resulting paths are sent to the task assignment algorithm.

3 Trajectory Assignment for Exploration

To gather information about the environment while accomplishing a mission, the system needs to generate and assign trajectories that balance gathering information about the environment with mission completion. This balance is a common problem when planning in uncertain environments. A common approach to achieve this balance is to provide a bonus in the cost function for exploration, based on the model uncertainty in the regions traversed by a trajectory [13]. This approach requires a weight be chosen for the bonus term in the cost function, and often this weight must be tuned manually to achieve satisfactory performance.

The approach taken in this application is to realize wind fields from the probabilistic model of the environment. These sampled models are used by several MCRRT instances in parallel. The planners run for a fixed period and return one or more solutions which are described by particle trajectories, capturing the distribution of cost for a given trajectory. The task assignment system must then make a choice over the resulting set of candidate trajectories.

The choice of an action from a candidate set with uncertain cost describes the multi-armed bandit problem. Optimal solutions to this problem exist when the choices and their reward distributions are constant [16]. Because unique trajectories are returned by the planner after each run, the action space is effectively infinite in dimension and strong claims of convergence to the optimal value cannot be made. A finite number of trajectories is returned, however, as well as a probabilistic description of the cost of each trajectory. A trajectory is chosen by randomly sampling a cost from the distribution at the terminal node of each candidate and selecting the trajectory corresponding to the minimum of the sampled costs. While this does not explicitly value the information gathered, the sampling step approximates a selection rule which matches probability of selection with probability that a trajectory is optimal. This approach was explored by Granmo and Berg for non-stationary problems [17]. The trajectory selection process is depicted in Fig. 3.

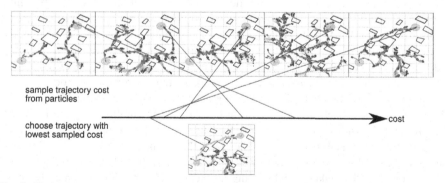

Fig. 3. Trajectory costs are sampled from the particle distribution at the terminal node. The trajectory from which the minimum cost was sampled is selected for execution.

4   Environment Model

The final component of the system is an environmental model which can be sampled for planning and can be updated using in situ observations gathered by the sUAS. Model-assimilation approaches such as the Ensemble Kalman filter (EnKF) provide probabilistic forecasts of the environmental state and the ability to refine state estimates as new observations are available [18].

Because the focus of this work is integrating the planning and assignment algorithms, a surrogate system is employed which uses a Kalman filter to estimate weights for a priori defined basis functions which are used to model the deterministic component of the wind field [19]. This provides capability outwardly similar to an EnKF while being simpler to implement for testing. It can also be used in applications where computational limitations preclude the use of a full EnKF weather model, though the approach used here can only interpolate rather than predict the atmospheric state.

Both the true and estimated environment are modeled as a uniform flow with random perturbations superimposed. The perturbations are described by Gaussian radial basis functions. To simulate an environment where all of the degrees of freedom are not perfectly captured, as is common in weather models, the model includes half the number of basis functions as the true environment and the bases are not located at the same points. The true wind field does not evolve with time in the simulations performed in this paper.

5   Simulations

The weather model, MCRRT planner, and task assignment algorithm are implemented in a numerical simulation where a fleet of sUAS must traverse a complex wind field while minimizing travel time, simulating package delivery or resupply. The weather model is initialized with no knowledge of the environment and model covariance which reflects climatological variation in the wind.

To approximate an sUAS with a closed-loop control system the aircraft dynamics in both planning and simulation are simplified to first order with decoupled longitudinal and lateral motion. Aircraft states are inertial position, heading, and airspeed. Control inputs are turn rate, climb rate and speed rate. Environmental inputs are the mean wind components and random wind disturbances. To simplify the simulation the wind vector is directly observed, with additive noise equivalent to inferring it from the difference of inertial and air-relative velocity, and is used to update the environmental model.

Simulations are conducted in an urban environment approximating Minneapolis, Minnesota (Fig. 4). Each mission begins at the same point and flies to a point located 1.2 km away. Missions are completed sequentially so that each trajectory is planned using the environmental model as it was estimated after the previous mission. Reusing the same start and goal points requires the system to actively gather information about the environment. The takeoff and landing are neglected – missions begin and end at flying speed and 10 m altitude.

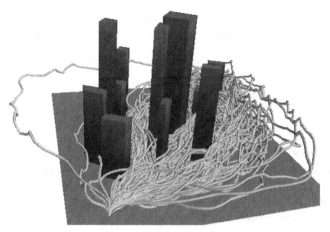

Fig. 4. One hundred sequential simulations are conducted in an urban environment approximating Minneapolis, Minnesota.

6   Results

Figure 4 shows flight paths taken by the aircraft in one hundred simulations. A qualitative examination of the paths shows that most missions follow one of several heavily used routes while a few missions fly much farther. The commonly used trajectories have similar cost, so randomly sampling trajectory costs will frequently result in selection of one of these routes. The longer trajectories result from infrequent instances where the planner uses a possible but not likely realization of the environment in which these regions have very favorable winds.

Figure 5 shows the mean absolute error between the true and modeled wind field used for planning, averaged over each mission. The large initial error is rapidly eliminated as the filter accurately estimates the uniform wind field component after a single mission. Correcting overfitting of the perturbations requires several more missions, with the wind

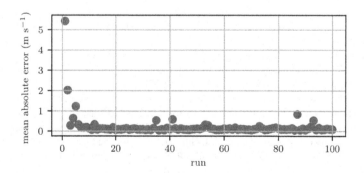

Fig. 5. Mean absolute error between the modeled wind and true wind experienced by the aircraft during each mission.

field error converging after ten missions. Occasional spikes (e.g. run 41) occur when the aircraft is tasked to an information-gathering trajectory through a poorly explored part of the wind field.

7 Conclusions

This paper presents the development of a dynamic data driven applications system for sUAS operations in urban environments which integrates planning, task assignment, and a weather model updated with in situ observations. By sampling wind fields from a probabilistic environmental model, using a particle-based trajectory planner, and selecting trajectories on the basis of sampled costs, the system can generate trajectories which visit potentially favorable regions in the environment while accomplishing a mission. Simulations in an urban environment show that the system is able to reduce the wind field error experienced by a group of sUAS completing missions representative of delivery or resupply.

The framework developed is intended to enable further investigation of the DDDAS paradigm applied to flight in uncertain wind fields. Further research is intended to explore the performance of MCRRT in comparison to other probabilistic planners, the use of time-varying and more realistic wind fields, incorporation of a physics-based model-assimilation system, and the effect that improving the wind field estimate has on mission performance. Finally, the system is being implemented on an sUAS for field testing.

References

1. Adkins, K.A.: Urban flow and small unmanned aerial system operations in the built environment. Int. J. Aviat. Aeronaut. Aerosp. 6(1), 10 (2019)
2. McGrath, B.E., Cybyk, B.Z., Frey, T.M.: Environment-vehicle interaction modeling for unmanned aerial system operations in complex airflow environments. Johns Hopkins APL Tech. Digest (Appl. Phys. Lab.) 31(2), 115–131 (2012)
3. Watkins, S., Loxton, B., Abdulrahim, M., Bil, C., Milbank, J.: Flow fields in complex terrain and their challenges to micro flight. In: AIAA Guidance, Navigation and Control Conference, August 2008
4. Dobrokhodov, V., Jones, K.D., Walton, C., Kaminer, I.I.: Energy-optimal trajectory planning of hybrid ultra-long endurance uav in time-varying energy fields. In: AIAA Scitech 2020 Forum (2020)
5. Pichugina, Y.L., et al.: Assessment of NWP forecast models in simulating offshore winds through the lower boundary layer by measurements from a ship-based scanning Doppler lidar. Mon. Weather Rev. 145(10), 4277–4301 (2017)
6. Glasheen, K., Pinto, J., Steiner, M., Frew, E.: Assessment of finescale local wind forecasts using small unmanned aircraft systems. J. Aerosp. Inf. Syst. 17(4), 182–192 (2020)
7. González-Arribas, D., Soler, M., Sanjurjo-Rivo, M.: Robust aircraft trajectory planning under wind uncertainty using optimal control. J. Guidance Control and Dyn. 41(3), 673–688 (2018)
8. Al-Sabban, W.H., Gonzalez, L.F., Smith, R.N.: Wind-energy based path planning for unmanned aerial vehicles using markov decision processes. In: 2013 IEEE International Conference on Robotics and Automation, pp. 784–789 (2013)
9. Darema, F.: Grid computing and beyond: the context of dynamic data driven applications systems. Proc. IEEE 93(3), 692–697 (2005)

10. Blasch, E.: DDDAS advantages from high-dimensional simulation. In: Proceedings of the 2018 Winter Simulation Conference, pp. 1418–1429 (2018)
11. Frew, E.W., Argrow, B., Houston, A., Weiss, C.: Toward an autonomous airborne scientist for studying severe local storms (Invited). In: 8th AIAA Atmospheric and Space Environments Conference (2016)
12. Singh, V., Willcox, K.E.: Methodology for path planning with dynamic data-driven flight capability estimation. AIAA J. **55**(8), 2727–2738 (2017)
13. Lawrance, N.R.J., Sukkarieh, S.: Simultaneous exploration and exploitation of a wind field for a small gliding UAV. In: AIAA Guidance, Navigation and Control Conference, August 2010
14. Beard, R.W., McLain, T.W.: Implementing Dubins airplane paths on fixed-wing UAVs. In: Valavanis, K.P., Vachtsevanos, G.J. (eds.) Handbook of Unmanned Aerial Vehicles, pp. 5–15. Springer, Dordrecht (2013). https://doi.org/10.1007/978-90-481-9707-1_120
15. Park, S., Deyst, J., How, J.P.: Performance and lyapunov stability of a nonlinear path following guidance method. J. Guidance Control Dyn. **30**(6), 1718–1728 (2007)
16. Kuleshov, V., Precup, D.: Algorithms for multi-armed bandit problems, arXiv: 1402.6028 (2014)
17. Granmo, O.C., Berg, S.: Solving non-stationary bandit problems by random sampling from sibling Kalman filters. In: García-Pedrajas, N., Herrera, F., Fyfe, C., Benítez, J.M., Ali, M. (eds.) IEA/AIE 2010. LNCS (LNAI), vol. 6098, pp. 199–208. Springer, Heidelberg (2010). https://doi.org/10.1007/978-3-642-13033-5_21
18. Houtekamer, P.L., Mitchell, H.L.: Data assimilation using an ensemble Kalman filter technique. Mon. Weather Rev. **126**(3), 796–811 (1998)
19. Bird, J.J., Richardson, S.J., Langelaan, J.W.: Estimating the vertical structure of weather-induced mission costs for small UAS. Sensors **19**(12), 1–30 (2019)

Plenary Presentations - Section 3: Energy Systems

Microgrid Operational Planning Using Deviation Clustering Within a DDDAS Framework

Joshua Darville$^{(\boxtimes)}$ and Nurcin Celik🆔

University of Miami, Coral Gables, FL 33124, USA
jmd437@miami.com, celik@miami.edu

Abstract. As climate change progresses and the global population continues to increase, meeting the energy demand is an issue that has been brought to the forefront of the conversation. Microgrids (MGs) are groundbreaking tools that have risen in popularity to combat this crisis by capitalizing on renewable, distributed energy resources to efficiently satisfy the energy demand from environmental sensors via telemetry. In this work, we present a deviation clustering (DC) algorithm within a dynamic data-driven application systems (DDDAS) framework to reduce the length of the MG dispatch model's planning horizon while retaining the temporal characteristics of the initial load profile. The DDDAS framework allows for the adjustment of the current dispatch decisions in near real-time. We develop two modules embedded within this framework; the first is a proposed rule-based policy (RBP) that modifies the sensing strategy and the second is the DC algorithm which reduces the execution time of the MG simulation. Numerical analysis was conducted on the IEEE-18 bus test network to assess the performance of the proposed framework and determine an appropriate threshold for clustering. The limitations of the presented framework were also determined by comparing the tradeoff between its the speed of the solver's solution time and the accuracy of the resulting solution. The results indicate a decrease in solution time within the desired accuracy limits when using the proposed approach as opposed to traditional load dispatch.

Keywords: Microgrids · Clustering algorithms · Data analytics · Climate change · Distributed feedback devices

1 Introduction

Energy surety remains the primary concern for many countries. In the wake of existing factors such as the rising global population [1], high frequency of natural disasters [2], and accelerating climate change due to carbon emissions (CO_2) [3], the utilization of distributed energy resources (DERs) into existing main grid technology is essential to effectively sustain the global population. Moreover, unexpected factors such as the COVID-19 virus [4] have re-emphasized the need for a quicker response to real-time situations as many people continually remain in quarantine consuming power (hence increasing residential demand). This dilemma presents both a challenge to reliable energy systems in

© Springer Nature Switzerland AG 2020
F. Darema et al. (Eds.): DDDAS 2020, LNCS 12312, pp. 77–84, 2020.
https://doi.org/10.1007/978-3-030-61725-7_11

times of crisis and an opportunity to utilize a load profile generated by the quarantined clusters for operational planning. Thus, understanding the parallel characteristics across various applications, is crucial for innovation [5]. Microgrids are sub-networks that utilize DERs in parallel with the main grid to efficiently dispatch power, ensuring reliable distribution with quicker response time than their traditional, manual counterparts. Therefore, the challenge to obtain real-time situational awareness requires the regulation of large heterogeneous data for anomaly detection within the microgrid (MG) system. Consequently, the MG simulation will need to steer the instrumentation to acquire the most relevant sensory data at the appropriate fidelity for near real-time decision making.

The powerful paradigm, Dynamic Data-Driven Application Systems (DDDAS), first introduced by [6] resolves this challenge in a holistic manner [7]. DDDAS equips the proposed framework with the ability to ascertain how the system and environmental data should be harvested as the MG simulation receives near real-time data from the MG system. Furthermore, DDDAS has had tremendous success across a vast and diverse spectrum of fields [4]. Examples of these fields include materials modeling [8], aerospace engineering [9], cybersecurity [10], smart cities [11, 12], cloud-data access [13, 14] and energy-aware optimization [1, 3, 15]. Similarly, derivatives of DDDAS such as [16, 17] are utilized within the context of bulk-power systems by dynamically receiving data into an executing MG simulation and utilizing an online learning algorithm to feed the database for faster future computations.

However, rapid future computations incur an engineering tradeoff between computational resources and the desired accuracy within an appropriate time as the MG dispatch model scales. For large scale bulk-power systems, this approach becomes less applicable as the error rises for a highly clustered load profile or becomes too computationally expensive to solve the initial load profile. Hence, it is imperative to efficiently cluster the initial load profile and consequently, the number of timesteps (blocks) throughout the planning horizon within an acceptable margin of error. Among the variety of clustering techniques, the most common is k-means use by [18] on spatial data to aggregate similar load profiles, and achieve accurate long-term load forecasts based on land use or location. However, [19] clusters based on the user's load characteristics to reduce the complexity of communication between the grid and the users. Previous studies throughout the literature further note the relationship between the scale of the MG dispatch model and the number of blocks that define the planning horizon [20].

Main contributions of this work are twofold. First, a rule-based policy (RBP) is presented to integrate the transmission system operator (TSO) into the considered DDDAS framework. Despite DDDAS's autonomous operational design for efficacy, anomalous data derived from various sensors (in error or fault) could result in blackouts, load spikes and/or a series of events leading toward an unplanned islanding. Thus, a human-in-the-loop system could be necessary. This necessity is represented by the TSO and is embedded within the proposed DDDAS framework. Second is the deviation clustering (DC) algorithm which clusters the initial load profile based on the standard deviation (σ) of similar load levels, enhancing the MG simulation's execution time. An engineering tradeoff between the speed of the solver's solution time and the accuracy of the resulting solution was developed to evaluate this performance of the presented approach.

This study is organized as follows. In Sect. 2, the various modules embedded in the MG framework design are outlined including the rule-based policy and the deviation clustering algorithm. In Sect. 3, numerical analysis is used to examine the engineering tradeoff between the speed of the solver's solution time and the accuracy of the resulting solution along with the benefit of using the DC algorithm. Finally, Sect. 4 concludes the results of this study.

2   Microgrid Framework Design

The proposed framework can be described via three cycles (see Fig. 1.). Cycle 1 is the main loop that integrates the MG Simulation with the DC algorithm and the RBP. Initially, near real-time data from the MG system is fed into the MG Simulation. The simulation produces the load profile according to the received data, which is then fed into the DC algorithm. After DC processes the initial load profile, the newly clustered profile is sent to the RBP as depicted in Fig. 1.

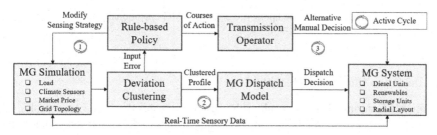

Fig. 1. Proposed MG operational planning within a DDDAS framework

The RBP then determines whether to continue the operation with cycle 2 or cycle 3, which reflects autonomous operation or some degree of TSO intervention, respectively. The MG dispatch model used in cycle 2 is based on [16] with an extension for energy storage capabilities. Both cycles 2 and 3 are mutually exclusive, and the unselected cycle will become inactive. As cycle 1 recursively scrutinizes the data according to the RBP, cycle 2 typically follows utilizing the MG dispatch model for decision-making unless the MG simulation receives anomalous data; In this case, cycle 3 would be chosen to involve some degree of TSO intervention.

The DDDAS paradigm supports this symbiotic, feedback loop requesting information unique to potential anomalies while receiving near real-time data. This two-way communication feature of DDDAS helps to better mimic the real-world MG system by capturing the current system's state and investigating extreme values to revise the current MG dispatch decisions. The RBP determines the operation plan, categorized by the risk associated with data, where the conditions are predicated on the tradeoff of using the DC algorithm.

2.1   Rule-Based Policy

In Fig. 2, which is nested in Fig. 1, the proposed RBP chooses which cycle should be used to determine the MG operational plan based on the load input error before and after clustering (Dt). The RBP is categorized into three major abnormality levels as low, medium, and high. Cycle 2 utilizes the MG dispatch model decisions when there is low risk for efficiency. However, cycle 3 integrates the TSO when there is a potentially higher risk. TSO may then follow the suggested courses of action from the RBP or make an informed decision having been provided with alternatives. The courses of action associated with each abnormality level are outlined in Fig. 2 and a subset of the initial load reflecting public safety facilities (Dcrit) is energized despite the risk.

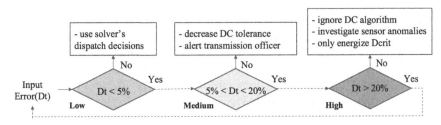

Fig. 2. Rule-based policy to determine MG operational plan

2.2 Deviation Clustering Algorithm

Deviation Clustering (DC) is an algorithm used to cluster the initial load profile to reduce the length of the planning horizon while retaining the initial load's temporal characteristics as explained in Table 1.

Table 1. Algorithm for Deviation Clustering.

Input: x load profile, σ threshold
1. Initialize counter
2. Initialize an empty array (no load profile)
3. Add the first element of x to the empty array
4. Conduct a pairwise comparison between the elements of x
5. If the pair's standard deviation is $< \sigma$, cluster the load
6. Else add the current element from x to begin new cluster
7. Conduct another pairwise comparison on x
8. If the elements in the pair are not equal, increase the counter
Output: the clustered load profile, the new planning horizon in blocks

In summary, DC clusters the load profile based on the standard deviation (σ) of sub-clusters throughout the planning horizon, where σ is the threshold value for all sub-clusters. As σ increases, so does the size of each sub-cluster resulting in fewer blocks to define the planning horizon. Moreover, the clustering occurs chronologically to preserve the temporal characteristics of the initial load profile.

3   Numerical Analysis

The IEEE-18 is selected as the testbed for this study where the data can be found at [22] for replicability purposes. After collecting the data, the proposed approach for MG operational planning was applied to examine the effects of implementing the DC algorithm within a DDDAS framework.

3.1   Deviation Clustering Tradeoff

When utilizing the DC algorithm, a varying degree of distortion in the initial load profile was observed by incrementing the sigma value as shown in Fig. 3. As previously mentioned, sigma value (σ) is a threshold for all sub-clusters.

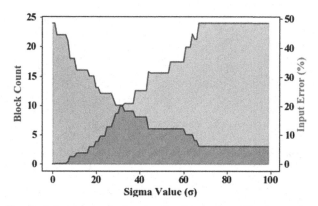

Fig. 3. Tradeoff analysis between reducing the planning horizon (block count) and retaining the initial information (input error) at various sigma values (σ)

In Fig. 3, the sigma value (σ) acts as a control parameter for the DC algorithm used to adjust the degree of clustering. The resultant level of distortion is captured by the input error and the resultant length of the planning horizon is captured by block count simultaneously. Input error captures change in the load profile between the MG simulation and the MG system as previously mentioned in Fig. 2. Block count is defined as $BC = 24 \ blocks/t_{hours}$ where its minimum is set as 24 blocks per day. Notably, this approach scales to consider smaller hourly time-steps. This allows for the realization of short-term MG operational planning. For example, a 1-min schedule would contain 1440 blocks, since $BC = 24 \ blocks/1/60 \ h = 1440 \ blocks$. Hence, it is imperative to find a suitable (σ) which effectively utilizes computational resources during nominal operation.

Similarly, the intersection between the block count and input error reflects the σ at which the tradeoff no longer exists because it shares an equivalent response relative to their scales. Since the σ is directly proportional to the input error but inversely proportional to the block count, the point of intersection (POI) will vary for each initial load profile. A single replication of the load profile was used in Fig. 3 and the best σ was determined to within [0, 30], which up to the POI; this interval reflects low to medium risk and gives preference toward accuracy instead of speed. Conversely, a high risk is associated with σ outside [0, 30] which reflect preference toward speed instead of accuracy. Designating the appropriate range based on the POI updates σ and consequently the proposed DC and RBP modules according to the most recent data. Additionally, this preferred region of operation can be adjusted before the POI by the TSO as a safety factor.

3.2 Utility of Deviation Clustering

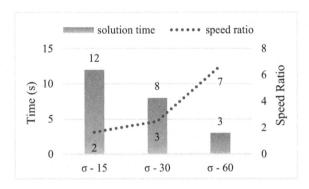

Fig. 4. DC's effect on solution time for the MG Dispatch model

In Fig. 4, we observe a decrease in solution time at higher σ values which consequently enhances the execution speed of the MG application reaffirming the previous observation in Fig. 3. The speed ratio is defined as the solution time of traditional dispatch where σ = 0 divided by the new solution time post deviation clustering, to capture any improvement. For example, a speed ratio of 2 at σ = 15 indicates that clustering at σ = 15 results in obtaining a solution twice as fast compared to traditional dispatch σ = 0. Conversely, σ results are directly proportional to the speed ratios which validates their use as control parameters for clustering and consequently the scale of the MG dispatch model. It should be noted that this benefit of obtaining a faster solution is limited by level of risk incurred previously mentioned in Fig. 3 and reflected in Table 2 with increasing output error, where output error is the error change in dispatch decision with the initial, unfiltered load profile. The MG simulation benefit of solution speed and limitation of information distortion using the DC module are summarized in Table 2, for the TSO to determine acceptable risk independent of the regions outlined by the proposed RBP module in Fig. 2.

Table 2. Summary of the DC effect on the MG application.

Load Profile	Block Count	Input Error	Speed Ratio	Output Error
Sigma = 0	24	–	–	–
Sigma = 15	16	3.7	2	2.8
Sigma = 30	10	17.4	3	7.23
Sigma = 60	6	35.2	7	9.6

4 Conclusion

This study presents a symbiotic benefit between a microgrid simulation and its execution in relation to data updated from a real system, within a dynamic data-driven application systems (DDDAS) framework. The DDDAS paradigm was applied to a microgrid (MG) simulation using two modules, a deviation clustering (DC) algorithm to reduce the dispatch model's scale, consequently enhancing the MG simulation's execution time, and a rule-based policy (RBP) to blend the transmission system operator (TSO) with smart grid operation design. Figure 1 provides an overview of all the modules within the proposed DDDAS framework for MG operational planning. The proposed DC algorithm clusters the initial load profile using the standard deviation as a control parameter for each sub-cluster.

Numerical analysis was conducted on the IEEE-18 bus test network and standard deviation within [0, 30] was selected based on the engineering tradeoff between the speed of the solver's solution time and the accuracy of the resulting solution. Furthermore, it was observed that the temporal characteristics of the initial load profile were retained at $\sigma = 15$ but not $\sigma = 60$ since the input error increases from 3.7% to 35.2%. Moreover, the DC algorithm generates a solution 50% faster with a 3.7% risk at $\sigma = 15$ when compared to traditional forms of microgrid dispatch. Numeral analysis has shown that standard deviation was directly proportional to input error but inversely proportional to block count, which reflects distortion in the load profile and the length of the planning horizon, respectively. Hence, these intervals can be used to develop conditions for the proposed RBP and detect anomalies other than those resulting the DC algorithm including the ones resulting in load spikes, blackouts and/or unplanned islanding.

References

1. Darville, J., Celik, N.: Simulation optimization for unit commitment using a region-based sampling (RBS) algorithm. In: Proceedings of the 2020 Institute of Industrial and Systems Engineers (2020)
2. Damgacioglu, H., Alyamani, T., Celik, N.: Evaluation of renewable energy policies using agent-based simulation - a case study of the state of Texas. In: Proceedings of the IIE Annual Conference, p. 154 (2015)
3. Celik, N., Thanos, A.E., Saenz, J.P.: DDDAMS-based dispatch control in power networks. Procedia Comput. Sci. **18**, 1899–1908 (2013)

4. Blasch, E., Ravela, S., Aved, A. (eds.): Handbook of Dynamic Data Driven Applications Systems. Springer, Cham (2018). https://doi.org/10.1007/978-3-319-95504-9
5. Darema, F.: On the parallel characteristics of engineering/scientific and commercial applications: differences, similarities and future outlook. In: Keane, J.A. (ed.) Parallel Commercial Processing, United Kingdon (1996)
6. Darema, F.: Dynamic data driven applications systems: a new paradigm for application simulations and measurements. In: Bubak, M., van Albada, G.D., Sloot, P.M.A., Dongarra, Jack (eds.) ICCS 2004. LNCS, vol. 3038, pp. 662–669. Springer, Heidelberg (2004). https://doi.org/10.1007/978-3-540-24688-6_86
7. Blasch, E.P., Aved, A.J.: Dynamic data-driven application system (DDDAS) for video surveillance user support. Procedia Comput. Sci. **51**(1), 2503–2517 (2015)
8. Li, X., Tran, P.H., Liu, T., Park, C.: Simulation-guided regression approach for estimating the size distribution of nanoparticles with dynamic light scattering data. IISE Trans. **49**(1), 70–83 (2017)
9. Blasch, E.: DDDAS advantages from high-dimensional simulation. In: Proceeding- Winter Simulation. Conference, vol. 2018-decem, pp. 1418–1429 (2019)
10. Blasch, E., Al-Nashif, Y., Hariri, S.: Static versus dynamic data information fusion analysis using DDDAS for cyber security trust. Procedia Comput. Sci. **29**, 1299–1313 (2014)
11. Fujimoto, R., et al.: Dynamic data driven application systems for smart cities and urban infrastructures. In: Proceedings - Winter Simulation Conference, Oecd 2011, pp. 1143–1157 (2016)
12. Hunter, M., Biswas, A., Fujimoto, R.: Energy efficient middleware for dynamic data driven application systems. In: Proceedings - Winter Simulation Conference, vol. 2018-Decem, pp. 628–639 (2019)
13. Yavuz, A., et al.: Advancing self-healing capabilities in interconnected Microgrids via DDDAS with relational database management. In: Proceedings of the 2020 Winter Simulation Conference (2020)
14. Aved, A.J.: Scene understanding for real time processing of queries over big data streaming video, University of Central Florida (2013)
15. Shi, X., Damgacioglu, H., Celik, N.: A dynamic data-driven approach for operation planning of microgrids. Procedia Comput. Sci. **51**(1), 2543–2552 (2015)
16. Damgacioglu, H., Bastani, M., Celik, N.: A dynamic data-driven optimization framework for demand side management in microgrids. In: Blasch, E., Ravela, S., Aved, A. (eds.) Handbook of Dynamic Data Driven Applications Systems, pp. 489–504. Springer, Cham (2018). https://doi.org/10.1007/978-3-319-95504-9_21
17. Thanos, A.E., Bastani, M., Celik, N., Chen, C.: Framework for Automated Control in Microgrids. IEEE Trans. Smart Grid **8**(1), 209–218 (2017)
18. Ye, C., Ding, Y., Wang, P., Lin, Z.: A data-driven bottom-up approach for spatial and temporal electric load forecasting. IEEE Trans. Power Syst. **34**(3), 1966–1979 (2019)
19. Zhou, K., Chen, Y., Xu, Z., Lu, J., Hu, Z.: A smart-community demand respsonse load scheduling method based on consumer clustering. In: 2nd IEEE Conference on Energy Internet Energy System Integration EI2 2018 – Proceedings, pp. 1–4 (2018)
20. Shao, C., Feng, C., Wang, X.: Load state transition curve based unit commitment for power system production cost modeling (2019)

Dynamic Data-Driven Self-healing Application for Phasor Measurement Unit Networks

Yanfeng Qu$^{(\boxtimes)}$, Xin Liu, Jiaqi Yan, and Dong Jin

Illinois Institute of Technology, Chicago, IL 60616, USA
{yqu9,xliu125,jyan31}@hawk.iit.edu, dong.jin@iit.edu

Abstract. This paper describes an approach to apply the dynamic data-driven applications systems (DDDAS) paradigm to enhance cyber security and resilience of wide-area monitoring systems in electrical grids. In particular, we explore a DDDAS-aware application to self-heal phasor measurement unit (PMU) networks that monitor the states of power systems in real-time. The application is built on top of a novel software-defined networking (SDN) architecture. The main components include a dynamic data-driven model that efficiently abstracts the PMU network behavior at run time and an optimization-based solution to quickly reconfigure network connections to restore the power system observability. The application also compresses network updates of the recovery plan to further reduce the recovery time. We develop a prototype system in a container-based network testbed and evaluate the recovery time of the self-healing application using the IEEE 30-bus system.

Keywords: Dynamic data driven application systems ·
Software-defined networking · Phasor measurement unit · Smart grid
resilience and security

1 Introduction

Phase measurement units (PMU) have been increasingly and rapidly deployed in the wide-area monitoring systems to capture the states of electric grids in real-time. PMUs are time-synchronized by GPS timestamps and measure power system states, such as magnitudes and phase angles of current and voltage at each bus, at rates between 30 and 240 Hz. The measurements are then aggregated at phasor data concentrators (PDC) and eventually transmitted to the control center to support state estimation and other critical control and analytic applications. Recent studies reveal that PMU networks are vulnerable to different types of cyber-attacks [1,2], which negatively impact the visualization and situational awareness of power systems.

To address this challenge, we develop a self-healing PMU network scheme with the objective of preventing the propagation of the attacks and maintaining

© Springer Nature Switzerland AG 2020
F. Darema et al. (Eds.): DDDAS 2020, LNCS 12312, pp. 85–92, 2020.
https://doi.org/10.1007/978-3-030-61725-7_12

the complete observability of the power system. We take a DDDAS-based approach to design the self-healing scheme. DDDAS stands for dynamic data-driven
applications systems, which is a paradigm that involves dynamically incorporating real-time data into computations in order to steer the measurement and
control process of an application system [3]. The DDDAS concept has been
successfully applied to many emerging application areas over decades, such as
smart cities, manufacturing, transportation, health care, critical infrastructures,
and many others [4,5].

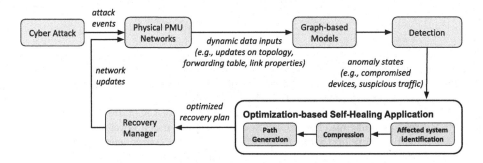

Fig. 1. DDDAS-aware PMU network self-healing application design

Figure 1 depicts the design of our DDDAS-aware self-healing PMU network.
The communication network is represented as a dynamic data-driven model that
efficiently abstracts the physical PMU network behavior (e.g., packet forwarding) under a dynamic system environment (e.g., network updates caused by
cyber-attacks, recovery plans, and other operations). The graph-based model is
capable of accepting real-time data at execution time as system states evolve.
When the model enters into an abnormal state (e.g., dropped or suspicious traffic from compromised devices), the self-healing scheme is triggered to isolate the
traffic from those PMUs and PDCs. The scheme consists of three steps. First,
it identifies the portion of the network affected by the cyber incident, such as
the list of PMUs to reconnect; Second, it solves an optimization problem to
compute the destination PDC for each PMU in the list as well as the immediate switches by meeting the specified device and network operation constraints.
Third, it generates an optimal recovery plan to restore power system observability and translate them into network updates for each affected switch. As
a result, the scheme steers the control and measurement process by installing
network updates on the physical network to self-heal the PMU systems. The
updated measurement data and control events are then fed into the graph-based
model for further processing. An effective feedback loop is thus enabled to steer
the entire self-healing process.

One key component to support this DDDAS-based PMU network self-healing
application is the underlying software-defined networking (SDN) based communication infrastructure. SDN is a programmable open-source approach to design-

ing, building, and managing communication networks [6]. SDN decouples the network control from the forwarding functions in network devices and offloads its decision functions to a logically centralized SDN controller. With the increasing size and complexity of the communication networks for wide-area control and monitoring systems, SDN has been increasingly investigated to improve their resilience and security [7–9]. The SDN controller provides the global network visibility that enables us to develop the optimization-based scheme to self-heal the PMU network connection against cyber-attacks. The communication network is composed of a set of SDN switches that enable a quick execution of the recovery plan through SDN's direct network programmability. Moreover, our scheme also applies a rule compression mechanism that compresses the SDN network updates of the recovery plan to further reduce the recovery time. Finally, we develop a proof-of-concept system in a container-based SDN emulation testbed and conduct performance evaluation using the IEEE 30-bus system. The PMU network connection is successfully recovered even when half of the PDCs are compromised, and the recovery time including the plan generation and network updates installation is all within 850 μs.

The remainder of the paper is organized as follows. Section 2 introduces an SDN-based architecture design that enables fast self-healing of PMU networks. Section 3 describes the DDDAS-aware self-healing application including the system model, SDN rule compression method, and optimization model formulation. Section 4 presents the experimental results for performance evaluation. Section 5 concludes the paper with future works.

2   SDN-Based PMU Network Architecture

We present an SDN-based network architecture to automatically self-heal PMU connections and preserve power system observability. This is useful to handle the growing cyber-attacks in wide-area monitoring and control systems that comprise PMU/PDC devices to drop and manipulate measurement data and control messages. Figure 2 depicts the architecture design that consists of five layers. The PMUs measure the states of the underlying power system and the measurements are aggregated at PDCs through the communication network layer, which is composed of a set of SDN-enabled switches to enable direct network programmability. The novelty of the design is mainly at the control layer, in which we integrate an SDN controller to the existing power grid controller. As a result, we now have global visibility and centralized control over the underlying communication network including the end-hosts (i.e., PMU and PDC) and the networking devices (e.g., switches, routers, gateways, and other middle boxes). Within the SDN controller, we develop an optimization-based self-healing scheme to reconfigure the PMU network against compromised or faulty devices. Upon detection of compromised devices, the scheme quickly generates a recovery plan that contains optimal communication path updates to reconnected lost PMUs to PDCs. The scheme also employs a compression module to reduce the number of SDN rules to be installed to further reduce the recovery time.

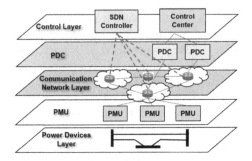

Fig. 2. An SDN-based self-healing PMU network architecture

3   System Modeling and Problem Formulation

3.1   System Model and Power System Observability

The power transmission network is represented by a graph $G_T = <B \cup U, T_U>$, where B is the set of buses, U is the set of PMUs, and T_U is a $|B| \times |U|$ connectivity matrix.

$$t_U[i,j] = \begin{cases} 1, & b_i \ u_j \text{ are connected} \\ 0, & \text{otherwise} \end{cases} \tag{1}$$

The communication network is represented by another graph $G_C = <U \cup D \cup S, L>$, where each PMU connects to a bus; D is the set of PDCs; and S is the set of SDN switches. L is a connectivity matrix merged via common columns from a $|U| \times |S|$ matrix, a $|S| \times |S|$, and a $|D| \times |S|$ matrix.

$$l[i,j] = \begin{cases} 1, & (u_i \text{ and } s_j) \text{ or } (s_i \text{ and } s_j) \text{ or } (d_i \text{ and } s_j) \text{ are connected} \\ 0, & \text{otherwise} \end{cases} \tag{2}$$

We represent the recovery plan as the following binary variable matrix X

$$x_{ij} = \begin{cases} 1, & u_i \text{ connects to } d_j \\ 0, & \text{otherwise} \end{cases} \tag{3}$$

A bus is observable if it can be measured by a PMU or estimated by the PMU located on an adjacent bus. Also, measurement data by the PMU has to be reported to a PDC. The power system is observable if all buses are observable. For each bus i, let $A(i)$ denote a set of its adjacent buses and the bus i itself. We define the power system observability as follows.

$$O = \wedge_{\forall i \in B, \forall j \in A(i)}((\vee_{\forall k \in U} t_U[j,k]) \wedge (\vee_{\forall l \in D} x_{k,l})) \tag{4}$$

3.2 Optimization Model and Formulation

We assume the power system is observable before a cyber attack. The attack event compromises a set of PDCs, $D_c \subseteq D$, and triggers the detection system. We then further identify a set of disconnected PMUs, $U_d \subseteq U$, which reduces the power system observability. Observability redundancy exists in the power system because a bus may be monitored by multiple PMUs or estimated through measurements from other related PMUs. Therefore, reconnecting a subset of PMUs in U_d can restore the complete observability. The self-healing scheme computes a recovery plan in the form of a set of updated communication paths $p = \{p_1, p_2, ..., p_n\}$, where $p_1 \in U_d$ and $p_n \in D \setminus D_c$, and each tuple $(p_i, p_{i+1}) \in L$ is a communication link segment. The SDN controller can directly program the switches and install updated rules to realize these paths. Certain paths in the recovery plan may involve a common switch, and it is likely that those paths re-routes different PMUs to the same destination PDC. Hence, we consider using wildcards in the source field of the corresponding SDN rules to further reduce the number of network updates.

We expand $x_{i,j}$ to a new binary decision variable $y_{s,i,j,k}$ defined as follows:

$$y_{s,i,j,k} = \begin{cases} 1, & u_i \text{ reconnects to } d_j \text{ through port } k \text{ of switch } s \\ 0, & \text{otherwise} \end{cases} \tag{5}$$

where s is the switch, i is the source PMU, j is the destination PDC, and k is the switch out-port. For simplicity, we assume that every switch has the same number of out-ports. Based on switch s and port k, we define a function, $n(s, k)$, to map the next hop of $p(i)$ in communication path p is $p(i+1)$.

We assume the SDN controller can install rules on switches in parallel. Let the auxiliary variable Z indicate the maximum number of rules to install on each switch. The objective is to minimize Z with the following constraints.

$$\min : Z$$
$$s.t. \ \forall s \in S : Z \geq \sum_{j \in D \setminus D_c} \sum_k \cup_i y_{s,i,j,k} \tag{6}$$

Constraint of Power System Observability. Assume that each bus is attached to one PMU, we revise Eq. 4 and obtain the following constraint.

$$\forall i \in U_d : \sum_{i \in N(i)} \sum_{j \in D \setminus D_c} \vee_s \vee_k y_{s,i,j,k} \geq 1 \tag{7}$$

where $N(i)$ denotes a set of PMUs including PMU i and all its neighboring PMUs.

Constraint of Switch Forwarding. For each switch s, it takes at most one port to forward the measurement data from PMU i. Note that each PMU can connect up to one PDC.

$$\forall s \in S, \forall i \in U_d, : \sum_{j \in D \setminus D_c} \sum_k y_{s,i,j,k} \leq 1 \tag{8}$$

Constraints of Communication Path. Assume that a source PMU i connects to switch $\alpha(i)$ and its destination PDC j connects to switch $\alpha(j)$. For switch $\alpha(i)$, the difference in the number of output flows and input flows is

$$\forall i \in U_d : \sum_k \sum_{j \in D \setminus D_c} y_{\alpha(i),i,j,k} - \sum_u \sum_v \sum_{n(s,k)=\alpha(i)} y_{s,u,v,k} = \sum_{j \in D \setminus D_c} V_s \vee_k y_{s,i,j,k} \tag{9}$$

For switch $\alpha(j)$, the difference in the number of output flows and input flows is

$$\forall j \in D \setminus D_c : \sum_u \sum_v \sum_{n(s,k)=\alpha(j)} y_{s,u,v,k} - \sum_i \sum_k y_{\alpha(j),i,j,k} = \sum_i V_s \vee_k y_{s,i,j,k} \tag{10}$$

For all other switches in the communication path, the number of output flows is equal to the number of input flows.

$$\forall p \notin \{\alpha(i)\} \wedge p \notin \{\alpha(j)\}, \forall i \in U_d, \forall j \in D \setminus D_c :$$

$$\sum_i \sum_j \sum_k y_{p,i,j,k} - \sum_i \sum_j \sum_{n(s,k)=p} y_{s,i,j,k} = 0 \tag{11}$$

4   Evaluation

4.1   Experimental Setup

We develop a prototype system in an SDN emulation testbed, and place our self-healing scheme as an application in the SDN controller. We use the GNU Linear Programming Kit (GLPK) solver for the ILP problem formulated in Sect. 3.2. To conduct evaluation experiments, we generate a PMU network based on the IEEE 30-bus system. We place one PMU on each bus, and then get the neighboring PMU list according to the adjacent matrix of each bus in the transmission system. We now apply the minimum set cover problem to obtain the least number of PMU sets. We also place one PDC in each set and connect the PDC to PMUs through a switch. All the switches are connected using a ring topology. The original power transmission system is shown in Fig. 3(a), and the constructed PMU network is shown in Fig. 3(b), which is composed of 30 PMUs, 10 PDCs, and 10 switches.

4.2   Performance Evaluation of PMU Network Self-healing Scheme

Model Computational Time is the time spent on the optimization model execution to produce the recovery plan of reconnecting the necessary PMUs to restore power system observability. We vary the number of compromised PDCs from 1 to 5, and run 30 experiments for each case. The means and standard deviations are plotted in Fig. 4(a). We can observe that the PMU network is successfully recovered for all the experiments, even when for the cases when half

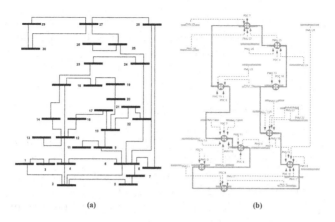

Fig. 3. PMU network construction from the original transmission network (a) IEEE 30-bus system, to (b) PMU network

of the PDC (i.e., 5 out of 10) are compromised. The average computational time is fast, from 265.6 ms to 643.4 ms, with the standard deviation around 20%. With the growing number of compromised PDCs, the computational time increases at first because the generated recovery paths become more complex. However, when the computational time does not keep increasing as more compromised PDCs do not always result in more PMUs to recover.

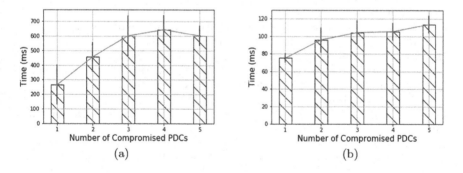

Fig. 4. Recovery plan: (a) computational time, and (b) installation time

Rule Installation Time is the time spent on realizing the recovery plan in the PMU network, including the rule generation at the SDN controller, the rule transmission from the controller to the switches, and the actual rule installation on the switches. We again vary the number of compromised PDCs from 1 to 5, and run 30 experiments for each case. The results are plotted in Fig. 4(b). We observe that it takes 75.1 ms to 113.4 ms on average to install the recovery plan. The standard deviation is within 10%. The installation time increases as the number of compromised PDCs grows. Compared with the computational time, the installation time is much faster in general. The total time to generate and install the recovery plan is quick in general as all the experiments complete within 850 µs.

5   Conclusion and Future Works

We apply the DDDAS paradigm to protect PMU networks and restore the power system observability. Our DDDAS-aware network self-healing application considers both the power system and communication network characteristics with the help of an SDN-based cyber-infrastructure. The current version focuses on PMUs in the power transmission systems and we will extend it to micro PMUs on the distribution systems and microgrids.

Acknowledgment. This work is partly sponsored by the Air Force Office of Scientific Research (AFOSR) under Grant YIP FA9550-17-1-0240, the National Science Foundation (NSF) under Grant CNS-1618631, and the Maryland Procurement Office under Contract No. H98230-18-D-0007.

References

1. Khan, R., Maynard, P., Mclaughlin, K., Laverty, D., Sezer, S.: Threat analysis of blackenergy malware for synchrophasor based real-time control and monitoring in smart grid. In: Proceedings of the 4th International Symposium for ICS and SCADA Cyber Security Research (2016)
2. Liu, X., Li, Z.: False data attacks against AC state estimation with incomplete network information. IEEE Trans. Smart Grid **8**(5), 2239–2248 (2017)
3. Darema, F.: Dynamic data driven applications systems: a new paradigm for application simulations and measurements. In: Bubak, M., van Albada, G.D., Sloot, P.M.A., Dongarra, J. (eds.) ICCS 2004. LNCS, vol. 3038, pp. 662–669. Springer, Heidelberg (2004). https://doi.org/10.1007/978-3-540-24688-6_86
4. Blasch, E., Ravela, S., Aved, A. (eds.): Handbook of Dynamic Data Driven Applications Systems. Springer, Cham (2018)
5. Fujimoto, R., et al.: Dynamic data driven application systems: research challenges and opportunities. In: Proceedings of the 2018 Winter Simulation Conference (WSC), pp. 664–678 (2018)
6. McKeown, N., et al.: Openflow: enabling innovation in campus networks. ACM SIGCOMM Comput. Commun. Rev. **38**(2), 69–74 (2008)
7. Lin, H., et al.: Self-healing attack-resilient PMU network for power system operation. IEEE Trans. Smart Grid **9**(3), 1551–1565 (2018)
8. Sarailoo, M., Wu, N.E.: An algorithm for resilient sensor network upgrade with fewest PMUs. In: Proceedings of the 2017 Resilience Week (RWS), pp. 77–82 (2017)
9. Qu, Y., Liu, X., Jin, D., Hong, Y., Chen, C.: Enabling a resilient and self-healing PMU infrastructure using centralized network control. In: Proceedings of the 2018 ACM International Workshop on Security in Software Defined Networks & Network Function Virtualization, pp. 13–18 (2018)

Interpretable Deep Attention Model for Multivariate Time Series Prediction in Building Energy Systems

Tryambak Gangopadhyay[1(⊠)], Sin Yong Tan[1], Zhanhong Jiang[2], and Soumik Sarkar[1]

[1] Department of Mechanical Engineering, Iowa State University, Ames, IA 50011, USA
{tryambak,tsyong98,soumiks}@iastate.edu
[2] Data Sciences and Product Development, Johnson Controls, Milwaukee, WI 53202, USA
zhanhong.jiang@jci.com

Abstract. Multivariate time series prediction has important applications in the domain of energy-efficient building technology. With the buildings consuming large amounts of electrical energy, it is critical to reducing energy consumption and economic costs while ensuring a better quality of urban living standards. As sensor-actuator rich, smart buildings are becoming complex dynamic data-driven applications systems (DDDAS), accurate and interpretable data-driven decision-making tools can have immense value. In this context, we develop a novel deep learning model that can explicitly capture the temporal correlations through LSTM layers. The model can isolate the important timesteps in the input time series for prediction. Also, it is critical to identify the contributions of different variables in the multivariate input. Our proposed model based on attention mechanisms can simultaneously learn important timesteps and variables. We demonstrate the results using a public multivariate time series dataset collected from an air handling unit in a building heating, ventilation, and air-conditioning (HVAC) system. The model with enhanced interpretability does not compromise with the prediction accuracy. The interpretations are validated from a domain knowledge perspective.

Keywords: Attention · LSTM · Interpretability

1 Introduction

Dynamic data-driven applications systems (DDDAS) depend on time-series data of different sensors to accurately predict the behavior of complex engineering

This work has been supported in part by the U.S. Air Force Office of Scientific Research under the YIP grant FA9550-17-1-0220. Any opinions, findings and conclusions or recommendations expressed in this publication are those of the authors and do not necessarily reflect the views of the sponsoring agency.

© Springer Nature Switzerland AG 2020
F. Darema et al. (Eds.): DDDAS 2020, LNCS 12312, pp. 93–101, 2020.
https://doi.org/10.1007/978-3-030-61725-7_13

systems [1,2]. When the data is large-scale and high-dimensional with complex underlying interactions, physics-based modeling, or specific data-driven analyses may not be feasible. During such a scenario, deep learning models can be used for multivariate time series prediction, which finds applications in performance monitoring of engineering systems [3] and other domains [4,5]. In addition to accuracy, the interpretability of the prediction outcomes is essential to gain domain insights and develop user trust in implementing the models.

The thermal dynamic model has played a critical role in building heating, ventilation, and air-conditioning (HVAC) systems to capture the underlying heat transfer relationships and serve advanced control strategies [6]. Hence, it is always a popular research topic. Generically, such modeling includes two types of methods - physical dynamics of the integral-differential equations with respect to energy and mass, and data-driven models based on time series measurements of environmental sensors [7,8]. Leveraging either of them enables us to predict the temperature evolution and energy consumption and design effective optimal controllers for the system. With the emergence of deep learning techniques, numerous research works have paid considerable attention to this area by adopting different deep neural networks to improve the modeling capability [9–11]. Although the prediction accuracy has been improved compared with the traditional methods, the interpretability of deep learning models remains unclear to most domain engineers [12]. Interpretability is important as it can provide a way to capture the underlying physical relationships among all measured variables without requiring much physics knowledge [13]. Hence, accurate prediction and interpretability should be simultaneously taken into account when designing a new model.

Long Short Term Memory (LSTM) networks can effectively capture the long-term temporal dependencies in multivariate time series [14]. LSTM has been utilized in different applications [15,16]. Attention-based model [17] was initially introduced for neural machine translation to overcome the bottleneck of the Encoder-Decoder model [18,19], which encodes information from all input time-steps in a single fixed-length vector. Inspired by this work, attention based models have been proposed for time series prediction [20–24]. Though these approaches have temporal attention, they do not have spatial attention to align directly with the output, limiting the ability of the model to capture spatial correlations explicitly. Some models [25] have only spatial attention. Also, some models are non-causal [20,22] or non-scalable [21] with no domain knowledge verification of the computed interpretations.

In this paper, we propose a novel spatiotemporal attention model that is accurate and provides spatiotemporal interpretations. The causal model can simultaneously soft search for the most relevant time-steps and variables with the spatial and temporal attentions aligned directly to the output [26]. The model is jointly trained in a unified architecture with attention weights learning the temporal and spatial contributions. To the best of our knowledge, this is the first work on attention-based time series models for interpretability in building energy prediction problems. The interpretability results are verified from a domain knowledge perspective. In general, the proposed model can be applied in different DDDAS utilizing multivariate time series data. Notably, it will significantly help advance the smart building HVAC optimal controller design. Data-driven control techniques, such as learning-based model-predictive control (MPC) or model-based reinforcement learning (MBRL) have emerged as the state-of-the-art in building energy management and control systems. The accuracy of the dynamic model significantly affects the control performance. A diverse set of deep learning models have been adopted accordingly while lacking interpretability in many existing works. Hence, the proposed model can be incorporated into the optimal control framework to minimize the energy consumption or cost and maintain thermal comfort requirements. Our model's enhanced interpretability delivers more useful insights regarding the impact of physical and interpretable model parameters on the modeling and control performance for these frameworks.

2   Model

2.1   Notations and Problem Formulation

We denote by $\mathbf{X} = [\mathbf{x}^1, \mathbf{x}^2, ..., \mathbf{x}^N]^\top \in \mathbb{R}^{N \times T_x}$, the compact form of all time series, where T_x and N signify the total input sequence length and the number of input variables respectively, $\mathbf{x}^i = [x_1^i, x_2^i, ..., x_{T_x}^i]^\top \in \mathbb{R}^{T_x}, i \in \{1, 2, ..., N\}$ signifies time series associated with each input variable. To represent all input variables at time step $t \in \{1, 2, ..., T_x\}$, with a slight abuse of notation, we denote by $\mathbf{x}_t = [x_t^1, x_t^2, ..., x_t^N]^\top \in \mathbb{R}^N$. Therefore, the time series can also be expressed as $\mathbf{X} = [\mathbf{x}_1, \mathbf{x}_2, ..., \mathbf{x}_{T_x}]^\top$. With $\mathbf{X}$ as input, we predict the output $\mathbf{y} \in \mathbb{R}$ at future time-step $(T_x + 1)$.

2.2   Spatiotemporal Attention (ST-Att) Model

The original *temporal* attention mechanism [17] was proposed to be used after the encoder. The attention weight of each encoder hidden state can be calculated by Eq. 1.

$$\alpha^t = \frac{\exp(a^t)}{\sum_{l=1}^{T_x} \exp(a^l)}, \quad \mathbf{s} = \sum_{t=1}^{T_x} \alpha^t \mathbf{h}_t. \tag{1}$$

The probability α^t reflects how much the output $\mathbf{y}$ is aligned to the input $\mathbf{x}_t$. In other words, α^t shows the importance of $\mathbf{h}_t$ in deciding the prediction $\mathbf{y}$. Here, the encoder hidden state is denoted by $\mathbf{h} \in \mathbb{R}^m$. The associated energy a^t is computed using an alignment model (feed-forward neural network). The *temporal context* vector $\mathbf{s}$ aggregates the information of all the input time-steps.

Recently, some models [20,27] have been proposed to incorporate spatial attention in the encoding phase. The *spatial* attention mechanism can determine the relative contributions of different input variables in multivariate time series prediction. At time-step $t - 1$, the encoder hidden and cell states are denoted as

$\mathbf{h}_{t-1} \in \mathbb{R}^m$ and $\mathbf{c}_{t-1} \in \mathbb{R}^m$ respectively. Given the i-th attribute time series $\mathbf{x}^i$ of length T_x, the spatial attention β_t^i at time-step t is computed as following.

$$e_t^i = \mathbf{v}_e^\top \tanh(W_e[\mathbf{h}_{t-1}; \mathbf{c}_{t-1}] + U_e \mathbf{x}^i), \ \beta_t^i = \frac{\exp(e_t^i)}{\sum_{o=1}^N \exp(e_t^o)} \tag{2}$$

This spatial attention approach suffers from two major limitations. Firstly, the *causality* is broken by using $\mathbf{x}^i, 1 \leq i \leq N$ covering the whole length of T_x to compute the spatial attention weights (Eq. 2) which are used to calculate the *weighted* time series $\hat{\mathbf{x}}_t$ at time-step t. Secondly, there is no direct alignment of the *spatial context* vector with the output time series. Therefore, the spatial relationships between input and output can only be captured implicitly after computing the hidden states.

The two limitations stated above can be addressed by introducing a novel spatiotemporal attention model (Fig. 1) where both the spatial and temporal attentions are aligned directly with the output variable [26]. Instead of having spatial attention in the encoder layer, we have spatial attention in parallel to the temporal attention in the prediction phase. The inputs to the spatial and temporal attention are spatial and temporal embeddings, respectively, which are generated independently. We compute the spatial embeddings by using feed forward neural network for each feature $\mathbf{x}^i = [x_1^i, x_2^i, ..., x_{T_x}^i]^\top \in \mathbb{R}^{T_x}, i \in \{1, 2, ..., N\}$. From $\mathbf{X} = [\mathbf{x}^1, \mathbf{x}^2, ..., \mathbf{x}^N]^\top$, the embeddings for all variables are computed as $\mathbf{D} = [\mathbf{d}^1, \mathbf{d}^2, ..., \mathbf{d}^N]^\top$, where $\mathbf{d}^i \in \mathbb{R}^m$. Given the input time series $\mathbf{X} = [\mathbf{x}_1, \mathbf{x}_2, ..., \mathbf{x}_{T_x}]^\top$, the encoder computes the temporal embeddings (hidden states) independently. The encoder consists of two stacked LSTM layers. At time-step t, the input to the encoder is $\mathbf{x}_t = [x_t^1, x_t^2, ..., x_t^N]^\top \in \mathbb{R}^N$. In the encoder, the hidden states computed by the first LSTM layer act as inputs for the second LSTM layer. The sequence of temporal embeddings is expressed as as $\mathbf{H} = [\mathbf{h}_1, \mathbf{h}_2, ..., \mathbf{h}_{T_x}]^\top$, where $\mathbf{h}_t \in \mathbb{R}^m$.

The i-th spatial attention weight β^i is calculated, where $\mathbf{d}^i \in \mathbb{R}^m$ the spatial embedding for i-th feature. ReLU activation function is used. Then, the spatial context vector is computed.

$$e^i = \text{ReLU}(W_e^\top \mathbf{d}^i + b_e), \ \beta^i = \frac{\exp(e^i)}{\sum_{o=1}^N \exp(e^o)}, \ \mathbf{g} = \sum_{i=1}^N \beta^i \mathbf{d}^i \tag{3}$$

To get the temporal attention weight α^t corresponding to the hidden state $\mathbf{h}_t$, the associated energy a^t is computed as follows:

$$a^t = \text{ReLU}(W_a^\top \mathbf{h}_t + b_a) \tag{4}$$

where $\mathbf{h}_t \in \mathbb{R}^m$ the temporal embedding for t-th input time-step. Thereafter, the attention weights α^t for $t \in \{1, 2, ..., T_x\}$ are calculated followed by the temporal context vector $\mathbf{s}$ according to Eq. 1. The spatial and temporal context vectors are concatenated before prediction. The proposed approach scales well with an increase in the number of variables, and the complexity does not increase significantly after adding the spatial attention to the temporal one.

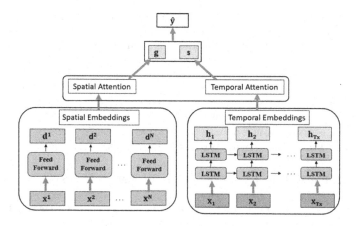

Fig. 1. Illustration of the proposed spatiotemporal attention (ST-Att) Model.

3 Experiments

3.1 Dataset

We use a public multivariate time series dataset collected from an air handling unit in a building heating, ventilation, and air-conditioning (HVAC) system [28]. This dataset consists of 9 variables - average zone temperature (AZT), outside air temperature (OAT, $°F$), return air temperature (RAT, $°F$), outside air damper command (OADC), cooling valve command (CVC), discharge air temperature (DAT, $°F$), supply fan speed command (SuFSC), discharge air static pressure (DASP), and return fan speed command (ReFSC). The input is the multivariate time series of T_x time-steps, and the output is the average zone temperature for the upcoming time-step. The training, validation, and test sizes are approximately 20,932, 6,977, and 6,978, respectively.

3.2 Baseline Models and Results

Baseline Models: For comparison, we use several baseline models including Epsilon-Support Vector Regression with Radial Basis Function kernel (SVR-RBF), LSTM model and LSTM with temporal attention (LSTM-Att) model. The hidden state dimensions for the LSTM and LSTM-Att models are kept same as that of ST-Att model.

Empirical Results: We find the optimal set of hyper-parameters for ST-Att after doing several experiments. The hidden state dimensions of LSTM layers in the encoder are kept the same for simplicity, and the dimension of 128 gives better results in our experiments. A dropout layer (0.2) is used after each LSTM layer to prevent overfitting. For training the model, we use Adam optimizer with a constant learning rate of 0.001, batch size of 256, and each model is

Table 1. Empirical results with $T_x = 5$. Each model was trained three times, to obtain the average and standard deviation of each evaluation metric. Tr.Time/epoch: Train Time/epoch, Num. Params: Number of trainable parameters

Model	RMSE	MAE	R^2 Score	Num. Params	Tr. Time/epoch	Test time
SVR-RBF	0.1376 ± 0.0000	0.1149 ± 0.0000	0.9868 ± 0.0000	-	0.188 s	0.029 s
LSTM	0.0428 ± 0.0030	0.0330 ± 0.0036	0.9987 ± 0.0002	202,369	2.506 s	0.264 s
LSTM-Att	0.0462 ± 0.0015	0.0346 ± 0.0024	0.9985 ± 0.0001	202,498	2.712 s	0.282 s
ST-Att	0.0423 ± 0.0021	0.0311 ± 0.0018	0.9987 ± 0.0001	203,523	2.795 s	0.252 s

Table 2. Spatial attention weight distribution from ST-Att.

Variables	AZT	OAT	RAT	OADC	CVC	DAT	SuFSC	DASP	ReFSC
Att. weight (%)	**11.76**	7.02	7.48	**20.26**	9.13	**14.73**	8.99	9.28	**11.26**

trained for 100 epochs. Through experiments, we optimize the input sequence length to $T_x = 5$. Three metrics are used for evaluations in our paper, including root mean square error (RMSE), mean absolute error (MAE), and coefficient of determination or R-squared score (R^2). Table 1 presents the empirical results. Both training time per epoch and testing time are provided for each model, except for SVR-RBF, where the total training time is presented instead. ST-Att shows better performance than all the baseline models on all three evaluation metrics. Table 1 also shows that ST-Att is computationally tractable.

Interpretability: The temporal attention weights are found to be almost equally distributed across all the input time-steps. It highlights that most likely, the correlation is weakly depending on time as the dataset has a quite high sampling frequency (one minute). It can be attributed to the slow thermal dynamics in the zone and the impact of the building mass absorbing heat to resist the quick change of the zone temperature. From Table 2, with the average zone temperature (AZT) as the output variable, the most relevant variables found by ST-Att are outside air damper command (OADC), discharge air temperature (DAT), return fan speed command (ReFSC), and itself. From domain knowledge, DAT affects AZT as these two variables have a direct physics relationship based on the heat transfer equation. During summer, in most building systems, the discharge air is directly pumped to the zone without reheating. Return air temperature (RAT) indicates the temperature of zone air circulated back to the central system. During the summer time, RAT is similar to the outside air temperature (OAT). Only part of the return air is mixed with the fresh outside air to generate the mixed air as the return air has a relatively higher level of CO_2. The mixed air is then cooled down by the cooling valve to become discharge air. OADC and ReFSC determine the required amount of fresh outside air and return air to maintain indoor comfort. Thus, AZT is significantly affected by OADC and ReFSC. In contrast, the cooling valve command (CVC) controlling the cooled water flow rate directly affects the mixed air temperature instead of the zone temperature. Thus, CVC has a smaller attention weight. The supply fan speed command (SuFSC) is a crucial indicator for the airflow rate and has its attention weight closer to that of DASP, which has more impact on the airflow rate than OAT and RAT.

4 Conclusion

In this paper, we propose a novel spatiotemporal attention model to incorporate interpretability along with generating accurate predictions in building energy prediction problems. We use LSTM to capture the temporal correlations in a sequence, and on top of that, the temporal and spatial attention weights are directly aligned with the output variable to provide spatiotemporal interpretations. Since the proposed technique is data-driven, it can be applied to any DDDAS utilizing multivariate time series. The interpretations provided by this model can be a significant benefit to the domain experts in understanding how different features and timesteps contribute to the predictions for diverse DDDAS.

References

1. Darema, F.: Dynamic data driven applications systems: new capabilities for application simulations and measurements. In: Sunderam, V.S., van Albada, G.D., Sloot, P.M.A., Dongarra, J.J. (eds.) ICCS 2005. LNCS, vol. 3515, pp. 610–615. Springer, Heidelberg (2005). https://doi.org/10.1007/11428848_79
2. Darema, F.: Grid computing and beyond: the context of dynamic data driven applications systems. Proc. IEEE 93(3), 692–697 (2005)
3. Gonzalez-Vidal, A., Jimenez, F., Gomez-Skarmeta, A.F.: A methodology for energy multivariate time series forecasting in smart buildings based on feature selection. Energy Build. 196, 71–82 (2019)
4. Bahadori, M.T., Lipton, Z.C.: Temporal-clustering invariance in irregular healthcare time series. arXiv preprint arXiv:1904.12206 (2019)
5. D'Urso, P., De Giovanni, L., Massari, R.: Trimmed fuzzy clustering of financial time series based on dynamic time warping. Ann. Oper. Res. 1–17 (2019)
6. Massano, M., Macii, E., Patti, E., Acquaviva, A., Bottaccioli, L.: A grey-box model based on unscented Kalman filter to estimate thermal dynamics in buildings. In: 2019 IEEE International Conference on Environment and Electrical Engineering and 2019 IEEE Industrial and Commercial Power Systems Europe (EEEIC/I&CPS Europe), pp. 1–6. IEEE (2019)
7. Afroz, Z., Shafiullah, G.M., Urmee, T., Higgins, G.: Modeling techniques used in building HVAC control systems: a review. Renew. Sustain. Energy Rev. 83, 64–84 (2018)
8. Jiang, Z., et al.: Data-driven thermal model inference with ARMAX, in smart environments, based on normalized mutual information. In: 2018 Annual American Control Conference (ACC), pp. 4634–4639. IEEE (2018)
9. Mocanu, E., Nguyen, P.H., Gibescu, M., Kling, W.L.: Deep learning for estimating building energy consumption. Sustain. Energy Grids Net. 6, 91–99 (2016)

10. Jiang, Z., Lee, Y.M.: Deep transfer learning for thermal dynamics modeling in smart buildings. arXiv preprint arXiv:1911.03318 (2019)
11. Mtibaa, F., Nguyen, K.-K., Azam, M., Papachristou, A., Venne, J.-S., Cheriet, M.: LSTM-based indoor air temperature prediction framework for HVAC systems in smart buildings. Neural Comput. Appl. 1–17 (2020)
12. Fan, C., Xiao, F., Yan, C., Liu, C., Li, Z., Wang, J.: A novel methodology to explain and evaluate data-driven building energy performance models based on interpretable machine learning. Appl. Energy **235**, 1551–1560 (2019)
13. Fan, C., Sun, Y., Zhao, Y., Song, M., Wang, J.: Deep learning-based feature engineering methods for improved building energy prediction. Appl. Energy **240**, 35–45 (2019)
14. Malhotra, P., Vig, L., Shroff, G., Agarwal, P.: Long short term memory networks for anomaly detection in time series. In: European Symposium on Artificial Neural Networks, Computational Intelligence and Machine Learning. Bruges (Belgium), pp.89. Presses universitaires de Louvain, 22–24 April 2015 (2015)
15. Shook, J., Wu, L., Gangopadhyay, T., Ganapathysubramanian, B., Sarkar, S., Singh, A.K.: Integrating genotype and weather variables for soybean yield prediction using deep learning. bioRxiv (2018)
16. Gangopadhyay, T., Locurto, A., Michael, J.B., Sarkar, S.: Deep learning algorithms for detecting combustion instabilities. In: Mukhopadhyay, A., Sen, S., Basu, D.N., Mondal, S. (eds.) Dynamics and Control of Energy Systems. EES, pp. 283–300. Springer, Singapore (2020). https://doi.org/10.1007/978-981-15-0536-2_13
17. Bahdanau, D., Cho, K., Bengio, Y.: Neural machine translation by jointly learning to align and translate. arXiv preprint arXiv:1409.0473 (2014)
18. Cho, K., et al.: Learning phrase representations using RNN encoder-decoder for statistical machine translation. arXiv preprint arXiv:1406.1078 (2014)
19. Sutskever, I., Vinyals, O., Le, Q.V.: Sequence to sequence learning with neural networks. In: Advances in Neural Information Processing Systems, pp. 3104–3112 (2014)
20. Qin, Y., Song, D., Chen, H., Cheng, W., Jiang, G., Cottrell, G.: A dual-stage attention-based recurrent neural network for time series prediction. arXiv preprint arXiv:1704.02971 (2017)
21. Singh, R., Lanchantin, J., Sekhon, A., Qi, Y.: Attend and predict: understanding gene regulation by selective attention on chromatin. In: Advances in Neural Information Processing Systems, pp. 6785–6795 (2017)
22. Song, H., Rajan, D., Thiagarajan, J.J., Spanias, A.: Attend and diagnose: clinical time series analysis using attention models. In: Thirty-Second AAAI Conference on Artificial Intelligence (2018)
23. Shook, J., Gangopadhyay, T., Wu, L., Ganapathysubramanian, B., Sarkar, S., Singh, A.K.: Crop yield prediction integrating genotype and weather variables using deep learning. arXiv preprint arXiv:2006.13847 (2020)
24. Gangopadhyay, T., Tan, S.Y., Huang, G., Sarkar, S.: Temporal attention and stacked LSTMs for multivariate time series prediction. In: NeurIPS Workshop on Modeling and Decision-Making in the Spatiotemporal Domain. NeurIPS (2018)
25. Zhang, X., Liang, X., Zhiyuli, A., Zhang, S., Xu, R., Wu, B.: At-LSTM: an attention-based LSTM model for financial time series prediction. In: IOP Conference Series: Materials Science and Engineering, vol. 569, pp. 052037. IOP Publishing (2019)
26. Gangopadhyay, T., Tan, S.Y., Jiang, Z., Meng, R., Sarkar, S.: Spatiotemporal attention for multivariate time series prediction and interpretation. arXiv preprint arXiv:2008.04882 (2020)

27. Jun, H., Zheng, W.: Multistage attention network for multivariate time series prediction. Neurocomputing **383**, 122–137 (2020)
28. U.S. Department of Energy (DOE). Long-term data on 3 office air handling units. http://aiweb.techfak.uni-bielefeld.de/content/bworld-robot-control-software/ 21 July 2015

Overcoming Stealthy Adversarial Attacks on Power Grid Load Predictions Through Dynamic Data Repair

Xingyu Zhou$^{(\boxtimes)}$, Robert Canady$^{(\boxtimes)}$, Yi Li$^{(\boxtimes)}$, Xenofon Koutsoukos$^{(\boxtimes)}$, and Aniruddha Gokhale$^{(\boxtimes)}$

Department of EECS, Vanderbilt University, Nashville, TN 37235, USA
{xingyu.zhou,robert.e.canady,yi.li,xenofon.koutsoukos,
a.gokhale}@vanderbilt.edu

Abstract. For power distribution networks with connected smart meters, current advances in machine learning enable the service provider to utilize data flows from smart meters for load forecasting using deep neural networks. However, recent research shows that current machine learning algorithms for power systems can be vulnerable to adversarial attacks, which are small designed perturbations crafted on normal inputs that can greatly affect the overall performance of the predictor. Even with only a partial compromise of the network, an attacker could intercept and adversarially modify data from some smart meters in a limited range to make the load predictor deviate from normal prediction results. In this paper, we leverage the dynamic data-driven applications systems (DDDAS) paradigm and propose a novel data repair framework to defend against these kinds of adversarial attacks. This framework complements the predictor with a self-representative auto-encoder and works in an iterative manner. The auto-encoder is used to detect and reconstruct the likely adversarial part in the input data. Different reconstruction results come up given different sensitivity levels in detection. As new data flows in each iterative time step, the service provider continuously checks the error of the previous prediction step and dynamically trades off between different detection sensitivity levels to seek an overall stable data reconstruction. Case studies on power network load forecast regression demonstrate the vulnerability of current machine learning algorithms and correspondingly the effectiveness of our defense framework.

Keywords: Power systems · Adversarial attacks · Load forecasting · Dynamic data repair

This work is supported in part by AFOSR DDDAS FA9550-18-1-0126 program. Any opinions, findings, and conclusions or recommendations expressed are those of the author(s) and do not necessarily reflect the views of the sponsor.

F. Darema et al. (Eds.): DDDAS 2020, LNCS 12312, pp. 102–109, 2020.
https://doi.org/10.1007/978-3-030-61725-7_14

1   Introduction

In modern smart grids, accurate load forecasting is critical for managing the infrastructure through targeted pricing and predictive maintenance. Advances in machine learning enable the service provider to utilize data flows from smart meters to perform load forecasting [9] using a deep learning model. However, recent research [6] reveals that current machine learning algorithms proposed for power system application scenarios can be vulnerable to adversarial attacks [11], which are inputs with small designed perturbations added to normal ones that can adversely affect the overall performance of the predictor [7,10]. In partially compromised hierarchical power networks, an attacker could intercept and maliciously modify data from some smart meters with small perturbations that can still make the load predictor deviate from normal prediction results.

To address these issues, we adopt the dynamic data-driven applications systems (DDDAS) paradigm [3] in providing a novel data repair framework to defend against such kind of adversarial attacks as shown in Fig. 1. This framework extends our prior work [13] of a cloud-supported platform for sensor networks (e.g., smart grid networks) to formalize general resilience testing procedures under adversarial settings using the model-driven approach [4]. To the best of our knowledge, this work is the first to introduce such a kind of dynamic data repair against adversarial attacks [5], and make the following contributions in this paper.

- We present a framework that can formalize the security and resilience testing in distributed sensor networks under adversarial settings;
- We design an iterative dynamic data repair scheme of Dropout-Detect-Reconstruct-Tradeoff to boost the robustness of data using the DDDAS paradigm for ongoing predictions; and
- We conduct a case study for distributed power network load forecasting to demonstrate potential risks for machine learning predictors and the efficiency of our defensive data repair framework.

The rest of the paper is organized as follows. Section 2 illustrates the theoretical background of our adversarial attack setting and dynamic data repair framework in a step-by-step manner. Section 3 presents a case study to demonstrate the capabilities of our framework on a power distribution network. Finally, Sect. 4 concludes the paper and presents opportunities for future research.

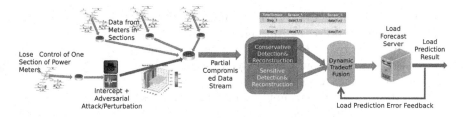

Fig. 1. Overall workflow for dynamic data repair under adversarial attack

2   Methodology

In this section we provide details of our approach. The techniques will be introduced following the execution order of attack and defense. Our predictor is based on deep learning. Specifically, the model absorbs data from distributed sensors and fetches their values from current and some time steps back to predict the total system load for the next time step.

2.1   Model of Stealthy Adversarial Attacks

To compromise the prediction system, an attacker intercepts and adds designed perturbations to the normal data flow. Without loss of generality, we assume that the attacker's goal is to maximize the load prediction deviation. For this scenario, larger ranges of input and output numerical value data space as well as the adoption of anomaly detectors leads to higher complexity in attack settings. To illustrate the vulnerabilities of the prediction system, we propose an attack method adapted from the most popular adversarial attack called FGSM (Fast Gradient Sign Method) [7], which generates adversarial perturbations using only one single equation: $\eta = \epsilon \cdot sign(\nabla_x J(\theta, x, y))$. Here θ represents the parameters of the model, x represents inputs to the model, y refers to the targets associated with x (for tasks with targets) and $J(\theta, x, y)$ is the goal loss function for deviating the neural network. The magnitude constraint added to the original sample is represented by ϵ.

With the presence of an anomaly detector, we reformulate an adversarial attack [13] as an optimization problem which attempts to find the best synthetic perturbations that maximize the prediction loss while keeping the modification magnitude at a small enough level so as to go undetected. Compared to the FGSM attack, we implement an iterative attack that allows each meter (value in input data array) to have its unique modification value because the input range may not be fixed. Our approach performs a number of iterations with small step ratio and updates the gradient sign method from the output of the previous iteration. Intermediate results are first checked with the detector to remove exposed parts and then sent into the next iteration for further exploration. This procedure eventually generates an adversarial but undetected data sample.

2.2   Resilient Detection and Reconstruction

To detect compromised sensors, we use an auto-encoder as the self-representation to build an anomaly detector. Auto-encoder models learn internal representations with the objective $AE(x) = x$ mapping to the input distribution itself. For the sensor network in our case study, we set individual detection thresholds for each meter reading. After training the auto-encoder using the training data, we use the training data to compute the fitting error (l_2 Norm) for all sensors and using maximum fitting deviation of each sensor as the error threshold for anomaly detection. During the prediction phase, the auto-encoder takes inputs and compares output residuals with the pre-computed thresholds and generates a list of sensors with the potential for adversarial attacks. In this way the detector judges whether specific sensors in the network are likely to be compromised.

Such a static detection is still vulnerable to stealthy attacks and can be made resilient when the input test sample first goes through a randomized dropout step [2]. The detection runs with controllable sensitivity levels. With $dctIter$ dropout iterations, if no less than $dctThres$ times the sensor has been marked as anomaly if would be returned as a high likely adversarial sensor. Different reconstruction results come up given different sensitivity levels in such a detection phase. In each detection iteration, a portion of the input data is randomly dropped out and a reconstruction is conducted using the remaining data. The residual between the original and the reconstructed data can be used to detect the likely adversarial part of data. Based on the detection results, the likely adversarial data part can be erased and reconstructed using the auto-encoder.

2.3   Iterative Dynamic Repair

The resilient detection and reconstruction procedure is configurable and sensitive to measurements. One key property for prediction tasks like load forecasting is that as new data flows in continuously, the system can utilize new data to validate the quality of previous predictions for which the DDDAS paradigm [3] is best suited to provide adaptive data repair against adversarial attacks as shown in Algorithm 1.

For the resilient detection and reconstruction, given a fixed dropout rate, the sensitivity can be adjusted with the number of detection iteration ($dctIter$) and the detection iteration threshold ($dctThres$). Given the infinite number of combination settings for the resilient detection, we consider three settings with the least computation burden (sensitivity from high to low): (1) $x1in2t \leftarrow resCor(x, dctIter = 2, dctThres = 1)$ and (2) $x1in1t \leftarrow resCor(x, dctIter = 1, dctThres = 1)$ and (3) $x2in2t \leftarrow resCor(x, dctIter = 2, dctThres = 2)$. We implement adjustments in iterative time steps to seek a balanced trade-off between sensitivity levels. The overall prediction result with dynamic repair is computed as a weighted sum of these three resilient reconstructions [12]. For each time step, the system checks the previous prediction deviations from these three levels and allocates higher weights for the least deviated reconstruction level.

3   Empirical Validation of the Claims

3.1   Power System Setting

For data collection, we conduct a detailed simulation of an electric distribution system using GridLAB-D provided by the Pacific Northwest National Laboratory (PNNL) [8]. We selected the prototypical feeder of a moderately populated area $R1$-12.47-3, and included representative residential loads like heating, ventilation and air conditioning (HVAC) systems to the distribution network model [1]. In

Algorithm 1. Dynamic Repair ($dynRepair$)

Require: x: original observation data flow; f: predictor; $NumTime$: number of execution time steps; $resCor$: resilient correction function; $ErrThres$: ideal prediction error threshold; $return$: return function for each time step; y: ground truth value.

1: $\alpha = [1.0, 0.0, 0.0]$, $\alpha_{bias} = 0.05$, $x \leftarrow x[0], t \leftarrow 1$
2: $pred, pred1in1, pred1in2, pred2in2 \leftarrow EmptyList$
3: $x1in1t \leftarrow resCor(x, dctIter = 1, dctThres = 1), pred1in1.append(f(x1in1t))$
4: $x1in2t \leftarrow resCor(x, dctIter = 2, dctThres = 1), pred1in2.append(f(x1in2t))$
5: $x2in2t \leftarrow resCor(x, dctIter = 2, dctThres = 2), pred2in2.append(f(x2in2t))$
6: $pred[0] \leftarrow pred1in1t * \alpha[0] + pred1in2t * \alpha[1] + pred2in2t * \alpha[2]$
7: **while** $t < NumTime$ **do**
8:     $resPre1 \leftarrow abs(pred[t-1] - y[t-1], resPre2 \leftarrow abs(pred[t-2] - y[t-2]$
9:     **if** $t > 1$ **and** $resPre1 > ErrThres$ **and** $resPre1 > resPre2$ **then**
10:       $res1in1 \leftarrow abs(pred1in1[t-1] - y[t-1])$
11:       $res1in2 \leftarrow abs(pred1in2[t-1] - y[t-1])$
12:       $res2in2 \leftarrow abs(pred2in2[t-1] - y[t-1])$
13:       $idx = argmin([res1in1, res1in2, res2in2])$
14:       $\alpha \leftarrow \alpha - \alpha_{bias}, \alpha[idx] \leftarrow \alpha[idx] + 3 * \alpha_{bias}$
15:     **end if**
16:     $x \leftarrow x[t]$
17:     $x1in1t \leftarrow resCor(x, dctIter = 1, dctThres = 1), pred1in1.append(f(x1in1t))$
18:     $x1in2t \leftarrow resCor(x, dctIter = 2, dctThres = 1), pred1in2.append(f(x1in2t))$
19:     $x2in2t \leftarrow resCor(x, dctIter = 2, dctThres = 2), pred2in2.append(f(x2in2t))$
20:     $pred[t] \leftarrow f(x1in1t) * \alpha[0] + f(x1in2t) * \alpha[1] + f(x2in2t) * \alpha[2]$,
21:     $return(pred[t]), t \leftarrow t + 1$
22: **end while**

---

summary, our distribution model has a total of 109 commercial and residential user loads. Smart meters are connected to end users and their usage data reports are transmitted to the upper-level control center in a hierarchical manner. For each hourly time step, the prediction model takes load data from distributed meter readings in the past 24 h and also takes into account the temperature data for the same period of time. We build a load forecasting model for this power distribution network using a relatively large LSTM deep neural network (with 3 LSTM layers of 150 units and 2 fully-connected layers of 200 units). The predictor on the clean data generates a mean squared error (MSE) of 0.1255 (Mega Volt Amp) on the test data set for a total of 216 time steps.

The attack scenario is a manipulation of sensor data under reasonable constraints with full knowledge of the prediction and detection model. In each time step, the attacker can manipulate a fixed number of meters in the network (10%–50% in our experiments). Moreover, for each meter, the attacker is allowed to deviate the meter reading by a limited level of 20%. Under these constraints, we generate stealthy adversarial examples using the iterative attack method.

3.2   Evaluating Reconstruction and Repair

We evaluate our dynamic data repair framework on various settings under strong attacks with a maximum modification ratio of 20% for compromised sensors. Figure 2 shows the prediction results when 40% of sensors in the network are compromised in two ways: (a) shows absolute prediction deviations from normal prediction results, and (b) shows mean absolute prediction deviations from normal prediction results of current prediction and all the ones prior to the current time step. Even with a large portion of 40% sensors compromised, the adversarial impact can still be mitigated to an overall practical level of 0.3 (Mega Volt Amp).

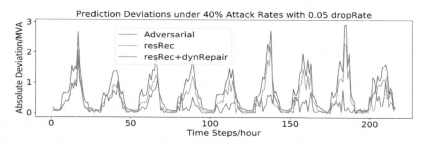

(a) Absolute Prediction Deviation from Original Prediction

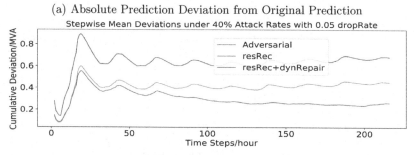

(b) Cumulative Mean Absolute Deviation from Original Prediction

Fig. 2. Predictions under 40% compromise and 5% detection dropout rate

We present experimental results under more flexible settings in Table 1, which shows results under four levels of detection dropout rate: 5%, 10%, 20%, 30% with 20, 40, 60, 80 reconstruction cycles. The error metric we chose is the most commonly used mean squared error (MSE) over the test dataset. For different attack rates, the best defense settings are marked in dark black. We can see that low detection dropout rates with more detection cycles usually show more stable prediction performances. From the figures we can also see that adversarial impacts in this load forecast case usually occurs at peak points. Further, the data repair framework successfully decreases prediction deviations at these vulnerable points without much impact on other locations.

The experimental results also clearly show the trade-off caused by the iterative data repair. With a large number of detection iterations, the chance of being totally stealthy for an adversarial sensor is reduced to a negligible level. Meanwhile, low threshold settings lead to obvious negative impacts caused by false alarms. From our experiments, the upper bound of this repair is determined by the performance of this self-representation model (auto-encoder here) and therefore we can see that dynamic repair does not always show best performance when the compromised sensor ratio is relatively low. This sensitive repair might lead to an unstable prediction performance over detection iterations in each time step. As shown in our experiments, this potential risk is most obvious when the detection dropout rate is high. As a result, the combination of a relative low detection dropout rate along with more iterations would usually lead to smoother and more stable performance.

Table 1. Prediction Mean Squared Error (MSE) under different settings

Drop/%	adv/%	natErr	advErr	resRec/numCycle				resRec+dynRepair/numCycle			
				20	40	60	80	20	40	60	80
5	10	0.126	0.173	0.152	0.144	0.142	**0.141**	**0.146**	0.147	0.150	0.149
	20	0.126	0.311	0.211	0.163	0.148	**0.143**	0.170	0.159	0.155	**0.149**
	30	0.126	0.538	0.380	0.300	0.257	**0.232**	0.281	0.216	0.197	**0.188**
	40	0.126	0.921	0.729	0.626	0.559	**0.523**	0.566	0.442	0.345	**0.301**
	50	0.126	1.329	1.090	0.979	0.909	**0.862**	0.876	0.719	0.581	**0.500**
10	10	0.126	0.171	0.139	**0.137**	0.138	0.139	0.152	0.148	**0.146**	0.147
	20	0.126	0.311	0.174	0.144	**0.139**	0.139	0.158	**0.150**	0.152	0.168
	30	0.126	0.538	0.310	0.236	0.211	**0.200**	0.224	0.183	**0.179**	0.179
	40	0.126	0.921	0.632	0.524	0.481	**0.464**	0.406	0.293	0.270	**0.267**
	50	0.126	1.329	0.984	0.859	0.808	**0.784**	0.688	0.526	0.477	**0.455**
20	10	0.126	0.173	**0.139**	0.146	0.145	0.145	**0.140**	0.153	0.150	0.151
	20	0.126	0.311	0.142	0.139	**0.138**	0.171	**0.160**	0.300	0.308	0.286
	30	0.126	0.538	0.229	**0.201**	0.216	0.218	**0.182**	0.192	0.229	0.273
	40	0.126	0.921	0.541	0.473	0.459	**0.457**	0.912	0.994	0.803	**0.760**
	50	0.126	1.329	0.850	0.777	0.767	**0.759**	0.567	**0.527**	0.559	0.579
30	10	0.126	0.173	**0.139**	0.140	0.139	0.139	0.147	0.140	**0.138**	0.142
	20	0.126	0.311	**0.138**	0.138	0.139	0.139	0.150	0.148	0.139	**0.139**
	30	0.126	0.538	0.219	0.201	0.202	**0.201**	0.197	**0.184**	0.197	0.213
	40	0.126	0.921	0.521	0.491	0.488	**0.485**	**0.378**	0.388	0.429	0.462
	50	0.126	1.329	0.876	0.842	**0.840**	0.838	**0.598**	0.644	0.699	0.786

An important property of our approach is that it takes advantage of existing pre-trained models in a resilient way, which means it can be combined with other defense techniques with no constraints. It is a generalized model deployment strategy to improve robustness that is easily transferable to other learning settings.

4 Conclusion

This paper demonstrated how to analyze and improve the robustness of learning-based prediction models in power distribution networks using the DDDAS paradigm. Given the existence of threats from stealthy adversarial attacks, we first designed a resilient detection and reconstruction strategy using randomization elements. We then proposed a practical, iterative dynamic data repair strategy to seek an optimal trade-off between reconstruction results from different sensitivity levels. Our work not only shows the importance of introducing randomization elements to increase robustness in learning-based systems but also the effectiveness of deviation feedback for predictions on-the-fly. Even though our defense framework has shown promising results, the computation cost for an optimal defense efficiency can be very high thereby requiring new approaches to simplify and accelerate computations for real time applications.

References

1. https://github.com/gridlab-d/Taxonomy_Feeders (2015). Accessed October 2019
2. Athalye, A., Carlini, N., Wagner, D.: Obfuscated gradients give a false sense of security: circumventing defenses to adversarial examples. arXiv preprint arXiv:1802.00420 (2018)
3. Blasch, E., Bernstein, D., Rangaswamy, M.: Introduction to dynamic data driven applications systems. In: Blasch, E., Ravela, S., Aved, A. (eds.) Handbook of Dynamic Data Driven Applications Systems, pp. 1–25. Springer, Cham (2018). https://doi.org/10.1007/978-3-319-95504-9_1
4. Broll, B., Whitaker, J.: DeepForge: an open source, collaborative environment for reproducible deep learning (2017)
5. Carlini, N., Wagner, D.: Adversarial examples are not easily detected: bypassing ten detection methods. In: Proceedings of the 10th ACM Workshop on Artificial Intelligence and Security, pp. 3–14. ACM (2017)
6. Chen, Y., Tan, Y., Zhang, B.: Exploiting vulnerabilities of load forecasting through adversarial attacks. In: Proceedings of the Tenth ACM International Conference on Future Energy Systems, pp. 1–11. ACM (2019)
7. Goodfellow, I.J., Shlens, J., Szegedy, C.: Explaining and harnessing adversarial examples. arXiv preprint arXiv:1412.6572 (2014)
8. Schneider, K.P., Chen, Y., Chassin, D.P., Pratt, R.G., Engel, D.W., Thompson, S.E.: Modern grid initiative distribution taxonomy final report. Technical report. Pacific Northwest National Laboratory (2008)
9. Sevlian, R., Rajagopal, R.: A scaling law for short term load forecasting on varying levels of aggregation. Int. J. Electr. Power Energy Syst. 98, 350–361 (2018)
10. Szegedy, C., et al.: Intriguing properties of neural networks. arXiv preprint arXiv:1312.6199 (2013)
11. Vorobeychik, Y., Kantarcioglu, M.: Adversarial machine learning. Synth. Lect. Artif. Intell. Mach. Learn. 12(3), 1–169 (2018)
12. Zhang, H., Yu, Y., Jiao, J., Xing, E.P., Ghaoui, L.E., Jordan, M.I.: Theoretically principled trade-off between robustness and accuracy. arXiv preprint arXiv:1901.08573 (2019)
13. Zhou, X., et al.: Evaluating resilience of grid load predictions under stealthy adversarial attacks. In: 2019 Resilience Week (RWS), vol. 1, pp. 206–212. IEEE (2019)

Plenary Presentations - Section 4: Materials Systems

Uncertainty Analysis of Self-healed Composites with Machine Learning as Part of DDDAS

Sameer B. Mulani$^{(\boxtimes)}$, Samit Roy, and Bodiuzzaman Jony

The University of Alabama, Tuscaloosa, AL 35487, USA
{sbmulani,sroy}@eng.ua.edu, jbodiuzzaman@crimson.ua.edu

Abstract. This research integrates deep artificial neural network (ANN) with the analytical solution for the stresses during the delamination of a thermoset composite double cantilever beam to carry out uncertainty analysis. Currently, micro-fiber composite (MFC) piezo patches act as sensors and actuators in the self-healing system. The same MFCs sense the initiation of the damage (delamination) during the dynamic loadings (operation) and initiate the healing process in the composite by high-frequency vibrations. During the healing, the thermoplastic healing materials (Polycaprolactone and shape memory polymer) close the gap between fracture surfaces and bond the surfaces together. Composites' failure is a complex phenomenon due to material non-homogeneity at micro-scales. Due to uncertainties, the damage parameters like critical stresses, the critical load which initiates the damage, and damage zone length remain uncertain. Deep ANN coupled with an analytical model will efficiently, and in real time, be able to quantify the uncertainties in critical load as well as damage zone length. For uncertainty propagation, material properties, as well as traction separation law parameters, are assumed to be uncorrelated Gaussian distributed random variables. The same deep ANN will be used to carry out parameter identification (i.e., traction separation law) in the future. Hence, the material law, damage prediction, and healing form a dynamic feedback loop, which, along with uncertainty quantification, constitutes a robust dynamic-data-driven system.

Keywords: Composite laminates · Uncertainty analysis · Deep ANN · Cohesive layer · Delamination

1 Introduction

The use of composite structures has been increased exponentially in many disciplines such as aerospace, automotive, marine, and sports, due to its high stiffness/strength to weight ratio, tailorability, and durability [1]. However, these benefits are susceptible to various types of manufacturing defects, e.g., fiber misalignment, voids, thermal stresses due to the curing, as well as in-plane laminated construction of the composite structures results in inherent vulnerability to out-of-plane loadings such as those experienced under dynamic impact events. Also, there exist various thermal, hygrothermal, and aging effects, which could eventually lead to the formation of considerable internal

© Springer Nature Switzerland AG 2020
F. Darema et al. (Eds.): DDDAS 2020, LNCS 12312, pp. 113–120, 2020.
https://doi.org/10.1007/978-3-030-61725-7_15

damage (macro and micro-cracks) [2] and compromise the structural integrity and service life [3] of laminated composite structures. The current regular intensive inspection of the composite components to detect and repair damages is inefficient and costly. To alleviate this inspection and repair, the researchers have explored biologically inspired self-healing concepts as an alternative to traditionally expensive repair techniques. In self-healing composite systems, the activation of self-healing in the damaged laminate (with the delamination) can be carried out based on the data collected from the sensors. To carry out decisions of self-healing activation, the analytical model will be utilized computationally efficient to obtain damage parameters in real-time.

In self-healing composite systems, the activation of self-healing in the damaged laminate (with the delamination) can be carried out based on the data collected from the sensors. To carry out decisions of self-healing activation, the predictive numerical models (finite element model or analytical) of the composite should be computationally efficient where the damage quantification, as well as the cohesive failure stresses, are estimated with the confidence in real-time.

The composite structure is significantly affected by the presence of uncertainties across various length scales, such as the variability of constituents (fiber and matrix) properties in micro-scale, the variability in thickness, and orientations of the plies in meso-scale, and the loads and boundary conditions in macro-scale. And, some of the traditional approaches for UQ using the probabilistic approach in composites are the Monte Carlo Simulation (MCS), perturbation methods, and spectral methods. Among these techniques for UQ, the spectral approach known as Polynomial Chaos Expansion (PCE) is computationally efficient and yields suitable accuracy even for random inputs with a high coefficient of variation.

Delamination is one of the major failures of the composite structures and generally caused by the interlaminar shear stresses at the mid-plane (Mode-II) or transverse stresses (Mode-I) or a combination of both. As an initial effort, the research will be focused on Mode-I delamination failure. Cohesive zone models offer themselves as tools for the investigation of crack initiation and propagation in quasi-brittle materials. The opening of the crack is described in terms of a nonlinear stress-displacement relationship, which has a significant softening phase due to damage zone formation; the fracture process zone approach of Needleman [4] and Tvergaard et al. [5] involves attributing a traction-separation law to the interface. Hence, the cohesive zone modeling is an excellent tool for the investigation of local fracture processes in fiber-reinforced composite delamination.

Recently, ANNs were utilized to replace computationally exhaustive calculations like finite element method (FEM), aeroelasticity, and coupled FEM-boundary element method. The ANN can capture the complicated relationship between inputs and outputs, especially if the dimensions of the inputs and outputs are huge, where traditional mathematics cannot capture the relationship. The ANN helps us to carry out optimization using heuristic algorithms as compared to gradient-based optimization methods and uncertainty quantification efficiently, especially for computationally intensive simulations.

The main objective of the current research is to build a stochastic framework to carry out the damage analysis of Double Cantilever Beam (DCB) composite specimens within the Dynamic Data-Driven Applications Systems (DDDAS) paradigm. To increase the computational efficiency multifold, deep ANN is utilized to replace the analytical model with a surrogate model. This flexible framework will help us to use the analytical damage analysis model, the FEM model, or experimental results interchangeably. The bond between two laminas is modeled as a cohesive layer, and cohesive crack models offer themselves as tools for the investigation of fracture in quasi-brittle materials, such as thermoset polymer composites.

2 Analytical Solution for Cohesive Layer of DCB Model

The analytical solution of the half double cantilever beam (DCB) model was developed (see Fig. 1a) with the modification of the model developed by Roy and Wang [6]. The associated bilinear traction-separation law is shown in Fig. 1(b). Among all the traction separation laws (linear, exponential, tri-linear, etc.), the bi-linear traction-separation law makes the calculation more efficient and tractable for DCB specimens. Due to this reason, the bi-linear traction-separation law was used for the analytical modeling of the half DCB specimen. The DCB specimen is divided into three separate zones (see Fig. 1(a)): debond zone, damage zone, and elastic zone, and the traction separation relationship (cohesive stress and crack tip opening relationship) was employed in these three zones according to the fracture mechanics. The beam is modeled using Euler Bernoulli's fourth-order differential beam equation with boundary conditions located at the boundaries of these zones.

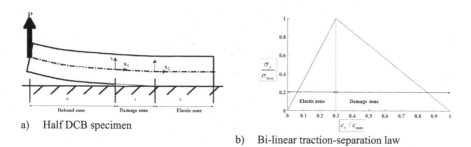

a)   Half DCB specimen

b)   Bi-linear traction-separation law

Fig. 1. DCB model description.

Invoking the symmetry, the deformation of the upper half of the DCB specimen can be given by the following equation.

$$\frac{d^4 v}{dx^4} = \frac{b\sigma_y}{D_{11}} \tag{1}$$

where v is the deflection of the beam, σ_y is the cohesive stress, D_{11} is the effective bending stiffness of the beam in the longitudinal (fiber) direction, and b is the width of the beam. Using the cohesive traction separation relationship in three different regions of the beam, the solution of (1) can be given by the following three Eqs. 2, 3 and 4.

$$v(x) = \frac{P(x+a)^3}{6D_{11}} + C_1(x+a) + C_2, -a \leq x < 0 \tag{2}$$

$$v(x) = \left.\begin{array}{c} v_{max} + C_3 sinh(\lambda_1 x) + \\ C_4 cosh(\lambda_1 x) + C_5 sin(\lambda_1 x) \\ + C_6 cos(\lambda_1 x) \end{array}\right\}, 0 \le x \le l \qquad (3)$$

$$v(x) = e^{-\lambda_2 x}[C_7 sin(\lambda_2 x) + C_8 cos(\lambda_2 x)], l \le x \le l + c \qquad (4)$$

where P is force, a is the pre-crack length, C_1 to C_8 are the integration constants.

The boundary conditions at $x = 0$ and $x = l + c$ and continuity conditions at the intersections ($x = 0, x = l$) were simultaneously imposed, to get the solution of the equations and find the unknown constants (damage zone length l and the critical force applied on the beam at crack initiation, P_{crit} and eight unknown integration constants $(C_1 - C_8)$).

After the applications of the boundary and continuity conditions, the solution $v(x)$ resulted in ten equations with nonlinear terms in it. Due to the nonlinearity of the system, a numerical predictor-corrector method was implemented to solve the set of ten equations and evaluate the eight unknown constants of integration and two and cohesive zone parameters, l and P_{cr}. A flow chart of the algorithm that was implemented to find the integration constants is given below in Fig. 2.

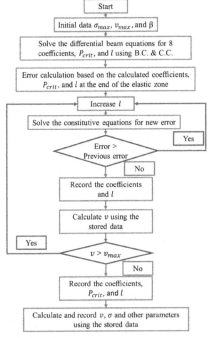

Fig. 2. Flowchart to find the critical cohesive parameters in the DCB configuration by using the bi-linear traction separation law.

3 DCB Model Description

The proposed framework was applied to a carbon fiber unidirectional (0^0_{16}) composite DCB specimen, where the uncertainties were assumed in material properties apart from the traction separation law. The probability density functions (PDF) of transverse stress (σ_y), damage zone length (l), and critical load (P_{crit}) were obtained using simple LHS, and sampling with ANN surrogates. The random input variables were the effective bending stiffness D_{11}, maximum cohesive stress σ_{max}, the ratio of the opening displacement (v) at the maximum stress point to the maximum crack tip opening displacement (v_m) β, half-thickness of the beam (b), the maximum crack tip displacement (v_m), and the pre-crack length (a).

The dimensions of the unidirectional IM-7 carbon fiber reinforced composite DCB beam were 215.9 mm × 38.1 mm × 4.5 m. The full-beam was manufactured using sixteen layers of unidirectional IM-7 carbon fiber fabric, and SC-780 two-phase toughened epoxy was used for the composite fabrication [7]. Thermoplastic polycaprolactone and polyurethane shape memory polymer were dispersed in the thermoset epoxy during the manufacturing to provide self-healing functionality. The length of the initial debond zone or the pre-crack (a) was 38.1 mm. The analysis was performed using the quasi-static displacement condition at the left edge of the beam, which aligned with the experimental conditions.

4 Uncertainty Quantification Using Latin Hypercube Sampling Technique

The uncertainty quantification was carried out using three approaches: 1) simple LHS sampling and 2) Deep ANN as a surrogate model. The random input variables are given in Table 1 and were assumed to be uncorrelated Gaussian distributed variables.

Table 1. Uncorrelated Gaussian input random variables.

	Mean	Standard deviation
Effective bending stiffness, D_{11} (N/mm²)	$27.5*10^3$	2.75
Maximum cohesive stress, σ_{max} (N/mm²)	40.0	4.0
The ratio of the crack tip displacement at the maximum stress point (v) to the maximum crack tip displacement (v_m), β	0.25	0.07
Half-thickness of the beam, t (mm)	2.25	0.1
Pre-crack length, a (mm)	38.1	0.2
Maximum crack tip displacement, v_m (mm)	0.12	0.01

To ascertain the converged results, LHS was carried out using a different number of samples. The violin plots are provided in Fig. 3, where one can see the convergence of different responses like transverse stress (σ_y) at a distance 0.2 mm from the crack-tip, and critical load (P_{crit}). In violin plots, the scaled PDFs are plotted on the y-axis along with the means and one standard deviation band about the means. The violin plots provide not only the convergence of means and standard deviations but also the PDFs convergence. The convergence of transverse stress, damage zone length, and critical load requires 250, 1000, 5000, and 5000 samples, respectively. Hence, the responses obtained with 10,000 LHS samples were taken for the comparison with Deep ANN study. Means and standard deviations for transverse stress (σ_y) at a distance 0.2 mm from the crack-tip, damage zone length (l), and critical load (P_{crit}) are provided in Table 2.

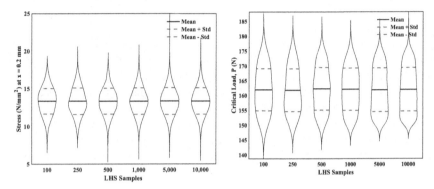

Fig. 3. Violin plots for LHS simulation.

Table 2. Response statistics using LHS 10,000 samples.

	Mean	Standard deviation
Transverse stress (σ_y) at a distance 0.2 mm from the crack-tip (N/mm^2)	13.3527	1.7538
Damage zone length (l) (mm)	0.6014	0.0303
Critical load (P_{crit}) (N)	162.0734	7.3562

5 Deep Artificial Neural Network

Different types of ANNs were used as surrogate models to replace the analytical solution of the DCB model. The main steps involved in UQ with ANNs are 1) Training data generation, 2) Training ANN, and 3) Simulation with ANN. One has to carry out training data generation and training ANN iteratively until the convergence criteria are met. Before carrying out the training of the Deep ANN, the data was normalized with data' (inputs and outputs) means and standard deviations. From earlier studies, it was found that the critical load and damage zone length required a higher number of samples to obtain their stochastic responses and had convergence issues. Initially, multi-input-single-output ANNs were tried, and then afterward, multi-input-multi-output ANNs were established.

Initially, multi-input-single-output Deep ANNs were used to model the damage zone length and critical load separately using five hidden layers of Tansig activation function with the number of neurons = [20 14 8 8 6] in hidden layers. This combination of hidden layers and the number of neurons was achieved by trial and error while looking at the convergence of ANN. The means and standard deviations for damage zone length and critical loads are given in Table 3. The PDFs for damage zone length and critical load are depicted in Fig. 4. Afterward, multi-input-multi-output Deep ANNs were trained for damage zone length and critical load simultaneously; the required number of hidden layers became six, and the number of neurons in the hidden layers changed as [20 14 10 8 8 6] and [20 14 12 8 8 6] for 500 and 1000 training samples, respectively. The PDFs means, and standard deviations remained the same for multi-input-single-output Deep ANNs. The means and standard deviations of damage zone length and critical load for Deep ANN were always bounded by the means and standard deviations of the training data.

Table 3. Uncorrelated Gaussian input random variables.

	Mean	Standard deviation
Damage length (mm); number of samples for training = 100	0.6002	0.0232
Damage length (mm); number of samples for training = 500	0.6015	0.0313
Damage length (mm); number of samples for training = 1000	0.6011	0.0278
Critical load (N); number of samples for training = 500	162.3058	7.1801
Critical load (N); number of samples for training = 1000	162.1381	7.1597

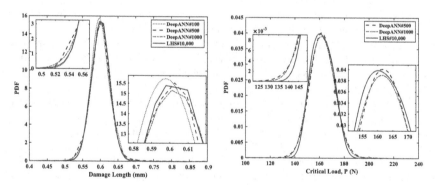

Fig. 4. PDFs of damage length and critical load using Deep ANNs.

6   Conclusions

To our knowledge, this is the first study where polynomial chaos using the least-squares approach and artificial neural network applied to damage characterization of carbon fiber composite DCB model using an analytical solution. With cohesive zone parameters determined from the experimental data, the analytical solution was then used to compute responses like transverse stresses along the DCB, transverse displacements (v), damage zone length, and critical load. The material and geometric properties, including traction separation law parameters, were assumed to be uncorrelated Gaussian distributed random variables.

The surrogate model described in this paper is built using Deep ANN to predict the stochastic transverse stresses, damage zone length, and critical load required to initiate fracture. In our future work, during predictive self-healing using the DDDAS paradigm, the MFC sensors will provide the current delamination length. The delamination length will be used as input to the ANN surrogate model to predict the critical load that will initiate the crack for that specific delamination length. If the applied operational load is greater than this critical load, then self-healing will be activated. In this manner, the self-healing activation will be dynamic data driven, based on sensors data. Further, the cohesive zone properties like traction separation law parameters can be obtained using Bayesian inference or optimization so that the cohesive zone properties can be updated based on the number of healing cycles employed, which in turn, is based on the dynamic data stream as mentioned above. Future work will also be directed towards implementing and integrating the damage sensing module and the dynamic data-driven damage prognosis module within the intelligent self-healing system. Preliminary developments in the damage prognosis module have shown promising results.

References

1. Kanoute, P., Boso, D., Chaboche, J., Schrefler, B.: Multiscale methods for composites: a review. Arch. Comput. Methods Eng. **16**, 31–75 (2009)
2. Trask, R., Norris, C., Bond, I.: Stimuli-triggered self-healing functionality in advanced fibre-reinforced composites. J. Intell. Mater. Syst. Struct. **25**(1), 87–97 (2014)
3. Li, G., Muthyala, V.: Impact characterization of sandwich structures with an integrated orthogrid stiffened syntactic foam core. Compos. Sci. Technol. **68**(9), 2078–2084 (2008)
4. Needleman, A.: An analysis of decohesion along an imperfect interface. J. Mech. Phys. Solids **38**(3), 289–324 (1990)
5. Tvergaard, V., Hutchinson, J.: Effect of t-stress on mode i crack growth resistance in a ductile solid. Int. J. Solids Struct. **31**, 823–833 (1994)
6. Roy, S., Wang, Y.: Analytical solution for cohesive layer model and model verification. Polym. Polym. Compos. **13**(8), 741–752 (2005)
7. Thapa, M., Jony, B., Mulani, Sameer B., Roy, S.: Development of intelligent and predictive self-healing composite structures using dynamic data-driven applications systems. In: Blasch, E., Ravela, S., Aved, A. (eds.) Handbook of Dynamic Data Driven Applications Systems, pp. 173–191. Springer, Cham (2018). https://doi.org/10.1007/978-3-319-95504-9_9

Active Search Methods to Predict Material Failure Under Intermittent Loading in the Serebrinksy-Ortiz Fatigue Model

Stephen Guth and Themistoklis Sapis[✉]

Massachusetts Institute of Technology, Cambridge, MA 02139, USA
tsapsis@mit.edu
http://sandlab.mit.edu/

Abstract. The rainflow counting algorithm for material fatigue is both simple to implement and extraordinarily successful for predicting material failure times. However, it neglects memory effects and time-ordering dependence, and therefor runs into difficulties dealing with intermittent loads, especially those with long tailed distributions. In this report, we use the Serebrinsky-Ortiz model of material fatigue to introduce a partial analytical solution for deterministic intermittent loads, which greatly improves integration speed while still conservatively identifying early failures. Additionally, we apply recent advances in optimal experimental design both to gain insight into how rare events lead to extreme early material failure, and to estimate the long tail of the distribution of failure times.

Keywords: Fatigue · Rare events · Extreme events · Intermittent events · Active search · Optimal experimental design

1 Introduction

The modern energy industry increasingly relies on enormously capital intensive structures, which are placed in extreme conditions and subject to extreme loads that vary throughout the structure's expected lifetime. Failure costs are astronomical, including forgone profits, legal penalties, tort payouts, and reputation damage [9]. Minimizing lifetime costs require safe-life engineering and a conservative assessment of failure probabilities. Unfortunately, while material fatigue is a major contributor to failure, non destructively measuring fatigue is both difficult and expensive [25].

For many classes of structure, fatigue loads have important intermittent stochastic character [1,10,24]. In particular, traditional frequency domain approaches have difficulty predicting the fatigue lifetime effects of intermittent loading, which have important dependence on time-ordering.

A major limitation to simulating the effects of intermittent loading is the time cost of Monte Carlo simulations, which grows quickly in the dimension of the

© Springer Nature Switzerland AG 2020
F. Darema et al. (Eds.): DDDAS 2020, LNCS 12312, pp. 121–131, 2020.
https://doi.org/10.1007/978-3-030-61725-7_16

search space. Alternative approaches include statistical linearization [6,17,22], hierarchical modeling [18,26], structured sampling methods [19], and optimal experimental design [2,11,13,15,23].

In this work, we will develop a computational scheme for the fatigue model developed by Serebrinksy and Ortiz with important time-ordering effects. To speed computation, we will develop an analytical method based on both statistical linearization and domain decomposition into quiescent and extreme load increments. This method will allow for efficiently computing the failure time for deterministic intermittent loads. Finally, we will show how an appropriately designed active search scheme can capture the long tail behavior of early fatigue failure with only a small number of numerical experiments.

2   Analytical Method for Deterministic Load

2.1   Serebrinsky-Ortiz Model

Consider a single finite element with one dimensional linear loading. The applied load (stress) is a continuous random process given by $\sigma(t; \omega)$ and the corresponding strain $\delta(t; \omega)$ depends on the element's constitutive relation. The argument for this random process are $t \in [0, T_{max}]$, the time variable and $\omega \in \Omega$, an element from the probability space (i.e., the random argument). Further, this constitutive relation depends on the fatigue state of the material; after some number of loading/unloading cycles N_{fail}, the material stiffness will degrade and eventually the material will fail. Our interest is in the relationship between the load $\sigma(t; \omega)$ and the failure time N_{fail}.

The Serebrinsky-Ortiz model, detailed in Serebrinsky, et al. (2005) [12,21], is a constitutive relationship between applied stress, σ, material strain, δ, and material stiffness parameters K^+ and K^-, given by

$$\dot{\sigma} = \begin{cases} K^- \dot{\delta} & \dot{\delta} < 0 \\ K^+ \dot{\delta} & \dot{\delta} > 0 \end{cases} \tag{1}$$

$$\dot{K}^+ = \begin{cases} (K^+ + K^-)\frac{\dot{\delta}}{\delta_a} & \dot{\delta} < 0 \\ -K^+ \frac{\dot{\delta}}{\delta_a} & \dot{\delta} > 0 \end{cases} \tag{2}$$

where δ_a is the fatigue endurance length.

In particular, K^- is assumed to be constant during unloading. These equations model fatigue-crack nucleation and growth via loading-unloading hysteresis. Critical material failure occurs when the parametric stress-strain curve $(\delta(t), \sigma(t))$ crosses a certain coherent envelope.

An example form for the coherent envelope is described by the uber relation

$$\sigma^* = e\sigma_c \frac{\delta}{\delta_c} \exp -\frac{\delta}{\delta_c}, \tag{3}$$

with constants δ_c, σ_c characterizing the material and constant $e \approx 2.718$.

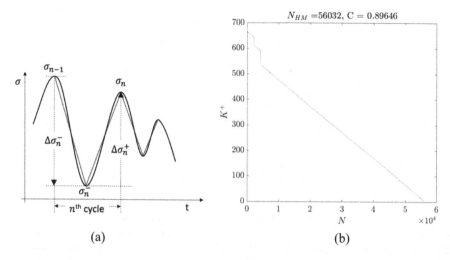

(a)   (b)

Fig. 1. a) Illustration of the linear approximation $\Delta\sigma_n^{\pm}$, derived from $\sigma(t)$. b) Sample time evolution of K^+ for the Serebrinsky-Ortiz model, for an intermittent load signal. Note the two discontinuous jumps near $t = 0.25 \times 10^4$ and $t = 0.5 \times 10^4$, which correspond to intersections with the ascending leg of the coherent envelope.

This cohesive envelope has an ascending limb (approximately $\delta < \delta_c$) and a descending limb (approximately $\delta > \delta_c$). If the stress-strain curve crosses the ascending limb, material fatigue accumulates discontinuously, and δ jumps (if possible) to say under the cohesive envelope. If the stress-strain curve crosses in the descending limb, however, there is no greater value of δ, and the material fails.

Equations 2 may be integrated between two local maxima σ_n^+ and σ_{n+1}^+ to give the update rule:

$$K_n^+ = K_n^- - \exp(\frac{\Delta\sigma_n^-}{\delta_a K_n^-})(K_n^- - K_{n-1}^+) - \frac{\Delta\sigma_n^+}{\delta_a}. \tag{4}$$

Figure 1(b) exhibits a clear linear regime in which the evolution of K^+ satisfies a simple linear relationship:

$$K_n^+ - K_{n-1}^+ \approx \Delta K. \tag{5}$$

The remaining regions, corresponding to the discontinuous jumps in Fig. 1 (b), correspond to intersections of the (σ, δ) curve with the coherent envelope. This breakdown of an intermittent process into a linear region and an extreme region parallels the probabilistic decomposition framework developed by Mohamad and Sapsis (2015) [16] and others [14].

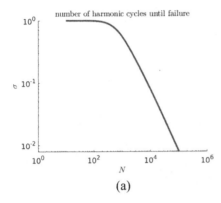
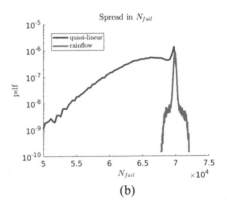

(a)   (b)

Fig. 2. a) Sample SN plot for the Serebrinksy-Ortiz fatigue model with uber coherent envelope. b) Comparison of the distribution of error times between the analytic model and rainflow counting. The full integration pdf overlaps the analytic model completely. Note that rainflow counting fails to capture the long left tail.

In order to use this approximate analytical algorithm, we will require an estimate of the stiffness slope ΔK, the mean change in K^+ per loading/unloading cycle. To find ΔK, we merely need to consult the graph in Fig. 1, and estimate the slope of the linear regions. This approach requires access to the time history of K^+ during an experiment or numerical simulation.

Alternately, an analytical estimate for ΔK may be obtained by combining the statistics of the load process (via a Rice-type formula) with a linearization of Eq. 4.

Taken together, Eqs. 4 and 5, along with a rule that identifies local maxima that may potentially intersect the coherent envelope, represent an algorithm for identifying the failure time of a material subject to a known load signal. This algorithm can be run on consumer desktop hardware in seconds–the major speed bottleneck is running the heuristic which filters out local maxima which are unlikely lead to intersections with the coherent envelope.

2.2   Comparison to Palmgren-Miner Rule

A simple method to compute the fatigue effects of intermittent signals is the Palmgren–Miner Rule, given by

$$\sum_i \frac{n_i}{N_{fi}} = C, \tag{6}$$

where n_i is the number of cycles with amplitude corresponding to bin i, and N_{fi} is the number of cycles until failure corresponding to harmonic loading with the same amplitude. This method allows for calculation of equivalent fatigue by breaking the load signal into individual cycles, each of whose contributions is separately determined by reference to the SN-Curve [7]. The well known rainflow counting algorithm, developed by Endo and Matsuishi [8], implements this rule by breaking a given signal into the corresponding set of increments.

Figure 2 (b) shows the relative errors introduced by approximating the Serebrinsky-Ortiz fatigue model by the rainflow counting method and by the analytical threshold-slope approximation. While both methods predict the mode of the distribution well, rainflow counting substantially underestimates the variance–in particular by discounting the early failure times associated with the long left tail.

3   Output-Weighted Optimal Experimental Design

3.1   Overview

We will address two primary goals for fatigue modeling. First, for a given distribution of load signals, we would like to estimate the distribution of N_{fail}, $f_N(n)$, especially the long tail of early failures. Second, we would like to identify certain characteristics of the load signals that lead to early failure–that is, we would like to identify early failure precursors.

If we had access to an exact expression for the material's coherent envelope, we could compute a distribution of failure times analytically, by finding the joint pdf of ascending and descending leg intersections and marginalizing for the failure time pdf. While this approach gives the advantage of easy updates if the coherent envelope or load statistics are changed, it has the disadvantage of requiring a very accurate estimate of the material's coherent envelope, an abstract function that is difficult to measure directly.

Instead, we will attempt to estimate the failure time pdf directly by performing (numerical) experiments. This will serve two purposes. First, the experimental design suggested will be (somewhat) agnostic to the underlying theoretical model; that is to say, the experimental design will be robust to some model misspecification. Second, assuming that the Serebrinsky-Ortiz model is a good fit for the material fatigue lifetime, the proposed experimental design will also allow for an estimation of the coherent envelope.

Standard Monte Carlo techniques for estimating probability density functions (pdfs) will require a large number of simulations, each of which is expensive even with the analytical approximation. Instead, we will use a active search methodology that accurately models the long tail of the distribution $f_N(n)$ without a large number of experiments.

3.2 J-Spike Model

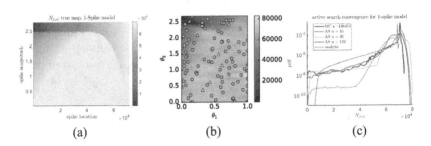

(a)   (b)   (c)

Fig. 3. a) Failure time of the 1-spike model, for different values of spike magnitude and location. b) Graphical representation of surrogate model after 104 black box evaluations. c) Sample pdf of surrogate function derived from active search with Q criterion goal, compared against Monte Carlo simulation of the 1-spike model.

It will be useful to define a class of intermittent signals called the J-spike model, which take the form

$$\sigma^J(t) = B + \sum_i^p a_i \cos(\omega_i t + \phi_i) + \sum_j \alpha_j^J G(t - \beta_j T_{max}) \tag{7}$$

This signal may be broken into a DC offset term, a narrowbanded background sum of sinusoids, and J distinct localized spikes with shape $G(t)$. We will assume that $G(t)$ is unimodal, and has small width relative to the characteristic background wavelength. Further, we will assume that the β_j and α_j are random variables drawn, respectively, from a uniform distribution, and a hand-turned Rayleigh distribution.

Note that for fixed J, the J-spike model does *not* satisfy the independent spike hypothesis.

3.3   Problem Setup

Let us consider the J-spike model described above in Sect. 3.2, restricted to the case $J = 1$. This is a space of signals with two parameters: the location of the spike α_1, and the magnitude of the spike β_1. We will let α_1 be drawn uniformly on the range $[0, 7.2e4]$ (slightly longer than the background failure time), and let β_1 be drawn from the Rayleigh distribution with tuned scale parameter. This scale parameter is tune so that few signals will have a maximum load that exceeds σ_c, but many signals will have one peak that reaches an appreciable fraction of σ_c.

Figure 3 shows the true map from the parametrized 1-spike signal to N_{fail}. This map clearly shows how both the magnitude and time-history of an intermittent load spike work together to affect the material failure time N_{fail}.

We will use use the Gaussian Process package developed by Blanchard and Sapis [3, 4] to construct a surrogate function $\tilde{N}(\alpha_1, \beta_1)$ so that for corresponding stress signals, $\tilde{N} \approx N_{fail}$.

Briefly, at each step the algorithm will create an intermediate surrogate model $\tilde{N}^i$ with Gaussian Mixture Model (GMM) form. It will then choose a parameter pair $x = (\alpha_1, \beta_1)$ by minimizing the Q-criterion, developed by Themistoklis Sapsis [20] and given by

$$Q[\sigma_N^2] = \int \frac{p_x(x)}{p_{N_0}(N_0(x))} \sigma_N^2(x; h) dx. \tag{8}$$

Finally, the algorithm will simulate the fatigue lifetime of the material using the chosen parameters, and update the surrogate model.

Unlike the Kullbeck-Liebler divergence, which selects experiments to maximum mutual information with the surrogate [5], the Q-criterion attempts to minimize the variance of the surrogate model along its entire support. In particular, this causes the Q-criterion to reduce the uncertainty in the tails of the surrogate model faster than other information theoretic metrics.

Finally, in order to simulate the scenario where we are cost limited by the difficulty of physical experiments, we will focus on small $n < 100$ simulations. Therefore, will should not expect to fit the map in Fig. 3 perfectly. Instead, we will seek to make a qualitative fit that matches a few of the major features, and the long tail behavior of the derived failure time pdf.

To this end, we will consider three error metrics. First, we will compare the recovered pdf to a high quality pdf generated by a Monte Carlo sampling strategy with $N = 138450$ samples. Unfortunately, typical error norms such as l_2 or KL divergence will overemphasize errors in the mode of the distribution, to the exclusion of fitting the long tail. To address with, we will also consider a 'tail mass' error metric, which compares the true mass and the recovered mass of the pdf long tail past some fixed threshold. Finally, we will compare the error between the recovered GMM map and the true map (constructed via careful grid sampling). While we shouldn't except close agreement (due to the issues mentioned above), a qualitative match for the recovered map is important to our subgoal of describing the particular load sequences that lead to early material failures.

3.4   Results

Figure 3 shows the evolution of the surrogate pdf trained on 1-spike model signals as the number of samples increases, compared to both a high quality Monte Carlo simulation and an analytically determined pdf.

While the analytical pdf has qualitative agreement with the truth, it fails to reproduce the magnitude of the long left tail due to very tight tuning requirements. In comparison, after just 60 experiments the left tail has been matched in both shape and magnitude.

In Fig. 4, the l_2 error in the recovered pdf and recovered mapping is shown for three sampling methods: Q-criterion active search, (fixed) Latin hypercube

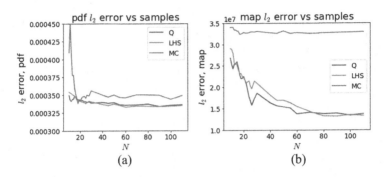

Fig. 4. l_2 error of a) the recovered pdf and b) the recovered mapping. Note that l_2 error of the pdf is a very poor error metric, because it ignores the long tail.

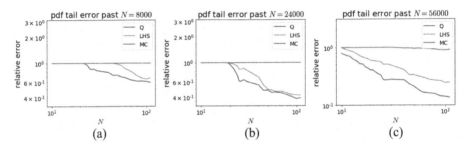

Fig. 5. Error in the recovered pdf tail mass, for three different thresholds a) $N = 8000$, b) $N = 24000$, c) $N = 56000$. Note that while both Latin hypercube sampling (LHS) and Q-criterion active search outperform simple random samples, active search generally outperforms LHS in the region of interest ($20 < N < 100$ samples).

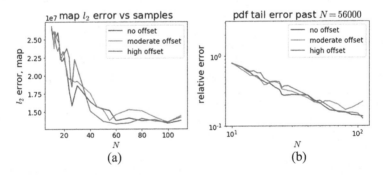

Fig. 6. Comparison of the recovered 1) map and b) tail error for different choices of the GMM fitting offset. Dependence on the zero value for GMM fitting was nearly nonexistent.

sampling (LHS), and simple Monte Carlo (MC) sampling. While both Q-criterion and LHS significantly outperform MC, there is little difference between LHS and Q-criterion sampling on the l_2 error. This is because, as previously noted, l_2 error preferentially weighs the mode of the distribution relative to the tails.

In Fig. 5, we compare the tail mass of the recovered pdf from each sampling methods. Immediately, we note that MC sampling completely fails to identify the long the tails at all. Q-criterion active search slightly outperforms fixed LHS, though the size of the gap changes depending on the particular long-tail cutoff and number of samples.

We previously hypothesized that the broad plateau region of the true map (see Fig. 3) might cause problems for the GMM fitting. Indeed, there are occasional fitting outliers in the $10 < N < 20$ region where the Q criterion significantly overestimates the tail mass of the recovered pdf (not shown).

To test this, we ran the Q criterion active search with three different fitting step offsets: $\bar{n} = 0$, $\bar{n} = 71,000$, and $\bar{n} = 40,000$. These choices represent no offset, the approximate distribution mode, and a compromise midpoint. Figure 6 shows the l_2 map error and tail error associated with each offset. it is clear that while the fitting offset changes the exact surrogate GMM fit, the output pdf tails are relatively insensitive to the details of the surrogate fitting.

Future work should be done to investigate the balance between more powerful models (GMM with more radial basis functions) and numerical instability during the fitting step.

4 Conclusion

We showed that rainflow counting disagrees with direct integration when predicting material fatigue failure in the presence of intermittent loads. In particular, we showed that rainflow counting substantially underestimates both the variance of N_{fail}, and the probability of extreme leftward deviations–the long tail.

On the other hand, we showed that an analytic algorithm based on domain decomposition had similar computational advantages but substantially less accuracy loss. In particular, the analytic algorithm captured the long tail caused by intermittent spikes in the loading signal.

Additionally, we used an active search package to learn a function mapping parametrized load signals into predicted failure times. This active search approach required only a small number of (numerical) experiments, and did not require prior knowledge of the material coherent envelope. While the results of this experimental design do not exactly reproduce the correct pdf, they do capture the long tail using significantly fewer experiments than traditional Monte Carlo approaches.

In the future, this approach should be extended to more complicated structures consisting of multiple finite elements. This extension will require more complicated input space parametrizations, but it would allow calculating the fatigue lifetime of real structures, such as oil risers and wind turbines, in the presence of intermittent loading with known distributions.

References

1. Khan, R.A., Ahmad, S.: Dynamic response and fatigue reliability analysis of marine riser under random loads. In: Volume 2: Structures, Safety and Reliability; Petroleum Technology Symposium of International Conference on Offshore Mechanics and Arctic Engineering (June 2007)
2. Forrester , A.I.J., Sóbester, A., Keane, A.J.: Exploring and exploiting a surrogate, chap. 3, pp. 77–107. John Wiley & Sons Ltd. (2008)
3. Blanchard, A., Sapsis, T.P.: Output-weighted importance sampling for Bayesian experimental design and rare-event quantification (manuscript in preparation)
4. Blanchard, A., Sapsis, T.P.: Bayesian optimization with output-weighted importance sampling. J. Comput. Phys. (2020, submitted)
5. Chaloner, K., Verdinelli, I.: Bayesian experimental design: a review. Stat. Sci. **10**(3), 273–304 (1995)
6. Chernyshov, K.R.: Information-theoretic statistical linearization. Int. Fed. Autom. Control **49**(12), 1797–1802 (2016)
7. Ciavarella, M., D'antuono, P., Papangelo, A.: On the connection between Palmgren-Miner rule and crack propagation laws. Fatigue Fract. Eng. Mater. Struct. **41**(7), 1469–1475 (2018)
8. Endo, T., Mitsunaga, K., Takahashi, K., Kobayashi, K., Matsuishi, M.: Damage evaluation of metals for random or varying loading. Three aspects of rain flow method. In: Proceedings of the 1974 Symposium on Mechanical Behavior of Materials, pp. 371–380 (1974)
9. Lee, Y.G., Garza-Gomez, X., Lee, R.M.: Ultimate costs of the disaster: seven years after the deepwater horizon oil spill. J. Corp. Account. Financ. **29**(1), 69–79 (2018)
10. Weifei Hu, K.K.C., Zhupanska, O., Buchholz, J.H.J.: Integrating variable wind load, aerodynamic, and structural analyses towards accurate fatigue life prediction in composite wind turbine blades. Struct. Multidiscip. Optim. **53**(3), 375–394 (2016)
11. Huan, X., Marzouk, Y.M.: Simulation-based optimal Bayesian experimental design for nonlinear systems. J. Comput. Phys. **232**, 288–317 (2013)
12. Serebrinsky, S., Arias, I., Ortiz, M.: A phenomenological cohesive model of ferroelectric fatigue. Acta Mater. **54**, 975–984 (2006)
13. Jiang, S., Malkomes, G., Converse, G., Shofner, A., Moseley, B., Garnett, R.: Efficient nonmyopic active search. In: Proceedings of the 34th International Conference on Machine Learning, ICML 2017, vol. 70, pp. 1714–1723. JMLR.org (2017)
14. Joo, H.K., Mohamad, M.A., Sapsis, T.P.: Heavy-tailed response of structural systems subjected to stochastic excitation containing extreme forcing events. J. Comput. Nonlinear Dyn. **13**(9), 090914 (2018)
15. Malkomes, G., Schaff, C., Garnett, R.: Bayesian optimization for automated model selection. In: Hutter, F., Kotthoff, L., Vanschoren, J. (eds.) Proceedings of the 2016 Workshop on Automatic Machine Learning, AutoML 2016, co-located with 33rd International Conference on Machine Learning, ICML 2016, New York City, NY, USA, 24 June 2016, volume 64 of JMLR Workshop and Conference Proceedings, pp. 41–47. JMLR.org (2016)
16. Mohamad, M.A., Sapsis, T.P.: Probabilistic description of extreme events in intermittently unstable dynamical systems excited by correlated stochastic processes. SIAM/ASA J. Uncertain. Quantif. **3**, 709–736 (2015)
17. Murata, M., Nagano, H., Kashino, K.: Unscented statistical linearization and robustified Kalman filter for nonlinear systems with parameter uncertainties. In: 2014 American Control Conference, pp. 5079–5084 (June 2014)

18. Mohamad, M.A., Cousins, W., Sapsis, T.P.: A probabilistic decomposition-synthesis method for the quantification of rare events due to internal instabilities. J. Comput. Phys. **322**, 288–308 (2016)

19. Olsson, A., Sandberg, G., Dahlblom, O.: On Latin hypercube sampling for structural reliability analysis. Struct. Saf. **25**(1), 47–68 (2003)

20. Sapsis, T.P.: Output-weighted optimal sampling for Bayesian regression and rare event statistics using few samples. Proc. R. Soc. A **476**, 20190834 (2020)

21. Serebrinsky, S., Ortiz, M.: A hysteretic cohesive-law model of fatigue-crack nucleation. Scripta Mater. **53**(1), 1193–1196 (2005)

22. Spanos, P.D., Kougioumtzoglou, I.A.: Harmonic wavelets based statistical linearization for response evolutionary power spectrum determination. Probab. Eng. Mech. **27**(1), 57–68 (2012). The IUTAM Symposium on Nonlinear Stochastic Dynamics and Control

23. Vu, K.K., D'Ambrosio, C., Hamadi, Y., Liberti, L.: Surrogate-based methods for black-box optimization. Int. Trans. Oper. Res. **24**(3), 393–424 (2017)

24. Wolfsteiner, P.: Fatigue assessment of non-stationary random vibrations by using decomposition in Gaussian portions. Int. J. Mech. Sci. **127**, 10–22 (2017)

25. Zhang, R., Mahadevan, S.: Fatigue reliability analysis using nondestructive inspection. J. Strct. Eng. **128**(8), 957–965 (2001)

26. Zio, E., Pedroni, N.: Estimation of the functional failure probability of a thermal-hydraulic passive system by subset simulation. Nucl. Eng. Des. **239**, 580–599 (2008)

Dynamic Data-Driven Distribution Tracking of Nanoparticle Morphology

Chiwoo Park[1(✉)] and Yu Ding[2]

[1] Florida State University, Tallahassee, FL 32310, USA
cpark5@fsu.edu
[2] Texas A&M University, College Station, TX 77840, USA
yuding@tamu.edu

Abstract. We present a data-driven distribution tracking system that is capable of tracking the process quality in a chemical synthesis process for nanoparticles. In the process, the process quality is defined as a distribution of particle sizes and shapes, which influence the functionalities of nanoparticles. A system of tracking the distribution of nanoparticle sizes and shapes consists of three components: (a) *in situ* measurement system, (b) a mathematical model to represent nanoparticle sizes and shapes, their distributions and the temporal changes in the distributions, and (c) a statistical algorithm to estimate the model with *in situ* measurements. We will review the state-of-the-art approaches to tracking the time-varying distribution of particle sizes and shapes. The advance of the distribution tracking by combining complementary *in situ* instruments based on the DDDAS paradigm is discussed.

Keywords: Shape model · Distribution tracking · *in situ* metrology

1 Introduction

Nanoparticles are minuscule particles whose dimensions are less than 100 nm. The functional properties of nanoparticles are heavily influenced by their sizes and shapes, so one can fine-tune the functionalities by simply changing the sizes and shapes. The relation of nanoparticles to sizes and shapes has been studied for many promising applications. For example, the dependency of the surface plasmon property of metal nanoparticles on the particle's sizes was studied for photo-thermal destruction of cancer cells [2], and semiconductor nanoparticles of various sizes were tested as catalysts to promote carbon nanotube growth [9].

A promising method of producing nanoparticles in large quantities is a chemical growth process, known as the self-assembly process [1]. In the chemical growth, atoms and molecules are added to a reaction solution, and those small-scale objects randomly collide in the solution, following a diffusion or a random

We acknowledge support for this work from the AFOSR (FA9550-13-1-0075, FA9550-16-1-0110, FA9550-18-1-0144).

F. Darema et al. (Eds.): DDDAS 2020, LNCS 12312, pp. 132–139, 2020.
https://doi.org/10.1007/978-3-030-61725-7_17

Brownian motion. Some collisions could lead to merging or aggregations. The small-scale objects are aggregated to become larger nanoparticles through multiple stages of mergers. The growth process is influenced by many individualized and localized factors, including the movements of individual objects, local densities of small-scale objects, and the frequency and effectiveness of individual collisions. Because of all these, every single nanoparticle exhibits a unique growth, so that the final sizes and shapes of the nanoparticles resulting from a growth process are unlikely equal but are rather likely form a distribution of a wide span. Producing nanoparticles with a concentrated distribution in both size and shape has been long desired by materials scientists [8].

Producing nanoparticles with controlled sizes and shapes has been attempted experimentally [3], which is to repeat the cycles of trying different chemical recipes and then check particle outcomes by the means of imaging. However, a pure checking of the sizes and shapes of the final nanoparticles does not give any clue on why the outcomes are bad nor guide process improvement. We believe that tracking the sizes and shapes of nanoparticles in the transient period of a growth process provides a crucial clue on how the growth progresses. This paper introduces the problem of tracking the evolution of nanoparticle sizes and shapes, as represented in a time-varying dynamic distribution, and review the state-of-the-art approaches. The tracking problem discussed in this paper is different from the object tracking problem in computer vision [4,5,14], which seeks the trajectories of individual objects and their characteristics instead of the distribution of the characteristics. Our review in Sect. 2 is only focused on the problem of tracking the distribution. The advance of the distribution tracking by combining complementary *in situ* instruments based on the dynamic data driven application system (DDDAS) paradigm is discussed in Sect. 3.

2 Distribution Tracking of Nanoparticles

A system of tracking the time-varying distribution of nanoparticle sizes and shapes consists of three components: (a) *in situ* measurement system, (b) a mathematical model to represent nanoparticle sizes and shapes, their distributions and the temporal changes in the distributions, and (c) a statistical algorithm to estimate, in near real-time, the distribution models with *in situ* measurements. Section 2.1 introduces existing approaches on distribution tracking for both size and shape, and Sect. 2.2 reviews on distribution tracking for size only.

2.1 Shape Distribution Tracking

Measurement Instrument. For tracking nanoparticle shapes in time, an *in situ* imaging of nanoparticles at a nanometer spatial resolution is necessary. There are many microscopic imaging techniques with nano-meter spatial resolutions such as electron microscopes. Most of them had not equipped with *in situ* imaging capability, mainly because wet material samples from chemical processes running in liquid phases cannot be placed on the high vacuum environment of a microscope sample chamber. In order to image those wet samples in the conventional microscopes, special sample holders should be attached for adding *in situ* capability. For examples, a liquid cell sample holder have a very thin layer of liquid samples sandwiched by two silicon or graphene windows [18], and the windows isolate wet samples from the vacuum environment.

As illustrated in Fig. 1-(a), a micro-tubing can be placed to connect in between a reaction chamber and the liquid cell, through which a reaction solution is continuously pumped into the liquid cell. Therefore, the liquid cell will be replenished continuously with reaction solutions taken at different times of a chemical nanoparticle growth process, and taking microscope images of the samples in the liquid cell with an imaging interval would generate a sequence of images containing nanoparticles taken at different stages of the growth process.

Shape Model. Each of the images generated by an *in situ* microscope are analyzed to extract the outlines of nanoparticles in the images, using the state-of-the-art image segmentation approaches [10,12,16,19]. Each of the outlines does not only the size and shape information of the corresponding nanoparticle but also includes the pose of the nanoparticle, where the 'pose' implies the orientation and location of the nanoparticle in the image. The size and shape information can be achieved by discarding the pose information from the outline.

There are quite a few existing works in the shape modeling for nanoparticles. Here we introduce one modern approach. Park [11] represented the outline as a closed curve. A closed curve in $\mathbb{R}^2$ has the circular topology $\mathbb{S}^1$. Therefore, a closed curve can be represented by a parametric curve $\phi : \mathbb{S}^1 \mapsto \mathbb{R}^2$, where the parameter $\theta \in \mathbb{S}^1$ indicates a point on the closed curve, and $\phi(\theta) \in \mathbb{R}^2$ represents the coordinate of the point. To discard the location information from the curve, the closed curve is converted to the centroid distance function, $r : \mathbb{S}^1 \mapsto \mathbb{R}^+$,

$$r(\theta) = ||\phi(\theta) - c_\phi||,$$

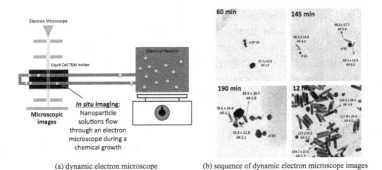

(a) dynamic electron microscope   (b) sequence of dynamic electron microscope images

Fig. 1. *In situ* electron microscope for measuring nanoparticle sizes and shapes at different stages of a nanoparticle growth process. Panel (a) shows a flow-through system attached on a conventional electron microscope that enables a realtime imaging, and panel (b) shows exemplary images from the system.

where $|| \cdot ||$ is the L2-norm, and $c_\phi = \frac{1}{2\pi} \int_{\mathbb{S}^1} \phi(\theta) d\theta$ represent the centroid of the closed curve. Let $\mathcal{R}$ represent a collection of all such centroid distance functions. The centroid distance function $r \in \mathcal{R}$ still contains the orientation of the corresponding closed curve. Let $\gamma : \mathbb{S}^1 \mapsto \mathbb{S}^1$ denote a diffeomorphism from $\mathbb{S}^1$ to $\mathbb{S}^1$ with a constant first derivative, and let Γ denote the space of all such diffeomorphisms. An $\gamma \in \Gamma$ defines a group action on $r \in \mathcal{R}$ in that $r \circ \gamma$ belongs to $\mathcal{R}$. In fact, the group action rotates the centroid distance function $r \in \mathcal{R}$. Therefore, the shape of a centroid distance function of $r \in \mathcal{R}$ can be represented as all rotational variants of r,

$$[r] = \{r \circ \gamma; \gamma \in \Gamma\}, \tag{1}$$

and the space of shapes can be defined as the quotient space, $\mathcal{R}/\Gamma$. The rotationally invariant distance of two shapes $[r_1]$ and $[r_2]$ in $\mathcal{R}/\Gamma$ is defined as

$$d_{\mathcal{R}/\Gamma}([r_1], [r_2]) = \min_{\gamma \in \Gamma} |(r_1 \circ \gamma) - r_2|,$$

where $|\cdot|$ is the L2-norm in $\mathcal{R}$. A centroid distance function r can be rotationally aligned to a reference centroid distance function $r_* \in \mathcal{R}$ by the partial Procrustes alignment with the distance $d_{\mathcal{R}/\Gamma}$, and the aligned r is achieved as $\tilde{r} = r \circ \tilde{\gamma}$, where $\tilde{\gamma} = \arg\min_{\gamma \in \Gamma} ||(r_i \circ \gamma) - r_*||$, and $\tilde{r}$ is used as the shape representation.

The shape of a nanoparticle is represented as a rotation aligned centroid distance function $\tilde{r}(\theta)$, and the shape evolution during a chemical growth process can be represented as a time series $\tilde{r}(\theta, t)$, which represents the shape observed at time t. Park [11] used the spline representation of the time series,

$$\tilde{r}(\theta, t) = \sum_{m=1}^{M} \sum_{n=1}^{N} \alpha_{m,n} a_m(t) b_n(\theta), t \geq 0 \text{ and } \theta \in [0, 2\pi),$$

where $a_m(t)$'s and $b_n(\theta)$'s are uniform B-spline basis functions with corresponding random coefficients $\alpha_{m,n}$, and M and N are tuning parameters controlling the number of the spline basis functions used. The vectorial representation of the model is

$$\tilde{r}(\theta, t) = (\boldsymbol{b}_\theta^T \otimes \boldsymbol{a}_t^T) \boldsymbol{\alpha},$$

where $\boldsymbol{\alpha} = (\alpha_{1,1}, \dots, \alpha_{M,1}, \dots, \alpha_{1,N}, \dots, \alpha_{M,N})^T$, $\boldsymbol{a}_t = (a_1(t), \dots, a_M(t))^T$, and $\boldsymbol{b}_\theta = (b_1(\theta), \dots, b_N(\theta))^T$. Park [11] pointed out that nanoparticles grow in size, so $\tilde{r}(\theta, t)$ should monotonically increase in time t. Let $\mathcal{Q}$ represent the set of all $\boldsymbol{\alpha}$ values to ensure the monotonicity given the fixed basis matrix $(\boldsymbol{b}_\theta^T \otimes \boldsymbol{a}_t^T)$. The unknown coefficient vector $\boldsymbol{\alpha} \in \mathcal{Q}$ defines the temporal evolution of a nanoparticle. The variation in the temporal evolution among multiple nanoparticles from the same growth process can be modeled by posing a probability distribution on $\boldsymbol{\alpha}$. The truncated multivariate normal distribution can be defined,

$$\boldsymbol{\alpha} \sim \mathcal{N}_{\mathcal{Q}}(\boldsymbol{\mu}, \boldsymbol{\Sigma}),$$

where $\mathcal{Q}$ is a support of $\boldsymbol{\alpha}$, $\boldsymbol{\mu}$ is the mean, and $\boldsymbol{\Sigma}$ is the covariance. More generally, one can use a nonparametric distribution such as a mixture,

$$\boldsymbol{\alpha} \sim \sum_{k=1}^{K} \beta_k \mathcal{N}_{\mathcal{Q}}(\boldsymbol{\mu}_k, \boldsymbol{\Sigma}_k),$$

where $\beta_k \geq 0$ is the mixture weight satisfying $\sum_{k=1}^{K} \beta_k = 1$. From the probability model, the probability distribution of $\tilde{r}(\theta, t)$ can be induced as

$$\tilde{r}(\theta, t) \sim \sum_{k=1}^{K} \beta_k \mathcal{N}_{\mathcal{Q}}((\boldsymbol{b}_\theta^T \otimes \boldsymbol{a}_t^T)\boldsymbol{\mu}_k, (\boldsymbol{b}_\theta^T \otimes \boldsymbol{a}_t^T)\boldsymbol{\Sigma}_k(\boldsymbol{b}_\theta \otimes \boldsymbol{a}_t)). \qquad (2)$$

For a fixed time t, it represents a probability distribution of nanoparticle sizes and shapes at time t. With the time t varying, it represents the temporal evolution of the probability distribution.

Statistical Algorithm. Suppose that there are N_t nanoparticles observed from the microscope image taken at time $t = 1, \ldots, T$. Let $\tilde{r}_{jt}(\theta)$ represent the rotationally aligned centroid distance function for the outline of the jth nanoparticle observed at time t. All the observations are $\mathcal{D} = \{\tilde{r}_{jt}(\theta); j = 1, \ldots, N_t, t = 1, \ldots, T\}$. Given the data, we want to estimate the distribution parameters $\{(\beta_k, \boldsymbol{\mu}_k, \boldsymbol{\Sigma}_k); k = 1, .., K\}$ of the mixture model (2). The expectation maximization algorithm would be a natural choice for the mixture model, if K is known. If K is unknown, a possible solution would be to use a model selection criterion such AIC and BIC to choose K, or a fully Bayesian approach can be taken to consider K as an unknown random variable. Park presented the exact Gibbs sampler for the posterior estimation of K along with the distribution parameters. For more details, please refer to the original paper [11].

2.2   Size Distribution Tracking

Measurement Instrument. When it comes to particle size, scattering techniques are more convenient and practical than microscope techniques. The scattering light techniques come with simpler sample preparation and data analysis steps than microscopic imaging. In addition, scattering machines can be loaded with a much larger volume of nanoparticle solution per each measurement than microscope techniques. Accordingly, the size distribution attained using the scattering techniques can base on a larger sample, so as to better represent the size distribution of the whole reaction solution.

One of the most commonly used scattering techniques for particle sizing is the dynamic light scattering. A sample solution is loaded into a dynamic light scattering machine, and a beam of lights is shot on the sample solution. The light beam is scattered by nanoparticles in the sample solution, and the intensities of the scattered light change in time due to the Brownian motion of nanoparticles in the solution. The autocorrelation of the temporal changes in the intensities is related to the sizes of the nanoparticles in the solution. The autocorrelation function can be analyzed to reveal the distribution of particle sizes in the form of a histogram. For more details, please refer to a relevant work [7].

Size Model. Let $x \in \mathbb{R}^+$ represents the size of a nanoparticle, and let $p_t(x)$ denote the probability density of the size at time t of a nanoparticle growth process. A simple and practical model for $p_t(x)$ may be a log-normal distribution,

$$p_t(x) = \frac{1}{\sqrt{2\pi\sigma_t^2}x} \exp\left\{-\frac{(\log x - \mu_t)^2}{2\sigma_t^2}\right\},$$

where $\mu_t \geq 0$ and $\sigma_t^2 \geq 0$ are the mean and variance of $\log x$. It has been popularly used for representing particle size distributions [6]. The simple parametric model is not good enough when $p_t(x)$ has multi-modalities, i.e., the density function has multiple local maxima. In that case, a non-parametric distribution such as a histogram can be used. Qian et al. [15] modeled the penalized B-spline model to represent the log probability density, $\log p_t(x) = \sum_{j=1}^{n} \alpha_{jt}B_j(x_i)$, where $B_j(x)$ is the jth B-spline basis function, and α_{jt} is the corresponding B-spline coefficient. The corresponding density of the size distribution is

$$p_t(x) = q_t \exp\left\{\sum_{j=1}^{n} \alpha_{jt}B_j(x_i)\right\}, \tag{3}$$

where $q_t > 0$ is a normalizing constant. The unknown coefficient vector, $\boldsymbol{\alpha}_t = (\alpha_{1t}, \ldots, \alpha_{nt})^T$, parameterizes the particle size distribution at time t, and the temporal change in $\boldsymbol{\alpha}_t$ characterizes the temporal evolution of the particle size distribution. The coefficient vectors can be spatially and temporally correlated. The consideration of the spatial and temporal correlation will be considered by means of incorporating the regularization terms in the statistical algorithms that will be discussed in the next section.

Statistical Algorithm. Suppose that nanoparticles undergoes a nanoparticle growth process, which makes the particle size change following the model (3), and dynamic light scattering measurements are achieved for the samples of nanoparticles taken from the process at time $t = 1, \ldots, T$. The measurement taken at time t can be analyzed by the existing scattering data analysis algorithm [7], and the outcome of the algorithm is a histogram of particle sizes at time t,

$$Y_t = (Y_{1t}, Y_{2t}, \ldots, Y_{mt}),$$

where Y_{it} represents the number of nanoparticles whose sizes range in the ith histogram bin, $[x_i - \delta, x_i + \delta]$. Each of the bin counts is naturally modeled as a Poisson random variable, $Y_{it} \sim Poisson(\lambda_{it})$, where the Poisson intensity $\lambda_{it} = p_t(x_i)$ is proportional to the sampling density p_t. The log likelihood is

$$L(\boldsymbol{\alpha}_t) = \sum_{i=1}^{m} Y_{it}p_t(x_i) - \sum_{i=1}^{m} \exp(p_t(x_i)).$$

Qian et al. [15] proposed to estimate all distribution parameters $\{\alpha_t; t = 1, ..., T\}$ jointly by maximizing the penalized log likelihood,

$$L(\{\alpha_t; t = 1, ..., T\}) = \sum_{t=1}^{T} L(\alpha_t) + \lambda \mathcal{P}(\{\alpha_t; t = 1, ..., T\}), \qquad (4)$$

where $\mathcal{P}(\{\alpha_t; t = 1, ..., T\}) = \sum_{t=1}^{T} \sum_{j=1}^{n} \eta(\alpha_{jt} - \alpha_{j(t+1)})^2 + (1 - \eta)(\alpha_{jt} - \alpha_{(j+1)t})^2$ is the smoothness penalty to ensure that the coefficient values do not have sudden jumps , and λ is a positive constant to determine the degree of the smoothness penalty. Qian et al. [15] proposed the alternating directional multiplier method (ADMM) algorithm to optimize the penalized likelihood function.

The penalized likelihood maximization is solved when the scattering measurements from time $t = 1$ to T are available. Therefore, the distribution is estimated after the whole growth process is completed. Qian et al. [17] proposed an online estimation algorithm to estimate α_t incrementally as soon as the measurements up to time t are available instead of waiting until all the measurements are collected. Qian et al. [17] used an autoregressive model to model the time-varying coefficient vector, $\alpha_t = \alpha_{t-1} + \epsilon_t$, where $\epsilon_t \sim \mathcal{N}(0, \sigma_t^2 I)$. With the autoregressive model, we would have a hidden Markov model linking $\{\alpha_t; t = 1, ..., T\}$ with the Poisson observation model (4). The online estimation algorithm of the Kalman filter type can be used to estimate the hidden Markov model [17].

3   Conclusion

This paper discusses the problem of tracking the time-varying distribution of particle sizes and shapes at different stages of a chemical growth process of nanoparticles. If the distribution can be tracked in realtime, it can be exploited for monitoring the growth process, a prerequisite leading to potential control of nanoparticle growth that produces nanoparticles with desirable sizes and shapes. The major challenges in achieving this goal are whether one can take the size and shape measurements in realtime during a growth process, how one effectively models the distributions of sizes and shapes, and how the mathematical model can be estimated as fast as the realtime measurements arrive. We review the recent developments addressing the three challenges. When only the particle sizes are concerned, quick scattering measurements followed by an online density estimation algorithm [17] can carry out a near real-time tracking of particle size distributions. When both shapes and sizes are concerned, realtime online distribution tracking is not yet available. Addressing this latter problem appears much more challenging, due to the high complexities in dealing with shapes. This challenge can be alleviated by a dynamic data-driven application systems (DDDAS) approach making use of multiple measurement instruments of complementary spatio-temporal resolutions. With multi-resolution instruments, one can primarily track the size distribution in realtime using a temporally fast instrument (e.g., the scattering light techniques), while triggering the estimate of shape distribution only when it is necessary [13].

References

1. Grzelczak, M., Vermant, J., Furst, E.M., Liz-Marzán, L.M.: Directed self-assembly of nanoparticles. ACS Nano **4**(7), 3591–3605 (2010)
2. Hirsch, L.R., et al.: Nanoshell-mediated near-infrared thermal therapy of tumors under magnetic resonance guidance. Proc. Nat. Acad. Sci. **100**(23), 13549–13554 (2003)
3. Jana, N.R., Gearheart, L., Murphy, C.J.: Seed-mediated growth approach for shape-controlled synthesis of spheroidal and rod-like gold nanoparticles using a surfactant template. Adv. Mater. **13**(18), 1389–1393 (2001)
4. Jia, B., Pham, K., Blasch, E., Chen, G., Shen, D.: Diffusion-based cooperative space object tracking. Opt. Eng. **58**(4), 041607 (2019)
5. Jia, B., Pham, K.D., Blasch, E., Shen, D., Wang, Z., Chen, G.: Cooperative space object tracking using space-based optical sensors via consensus-based filters. IEEE Trans. Aerosp. Electron. Syst. **52**(4), 1908–1936 (2016)
6. Kiss, L., Söderlund, J., Niklasson, G., Granqvist, C.: New approach to the origin of lognormal size distributions of nanoparticles. Nanotechnology **10**(1), 25 (1999)
7. Li, X., Tran, P.H., Liu, T., Park, C.: Simulation-guided regression approach for estimating the size distribution of nanoparticles with dynamic light scattering data. IISE Trans. **49**(1), 70–83 (2017)
8. Liu, L., Liang, H., Yang, H., Wei, J., Yang, Y.: The size-controlled synthesis of uniform mn2o3 octahedra assembled from nanoparticles and their catalytic properties. Nanotechnology **22**(1), 015603 (2010)
9. Nikolaev, P., et al.: Autonomy in materials research: a case study in carbon nanotube growth. NPJ Comput. Mater. **2**(1), 1–6 (2016)
10. Park, C., Huang, J.Z., Ji, J.X., Ding, Y.: Segmentation, inference and classification of partially overlapping nanoparticles. IEEE Trans. Pattern Anal. Mach. Intell. **35**(3), 669–681 (2013)
11. Park, C.: Estimating multiple pathways of object growth using nonlongitudinal image data. Technometrics **56**(2), 186–199 (2014)
12. Park, C., Ding, Y.: Automating material image analysis for material discovery. MRS Commun. **9**(2), 545–555 (2019)
13. Park, C., Ding, Y.: Dynamic data-driven monitoring of nanoparticle self assembly processes. Handbook of Dynamic Data Driven Applications Systems, 2nd eds. submitted (2020)
14. Park, C., Woehl, T.J., Evans, J.E., Browning, N.D.: Minimum cost multi-way data association for optimizing multitarget tracking of interacting objects. IEEE Trans. Pattern Anal. Mach. Intell. **37**(3), 611–624 (2014)
15. Qian, Y., Huang, J.Z., Ding, Y.: Identifying multi-stage nanocrystal growth using in situ TEM video data. IISE Trans. **49**(5), 532–543 (2017)
16. Qian, Y., Huang, J.Z., Li, X., Ding, Y.: Robust nanoparticles detection from noisy background by fusing complementary image information. IEEE Trans. Image Process. **25**(12), 5713–5726 (2016)
17. Qian, Y., Huang, J.Z., Park, C., Ding, Y.: Fast dynamic nonparametric distribution tracking in electron microscopic data. Ann. Appl. Stat. **13**, 1537–1563 (2019)
18. Ross, F.M.: Liquid Cell Electron Microscopy. Cambridge University Press, Cambridge (2016)
19. Vo, G.D., Park, C.: Robust regression for image binarization under heavy noise and nonuniform background. Pattern Recogn. **81**, 224–239 (2018)

Plenary Presentations - Section 5:
Physics-Based Systems Analysis

Machine Learning Algorithms for Improved Thermospheric Density Modeling

Herbert Turner[1](✉), Maggie Zhang[2](✉), David Gondelach[1](✉),
and Richard Linares[1](✉)

[1] Department of Aeronautics and Astronautics,
Massachusetts Institute of Technology, Cambridge, USA
{hmturner,dgondela,linaresr}@mit.edu
[2] Department of Electrical Engineering and Computer Science,
Massachusetts Institute of Technology, Cambridge, MA, USA
maggieqz@mit.edu

Abstract. Accurate estimation and prediction of the thermospheric density is crucial for accurate low Earth orbit prediction. Recently, Reduced-Order Models (ROMs) were developed to obtain accurate quasi-physical dynamic models for the thermospheric density. In this paper we explore the use of deep neural networks and autoencoders to improve the reduced-order models. Through the development of deep and convolutional autoencoders, we obtain improved low-dimension representations of a high-dimensional density state. In addition, we improve the prediction accuracy of the ROM using a deep neural network.

1 Introduction

Almost 63% of all functioning satellites reside in Low Earth Orbit between 250–1500 km above the Earth's surface. In much of this region, the orbit of the satellites can be drastically affected by drag from the Earth's thermosphere. For models to accurately determine and predict orbits, they must have a way to accurately estimate and predict thermospheric conditions that relate to the drag on the satellite. To estimate the thermospheric density, satellite tracking data can be used. At the same time, improved density forecast results in better orbit predictions that enables improved satellite tracking. This feedback loop in which measurements improve the density model and the model helps control the tracking instruments follows the Dynamic Data Driven Applications Systems (DDDAS) paradigm [3]. Here, we reinforce the cycle of satellite tracking, density estimation and orbit prediction, see Fig. 1, to improve space traffic management.

Currently, two types of thermospheric models exist: empirical and physics-based models. Empirical models use low-order parametrized mathematical formulations to estimate average behavior of the upper atmosphere. These models are much more computationally efficient, however, they have no forecasting

---

H. Turner and M. Zhang—These authors contributed equally to this work.

© Springer Nature Switzerland AG 2020
F. Darema et al. (Eds.): DDDAS 2020, LNCS 12312, pp. 143–151, 2020.
https://doi.org/10.1007/978-3-030-61725-7_18

capability which limits their effectiveness for real-time data assimilation and uncertainty quantification. Physics-based models, such as the Global Ionosphere-Thermosphere Model (GITM) solve the Navier-Stokes equations for discretized spatial grids. They enable forecasting and have been used with the DDDAS principles for data assimilation [2]. However, because of their high dimensionality, they are computationally expensive and require parallelization for real-time use.

Recently, Reduced-Order Models (ROMs) have been developed to obtain accurate quasi-physical dynamic models for the thermospheric density [12,13]. These models make use of Proper Orthogonal Decomposition (POD) to reduce the dimensionality and Dynamic Mode Decomposition (DMD) to train linear dynamic models

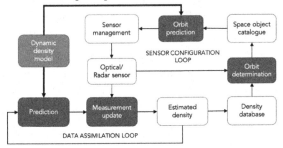

Fig. 1. Density estimation framework

to make significantly faster predictions. This enables efficient and accurate estimation of thermospheric densities using satellite tracking data [4]. However, POD and DMD are linear techniques while the thermospheric dynamics are highly nonlinear. Therefore the ROMs have limited accuracy.

In this work, we seek to improve the ROMs using machine learning (ML) techniques [5, 9–11]. We use deep autoencoders to better represent thermospheric data in a reduced space using non-linear dimensionality reduction. Improvements are made by using convolutional layers, which significantly reduce the number of trainable weights in our model. Utilizing the reduced data, we continue the density predictions using a deep feedforward neural network (NN) that includes activation functions to provide a nonlinear component. We optimize the hyperparameters of the network to obtain best results. The autoencoder and deep NN architectures developed in this work can be used as basis for recurrent autoencoders developments. In the following, the linear and machine-learning techniques are described and results are discussed. In future work, the methods will be incorporated to improve density forecasting and satellite orbit prediction. This enhances the feedback loop for real-time density estimation and satellite tracking.

2   Methodology

Reduced-order modeling of the neutral density consists of two main components: 1) reducing the dimensionality of the state space while retaining maximum information and 2) deriving a dynamical model for the reduced-order state. In this paper, we follow a data-driven reduced-order modeling approach using both linear and nonlinear techniques. We use 12-years of density data with a 1 h temporal resolution to derive the reduced-order model.

2.1 Dimensionality Reduction

Proper Orthogonal Decomposition. The concept of order reduction using POD is to project the high-dimensional system and its solution onto a set of low-dimensional basis functions or spatial modes, while capturing the dominant characteristics of the system. Consider the variation $\tilde{\mathbf{x}}$ of the neutral mass density $\mathbf{x}$ with respect to the mean value $\bar{\mathbf{x}}$:

$$\tilde{\mathbf{x}}(\mathbf{s}, t) = \mathbf{x}(\mathbf{s}, t) - \bar{\mathbf{x}}(\mathbf{s}) \tag{1}$$

where $\mathbf{s}$ is the spatial grid. A significant fraction of the variance $\tilde{\mathbf{x}}$ can be captured by the first r principal spatial modes:

$$\tilde{\mathbf{x}}(\mathbf{s}, t) \approx \sum_{i=1}^{r} c_i(t) \Phi_i(\mathbf{s}) \tag{2}$$

where Φ_i are the spatial modes and c_i are the corresponding time-dependent coefficients. The spatial modes Φ are computed using a SVD of the snapshot matrix $\mathbf{X}$ that contains $\tilde{\mathbf{x}}$ for different times:

$$\mathbf{X} = \begin{bmatrix} \tilde{\mathbf{x}}_1 & \tilde{\mathbf{x}}_2 & \cdots & \tilde{\mathbf{x}}_m \end{bmatrix} = \mathbf{U} \mathbf{\Sigma} \mathbf{V}^\top \tag{3}$$

where m is the number of snapshots. The spatial modes Φ are given by the left singular vectors (the columns of $\mathbf{U}$). The state reduction is achieved using a similarity transform:

$$\mathbf{z} = \mathbf{U}_r^{-1} \tilde{\mathbf{x}} = \mathbf{U}_r^\top \tilde{\mathbf{x}} \tag{4}$$

where $\mathbf{U}_r$ is a matrix with the first r POD modes and $\mathbf{z}$ is our reduced-order state. More details on POD can be found in [12].

Autoencoders. An autoencoder is a NN that takes an input vector, X, encodes it as vector V and then decodes it to vector X', which is an attempted reconstruction of the original vector [6]. It consists of two parts, an encoder and decoder, which we can define as transitions $\mathbb{F}$ and $\mathbb{G}$ such that given a loss function $\mathcal{L}$:

$$\mathbb{F} : X \rightarrow V \tag{5}$$

$$\mathbb{G} : V \rightarrow X' \tag{6}$$

$$\mathbb{F}, \mathbb{G} = \arg \min_{\mathbb{F}, \mathbb{G}} \mathcal{L}(X, X') \tag{7}$$

Throughout this work, we used mean squared error as our loss function, which is defined such that given a vector X and its reconstruction X of dimension d:

$$\mathcal{L}(X, X') = \frac{||X - X'||^2}{d} \tag{8}$$

We specifically looked at undercomplete autoencoders, autoencoders whose encoded dimension is less than the input dimension. Undercomplete autoencoders allow models to learn the most important features of the dataset. The advantages of an autoencoder over POD is that while POD finds orthogonal linear projections, autoencoders, if given nonlinear activation functions, are capable of learning nonlinear manifolds. As the factor of the dimensionality reduction is increased, the benefits of learning these nonlinear features becomes more and more apparent. However, care must be taken to ensure that the NNs are learning the useful information about the data and not simply memorizing the copying task. In each of the following networks, we took extra steps to address this problem.

Deep Autoencoder. We began with a feed-forward deep network architecture with a multilayer encoder and decoder with linear final activation functions. To address the issue of overfitting, we introduced batch normalization and dropout to our networks. Batch normalization fixes the mean and variance of each layer's inputs to values determined during training, addressing the issue of internal covariate shift and has been shown to have a regularizing effect on networks [7]. Dropout is used during training to prevent overfitting by randomly ignoring hidden nodes during the forward and backward pass [14]. The probability of dropping a node p_i is a tuned hyperparameter.

Convolutional Autoencoder. We also attempted dimensionality reduction through convolutional techniques. We added several convolutional layers to our encoder and decoder [6]. In the single channel version, we use a 3D filter and do element-wise multiplication and addition. Each convolution step will therefore result in a single number. In the multi-channel version, our input "layer" may have multiple "channels." Therefore, we use a four-dimensional "filter." The filter contains several "kernels." Each kernel is a 3D array of weights. Given output g and input x, the 3D convolution can be written such that

$$g_{i,j,k,c} = \sigma(w_c^T x_{i,j,k,c}) \tag{9}$$

where each pixel in a given channel output, $g_{i,j,k,c}$, is the matrix multiplication between the filter, c, and the input space centered around $x_{i,j,k,c}$. We experimented with various filter sizes including $3 \times 3 \times 3$ and $5 \times 5 \times 5$ and varied the number of channels. Every other filter used a stride of 2 in its convolution. This stride results in a dimensionality reduction that ideally filters out the least important features of the data. We continued to use a fully connected final encoder layer with linear activation function, and a deep fully connected decoder.

We also experimented with $1 \times 1 \times d$ filters, where d matched one of the dimensions of x. Using 1×1 filters is a form of dimensionality reduction included in Google's state of the art inception module [15]. Each convolution will reduce our data in one dimension to 1 per sample. Our 3D convolution then becomes:

$$g_{i,j,c} = \sigma(w_c^T x_{i,j,c}) \tag{10}$$

where each pixel in a given channel output, $g_{i,j,c}$, is the matrix multiplication between the filter, c, and the input space centered around $x_{i,j,c}$.

Hyperparameter Tuning. While our network weights are easily tuned using gradient descent, our hyperparameters are not differentiable, and therefore more difficult to optimize. Due to the size and variety of our networks, simpler grid searches and hand-tuned models were unlikely to find the optimum values, even with significant training time. Instead, we trained our networks using hyperopt. Hyperopt is a Python library for hyperparameter tuning [1]. It implements several methods for efficiently searching through a hyperparameter space, including Tree-structured Parzen Estimator (TPE) algorithm. Using hyperopt on MIT's HPC platform, Supercloud, we tuned our optimizer, learning rate, layer number and sizes, as well as the hyperparameters for batch normalization and dropout.

2.2   Prediction

The atmospheric density depends strongly on the space weather conditions. Therefore, to predict the future density, we look for a function that takes the current state $\mathbf{z}_k$ and space weather inputs $\mathbf{u}_k$ and returns the future state:

$$\mathbf{z}_{k+1} = \mathbf{f}(\mathbf{z}_k, \mathbf{u}_k) \tag{11}$$

where $\mathbf{z}_k$ is the reduced-state at epoch k: $\mathbf{z}_k = \mathbb{F}(\mathbf{x}_k)$.

Dynamic Mode Decomposition with Control. Dynamic Mode Decomposition with control (DMDc) enables us to derive a linear dynamical system that considers exogenous inputs:

$$\mathbf{z}_{k+1} = \mathbf{A}\mathbf{z}_k + \mathbf{B}\mathbf{u}_k \tag{12}$$

The dynamic matrix $\mathbf{A}$ and input matrix $\mathbf{B}$ can be estimated from output data, or snapshots, $\mathbf{z}_k$, rearranged into time-shifted data matrices. Let $\mathbf{Z}_1$ and $\mathbf{Z}_2$ be the time-shifted matrix of snapshots such that:

$$\mathbf{Z}_1 = \begin{bmatrix} \mathbf{z}_1\ \mathbf{z}_2 \cdots \mathbf{z}_{m-1} \end{bmatrix}, \quad \mathbf{Z}_2 = \begin{bmatrix} \mathbf{z}_2\ \mathbf{z}_3 \cdots \mathbf{z}_m \end{bmatrix}, \quad \mathbf{\Upsilon} = \begin{bmatrix} \mathbf{u}_1\ \mathbf{u}_2 \cdots \mathbf{u}_{m-1} \end{bmatrix} \tag{13}$$

where m is the number of snapshots and $\mathbf{\Upsilon}$ contains the corresponding inputs. Since $\mathbf{Z}_2$ is the time evolution of $\mathbf{Z}_1$ they are related through Eq. (12) such that:

$$\mathbf{Z}_2 = \mathbf{A}\mathbf{Z}_1 + \mathbf{B}\mathbf{\Upsilon} \tag{14}$$

Given $\mathbf{Z}_1$ and $\mathbf{Z}_2$, we can estimate matrices $\mathbf{A}$ and $\mathbf{B}$ in least-squares sense and obtain a linear reduced-order model (Eq. 11) that corresponds to the fixed timestep T used for the snapshots.

Deep Neural Network. As changes in atmospheric density and the effects of space weather on the density are highly complex and nonlinear, we chose to utilize a deep feedforward neural network (NN) for our prediction model. Such a NN is able to capture and learn nonlinear complexities using activation functions, with the goal of creating more accurate density predictions.

Architecture. In building a NN, there are several key components to consider: node layers, activation functions, and the loss function. We will now break down each component into its relevance in our algorithm. In the final iteration of hyperparameter tuning, we found a minimized loss while using one input layer of size 120, two hidden layers of size 40 then 20, and an output layer with 10, our reduced dimension.

As just having hidden layers with no activation function is equivalent to a single linear layer, we add a LeakyRelu activation function between each layer. After testing Sigmoid, Softmax, and Tanh activation functions, we saw errors several orders of magnitude larger than that of the linear prediction model. Our problem is a regression, so we do not use such activation functions as Sigmoid, Softmax, or Tanh and instead opt for a Relu variant. As our data has both positive and negative values, using Relu can lead to the vanishing gradient problem and we empirically found higher values of error in validation. Thus, to account for the negative values in our data, the LeakyRelu activation function has a positive slope for negative inputs. We found that this activation function with a slope of 0.3 for negative inputs yielded consistently fast training times and accurate predictions.

Training. We use a standard mean squared error (MSE) to compute the prediction loss and train the network. In addition, we use the Adaptive moment estimation (Adam) as our optimizer. Adam is a combination of RMSprop and Stochastic Gradient Descent with momentum. Past literature has shown Adam to reach an optimal solution more quickly than other optimizers [8]. Furthermore, we used a learning rate of 0.0005 that was determined through empirical testing.

Finally, to train our NN, we split the density data in a 70–15–15 ratio of train, validation, and test data respectively using randomized splitting. We use mini batch gradient descent with a batch size of 32 for training. With smaller batch sizes, there are more frequent weight updates at the cost of longer training times. Weighing these tradeoffs and the subsequent prediction accuracies, we find that a batch size of 32 is optimal. For our final models, we trained for 500 epochs.

2.3 Density Data

To train and test our NNs, we used two different density datasets generated using the NRLMSISE-00 (MSISE) and JB2008 density models, see [4]. Each dataset contains the hourly density over 12 years (one solar cycle) on a fixed $24 \times 20 \times 36$ grid in local solar time, latitude and altitude, see Table 1.

3 Results

3.1 Dimensionality Reduction

We first performed a dimensionality reduction from the full sample size of $24 \times 20 \times 36$ to a vector of length 10. We split our data into a training, validation, and test set. We chose POD reduced data, calculated on the training

Table 1. ROM characteristics: spatial grid and time period.

Base model	Local solar time [hr]		Latitude [deg]		Altitude [km]		Years
	Domain	Resolution	Domain	Res.	Domain	Res.	
NRLMSISE-00	[0, 24]	1.04	[–87.5, 87.5]	9.2	[100, 800]	20	1997–2008
JB2008	[0, 24]	1.04	[–87.5, 87.5]	9.2	[100, 800]	20	1999–2010

data, as our baseline. Our autoencoders were trained on the training data while hyperparameter optimization was done on the validation set. We found that the optimal architecture was the convolutional autoencoder using square filters. Table 2 shows the results for POD and three hyperopt-tuned models on the testing data for both the JB2008 and MSISE datasets. The POD performs better than most of the autoencoders on the JB2008 data. However, on the MSISE data, which is more nonlinear than the JB2008 data, the autoencoders all perform better. This highlights the ability of autoencoders to deal with nonlinearities. We also analysed the reconstruction accuracy of POD and our best model for a reduced dimension of 1. Table 2 shows that the autoencoder outperforms POD for data reduction to a single dimension. This emphasizes the benefit of non-linear dimensionality reduction for few dimensions.

Table 2. Reconstruction Loss (MSE) for reduced dimensions $r = 10$ and $r = 1$

Dimension	Model	JB2008	MSISE
10	POD	$8.82 * 10^{-5}$	$3.03 * 10^{-3}$
	Deep Autoencoder	$2.81 * 10^{-4}$	$7.60 * 10^{-5}$
	Square Convolutional Autoencoder	$6.28 * 10^{-5}$	$1.99 * 10^{-4}$
	1×1 Convolutional Autoencoder	$1.09 * 10^{-4}$	$1.21 * 10^{-4}$
1	POD	$1.10 * 10^{-1}$	1.03
	Square Convolutional Autoencoder	$1.59 * 10^{-2}$	$4.98 * 10^{-2}$

3.2 Prediction

We found that the MSE across the density data predictions using a NN consistently outperforms the MSE of using the DMDc method for predictions, see Fig. 2. Using both the POD reduction method and the 1×1 convolutional autoencoder, we trained and tested the NNs with JB2008 and MSISE reduced data. Especially, as we predict further time steps into the future, we find that for MSISE, the NN outperforms the DMDc by an even greater degree than for earlier time steps, see Table 3. Among JB2008 data, the NN is able to outperform the DMDc by reducing the error by 99.3% in the first time step while later prediction ratios decline as errors compound in the network.

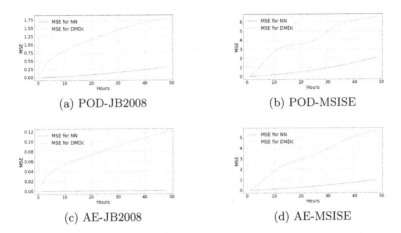

(a) POD-JB2008   (b) POD-MSISE

(c) AE-JB2008   (d) AE-MSISE

Fig. 2. MSE in reduced state prediction using DMDc and DNN for JB2008 and MSISE data reduced using POD or AE.

Table 3. Percentage reduction of MSE in reduced state prediction using DNN with respect to DMDc for different density data and encodings.

Density data	Encoding	Reduction of MSE [%]						
		1h	2h	4h	8h	16h	24h	48h
JB2008	POD	99.3	99.2	98.8	97.5	94.6	91.8	83.1
	AE	99.1	99.0	99.0	99.0	99.1	99.2	99.4
MSISE	POD	73.3	84.3	90.9	92.8	89.4	83.1	68.8
	AE	92.2	93.7	94.5	94.5	92.7	89.9	83.0

4   Discussion and Conclusions

We designed and trained deep and convolutional autoencoders that outperforms POD for the reduction of $24 \times 20 \times 36$ density data to an encoded dimension of 1 and 10. In addition, we found that thermospheric density predictions using our NN consistently outperformed the DMDc predictions over a 48 h time span using both JB2008 and MSISE data and both the POD and autoencoder reduced data. This shows that NNs can be trained efficiently to forecast thermospheric densities into the future. We plan to replicate training of our models to prove the convergence with parameters found during our research. This approach improves the reduced-order modeling of thermospheric densities, which enables improved density estimation and prediction and therefore more accurate orbit predictions. However, we also found that even a non-overfitted NN that performs well for one time step may perform poorly over multiple time steps. As our training error metric does not take into account previous data in training, the NN cannot optimize in a recurrent fashion. We will continue our work by developing recurrent networks that consider past predictions to improve the multi-step prediction performance. In addition, we will research a combination of our two networks, a LSTM-based autoencoder, and incorporate them into the thermospheric density estimation tool. In future work, the density prediction models can be applied in DDDAS fashion to improve resident space object tracking and vice versa.

References

1. Bergstra, J., Yamins, D., Cox, D.D.: Making a science of model search: hyperparameter optimization in hundreds of dimensions for vision architectures. In: Proceedings of the 30th International Conference on Machine Learning, vol. 28, p. I-115-I-123. JMLR (2013)
2. Bernstein, D., Ridley, A., Cutler, J., Cohn, A.: Transformative advances in DDDAS with application to space weather monitoring. University of Michigan (2015)
3. Blasch, E.: DDDAS advantages from high-dimensional simulation. In: 2018 Winter Simulation Conference (WSC), pp. 1418–1429. IEEE (2018)
4. Gondelach, D.J., Linares, R.: Real-time thermospheric density estimation viatwo-line element data assimilation. Space Weather 18(2), e2019SW002356 (2020)
5. Gonzalez, F.J., Balajewicz, M.: Deep convolutional recurrent autoencoders for learning low-dimensional feature dynamics of fluid systems (2018). arXiv preprint arXiv:1808.01346
6. Goodfellow, I., Bengio, Y., Courville, A.: Deep Learning. MIT Press, Cambridge (2016)
7. Ioffe, S., Szegedy, C.: Batch normalization: Accelerating deep network training by reducing internal covariate shift (2015)
8. Kingma, D.P., Ba, J.: Adam: A method for stochastic optimization (2014). arXiv preprint arXiv:1412.6980
9. Lee, K., Carlberg, K.T.: Model reduction of dynamical systems on nonlinear manifolds using deep convolutional autoencoders. J. Comput. Phys. 404, 108973 (2020)
10. Licata, R.J., Mehta, P.M.: Physics-informed machine learning with autoencoders and LSTM for probabilistic space weather modeling and forecasting. In: 100th American Meteorological Society Annual Meeting (2020)
11. Linares, R., Mehta, P.M., Godinez, H.C., Gondelach, D.J.: Koopman operator theory for thermospheric density modeling. In: Proceedings of the 29th AAS/AIAA Space Flight Mechanics Meeting, Ka'anapali, HI (2019)
12. Mehta, P.M., Linares, R.: A methodology for reduced order modeling and calibration of the upper atmosphere. Space Weather 15(10), 1270–1287 (2017)
13. Mehta, P.M., Linares, R., Sutton, E.K.: A quasi-physical dynamic reduced order model for thermospheric mass density via hermitian space-dynamic mode decomposition. Space Weather 16(5), 569–588 (2018)
14. Srivastava, N., Hinton, G., Krizhevsky, A., Sutskever, I., Salakhutdinov, R.: Dropout: A simple way to prevent neural networks from overfitting. J. Mach. Learn. Res. 15(56), 1929–1958 (2014)
15. Szegedy, C., et al.: Going deeper with convolutions (2014). arXiv preprint arXiv:1409.4842

Dynamic Transfer Learning from Physics-Based Simulated SAR Imagery for Automatic Target Recognition

Ali Ahmadibeni, Branndon Jones, Damiyelle Smith, and Amir Shirkhodaie[✉]

Tennessee State University, Nashville, TN 37209, USA
{aahmadib,bjone161,dsmit268}@my.tnstate.edu,
ashirkhodaie@tnstate.edu

Abstract. In this paper, we present a two-step deep learning technique in support of DDDAS for achievement of robust ATR via transfer learning using simulated SAR imagery. The first Deep Learning (DL) model performs noise suppression of input SAR images via a Multi-resolution Stacked Denoising Autoencoder (MSDAE) architecture. The second DL model includes a Multi-output Convolutional Neural Network (M-CNN) architecture suitable for multi-feature classification of ATR pertaining to the DDDAS paradigm. In this approach, we train each DL model independently, then, streamline this process as a standalone deep learning ATR classifier. Primarily, we employed the IRIS Electromagnetic (IRIS-EM) modeling and simulation system to systematically generate our own multi-look large-scale simulated SAR images of multi-platform (i.e., ground, aerial, and marine) vehicles. To improve situational awareness of a DDDAS with respect to ATR, we devised dynamic transfer learnings which employ a step-wise retraining inspired by the observational statistical sampling technique. In this paper, we demonstrate the efficiency and effectiveness of the proposed approach in performing multi-feature ATR of test target vehicles applicable to DDDAS. Lastly, we discuss our classification results using a streamlined denoising and classification system and justify its implication for the DL-based DDDAS.

Keywords: Deep learning · SAR · ATR · DDDAS · Image denoising · Convolutional neural networks

1 Introduction

The Synthetic Aperture Radar (SAR) system is typically an integral part of surveillance aircrafts, operating from a long distance that produces two-dimensional images from observed landscape targets by illuminating electromagnetic (EM) waves to an area and record the reflections (also called backscattering). Understanding and interpreting the SAR imagery using deep learning based computer vision systems for detection and classification purposes have witnessed great success in the past decade.

We propose a denoising autoencoder (DAE) model that performs the SAR image denoising and object shadow removal while preserving the object texture as an intermediate step before passing the images through the classifier. This operation provides

© Springer Nature Switzerland AG 2020
F. Darema et al. (Eds.): DDDAS 2020, LNCS 12312, pp. 152–159, 2020.
https://doi.org/10.1007/978-3-030-61725-7_19

the classifier model with more image pixel information to be trained on - resulting in achievement of a higher object classification accuracy.

DDDAS are distinctive predictive models taking advantage of a data assimilation feedback loop when discrete sensor data are available. Using sensor data error, the system attempts to drive the physical system simulation so that the trajectory of the simulation more closely follows the trajectory of the physical system [4].

In our work, we attempted to train our CNN model with limited scattered data. This is similar to situations in which the data is dynamically generated and become available for the training. This was accomplished by splitting the IRIS-SAR and the Denoised SAR datasets in various combinations and retrain our network using incremental transfer learning. This methods showed a promising result in increasing the accuracy and generalization of the classifier model for the purposes of object recognition and classification.

The remaining of this paper is organized in the following sections. We initially describe the aspects of our SAR dataset generation and annotation scheme. Then, we describe the SAR image denoising process using the MSDAE model and technical improvements involved in this model. Next, we introduce our multi-output CNN classifier model and discuss the results from dynamic data-driven scenarios for training. Lastly, the combined MSDAE + MCNN model is described for streamlining the denoising and classification process. Finally, we present the conclusion of this research work.

2 EM Modeling and Simulation

In the brevity of the space limitation here, the detailed aspects of the Synthetic SAR image dataset generation using IRIS physics-based modeling and simulation method is not covered in this paper. The interested readers are encouraged to review our papers [1, 2] for the details of our proposed approach. This section presents a brief introduction to the main key points of our synthetic SAR dataset. The IRIS-SAR dataset was produced using Intelligent Robotics Integrated Systems (IRIS) software developed at Tennessee State University [3]. The IRIS EM simulation engine implements an efficient Synthetic Aperture Radar Interface which offers full automation capability for achieving generated synthetic SAR imagery with uniformity, consistency, and reliability. Our dataset contains the simulated SAR imagery of 48 commercial airplanes, 58 small propeller aircrafts, 82 jet fighters, 29 civilian and 54 military helicopters, and 24 commercial and 28 military ground vehicles, and 32 civilian and military marine vehicles. In generation of this dataset, we used five elevation angles starting at $15°$ with increments of $15°$, twelve orientations (azimuth angle) around the Z axis starting at $0°$ with increments of $30°$, and also three slant ranges. Figure 1 depicts a sample set of simulated SAR images of different categories of objects from our IRIS CAD model bank.

IRIS-SAR dataset contains 63,900 images with 512×512 pixels resolution. The dataset presents multiple views of the objects (5 elevation * 12 azimuth * 3 slant ranges = 180 each per vehicle) for 355 CAD objects. Moreover, the three modalities of scanning (Reflectivity Map, Depth Map, and Height Map) are also composed as individual datasets. The Reflectivity Map (RM) is used as reference in the training of our denoising auto-encoder models. Although this dataset includes 3 slang ranges for each object,

Fig. 1. Top: samples of our CAD models, bottom: their corresponding simulated SAR images at 45° elevation angle.

we only used images with the shortest range of 100 m (21,300 images) for training of denoiser and classifier models.

3 Multi-resolution Stacked Denoising Auto-Encoder (MSDAE)

Auto-encoders are a type of neural networks commonly used for feature selection and extraction by learning to efficiently compress and encode data and also learn to how to reconstruct the data back from the encoded representation to another representation that is as close to the original input as possible. In this research, we use a multi-resolution stacked denoising auto-encoder (MSDAE) to denoise SAR imagery that carry very dense amounts of noise in their nature.

After designing and testing the single DAEs we came into the conclusion that increasing the depth of the network or filters count will not always necessarily improve the network performance. Stacked auto-encoders [5] was proposed to increase the network performance where the single network can't be improved on. Stacked denoising auto-encoders [6] have been proven to be very effective in the task of image denoising, in which the output of the previous auto-encoder is fed to the current auto-encoder as input.

Multi-Resolution Convolutional Neural Network (MRCNN) [9] is also a type of Multi-Input Neural Network architecture that processes images of different resolution as inputs. After experimenting with the promising MRCNN architectures, we decided to build a stacked version of this network architecture and called it Multi-resolution Stacked Denoising Auto-encoder (MSDAE). Figure 2 illustrates the MSDAE model architecture.

3.1 Training and Evaluation

The MSDAE model training was performed on 50 epochs that took 3.6 h on an NVIDIA GTX 1080 graphics card. Structural Similarity (SSIM) [7] and Peak Signal to-Noise Ratio (PSNR) index were primarily used as two of the most standard evaluation metrics in the area of image denoising. Furthermore, Mean Squared Error (MSE) and Pearson Correlation Coefficient (PCC) were used as pixel wise evaluation of the images. The final model was then trained by feeding the network with SAR imagery from the encoder side and the corresponding Reflectivity Map imagery as the output at the decoder side. After the training of the MSDAE model was done, we passed the main IRIS SAR dataset through this model to create a Denoised dataset for training of CNN classifiers in the next steps. In order to evaluate our denoising models, we compared the Reflectivity

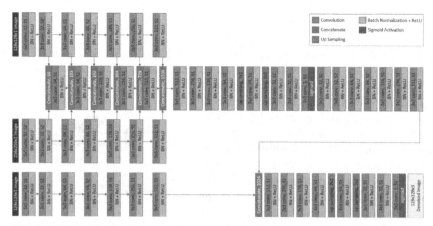

Fig. 2. Multi-resolution stacked Denoising auto-encoder (MSDAE) model Architecture

Map image as the reference and its corresponding Denoised SAR image from the model output. The MSDAE network performance compared to its previous variants is included in Table 1.

Table 1. Denoising models performance trained on IRIS SAR + RM datasets

Model name	SSIM	PSNR	MSE	PCC
Single AE	0.8852	24.27	314.67	0.9221
Double stacked AE	0.9178	23.46	376.45	0.9051
Triple stacked AE	0.9106	23.20	405.95	0.8972
MMRN	0.9463	26.77	174.58	0.9528
MSDAE	**0.9578**	**27.57**	**129.49**	**0.9537**
U-NET	0.9534	27.22	141.56	0.9486

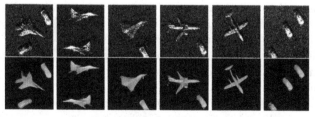

Fig. 3. Multi-resolution stacked Denoising auto-encoder (MSDAE) model performance. Top: simulated SAR images from IRIS-SAR dataset. Bottom: MSDAE output (Denoised SAR)

4 Target Classification

Our CNN model has a sequential architecture inspired by the VGG16 [8] model with filter sizes up to 512. Drop out layer with 0.2 factor is used as regularization layer after each convolutional block (Fig. 3). Two fully connected layers with size 1024 followed by a Softmax layer are at the end of the model. ReLU as activation function followed by a Batch Normalization layer was used after each convolutional layer. This model takes input images in size of 128 × 128 × 3. Figure 4 illustrates this network architecture. Adam optimizer was used in initial training with a decaying rate of 0.004, and a categorical cross entropy as its loss function.

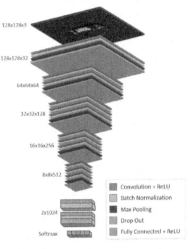

Fig. 4. The proposed CNN model architecture

4.1 Elevation Angle Dynamic Data Simulation

To evaluate our technique against such variability in input imagery space, we tested the performance of the network on all 5 elevation angles while training only on one elevation angle. This was done to simulate the condition in which the training data is only available from one elevation angle and new incoming data is captured in different elevation angles. Figure 5 illustrates the five elevation angles of our IRIS-SAR dataset. This training was done on IRIS-SAR and Denoised datasets separately. Next, using the dataset for each elevation angle, we studied the transfer learning method for training the model gradually for each elevation angle.

First we trained the model on 15°. Then we froze certain convolutional layers of the model and changed the top fully connected layers with new ones. We proceeded with training the model using 30° elevation. Then captured the performance results and continued the training for 45, 60, and 75° in the next steps. The plots in Fig. 6 illustrates the comparison of the results from with and without transfer learning for IRIS-SAR and Denoised dataset with elevation angle data separations. We can witness that when the learnt representations from previous trainings are used and transferred to the new training, the performance of the network improves gradually and its compatibility with the new dynamic data is increased.

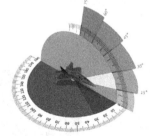

Fig. 5. Five elevation angles of IRIS-SAR dataset

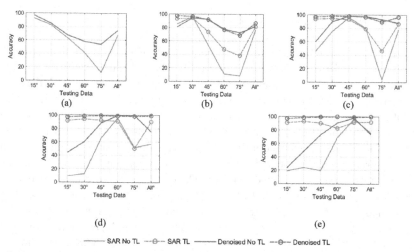

Fig. 6. Comparison of the results from with and without transfer learning applied for training IRIS-SAR and Denoised dataset witsh regards to elevation angle increments. Training using elevation angle with degrees a) 15°, b) 30°, c) 45°, d) 60°, e) 75°.

4.2 Azimuth Angle Dynamic Data Simulation

Next, we studied the effect of partial data training with respect to the azimuth (rotational) angle of the SAR scanning. Since the IRIS-SAR dataset contains the 12 azimuth observation angles with 30° increments, we labelled these angles into 3 groups with 0, 30, and 60° shifts. Figure 7 illustrates this scheme. Similar to the experiments with regards to the elevation angle in previous section, we also used transfer learning method for training our model with images with varying azimuth angles. Figure 8 illustrates the comparison of results for three separate azimuth angle bands.

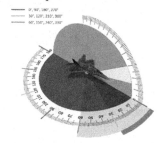

Fig. 7. Five elevation angles of IRIS-SAR dataset

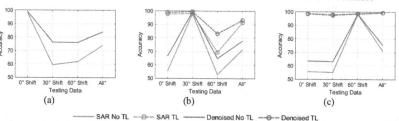

Fig. 8 Comparison of the results from with and without transfer learning applied for training IRIS-SAR and Denoised dataset with regards to azimuth angle shifts. Training using elevation angle with degree shifts of a) 0°. b) 30°. c) 60°.

5   Multi-output Classification

In this section, we present the multi output network architecture based on our proposed CNN model to perform classification of test objects based on their category, as well as their observed elevation, and azimuth angles. To achieve this goal, we used the convolutional blocks of the CNN model and added 2 more branches of fully connected layer with Softmax layer at the end of each branch. This network learns the features from each image and incorporates features with 3 labels that each input image has. The results from the IRIS-SAR and Denoised dataset trainings are presented in Tables 2, 3 and 4 for each of the three branches. Based on this model a higher classification accuracy was achieved when the network was trained based on the Denoised dataset and then compared to the model trained based on the IRIS-SAR dataset. Thus, we concluded that putting a MSDAE model before the classifier model can increase the classifiers accuracy. A 3.9 percent accuracy decrease was also captured in the elevation angle classification when tested based on the Denoised dataset and compared to the IRIS-SAR dataset that was logical since the SAR images contained test objects with their shadows that provided more information for the network to generalize its learning.

Table 2. Performance of the MCNN model on object category classification

Class	IRIS-SAR	Denoised
E15	100	98.6
E30	100	91.5
E45	100	94.7
E60	98.9	95.7
E75	100	99.2
Total Average	**99.8**	95.9

Table 3. Performance of the MCNN model on object elevation angle classification

Class	IRIS-SAR	Denoised
Airplane	96.9	96.2
Ground Vehicle	98.9	100
Helicopter	99.4	99.8
Jet Fighter	97.7	99.8
Small Propeller	98.3	98.7
Total Average	98.2	**99.0**

Table 4. Performance of the MCNN model on object azimuth angle classification

Class	R000	R030	R060	R090	R120	R150	R180	R210	R240	R270	R300	R330	Ave.
IRIS-SAR	98.2	99.2	97.7	97.9	99.6	95.6	98.1	98.0	98.6	99.0	100	99.6	98.5
Denoised	99.6	99.6	98.9	98.3	97.4	98.5	96.3	100	100	98.7	98.9	99.6	**98.8**

In order to streamline the denoising and classification process, we lastly combined the MSDAE and MCNN models together. This final model takes SAR image as input and outputs the Denoised SAR image and classification result based on object category, elevation, and azimuth observational angles. The MSDAE is trained on synthetic SAR and RM images. Then, the generated denoised SAR images using this network was used to train the MCNN model.

6 Conclusion

In this paper, we showed that by proper training of the MSDAE and CNN model we can streamline the denoising and classification into one single process. We also experimented that by placing the denoising model before feeding the images to the classifier model, it can further improve the classification accuracy. Lastly, we presented our experimental results based on DDDAS paradigm that showed by using denoised data for training, higher levels of generalization in classification is acquired when limited data is gradually available for DL training.

Acknowledgement. This research work is currently sponsored by the Office of Naval Research under research grant account: N00014-18-1-2738. The ONR program manager is Dr. Martin Kruger. The authors also thanks Mr. Antony Smith, director of ONR HBCU Office for the support of this project.

References

1. Jones, B., Ahmadibeni, A., Shirkhodaie, A.: Marine vehicles simulated SAR imagery datasets generation. In: SPIE Defense + Commercial Sensing, Ocean Sensing and Monitoring XII. paper 11420–24, 22 April (2020)
2. Ahmadibeni, A., Borooshak L., and Shirkhodaie, A.: Aerial and ground vehicles synthetic SAR dataset generation for automatic target recognition. In: SPIE Defense + Commercial Sensing, Algorithms for Synthetic Aperture Radar Imagery XXVII, paper 11393–20, April (2020)
3. Shirkhodaie, A.: IRIS – Intelligent Robotics Interface Systems. Developed at Tennessee State University, Department of Mechanical and Manufacturing Engineering (2006)
4. Blasch, E., Seetharaman, G., et al.: Dynamic Data Driven Applications Systems (DDDAS) modeling for Automatic Target Recognition. In: Proceedings SPIE, vol. 8744 (2013)
5. Vincent, P., Larochelle, H., Bengio, Y., Manzagol, P.: Extracting and Composing Robust Features with Denoising Autoencoders. In: Proceedings of the International Conference on Machine Learning (2008)
6. Vincent, P., et al.: Stacked denoising autoencoders: learning useful representations in a deep network with a local denoising criterion. J. Mach. Learn. Res. **11**, 3371–3408 (2010)
7. Wang, Z., Bovik, A.C., Sheikh, H.R., Simoncelli, E.P.: Image quality assessment: from error visibility to structural similarity. IEEE Trans. Image Process. **13**(4), 600–612 (2004)
8. Simonyan, K., Zisserman, A.: Very deep convolutional networks for large-scale image recognition. arXiv: 1409.1556 (2016)
9. Ahmadibeni, A., Borooshak L., Jones, B., Shirkhodaie, A.: Automatic target recognition of aerial vehicles based on synthetic SAR imagery using Hybrid Stacked Denoising Autoencoders. In: SPIE Defense + Commercial. Sensing, Alg. for Synthetic Aperture Radar Imagery XXVII, paper 11393.25 April (2020)

Plenary Presentations - Section 6: Imaging Methods and Systems

Uncertainty Estimation for Semantic Segmentation of Hyperspectral Imagery

Aneesh Rangnekar$^{(\boxtimes)}$ ⓘ, Emmett Ientilucci, Christopher Kanan, and Matthew J. Hoffman

Rochester Institute of Technology, Rochester, NY, USA
aneesh.rangnekar@mail.rit.edu, emmett@cis.rit.edu
{kanan,mjhsma}@rit.edu

Abstract. As a step in a Dynamic Data-Driven Applications Systems (DDDAS) method to characterize the background in a vehicle tracking problem, we extend the application of deep learning to a hyperspectral dataset (the AeroRIT dataset) to evaluating network uncertainty. Expressing uncertainty information is crucial for evaluating what additional information is needed in the DDDAS algorithm and where more resources are required. Hyperspectral signatures tend to be very noisy, when captured from an aerial flight and a slight shift in the atmospheric conditions can alter the signals significantly, which in turn may affect the trained network's classifications. In this work, we apply Deep Ensembles, Monte Carlo Dropout and Batch Ensembles and study their effects with respect to achieving robust pixel-level identifications by expressing the uncertainty within the trained networks on the task of semantic segmentation. We modify the U-Net-m architecture from the AeroRIT paper to account for the frameworks and present our results as a step towards accounting for sensitive changes in hyperspectral signals.

Keywords: Hyperspectral · Uncertainty · Segmentation

1 Introduction

Instead of solely modeling vehicle movement or focusing on vehicle appearance for a vehicle tracking problem, we are working on adaptively modeling the background in a DDDAS [4] framework using hyperspectral data. This allows the possibility of identifying potential confusers and modifying the detection or tracking strategy. In this paper we describe efforts to characterize the background and the uncertainties in a classification problem. A fair amount of effort has been invested in applying deep learning methodologies to hyperspectral imagery for the purpose of learning scene representations towards aerial object detection and

Electronic supplementary material The online version of this chapter (https://doi.org/10.1007/978-3-030-61725-7_20) contains supplementary material, which is available to authorized users.

F. Darema et al. (Eds.): DDDAS 2020, LNCS 12312, pp. 163–170, 2020.
https://doi.org/10.1007/978-3-030-61725-7_20

tracking [13,17,18]. In this paper, we use the AeroRIT data set released in with SegNet and U-Net networks [1,13,16] trained for the task of semantic segmentation. However, AeroRIT also comes with the limitation of being a single flight line captured under clear atmospheric conditions. If the same set of trained networks are used to run inference on a similar dataset but under different atmospheric conditions, the outputs will, more than likely, vary. We visually verify this claim by applying one of the networks established in the paper (U-Net-m, discussed further in Sect. 3.2) to another flight line captured under cloudy atmospheric conditions in Fig. 1. We would ideally pre-process the images to ensure no atmospheric occlusions are present in the scene - for example, a cloud shadow removal algorithm, however we use this snapshot as a particular example to illustrate our goal in this paper. We observe that the network fails to recognize the correct set of classes in key areas of interest - for example, the region around the circular roundabout is predicted to be a building instead of a road. This can affect the flow of down-streaming tasks dependent on decision trees - do we want to look for vehicles at pixels classified as buildings? While the straight forward answer is a No, the approach can be altered if we could also be privy to information about the network's confidence (viz-a-viz, uncertainty) of the pixel's classification. This information may help in creating more robust inferences as other networks in down-streaming tasks would be aware of the prediction's uncertainty and can dynamically adapt to account for variations.

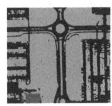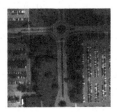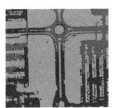

Fig. 1. Roundabout section from AeroRIT under sunny and cloudy atmospheric conditions. We observe the output of a network trained on the clear flight line to its cloud-occluded counterpart, (c)–(d), (e)–(f) respectively. The labels are roads (blue), cars (ivory), buildings (red) and vegetation (green). (Color figure online)

We train deep networks by minimizing the difference between the networks' prediction and the true distribution of labels and during evaluation, use the learnt set of weights for classification by selecting the class label corresponding to the maximum probability. However, this approach does not provide any information about the network's uncertainty of the predictions. Kendall *et al.* applied Bayesian deep learning to obtain the network's uncertainty for depth regression and semantic segmentation tasks [9,10]. We adopt their approach in this paper and analyze the effect of uncertainty quantification towards AeroRIT scene understanding.

2   Related Works

There are many areas of research that can be used to estimate the network's uncertainty, the most popular being: 1) forming ensembles [1, 7, 8, 19], 2) variational inference [2], and 3) K-FAC Laplace approximation [15]. We focus on the first type of approach - forming ensembles as it is relatively simpler to follow and easier to implement compared to the other areas. The core idea is to train a bunch of networks with different initializations on the same set of data and at test time, evaluate the final predictions as an average of the ensemble networks predictions. Gal and Ghahramani showed that using dropout across layers of the convolutional neural network (CNN) can act as approximate Bayesian interpretation [7]. This facilitates training a single network and using dropout at test time to create model ensembles. Kendall *et al.* further demonstrated that applying dropout at selective layers of the network instead of all layer further improves the predictions [9]. Lakshminarayanan *et al.* trained different networks separately for forming ensembles [11], and Huang *et al.* obtained sets of networks by taking *snapshots* at different intervals using cyclic learning rate schedule [12]. Recently, Wen *et al.* proposed to use multiple rank-1 matrices along with the core weight matrix to form ensembles as an alternative to existing methods [19]. Uncertainty estimation approaches [3, 6, 14] have already been applied in other areas of remote sensing. In this paper, we adopt deep ensembles [11], Monte-Carlo dropout based ensembles [1, 7] and batch ensembles [19] for estimating network uncertainty.

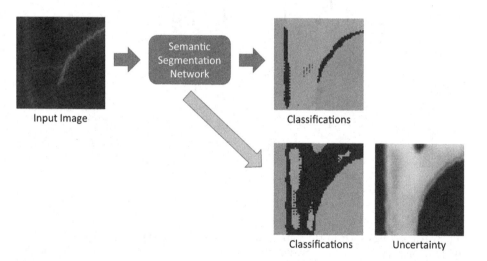

Fig. 2. Schematic overview of the uncertainty based pipeline. The standard flow is shown with blue arrows where the trained network predicts the pixel-wise labels. We augment the flow with a ensemble learning framework (orange) that eventually accounts for the uncertainty within the network. Brighter areas correlate to larger uncertainty - and as image chips corresponding to the racetrack are not present in the training set, the network is overall highly uncertain of its prediction. (Color figure online)

3   Estimating Uncertainty

3.1   Types of Uncertainties

Kendall and Gal expressed uncertainty into two subtypes - Aleatoric and Epistemic, in accordance with Kiureghian and Ditlevsen [5]. Aleatoric uncertainty corresponds to noise that is data-independent, for example, sensor noise, environmental noise, and cannot be reduced even if more data is collected. Epistemic uncertainty can be expressed as more data-dependent and model-based, and hence is widely modelled using ensembles. In our paper, we focus on epistemic uncertainty and use ensembles for estimation. Figure 2 outlays the overall framework.

3.2   Network Review

We use the U-Net-m architecture developed in AeroRIT [13] for its better performance among other networks. It contains 2 downsampling convolutional blocks, followed by a bottleneck layer and 2 upsampling blocks with skip connections. Each convolutional block contains two sets of convolutional kernels of 3 × 3, a Batch-Normalization layer and ReLU activation. We represent this structure in Fig. 3 (a).

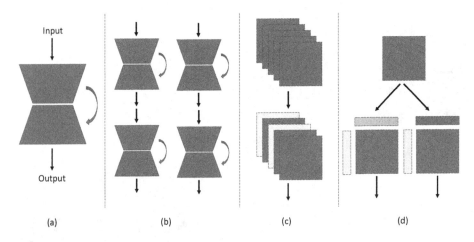

Fig. 3. All settings used in the paper: (a) U-Net-m, (b) 4 deep ensembles for [11], (c) MC-Dropout applied on the convolutional maps of (a) with *Spatial Dropout*, (d) Batch Ensembles with two sets of rank-1 matrices on weights of (a).

3.3   Deep Ensembles (DE)

This approach, proposed by Lakshminarayanan *et al.* [11], averages the predictions across networks trained independently starting from different initializations (Fig. 3 (b)). Every member of the deep ensembles is trained with the same hyperparameters as discussed in Sect. 4.1. At test time, we average the predictions to obtain the final set of predictions. Following all approaches that estimate uncertainty, we use entropy of the resulting distribution as the measure of uncertainty and use it in all the figures throughout this paper.

3.4   MC-Dropout (MCD)

Monte-Carlo Dropout is the less training-time alternative to Deep Ensembles. Instead of training separate copies of networks multiple times, Gal *et al.* [7,9] proposed to inject Bernoulli noise in form of Dropout over the activations of the network weights. In practice, we observed that applying spatial dropout instead of conventional dropout produced more better uncertainty estimates (Figs. 3 (c), X). Spatial dropout randomly drops an entire feature map from the list of feature maps as compared to individual elements in conventional dropout. We use the same set of hyperparameters as discussed in Sect. 4.1. At test time, we average the predictions obtained across a fixed set of runs with dropout enabled to obtain the final set of predictions.

3.5   Batch Ensembles (BE)

This approach was proposed by Wen *et al.* and works as an alternative to using Dropout for ensembles (Fig. 3 (d)). The core idea is to have a single *slow* matrix (W), which corresponds to the 2-D convolution kernel weight and two corresponding rank-1 matrices (r_i, s_i) that act as *fast* matrices:

$$\overline{W}_i = W \circ F_i, \text{ where } F_i = r_i s_i^\top, \tag{1}$$

and hence, we obtain $\overline{W}_i$ as the corresponding weight for ensemble i. The number of ensembles is equal to the number of sets of rank-1 matrices used and is very efficient in terms of model storage. During evaluation, similar to above, we repeat the mini-batch to correspond with total number of ensemble members and average the predictions.

4   Experiments and Results

4.1   Hyperparameters

We use all 51 bands available in the AeroRIT dataset chips in this paper - 31 visible and 20 infrared bands. All chips are clipped to a maximum of 2^{14}, and normalized between 0 and 1, before forward passing through the networks. All networks are initialized with Kaiming init, and the rank-1 matrices for BE are initialized to have a mean of 1 and standard deviation of 0.5 in accordance with the original paper. We use an initial learning rate of $1e^{-2}$: for DE and MCD, we train for 60 epochs with drops of 0.1 at 30, 40, 50th and for BS, we train for 120 epochs with drops of 0.1 at 50, 80, and 100th epoch. We train with standard cross-entropy loss (CE) for DE and MCD and use weighted CE only for the BE approach.

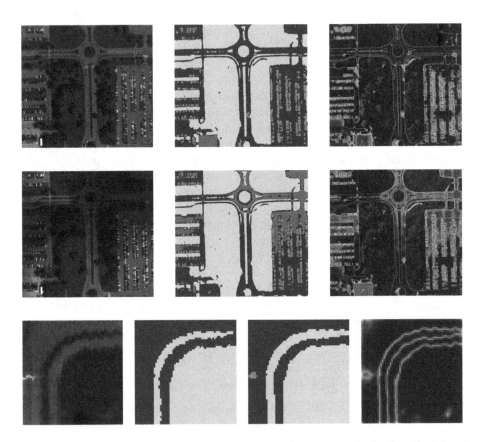

Fig. 4. Visualization of uncertainty estimates on the sunny and cloudy roundabout scenes from Fig. 1. (a) and (d) are the RGB rendered images, (b) and (e) are the corresponding network predictions while, (c) and (f) are the uncertainty maps. We also visualize an instance from (g) the AeroRIT test set with (h) corresponding ground truth label, (i) network predictions and (j) uncertainty map.

4.2 Results

We observe visual improvement over the scenes presented in Fig. 1 using 10 runs with MCD ensembles. The network predictions for the roundabout area show

Table 1. Results of techniques discussed in Sect. 3 compared to the baseline network from AeroRIT [13].

	Standard network	Deep ensembles	Monte carlo dropout	Batch ensembles
mIOU	70.62	71.41 ± 2.48	72.45 ± 1.56	69.05 ± 3.45

high uncertainty (Fig. 4 (f)) which is desired in this setting. This information can be used by down-steam tasks which can dynamically adapt to ensure continuity. Further, we also observe that the network uncertainty estimates are high for row Fig. 4 (g) as the road crossing has been incorrectly classified as belonging to the vehicle category. We also observe uncertainty around the boundaries of classes - this can possibly be due to the presence of mixed pixels. Table 1 shows us that all ensemble techniques are able to achieve near-par or higher performance than the conventional counterpart. We use mean IOU (mIOU) as the metric of interest (following [13]) and do not discuss metrics pertaining to uncertainty estimations (for example, Expected Calibration Error) for the scope of this paper. mIOU is the class-wise mean of the area of intersection between the predicted segmentation and the ground truth divided by the area of union between the predicted segmentation and the ground truth. To generate the results, we ran all ensembles 10 different times, with varying number of models for DE and MCD. We found 4 to be a sufficient set of models for DE and BE and 10 for MCD in our ablation studies.

5 Conclusion

We presented the extension of uncertainty estimation to hyperspectral remote sensing imagery as a first step towards dynamic scene adaptation under varying atmospheric conditions. Our next set of questions are as follows: 1) can we reduce uncertainty in mixed pixel areas to obtain a much precise map that can be passed to down-stream tasks? and 2) can we decrease the inference speed to get as close to a single forward pass of a network? 3) is it possible to design an end to end framework to adaptively shift between sensor modalities using uncertainty as an input?

Acknowledgements. This work was supported by the Dynamic Data Driven Applications Systems Program, Air Force Office of Scientific Research under Grant FA9550-19-1-0021. We gratefully acknowledge the support of NVIDIA Corporation with the donations of the Titan X and Titan Xp Pascal GPUs used for this research.

References

1. Badrinarayanan, V., Kendall, A., Cipolla, R.: Segnet: A deep convolutional encoder-decoder architecture for image segmentation. arXiv preprint arXiv:1511.00561 (2015)

2. Blundell, C., Cornebise, J., Kavukcuoglu, K., Wierstra, D.: Weight uncertainty in neural networks. arXiv preprint arXiv:1505.05424 (2015)
3. Cobb, A.D., et al.: An ensemble of bayesian neural networks for exoplanetary atmospheric retrieval. Astronomical J. **158**(1), 33 (2019)
4. Darema, F.: Dynamic data driven applications systems: a new paradigm for application simulations and measurements. In: Bubak, M., van Albada, G.D., Sloot, P.M.A., Dongarra, J. (eds.) ICCS 2004. LNCS, vol. 3038, pp. 662–669. Springer, Heidelberg (2004). https://doi.org/10.1007/978-3-540-24688-6_86
5. Der Kiureghian, A., Ditlevsen, O.: Aleatory or epistemic? does it matter? Structural Safety **31**(2), 105–112 (2009)
6. Fletcher, S., Lickley, M., Strzepek, K.: Learning about climate change uncertainty enables flexible water infrastructure planning. Nat. Commun. **10**(1), 1–11 (2019)
7. Gal, Y., Ghahramani, Z.: Dropout as a bayesian approximation: Representing model uncertainty in deep learning. In: international Conference on Machine Learning, pp. 1050–1059 (2016)
8. Huang, G., Li, Y., Pleiss, G., Liu, Z., Hopcroft, J.E., Weinberger, K.Q.: Snapshot ensembles: Train 1, get m for free. arXiv preprint arXiv:1704.00109 (2017)
9. Kendall, A., Badrinarayanan, V., Cipolla, R.: Bayesian segnet: Model uncertainty in deep convolutional encoder-decoder architectures for scene understanding. arXiv preprint arXiv:1511.02680 (2015)
10. Kendall, A., Gal, Y.: What uncertainties do we need in bayesian deep learning for computer vision? In: Advances in Neural Information Processing Systems, pp. 5574–5584 (2017)
11. Lakshminarayanan, B., Pritzel, A., Blundell, C.: Simple and scalable predictive uncertainty estimation using deep ensembles. In: Advances in Neural Information Processing Systems, pp. 6402–6413 (2017)
12. Loshchilov, I., Hutter, F.: Sgdr: Stochastic gradient descent with warm restarts. arXiv preprint arXiv:1608.03983 (2016)
13. Rangnekar, A., Mokashi, N., Ientilucci, E.J., Kanan, C., Hoffman, M.J.: Aerorit: a new scene for hyperspectral image analysis. IEEE Trans. Geosci. Remote Sens. **1**, 1–9 (2020)
14. Rao, V., Sandu, A.: A posteriori error estimates for dddas inference problems. Procedia Comput. Sci. **29**, 1256–1265 (2014)
15. Ritter, H., Botev, A., Barber, D.: A scalable laplace approximation for neural networks. In: 6th International Conference on Learning Representations, ICLR 2018-Conference Track Proceedings. vol. 6. International Conference on Representation Learning (2018)
16. Ronneberger, O., Fischer, P., Brox, T.: U-Net: convolutional networks for biomedical image segmentation. In: Navab, N., Hornegger, J., Wells, W.M., Frangi, A.F. (eds.) MICCAI 2015. LNCS, vol. 9351, pp. 234–241. Springer, Cham (2015). https://doi.org/10.1007/978-3-319-24574-4_28
17. Uzkent, B., Rangnekar, A., Hoffman, M.J.: Aerial vehicle tracking by adaptive fusion of hyperspectral likelihood maps. In: Proceedings of the IEEE Conference on Computer Vision and Pattern Recognition Workshops (CVPRW), pp. 233–242. IEEE (2017)
18. Uzkent, B., Rangnekar, A., Hoffman, M.J.: Tracking in aerial hyperspectral videos using deep kernelized correlation filters. IEEE Trans. Geosci. Remote Sens. **57**(1), 449–461 (2018)
19. Wen, Y., Tran, D., Ba, J.: Batchensemble: An alternative approach to efficient ensemble and lifelong learning (2020)

Spectral Super Resolution with DCT Decomposition and Deep Residual Learning

Raghunath Sai Puttagunta[1], Renlong Hang[1(✉)], Zhu Li[1(✉)],
Shuvra Bhattacharyya[2(✉)], and George York[3(✉)]

[1] University of Missouri-Kansas City, Kansas City, USA
{hangr,lizhu}@umkc.edu
[2] University of Maryland College Park, College Park, USA
ssb@umd.edu
[3] US Air Force Academy, Colorado Springs, USA
george.york@usafa.edu

Abstract. In this paper, we aim to reconstruct a hyperspectral image of multiple bands from an RGB image. This process of reconstruction of the hyperspectral image from RGB images is called Spectral Super Resolution (SSR). Using spectral super resolution, we can adapt the Dynamic Data Driven Applications System paradigm by using RGB cameras in surveillance instead of using hyperspectral cameras. This process is challenging because hyperspectral images have different information available in each band. There have been few works recently in SSR, most of them use a Convolutional Neural Network (CNN) to learn hyperspectral images from RGB image using a pixel wise loss function. The pixel wise loss function smooths the image which leads to loss of information in spectral bands. To overcome this in our work, we initially divide spectral bands into four subgroups and learn the hyperspectral image by learning the Discrete Coefficient Transform (DCT) coefficients of the hyperspectral image from RGB image using a residual dense network. Experiment results show our work using DCT based learning performs better than the state of the art HSCNN+ work [12].

Keywords: Spectral super resolution · Super resolution · DCT

1 Introduction

Hyperspectral Imaging has a lot of use cases in the area of remote sensing and surveillance. Hyperspectral images have rich information in their spectral bands which are used for high image tasks like image classification and object detection. These recognition and detection problems have significant use cases in the Department of Defense. Unmanned Aircraft Vehicle (UAV) is one of the examples of such use cases where we can automate and monitor surveillance of a location. Dynamic Data Driven Applications System (DDDAS) is one of the paradigms in which we want to have a dynamic feedback loop based on collecting the data, using the machine learning models to implement the high level tasks like classification and object detection and continuously optimize it.

© Springer Nature Switzerland AG 2020
F. Darema et al. (Eds.): DDDAS 2020, LNCS 12312, pp. 171–178, 2020.
https://doi.org/10.1007/978-3-030-61725-7_21

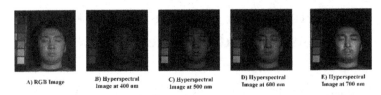

A) RGB Image   B) Hyperspectral Image at 400 nm   C) Hyperspectral Image at 500 nm   D) Hyperspectral Image at 600 nm   E) Hyperspectral Image at 700 nm

Fig. 1. Cave Dataset with RGB image and Hyperspectral Images at different frequencies

In hyperspectral imaging, it is hard to obtain an image of high resolution due to the hardware limitations of cameras. To reconstruct a high resolution of the hyperspectral images we can do it by either using a high resolution RGB images or low resolution hyperspectral images. The advantage of using RGB images is that devices that capture RGB images are cheaper compared to the ones capturing hyperspectral images. The task of reconstructing hyperspectral images from an RGB image is called Spectral Super Resolution. The task of SSR is challenging because each spectral band has different spectral information shown in Fig. 1. The recent works in SSR are using CNN's due to the recent emergence of deep learning. They used a pixel wise loss function to learn hyperspectral images. The pixel wise loss function smooths the image because of its characteristic to decrease the mean square error. This characteristic of the loss function leads to losing information during the reconstruction of the hyperspectral image. In our work, we decompose the spectral bands into four subgroups and learn the hyperspectral image by learning subgroups individually. The learning of the subgroups is done by learning the DCT coefficients of the hyperspectral image. The DCT coefficients are learned by using a deep residual network whose architecture is inspired by Enhanced Deep Residual Network (EDSR) [10]. DCT is an orthogonal transform which is generally used in image and video compression. DCT of an image has frequency separation properties which help us to learn hyperspectral images efficiently. Using our approach, we adopt the DDDAS paradigm in surveillance by instead of using an expensive hyperspectral camera we use an RGB camera and learn hyperspectral images in real-time and perform high-level vision tasks.

The rest of the paper is organized as follows. In Sect. 2 we review the related works in SSR. In Sect. 3 section we give a brief introduction of our novel DCT decomposition based SSR. In the results section, we compare our results with state of the art methods. In the final section, we provide conclusion of our work and future work that could be explored.

2   Related Works

The initial work on Spectral Super Resolution used interpolation methods [8] to predict information in spectral bands. The interpolation was done in the number of channels where 3 input RGB is converted to multiple channels by interpolation. In [2] they used hyperspectral priors to construct a sparse dictionary learning using K-SVD and then they used Orthogonal Matching Pursuit (OMP) on RGB images to get hyperspectral images. There have been few works using CNN's for SSR [1, 3, 4, 12, 14, 15, 17]. The initial work using CNN for SSR was done by [4] the architecture they used was inspired by the classification network Densenet [9]. They modified the architecture of the classification network to have a regression type of problem for predicting the spectral information of the bands. In [3] they used a CNN architecture that has residual networks that were inspired by ResNet [6]. They found out that previous work using Densenet architecture for SSR was overfitting the data so they used residual blocks to avoid overfitting of the data. Inspired by the work of UNet [11] in Image Segmentation [15] implemented a network structure which captures the spectral information in multiple scales. In Unet architecture, we initially downsample the features and then upsample them back to their original spatial size. The downsampling leads to a constant increase in the receptive field size of the network and by doing that we can find local and non-local information which could be used for finding the missing information in spectral bands.

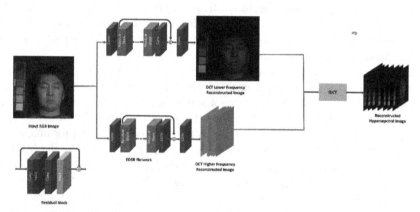

Fig. 2. Our Proposed Method where RGB image learns DCT Low Frequency and DCT High Frequency information

In HSCNN [14] they adapted VDSR architecture for SSR. In HSCNNN we need to do pre-processing where we need to do a spectral upsampling operation of converting from 3 channels to 31 channels. In [12] they do spectral upsampling by using a simple convolutional layer. HSCNN also fails to adapt to when using deeper sizes of the network this is also fixed in HSCNN+ . There are 3 different HSCNN+ architectures HSCNN-u, HSCNN-R, HSCNN-D. HSCNN-u is very similar to the work of HSCNN, the only difference is the spectral upsampling operator is replaced by a 1×1 convolutional filter. HSCNN-R we have a 3×3 convolutional layer as a spectral upsample operator and we also have multiple residual blocks and the architecture is very similar to EDSR. HSCNN-D adapts a dense network structure for the reconstruction of hyperspectral image. Both HSCNN-R and HSCNN-D are state of the art results in SSR for the NTIRE 2018 spectral reconstruction challenge [13].

In our work, we adapted a transform based learning where we transform images into the DCT domain and learn the SSR in the DCT domain. There have been few works for CNN based classification networks using DCT in [7] In Super Resolution there are few works that have used transform based learning. In [5] they constructed a CNN based Super Resolution where they learn the task via learning the DCT coefficients. In SR low resolution image and high resolution image they mostly share the same low frequency. In our work, we used domain transform learning for SSR.

3 Proposed Method

In this paper, we present our DCT transform based learning for Spectral Super Resolution which is shown in Fig. 2. Our proposed method instead of directly learning the pixel domain we do a DCT transform and learn the coefficients in the DCT domain DCT is an orthogonal transform and it converts an image in the pixel domain to the frequency domain. Most of the energy in DCT in is in low frequency components. Low frequency components are known to have most of the information most of the useful information in an image. In [5] they proposed that the low frequency information remains the same for low resolution and high resolution image and they adapted an SR based CNN to learn those missing high frequency image. The learning was done in the frequency domain and then converted back to the image domain using inverse DCT.

From Fig. 1 we can see that the images which are in 400 nm have different information in terms of pixel intensities when compared with 500 nm, 600 nm, 700 nm. So in our work, we decomposed the 31 bands into 4 subgroups with 1–8 bands as 1st group, 9–16 as 2nd group, 17–24 as 3rd group and 25–31 as 4th group. So we try to learn the subgroups DCT coefficient values from an RGB image. Generally, for images, we perform a 2D DCT but in our case, we perform a 1D DCT along with the bands of the hyperspectral image. This can be viewed as a channel-wise DCT operation on the hyperspectral image. So basically, we are grouping the 31 bands into 4 subgroups and then do DCT channel-wise on the subgroups. DCT has energy separation properties where we can separate low frequency information and high frequency information. So, after decomposing into subgroups we further decompose the DCT coefficients into low frequency information and high frequency information. In our work, we used the first DCT coefficient transform as low frequency information and rest coefficient transform as high frequency information. The first transform will have the most of the information in the image due to the energy property of the DCT. We indicate the low frequency transform as DC and other high frequency information as AC transform and we can see from Fig. 3 that most of the information is in DC transform and high frequency transform there isn't much information.

In our work, we have adapted network design which was inspired by the SR network called EDSR [10]. The architecture is very similar to EDSR except for having up sampling blocks. Our network has 3 convolutional layers with 3×3 as kernel size and a residual block which has 2 convolutional layers of 3×3 kernel size and one Rectified Linear unit (ReLU) activation function. We use a different number of residual blocks for low frequency and higher frequency components. For low frequency, we used 8 residual blocks in the network and for high frequency, we used 4 residual blocks. As shown in Fig. 2 our model learns the low frequency and high frequency DCT coefficients from 2 EDSR kinds of network and then we perform Inverse DCT on the frequency information and learn the hyperspectral image. Let the input RGB image be denoted as x and our ground truth is a hyperspectral image of 31 bands and is denoted by y and then we decompose the hyperspectral image into m subgroups and then we do DCT on each subgroup and DCT transform can be denoted as

$$Y_{k_{1,2,\ldots,m}} = \sum_{n=0}^{N-1} y_{n_{1,2,\ldots,m}} \cos\left[\frac{\pi}{N}\left(n + \frac{1}{2}\right)k\right] \quad (1)$$

In the above equation N denotes N-point DCT and it also implies the number of bands in each subgroup and m denoted the number of subgroups. The CNN tries to learn a non-linear relationship from input RGB image to DCT coefficient $\widehat{Y_k}$. The loss function we used to train the network was L1 Loss and is given by

$$L_1 = \frac{1}{N} \sum_{i=1}^{N} Y_{k_i} - f(x_i, \theta) \quad (2)$$

where Y_k and x_i denote the ith sample of the image. f denotes the mapping function of the CNN from the pixel RGB domain to the DCT coefficient domain Y_K. The θ represents the parameters involved in the training of the network.

4 Experiments and Results

4.1 Experimental Setup

For our experiments, we have used the CAVE dataset [16]. The CAVE dataset has 31 hyperspectral indoor images and has 31 bands ranging from 400 nm to 700 nm with a 10 nm difference in each band. Each image has a Spatial Resolution of 512 × 512. In CAVE dataset we divided the dataset into 21 images for training and 10 images for testing. In order to increase the number of samples for training samples for our network we randomly extract 500 64 × 64 patches from the images for both CAVE. For data augmentation, we also randomly flipped the patches vertically or horizontally. The receptive field sizes for our low frequency network and high frequency network were 39 and 23 respectively. The optimizer we used was Adam optimizer with default parameters and we used batch sizes of 32 for low frequency and high frequency networks. The Loss function we used was L1 loss and we used a learning rate of 1e-4 and exponentially decayed the loss by 0.90 every epoch.

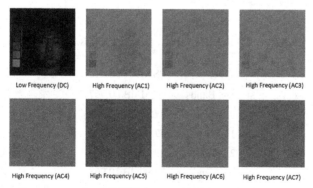

Fig. 3. DCT transform images from CAVE dataset showing low frequency and high frequency information.

4.2 Performance Evaluation

In our work, we have compared our results with state of the art HSCNN-R. For evaluating parameters, we have used metrics like Peak Signal to Noise Ratio (PSNR) and Structural Similarity Metrics (SSIM). From Table 1 we can observe that our network performs well when compared to the state of the art HSCNN-R. Our networks perform well when the band's wavelength range from 400–640 nm and doesn't work as well in wavelength of bands from 650–700 nm. We also implemented a transform based learning where we learn DCT coefficients of all bands instead of doing sub grouping. The PSNR of the DCT based learning without dividing into subgroups was 29 dB. Our grouping into bands works well because when we do DCT the bands have some co-relation information and DCT exploits it by separating the information into a low and high frequency which makes the learning easier. In bands with the higher spectrum, it is harder to separate the low frequency and high frequency information that's why our network works worse than HSCNN-R (Fig. 4).

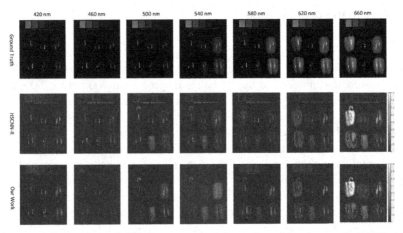

Fig. 4. Visual Comparison of different spectrum information of test images in CAVE dataset. From top to bottom we have ground truth difference map between ground truth and predicted image from HSCNN-R and our work

Table 1. Test Results on Cave Dataset

Type	PSNR	SSIM
1–8 Bands	35.61 dB	0.967
9–16 Bands	37.32 dB	0.980
17–24 Bands	37.89 dB	0.980
25–31 Bands	29.12 dB	0.924
All Bands	32.90 dB	0.968
HSCNN-R	32.27 dB	0.959

5   Conclusion and Future Work

In this paper, we proposed a DCT domain based learning for learning the DCT coefficient information by using a Residual Dense network. This one of the first work which used a DCT transform based learning for SSR. As we trained different network on each subgroup we can dynamically adapt our algorithm to learn only certain bands of the hyperspectral image which could be used in surveillance. The hyperspectral image in our case was divided into 4 subgroups and then further decomposed using DCT into low frequency and high frequency information. After learning the DCT coefficients we do inverse DCT on the learned coefficients so our learning is not end to end architecture. We performed test on benchmark dataset called CAVE dataset and we compared our work with state of the art HSCNN-R and we showed that our work has better performance than HSCNN-R. From our results we also showed that DCT works well with bands ranging from 400–640 nm but performance is not as good at higher spectrum. In future work we have to find better spectral resolution in higher spectral domain regions. In future work, we can also consider using other types of domain transform like wavelet transform to learn the textural information lost due to using pixel wise loss function.

References

1. Alvarez-Gila, A., van de Weijer, J., Garrote, E.: Adversarial net- works for spatial context-aware spectral image reconstruction from RGB. *CoRR*, abs/1709.00265 (2017)
2. Arad, B., Ben-Shahar, O.: Sparse recovery of hyperspectral signal from natural RGB images. In: Leibe, B., Matas, J., Sebe, N., Welling, M. (eds.) ECCV 2016. LNCS, vol. 9911, pp. 19–34. Springer, Cham (2016). https://doi.org/10.1007/978-3-319-46478-7_2
3. Can, Y.B., Timofte, R.: An efficient CNN for spectral reconstruction from RGB images. *CoRR*, abs/1804.04647 (2018)
4. Galliani, S., Lanaras, C., Marmanis, D., Baltsavias, E., Schindler, K.: Learned spectral super-resolution. *CoRR*, abs/1703.09470 (2017)
5. Guo, T., Mousavi, H.S., Monga, V.: Adaptive transform domain image super-resolution via orthogonally regularized deep networks. *CoRR*, abs/1904.10082 (2019)
6. He, K., Zhang, X., Ren, S., Sun, J.: Deep residual learning for image recognition. *CoRR*, abs/1512.03385 (2015)
7. Md Tahmid, H., Teng, S.W., Zhang, D., Lim, S., Lu, G.: Distortion robust image classification using deep convolutional neural network with discrete cosine transform. *CoRR*, abs/1811.05819 (2018)
8. Hou, H., Andrews, H.: Cubic splines for image interpolation and digital filtering. IEEE Trans. Acoustics, Speech, and Signal Processing, **26**(6), 508–517 (1978)
9. Gao, H., Liu, Z., Weinberger, K.Q.: Densely connected convolutional networks. *CoRR*, abs/1608.06993 (2016)
10. Lim, B., Son, S., Kim, H., Nah, S., Lee, K.M.: Enhanced deep residual networks for single image super-resolution. *CoRR*, abs/1707.02921, (2017)
11. Ronneberger, O., Fischer, P., Brox, T.: U-net: Convolutional net- works for biomedical image segmentation. *CoRR*, abs/1505.04597 (2015)
12. Shi, Z., Chen, C., Xiong, Z., Liu, D., Wu, F.: HSCNN+ : advanced cnn-based hyperspectral recovery from RGB images. In: The IEEE Conference on Computer Vision and Pattern Recognition (CVPR) Workshops, June 2018

13. Timofte, R., Gu, S., Wu, J., Gool, L.V.: Ntire 2018 challenge on single image super-resolution: methods and results. In: The IEEE Conference on Computer Vision and Pattern Recognition (CVPR) Workshops, June 2018

14. Xiong, Z., Shi, Z., Li, H., Wang, L., Liu, D., Wu, F.: HSCNN: CNN-based hyper- spectral image recovery from spectrally undersampled projections. In: 2017 IEEE International Conference on Computer Vision Workshops (ICCVW), pp. 518–525, October 2017

15. Yan, Y., Zhang, L., Li, J., Wei, W., Zhang, Y.: Accurate spectral super-resolution from single RGB image using multi-scale CNN. *CoRR*, abs/1806.03575 (2018)

16. Yasuma, F., Mitsunaga, T., Iso, D., Nayar, S.K.: Generalized Assorted Pixel Camera: Post-Capture Control of Resolution, Dynamic Range and Spectrum. Technical report, November 2008

17. Zhang, L., Lang, Z., Wang, P., Wei, W., Liao, S., Shao, L., Zhang, Y.: Pixel-aware deep function-mixture network for spectral super- resolution. *CoRR*, abs/1903.10501 (2019)

Active Scene Classification via Dynamically Learning Prototypical Views

Zachary A. Daniels[✉] and Dimitris N. Metaxas[✉]

Rutgers University, Piscataway, NJ 08854, USA
{zad7,dnm}@cs.rutgers.edu

Abstract. Scene classification is an important computer vision problem with applications to a wide range of domains including remote sensing, robotics, autonomous driving, defense, and surveillance. However, many approaches to scene classification make simplifying assumptions about the data, and many algorithms for scene classification are ill-suited for real-world use cases. Specifically, scene classification algorithms generally assume that the input data consists of single views that are extremely representative of a limited set of known scene categories. In real-world applications, such perfect data is rarely encountered. In this paper, we propose an approach for active scene classification where an agent must assign a label to the scene with high confidence while minimizing the number of sensor adjustments, and the agent is also embedded with the capability to dynamically update its underlying machine learning models. Specifically, we employ the Dynamic Data-Driven Applications Systems paradigm: our machine learning model drives the sensor manipulation, and the data captured by the manipulated sensor is used to update the machine learning model in a feedback control loop. Our approach is based on learning to identify prototypical views of scenes in a streaming setting.

Keywords: Computer vision · Scene classification · Prototype learning · Active vision · Active learning · Dynamic data driven applications systems

1 Introduction

1.1 Motivation

Scene classification is an important computer vision problem with applications to a wide range of domains including remote sensing, robotics, autonomous driving, defense, and surveillance. Many approaches to scene classification make simplifying assumptions about the data, and many of the algorithms for scene classification are ill-suited for real-world use cases. For example, many of the popular datasets for scene classification only consider single views of a scene sampled from a finite set of scene categories, and these views are often extremely representative of its scene category. In real-world applications, data is much noisier. Consider a robot designed to explore an indoor environment. If the robot is

© Springer Nature Switzerland AG 2020
F. Darema et al. (Eds.): DDDAS 2020, LNCS 12312, pp. 179–187, 2020.
https://doi.org/10.1007/978-3-030-61725-7_22

randomly placed within the environment, it might encounter views belonging to one of four categories: 1) *informative* views that are representative of the scene, 2) *uninformative* views that give little to no useful information about the scene (e.g., the robot is facing a blank wall), 3) *atypical* views that might be adversarial or misleading (e.g., the robot is looking through a doorway or window into a different type of scene), and 4) *incomplete* views that provide some information about the scene, but do not fully describe the scene (e.g., the robot sees a view which includes a sink, which can be indicative of either a kitchen or bathroom). The agent must be capable of intelligently exploring such complex environments, and this requires the agent to operate under an active vision paradigm [1–4,13]).

Likewise, closed set assumptions about scene categories are rarely satisfied in real-world applications. Sometimes, an agent will encounter a scene unlike any it has previously encountered. When the agent encounters such scenes, it should have the capability to update its internal knowledge and machine learning models. Similarly, for many real-world applications, training data might not be immediately available, and once again, the agent must have the capability to continuously update its internal models in a streaming manner (i.e., as every new data point is encountered). Thus, the agent should be capable of performing active learning [42].

1.2   Overview of Approach and Contributions

In this paper, we introduce and propose an initial solution for the problem of *active scene classification*. Active scene classification involves assigning a label to a scene, but unlike in traditional scene classification, instead of assuming a single, representative view of the scene as input to the scene classifier, we assume that an agent can manipulate its sensor to capture multiple views. In this paper, we consider a simple demonstration application whereby an agent is placed in the middle of an indoor room and can rotate 360° along a set axis. The sensor attached to the agent is a standard electro-optical RGB camera. We simulate the agent using a subset of the SUN360 dataset [46] of *panoramic* scene images. The goal of the agent is to assign a label to the scene with high confidence while minimizing the number of sensor adjustments.

We formulate a novel approach to this problem based on the Dynamic Data-Driven Applications Systems (DDDAS) paradigm [16]. In a feedback control loop, we employ a machine learning model that drives the sensor manipulation (by adjusting the orientation of the robot and as a result, its camera), and the data captured by the manipulated sensor is used to update the machine learning model. Our approach is built upon prototype learning (see [33] for an overview). The key technical contribution of this paper is a machine learning model that learns prototypical views of scenes in some given feature space. When the agent encounters a new view, it must decide whether:

- The new view is close enough to one of the *informative* prototypical views (i.e., views highly associated with a specific class) to confidently assign a label to the scene.

- The new view matches an *uninformative* prototypical view (i.e., a view that is commonly encountered but does not strongly correlate with a specific class, such as a blank wall) and offers little useful information.
- The new view is *atypical* of past views and should be treated as a new prototypical view.
- The new view provides some useful but *incomplete* information, and the agent's sensor must be adjusted to gather more information about the scene, so the model can make a decision with higher confidence.

Every time a scene is assigned a class label, the prototype-based machine learning model is updated using sensor data collected from all of the views of the given scene encountered up to and including the decision-making time step.

2 Related Work

2.1 Active Learning, Active Perception, Informative/Information-Theoretic Planning/Perception/Learning, and Dynamic Data-Driven Applications Systems for Scene Understanding

Our work is closely related to the active vision/perception paradigm [1–4,13]. Active vision is primarily concerned with modeling the task of visual perception as a dynamic and purpose-driven process whereby some set of observers actively control one or more imaging sensors. In the active vision literature, our problem setting is most similar to Li and Guo's work on active learning for scene classification [31] which extends the scene classification task to include an active learning component that improves a machine learning-based model when unexpected scenes are encountered. In contrast to our approach, [31] only operates on data consisting of clean, single views, and as such, there is no exploration of noisy scenes. Another problem that is similar to ours is the active scene recognition problem proposed by Yu et al. [48]. This approach exploits high-level knowledge (e.g., object information) in order to actively guide a machine learning-driven model's attention in scene images and videos in order to improve performance on the scene classification task. As with [31,48] assumes clean, single view images and video. Furthermore, [48] does not address situations where unknown scenes might be encountered. Other less-related works attempt to merge active learning/vision with the scene classification task. These works include [5,29,30,38,39,49]. Our work is also related to other important problems in active vision for scene understanding, including active scene exploration [25,43], viewpoint selection [10,15,44,45], and active object localization and recognition (e.g., [11,14,21,26,37]).

Our work is also related to informative planning (e.g., [6,7,34]), information-theoretic perception (e.g., [12,43]), and information-theoretic active learning (e.g., [32,35]). In each of these cases, the next set of actions/waypoints (planning), next set of sensor adjustments (perception), or next set of data samples (learning) are selected based on optimizing some information-related criteria.

Our method is related to these paradigms because it involves selecting the next view using a greedy entropy-based criterion.

As stated previously, our approach also follows the Dynamic Data-Driven Applications Systems (DDDAS) paradigm [16], which involves a feedback loop between sensor manipulation and a data-driven modeling component. Other works utilize the DDDAS paradigm for various tasks in scene understanding, but generally not scene classification. Such tasks include automatic target recognition and tracking (e.g., [8]), situational awareness (e.g., [9]), and environmental monitoring and weather forecasting (e.g., [18,19]), among many others.

2.2   Prototype Learning

Our work is based on prototype learning, a classic pattern recognition problem where predictions are made by comparing a query instance to a small set of prototypes/prototypical instances that are learned automatically from some training data. Prototype learning is similar to the k-nearest neighbor classification algorithm, but tries to reduce memory requires by identifying a small subset of the most representative training instances or a small set of abstract "prototype" vectors derived from the training data. Many works have explored this direction, including but not limited to: [17,22,24,27,28,33,40,41,47].

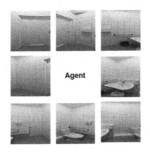

Fig. 1. An example scene from our dataset.

3   Problem Setup/Data

We utilize a subset of the SUN360 dataset [46] of *panoramic* scene images, which allows us to easily simulate manipulating an agent with a camera to obtain different views. We select 14 common scene categories, and annotate 36 instances for each scene category. For each instance, we extract eight views at evenly spaced intervals. Thus, our dataset consists of 504 scenes with a total of 4,032 images. We show an example scene in Fig. 1.

4   Methodology

We now outline our technical approach. The agent encounters a scene S consisting of a set of views V. Each view v has a score c_v, which quantifies the potential of that view to contain discriminative information about the scene. Initially, c_v is set to a constant (2 in our experiments). In our experiments, the first view is selected randomly. Our algorithm operates as follows:

Active Scene Classification with Prototypes Algorithm

▶ Extract features from the view image using a ResNet-50 convolutional neural network [23] pre-trained on the Places-365 dataset [50].

▶ If the set of prototypes is empty:

▶▶ Query a human for the scene category label, and make the view a prototype.

▶▶ Extract features for the remaining views of the scene.

▶▶ Update the prototype vectors using MacQueen's sequential k-means algorithm [20,36], or if any view is more than distance δ (a hyperparameter; 10 in our experiments) away from all existing prototypes in Euclidean space, use it to start a new prototype.

▶▶ For each prototype p, store a "support" histogram h_p of how many past instances have been assigned to the prototype (i.e., the prototype is the nearest prototype to the instance and the distance between the prototype and instance is less than δ) during exploration.

▷ Otherwise:

▶▶ Find the nearest prototype.

▶▶ Compute the discrete probability distribution π_p over all classes already encountered for the nearest prototype p_{near}. Recover the probability distribution for potential class assignments for the current view $\pi_{v_t} = \pi_{p_{near}}$ and the support histogram for the current view $h_{v_t} = h_{p_{near}}$ using the nearest prototype.

▶▶ Find the support histogram for the current scene h_{S_t} by summing the support histograms for all views already encountered. Normalize the histogram to get the probability distribution over potential class assignments for the scene: π_{S_t}.

▶▶ Compute the entropy of the scene-level probability distribution (π_{S_t}): e_{S_t}. If the entropy of the distribution is high, then we are not yet confident enough to make a prediction about the category of the scene. This is because either the prototypes associated with each of the seen views provide conflicting information (e.g., different predictions), or the prototypes are not discriminative for a single class (e.g., the prototype represents a blank wall).

▶▶ Compute an "evidence" score as $n_{S_t} = min(1, \frac{\sum_i h_{S_t}^i}{m})$. The evidence score is indicative of how much trust can be placed on the prototypes used to form the decision (i.e., confidence in the probability distribution associated with a set of specific prototypes). m is a hyperparameter (20 in our experiments) which corresponds to the minimum number of training views that should be associated with the prototypes to consider π_{S_t} "trustworthy".

▶▶ Perform a test to see if a prediction can be output. If $e_S < \epsilon$ (ϵ is a hyperparameter corresponding to the maximum entropy that can be tolerated; 1.6 in our experiments) and $h_S = 1$, then the model should have high confidence when outputting a prediction.

▶▶ If the scene-level tests pass:

▶▶▶ Output the prediction. Exploration ends.

▷▷ If the scene-level tests fail:

►►► Compute the entropy e_{v_t} and evidence scores n_{v_t} just for the current view and run the same tests as before using e_{v_t} and n_{v_t} instead of e_{S_t} and n_{S_t}. An additional test must be run to checks whether the distance to the nearest prototype is less than δ.

►►► If the view-level tests pass:

►►►► The single view provides very strong evidence in a favor of a specific class. Output the prediction for that class. Exploration ends.

▷▷▷ If both the scene-level and view-level tests fail:

►►►► Update the neighboring views' c_v score by averaging them with the entropy of the current view e_{v_t}. If the current view provides strong evidence in favor of a specific class, its neighboring scores will be more likely to provide strong evidence in favor of a specific class, and if the current view is not very discriminative for any class (e.g., it is a blank wall), then the neighboring views will be less likely to contain useful information.

►►►► Set the current view to the remaining view with the lowest c score

►►►► Repeat the procedure with the next view, and repeat until a prediction is output or no views remain.

►► When a prediction was output or no views remain unexplored:

►►► Use the feature vectors for each of the seen views of the scene to update the prototype vectors using MacQueen's sequential k-means algorithm while also updating the corresponding support histograms for each prototype (verifying the prediction with a human). If the instance is more than distance δ away from all existing prototypes in Euclidean space, use it to start a new prototype.

►►► Store the feature vectors and true classes of all of the seen views.

►►► After every k scenes (in our experiments, $k = 30$), do a full batch update of the support histograms for all prototypes using all past data (since prototypes can drift in feature space).

5   Experimental Results

We run our experiments over our 504 scenes. We randomize the order of the scenes, and we randomly pick the first view. For each scene, we record if the model made a correct prediction, the number of views it needed to examine before making a prediction, and the number of prototypes learned up to that scene. We report results in Fig. 2. We make a couple of general observations, most of which are to be expected:

- As the model encounters more scenes, its ability to correctly predict the scene category improves, and it achieves an accuracy rate of 55–65%.
- As the model encounters more scenes, it more efficiently explores the scene. By the final scene, on average, it only uses about four to five of the eight available views before confidently making a decision.
- The number of prototypes learned by the model grows much slower than the number of views encountered, so the learned prototypes efficiently encode useful scene information.

Fig. 2. Left: As the model encounters more scenes, it improves its ability to predict the scene category. **Center:** As the model encounters more scenes, it more efficiently explores the scene; ultimately only using on average about four to five of the eight available views before confidently making a decision. **Right:** The number of prototypes learned by the model grows much slower than the number of views encountered.

6 Conclusions and Future Work

We identified several ways the standard scene classification task is ill-suited for real world applications, and we proposed the active scene classification problem. We proposed a prototype-based method within the DDDAS paradigm as a first attempt to solve the active scene classification problem. In our DDDAS framework, sensors collect information about a scene, and this sensor data is used to learn and update a prototype-based model. In a feedback control loop, the prototype-based model determines how to adjust the sensors to collect more information about the scene. We showed the utility and feasibility of our method experimentally and demonstrated some promising results. However, active scene classification is far from solved, and our method has its limitations. First, we assume the features live in Euclidean space, which might not be a valid assumption. Instead, we should try to incorporate metric learning into our framework. Second, there are likely better ways to balance exploration and exploitation when learning the prototypes, e.g., via reinforcement learning. Third, many hyperparameters were set by hand; we envision performance could improve if we utilitized a hyperparameter optimization method.

References

1. Aloimonos, J., Weiss, I., Bandyopadhyay, A.: Active vision. IJCV **1**(4), 333–356 (1988)
2. Bajcsy, R.: Active perception. Proc. IEEE **76**(8), 966–1005 (1988)
3. Bajcsy, R., Aloimonos, Y., Tsotsos, J.K.: Revisiting active perception. Autonomous Robots **42**(2), 177–196 (2018)
4. Ballard, D.H.: Reference frames for animate vision. In: IJCAI, vol. 89 (1989)
5. Bappy, J.H., Paul, S., Roy-Chowdhury, A.K.: Online adaptation for joint scene and object classification. In: Leibe, B., Matas, J., Sebe, N., Welling, M. (eds.) ECCV 2016. LNCS, vol. 9912, pp. 227–243. Springer, Cham (2016). https://doi.org/10.1007/978-3-319-46484-8_14
6. Binney, J., Krause, A., Sukhatme, G.S.: Informative path planning for an autonomous underwater vehicle. In: ICRA (2010)

7. Binney, J., Krause, A., Sukhatme, G.S.: Optimizing waypoints for monitoring spatiotemporal phenomena. In: IJRR (2013)
8. Blasch, E., Seetharaman, G., Darema, F.: Dynamic data driven applications systems (DDDAS) modeling for automatic target recognition. In: Automatic Target Recognition XXIII, vol. 8744, p. 87440J. SPIE (2013)
9. Blasch, E.P., Aved, A.J.: Dynamic data-driven application system (dddas) for video surveillance user support. Procedia Comput. Sci. **51**, 2503–2517 (2015)
10. Brown, C.: Prediction and cooperation in gaze control. Bio. cybernetics (1990)
11. Caicedo, J.C., Lazebnik, S.: Active object localization with deep reinforcement learning. In: ICCV, pp. 2488–2496 (2015)
12. Charrow, B.: Information-theoretic active perception for multi-robot teams (2015)
13. Chen, S., Li, Y., Kwok, N.M.: Active vision in robotic systems: a survey of recent developments. IJRR **30**(11), 1343–1377 (2011)
14. Chen, X.S., He, H., Davis, L.S.: Object detection in 20 questions. In: WACV (2016)
15. Coombs, D.J., Brown, C.M.: Intelligent gaze control in binocular vision. In: ISIC. pp. 239–245. IEEE (1990)
16. Darema, F.: Dynamic data driven applications systems: a new paradigm for application simulations and measurements. In: Bubak, M., van Albada, G.D., Sloot, P.M.A., Dongarra, J. (eds.) ICCS 2004. LNCS, vol. 3038, pp. 662–669. Springer, Heidelberg (2004). https://doi.org/10.1007/978-3-540-24688-6_86
17. Decaestecker, C.: Finding prototypes for nearest neighbour classification by means of gradient descent and deterministic annealing. Pattern Recogn. **30**, 281–288 (1997)
18. Denham, M., Wendt, K., Bianchini, G., Cortés, A., Margalef, T.: Dynamic data-driven genetic algorithm for forest fire spread prediction. J. Computat. Sci. **3**(5), 398–404 (2012)
19. Douglas, C.C., et al.: DDDAS approaches to wildland fire modeling and contaminant tracking. In: Proceedings of the 2006 Winter Simulation Conference, pp. 2117–2124. IEEE (2006)
20. Duda, R.: Sequential k-means. http://www.cs.princeton.edu/courses/archive/fall08/cos436/Duda/C/sk_means.htm
21. Garcia, A., Vezhnevets, A., Ferrari, V.: An active search strategy for efficient object detection. In: CVPR. pp. 3022–3031 (2015)
22. Geva, S., Sitte, J.: Adaptive nearest neighbor pattern classific. In: IEEE TNN (1991)
23. He, K., Zhang, X., Ren, S., Sun, J.: Deep residual learning for image recognition. In: CVPR, pp. 770–778 (2016)
24. Huang, Y.S., et al.: A simulated annealing approach to construct optimized prototypes for nearest-neighbor classification. In: ICPR, vol. 4, pp. 483–487. IEEE (1996)
25. Jayaraman, D., Grauman, K.: Learning to look around: Intelligently exploring unseen environments for unknown tasks. In: CVPR, pp. 1238–1247 (2018)
26. Johns, E., Leutenegger, S., Davison, A.J.: Pairwise decomposition of image sequences for active multi-view recognition. In: CVPR, pp. 3813–3822 (2016)
27. Kohonen, T.: Improved versions of learning vector quantization. In: IJCNN (1990)
28. Kohonen, T.: The self-organizing map. In: Proceedings of the IEEE (1990)
29. Li, X., Guo, R., Cheng, J.: Incorporating incremental and active learning for scene classification. In: ICMLA, vol. 1, pp. 256–261. IEEE (2012)
30. Li, X., Guo, Y.: Adaptive active learning for image classification. In: CVPR (2013)

31. Li, X., Guo, Y.: Multi-level adaptive active learning for scene classification. In: Fleet, D., Pajdla, T., Schiele, B., Tuytelaars, T. (eds.) ECCV 2014. LNCS, vol. 8695, pp. 234–249. Springer, Cham (2014). https://doi.org/10.1007/978-3-319-10584-0_16

32. Lindley, D.V.: On a measure of the information provided by an experiment. Ann. Math. Stat. **27**, 986–1005 (1956)

33. Liu, C.L., Nakagawa, M.: Evaluation of prototype learning algorithms for nearest-neighbor classifier in application to handwritten character recognition. Pattern Recogn. **34**(3), 601–615 (2001)

34. Ma, K.C., Liu, L., Sukhatme, G.S.: Informative planning and online learning with sparse gaussian processes. In: ICRA (2017)

35. MacKay, D.J.: Information-based objective functions for active data selection. Neural Comput. **4**, 590–604 (1992)

36. MacQueen, J., et al.: Some methods for classification and analysis of multivariate observations. In: Proceedings of the Fifth Berkeley Symposium on Mathematical Statistics and Probability, vol. 1, pp. 281–297. Oakland, CA, USA (1967)

37. Mathe, S., Pirinen, A., Sminchisescu, C.: Reinforcement learning for visual object detection. In: CVPR, pp. 2894–2902 (2016)

38. Paul, S., Bappy, J.H., Roy-Chowdhury, A.K.: Efficient selection of informative and diverse training samples with applications in scene classification. In: ICIP, pp. 494–498. IEEE (2016)

39. Reineking, T., Schult, N., Hois, J.: Evidential combination of ontological and statistical information for active scene classification. In: KEOD, pp. 72–79 (2009)

40. Sato, A., Yamada, K.: Generalized learning vector quantization. In: NeurIPS (1996)

41. Sato, A., Yamada, K.: A formulation of learning vector quantization using a new misclassification measure. In: ICPR, vol. 1, pp. 322–325. IEEE (1998)

42. Settles, B.: Active learning literature survey. Tech. rep., University of Wisconsin-Madison Department of Computer Sciences (2009)

43. Sommerlade, E., Reid, I.: Information-theoretic active scene exploration. In: CVPR, pp. 1–7. IEEE (2008)

44. Wilkes, D., Tsotsos, J.K.: Active object recognition. In: CVPR, IEEE (1992)

45. Wixson, L.: Viewpoint selection for visual search. In: CVPR (1994)

46. Xiao, J., Ehinger, K.A., Oliva, A., Torralba, A.: Recognizing scene viewpoint using panoramic place representation. In: CVPR. pp. 2695–2702. IEEE (2012)

47. Yang, H.M., Zhang, X.Y., Yin, F., Liu, C.L.: Robust classification with convolutional prototype learning. In: CVPR, pp. 3474–3482 (2018)

48. Yu, X., Fermüller, C., Teo, C.L., Yang, Y., Aloimonos, Y.: Active scene recognition with vision and language. In: ICCV, pp. 810–817. IEEE (2011)

49. Zheng, C., Yi, Y., Qi, M., Liu, F., Bi, C., Wang, J., Kong, J.: Multicriteria-based active discriminative dictionary learning for scene recognition. IEEE Access (2017)

50. Zhou, B., Lapedriza, A., Khosla, A., Oliva, A., Torralba, A.: Places: a 10 million image database for scene recognition. IEEE TPAMI **40**(6), 1452–1464 (2017)

Plenary Presentations - Section 7: Learning Systems

Informative Ensemble Kalman Learning for Neural Structure

Margaret Trautner[1,2], Gabriel Margolis[1,3], and Sai Ravela[1(✉)]

[1] Earth Signals and Systems Group, Massachusetts Institute of Technology,
Cambridge, USA
ravela@mit.edu
[2] Department of Mathematics, Massachusetts Institute of Technology,
Cambridge, USA
[3] Department of Aeronautics and Astronautics,
Massachusetts Institute of Technology, Cambridge, MA, USA

Abstract. We characterize the stochastic dynamics of Neural Learning to develop Informative Ensemble Kalman Learning. Specifically, an adaptive Ensemble Kalman Filter replaces backpropagation to quantify uncertainty and maximize information gain during Learning. Demonstrating competitive performance on standard datasets, we show Structure Learning using the Informative Ensemble Kalman Learner quickly recovers the dynamical equations of the Lorenz-63 system *ab initio* from data. Results indicate that extending DDDAS key informative paradigm to optimize Learning Systems is promising.

Keywords: Deep learning · Ensemble Kalman Filter · Informative learning · Systems dynamics and optimization

1 Introduction

The use of data to dynamically control an executing model and, conversely, using the model to control the instrumentation process is a central tenet of Dynamic Data Driven Applications Systems. Applications such as Cooperative Autonomous Observing Systems (CAOS) embody this paradigm [1] in a stochastic system's dynamics and optimization (SDO) loop, maximizing information gain from model predictions to plan observations or select sensors for improved model estimation or reduction. Variously called informative-planning, -estimation, or -sensing, this approach improves nonlinear, high-dimensional stochastic process modeling and prediction, including systems with epistemic uncertainties.

Learning machines are in demand as surrogate or hybrid models for SDO, but SDO is rarely applied to Machine Learning. In particular, Neural Learning dynamics are also stochastic, nonlinear, and high-dimensional. Could DDDAS'

Support from ONR grant N00014-19-1-2273 and VTSIX INC are gratefully acknowledged.

© Springer Nature Switzerland AG 2020
F. Darema et al. (Eds.): DDDAS 2020, LNCS 12312, pp. 191–199, 2020.
https://doi.org/10.1007/978-3-030-61725-7_23

informative approach help machines learn better or faster? In addition to improving CAOS, we posit doing so would broadly impact Machine Learning.

From a systems perspective, training a neural network is parameter estimation [14], and backpropagation [10] restates the variational solution to multistage two-point boundary value problems [2] (2BVP). In practice, Learning implies stochastic dynamics (e.g., due to mini-batches) and the associated Fokker-Planck equations describe the evolution of parameter uncertainty. Much like in nonlinear dynamics, an ensemble approximation to the Fokker-Planck, e.g., the Ensemble Kalman Filter [3], can train a neural network. The benefits include adjoint-free Learning, parallelism, and quantified uncertainty.

The uncertainty quantification benefit implies that one could optimize Learning by maximizing information gain between the training error distribution and key variables. Doing so unifies several paradigms, including parameter selection (Feature/Model Selection), input selection (Relevance and Active Learning), and term/variable selection (Structure Learning). Thus, by analogy to informative approaches in DDDAS, *Informative Learning is the coupling of stochastic learning dynamics with maximization of information gain.*

Although this paradigm is not new from a DDDAS perspective, we cannot ignore the unifying formalism or practical benefits from a Machine Learning perspective. Due to space limitations, we refer the reader elsewhere [14] for details of the stochastic methodology and learning paradigms. Here, we focus on a few critical numerical examples.

First, we show that an adaptive version of the Ensemble Kalman Learner is competitive with backpropagation [10] on standard datasets. Second, we use Informative Ensemble Kalman Learning to learn the structure and parameters of a neural dynamical system [15]. We use numerical simulations of the Lorenz system [6] as training data to demonstrate successful generalization, extrapolation, and interpretation. We can do this because numerical solutions of dynamical systems with polynomial nonlinearities have exact Neural Networks [15]. Thus, neural structure learning reveals the dynamical equations (terms and coefficients). We show that the Informative Learning approach rapidly learns the Lorenz-63 equations to numerical accuracy, *ab initio*, from simulated data. It is both uncertainty aware and sparsity promoting but without iterative burdens, which is an exciting result.

The rest of this paper is as follows. Section 2 describes related work. Section 3 describes Ensemble Kalman Learning, and Sect. 4 uses it for Informative Structure Learning.

2   Related Work

There are connections between Informative Learning and Active Learning [13]. However, the latter does not embody a stochastic dynamical perspective. Informative Learning is related to applications in planning and estimation [1]; Learning has scarcely seen such methodology applied. The application of the Ensemble Kalman Filter [3] to Learning has received scant interest so far. However, adaptive Ensemble Kalman Learning proposed here offers competitive performance, and Informative Ensemble Kalman Learning is new. Ensemble Kalman Learning is itself related to Bayesian Deep Learning [16], but it remains distinct from the extant methodology that typically emphasizes variational Bayesian approaches or Bayesian Active Learning [13].

The stochastic dynamics of Learning naturally form a Markov chain [11]. Stochastic gradient descent using Kalman-SGD [7] and Langevin dynamics [17] have both been developed, but these are unrelated to our work. Finally, learning physics from data [8] is receiving some attention, but our proposed approach is new. Neural structure optimization has also received some attention [18], but our approach still appears to be novel. Note that the presented Informative Ensemble Kalman Learning paradigm is applicable wherever backpropagation is. In fact, it can be broadly applied to other learning systems as well.

3   Ensemble Kalman Learning

In this section, we describe a framework for Informative Learning briefly, referring the reader to details elsewhere [14]. Let us define a standard Neural Network as a N-stage process [2]:

$$x_{l+1} = F_{l+1}(x_l, u_l; \alpha_l) \quad y_N = x_N + \nu_N \quad 0 \le l < N \tag{1}$$

where $x_l \in \mathbb{R}^{n_{l,x}}$ are the layer l nodes, F_l is the function, $\alpha_l \in \mathbb{R}^{n_{l,\alpha}}$ are the weights and biases, $u_l \in \mathbb{R}^{n_{l,u}}$ represents feed-forward (e.g. ResNet) or feedback terms (e.g. recurrent network). The vector $y_N \in \mathbb{R}^{n_v}$ refers to (imperfect) training outputs with additive noise $\nu_l \in \mathbb{R}^{n_{l,\nu}}$. All subscripted variables $n.$ are positive integers. We may refer to the network as a single function embedding all layers:

$$x_N = F_{NN}(x_1, u; \alpha) \tag{2}$$

Here, α is the collection of network weights and biases, and a training sample s is $([x_1, y_N]_s)$. We are also interested in neural dynamical systems which are dynamical systems described at least in part by neural networks [15]. A special case is a discrete-time autonomous system:

$$x_{i+1} = F(x_i, u_i; \alpha) \quad y_i = h(x_i) + \nu_i \tag{3}$$

Where x_i is the network input at time step i, h is the observation operator and ν_i is additive observational noise. These equations also have standard systems interpretations in terms of state, parameter, and control input and measurement/output vectors. Please note that the network types defined here are necessary to apply DDDAS concepts to Learning in this paper, but the definitions are incomplete (e.g., missing stochastic neural dynamical system).

Training a neural network using backpropagation, although not commonly described as such[1], is equivalent to solving a two-point boundary value problem adjoined with the dynamics as mentioned above in Eqs. 1–3. However, it is challenging to be uncertainty aware or informative this way.

---

[1] See course at http://essg.mit.edu/ml.

An alternative to 2BVP is the ensemble approach [3,9] to Learning, which is akin to its use in parameter estimation for nonlinear dynamics and admits both stochastic dynamical and Bayesian estimation perspectives. Specifically, consider the Ensemble Kalman Filter (EnKF) [3,9], which fundamentally leverages a sample approximation to gradients for inference.

For the purpose of this discussion, we interpret Eq. 3 as a standard discrete dynamical system with Gaussian observational noise $\nu_i \sim \mathcal{N}(0, R = r^2 I)$. Defining $X_i = [x_{i,1} \ldots x_{i,E}]$ to be a matrix of E state (column) vector samples obtained by solving F model equations from an initial condition ensemble at the previous time step, and define an observational projection $Z_i = [h(x_{i,1}) \ldots h(x_{i,E})]$ and $Y = [y_{i,1} \ldots y_{i,E}]$ as an ensemble of observations[2]. We adopt the notation that $\tilde{Q}$ is a deviation matrix obtained by removing the mean column vector of Q from its columns. Then, the filter state estimate X_i^+ may be written as

$$X_i^+ = X_i + \tilde{X}_i \tilde{Z}_i^T [\tilde{Z}_i \tilde{Z}_i^T + R]^{-1}(Y_i - Z_i) = X_i M_{x,i} \tag{4}$$

The EnKF in Eq. 4 is a weakly nonlinear update, and it also enables building Lagged filters and smoothers equivalent to 2BVP [9]. For parameter estimation, let $A_i = [\alpha_1 \ldots \alpha_E]_i$ be the matrix of parameter samples at time-step i. The parameters are assumed to persist from one time step to the next in the absence of observation. Thus, the update is:

$$A_i^+ = A_i M_{\alpha, i+k} \; k > 0 \; (Parameter\ Estimation) \tag{5}$$

Here, an initial ensemble of parameters at initial condition and fixed control input sequence ($wlog$) is used for a $k - step$ ensemble simulation to derive a parameter update. The matrix R is just the observational covariance.

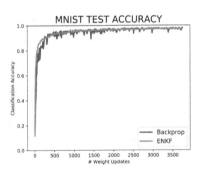

Fig. 1. The Ensemble Kalman Learner offers competitive performance on Boston Housing and MNIST datasets relative to backpropagation.

Parameter estimation immediately provides the basis for neural learning. In particular, consider A_1 to be the initial parameter ensemble (generated with a

---

[2] Perturbed observations are used here for simplicity. This is not strictly necessary.

first-guess Gaussian distribution) and B_i to be the minibatch of size S at iteration i. Then,

$$A_{i+1} = A_i \frac{1}{S} \sum_{s \in B_i} M_{\alpha,i,s} \ i > 0 \ (Learning) \tag{6}$$

In this formulation, $M_{\alpha,i,s}$ is the update produced at iteration i from the ensemble simulation of neural networks for each parameter ensemble member A_i and each training sample $[x_1, y_N]_{s \in B_i}$. Thus $S \times E$ parallel simulations are performed. The "noise model" (R) is used to specify a tolerance or performance index in achieving training outputs. The resulting A_{i+1} are then the parameters at iteration $i + 1$. The same approach are applicable to recurrent systems (with rollout) and neural dynamical systems. In contrast to 2BVP it is applicable to stochastic neural dynamical systems and learning systems in general.

Ensemble Kalman Learning has several interesting properties. Network linearization and analytical parameter gradients are unnecessary; loss functions are not limited. The directly-obtained uncertainty estimates further allow us to quantify information gain. In contrast to 2BVP, all layer weights update in parallel. Parallel simulations further reduce computational expense. For small parameter ensembles, the update is compact.

We conducted examples with the Boston Housing [4] and MNIST [5] datasets[3]. For Boston Housing, we use a neural network with two 32-neuron hidden layers, ReLU activations, least-squares loss function, minibatch of size 16, and 100-member parameter ensemble. IID zero-mean Gaussian with a standard deviation of 0.01 generates the initial parameter ensemble, and the target tolerance is $r = 0.01$. SGD with a learning rate of 0.1 in backpropagation. The results (see Fig. 1) show that the Ensemble Kalman Learner achieves a converged error similar to tuned backpropagation within five epochs.

The MNIST dataset [5] network architecture consists of two batch-normalized convolutional layers, max-pooling, and ReLU activations, followed by a single ReLU-activated linear layer of width 10, finally followed by a softmax-activated categorical output layer. We use a least-squares loss function, minibatch size 16, parameter ensemble size 1000, and a target error tolerance of 0.015 to match the observed performance of a highly-performing backpropagation-trained network. Furthermore, the target error tolerance adapts as ensemble variance reduces, up to a lower bound of 0.0015. SGD, with a learning rate of 1.0, is used for backpropagation. The Ensemble Kalman Learner achieves a final test accuracy of 97.1%, competing well with backpropagation at 97.9%. It does this while maintaining better stability at a high learning rate.

4 DDDAS: Informative Structure Learning

In this section, Informative Ensemble Kalman Learning is developed and applied to Neural Structure Learning, a difficult problem. For example, just learning $y = x^2$ with a $tanh$ activation node is hard ($tanh$ has no even Taylor expansion

---

[3] Obtain code from https://github.com/sairavela/EnsembleTrain.git.

terms). In general, a poor structural basis, poor interpretability, generalization, and extrapolation are all confounding factors. However, in the restricted setting of learning the structure of neural dynamical systems [15] trained from the non-trivial and large class of polynomial dynamics, these issues are overcome. Neural networks with multiplicative gates [15] represent dynamical systems with polynomial nonlinearities exactly. Therefore, learning neural structure from data generated by polynomial dynamics is exactly equal to recovering the polynomial equations (terms and coefficients). Here, consider the problem of learning neural structure and parameters from data generated by numerical solutions to the chaotic Lorenz-63 [6] system[4], which is defined as:

$$\dot{x}_1 = \sigma(x_2 - x_1), \quad \dot{x}_2 = \rho x_1 - x_2 - x_1 x_3, \quad \dot{x}_3 = -\beta x_3 + x_1 x_2. \tag{7}$$

Suppose the starting model is a second-degree polynomial with nine terms per equation $\mathbf{X} = \left(x_1, \ x_2, \ x_3, \ x_1 x_2, \ x_1 x_3, \ x_2 x_3, \ x_1^2, \ x_2^2, \ x_3^2\right)$. There are thus 27 unknown parameters $\{a_{ij}\}$, where i indexes $x_{1...3}$ and j indexes $\mathbf{X}$. The "true" Lorenz equations are simulated from an arbitrary initial condition $\mathbf{x_0} = (-1.1, 2.2, -2.7)$ with parameters $\sigma = 10$, $\rho = 28$, and $\beta = 8/3$, and time step $dt = 0.01$. The model equations are also simulated using a parameter ensemble of size 100, each initialized i.i.d. from Gaussian with mean 0 and variance 100. If the parameter matrix for the kth ensemble member is denoted $A_k := \left[a_{ij}^k\right]$, then $A_k \mathbf{X_t}$ are the predictions. The parameters are then updated using Eq. 4.

When the Ensemble Kalman Learner estimates all 27 possible parameters, the model system converges in approximately 85 iterations when we use an initial parameter mean 0, variance 100, and high-precision/small target variance of 1×10^{-10}. Actual parameters are recovered to within 3×10^{-4} with a posterior variance of 3.2×10^{-7} with the "wrong" term coefficients going to zero. Convergence was repeatable and, remarkably, required no additional sparsity constraints.

However, there are clear limitations. The initial model is arguably quite close to the true model because all true terms are given as options; in other words, the true model lies within the space of candidate models. In general, this is not the case, and the dimensionality of the starting model may be quite high.

The following Informative Ensemble Kalman Learning approach is a better. Instead of automatically updating all terms using Ensemble Kalman Learning, we automatically select a small initial subset of terms as candidates, then alternate between parameter estimation and term selection until achieving sufficient prediction accuracy. To select terms, we first quantify the pairwise mutual information between each of the structure terms and each of the current model's three training error variables. Pairwise conditional mutual information assumes Gaussian ensembles, but other approaches are feasible [12]. After that, greedy term selection maximizes the cumulative sorted pairwise mutual information while minimizing the number of terms selected. This is sparsity promoting but noniterative and akin to information selection criteria, and thus faster than classical

---

[4] Code may be found at http://github.com/sairavela/LorenzStructureLearn.

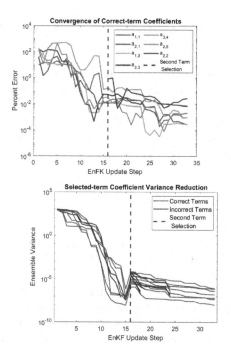

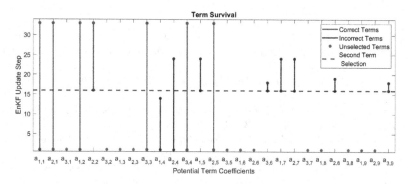

Fig. 2. Convergence of the true parameters and variance reduction of chosen terms for learning the structure of the Lorenz-63 system.

Fig. 3. Survival of terms over iterations. Green are the correct terms, red are unselected, and blue are terms selected and later rejected. (Color figure online)

sparse optimization. The chosen terms augment the system equations. Ensemble Kalman Learning proceeds for a specified variance reduction, at the end of which terms with parameter values approaching zero leave the system equations. The selection cycle repeats. Variances are then rescaled and balanced in the new parameter ensemble, and Ensemble Learning proceeds.

By alternating the maximization of information gain with Ensemble Learning, we recover the Lorenz system equations from the initial model $\dot{x}_{1...3} = 0$ within approximately 35 iterations requiring three or fewer selection steps. Not only is this more efficient but the incremental selection-rejection (prediction-correction) is automatic and overcomes the dimensionality concern. As shown in Fig. 2, the true equations were recovered with parameter estimates within 1%. The final system structure learned is structurally exact: $\dot{x}_1 = a_{11}x_1 + a_{12}x_2$, $\dot{x}_2 = a_{21}x_1 + a_{22}x_2 + a_{25}x_1x_3$, and $\dot{x}_3 = a_{33}x_3 + a_{34}x_1x_2$. The progression of term presence in the equations throughout the term selection process can be seen in Fig. 3.

5   Conclusions

DDDAS's informative optimization paradigm applies to neural Learning. We develop adaptive Ensemble Kalman Learning, and results on two standard datasets were comparable to stochastic gradient descent. Informative Learning promotes sparsity while maximizing information gain. We applied information gain to learn the Lorenz system equations *ab inito* quickly and incrementally without iterative optimization for selecting terms. In future work, discovering equations of natural hazards and other tractable inference models for Learning and Information Gain are of interest.

References

1. Blasch, E., Ravela, S., Aved, A. (eds.): Handbook of Dynamic Data Driven Applications Systems. Springer, Cham (2018). https://doi.org/10.1007/978-3-319-95504-9
2. Bryson, A., Ho, Y.C.: Applied Optimal Control. Hemisphere Publishing Corporation (1975)
3. Evensen, G.: The ensemble kalman filter: theoretical formulation and practical implementation. Ocean Dyn. **53**, 343–367 (2003)
4. Harrison Jr., D., Rubinfeld, D.L.: Hedonic housing prices and the demand for clean air. J. Environ. Econ. Manage. **5**(1), 81–102 (1978)
5. LeCun, Y., Bottou, L., Bengio, Y., Haffner, P.: Gradient-based learning applied to document recognition. Proc. IEEE **86**(11), 2278–2324 (1998)
6. Lorenz, E.N.: Deterministic nonperiodic flow. J. Atmospheric Sci. **20**(2), 130–141 (1963)
7. Patel, V.: Kalman-based stochastic gradient method with stop condition and insensitivity to conditioning (2015). https://doi.org/10.1137/15M1048239
8. Raissi, M., Perdikaris, P., Karniadakis, G.E.: Physics informed deep learning (part i): Data-driven solutions of nonlinear partial differential equations. arXiv preprint arXiv:1711.10561 (2017)
9. Ravela, S., McLaughlin, D.: Fast ensemble smoothing. Ocean Dyn. **57**(2), 123–134 (2007)
10. Rumelhart, D., Hinton, G., Williams, R.: Learning representations by back-propagating errors. Nature **323**(6088), 533–536 (1986)

11. Shwartz-Ziv, R., Tishby, N.: Opening the black box of deep neural networks via information (2017)
12. Tagade, P., Ravela, S.: A quadratic information measure for data assimilation. In: IEEE American Control Conference, pp. 598–603, Portland, USA (2014). https://doi.org/10.1109/ACC.2014.6859127
13. Tran, T., Do, T.T., Reid, I., Carneiro, G.: Bayesian generative active deep learning (2019)
14. Trautner, M., Margolis, G., Ravela, S.: Informative Neural Ensemble Kalman Learning (2020). arXiv:2008.09915, http://arxiv.org/abs/2008.09915
15. Trautner, M., Ravela, S.: Neural integration of continuous dynamics (2019). arXiv:1911.10309, http://arxiv.org/abs/1911.10309
16. Wang, H., Yeung, D.Y.: Towards bayesian deep learning: a survey (2016). arxiv:1604.01662, http://arxiv.org/abs/1604.01662
17. Welling, M., Teh, Y.W.: Bayesian learning via stochastic gradient langevin dynamics. In: ICML (2011)
18. Zhang, Q., Li, B., Wu, Y.: Evolutionary structure optimization of convolutional neural networks for deployment on resource limited systems. In: Huang, D.-S., Jo, K.-H., Zhang, X.-L. (eds.) ICIC 2018. LNCS, vol. 10955, pp. 742–753. Springer, Cham (2018). https://doi.org/10.1007/978-3-319-95933-7_82

Reachability Analysis Based Tracking: Applications to Non-cooperative Space Object Tracking

Zach Hall$^{(\boxtimes)}$ and Puneet Singla

Pennsylvania State University, State College, PA 16802, USA
zyh5059@psu.edu

Abstract. This paper presents a reachability set based method for tracking maneuvering space objects in the presence of sparse measurements. The proposed approach invokes the Dynamic Data Driven Application Systems (DDDAS) paradigm by dynamically integrating model forecasts due to uncertainties in maneuver capabilities with collected sensor data to search and track for a non-cooperative satellite in a control theoretic framework. The typically large time interval between measurements from ground stations presents significant problems for tracking satellites that have maneuvered during this interval. Using reachability set propagation techniques and a particle filter update scheme, an intelligently guided search algorithm is developed. This algorithm enables the systematic reduction of likely reachable states until measurements of the target are acquired and traditional tracking techniques can be resumed. Numerical simulations of a space-based sensor tasking scenario are given, however, the method is generic and can be extended to ground-based sensors or a combination of both ground and space-based sensors.

Keywords: Reachability · Target tracking · Uncertainty quantification

1 Introduction

Dynamic Data Driven Application Systems (DDDAS) provide an important avenue to detect, track and characterize resident space objects, by enabling mechanisms to infer their orbit, orientation, shape, and number, and simultaneously providing a data driven feedback loop about which future measurements are to be made to maintain the RSO uncertainties in the catalog below acceptable threshold values [14]. Such a framework comprises of an interplay between various algorithms and methods, catering to different SSA products. Reference [14] introduces a DDDAS paradigm for SSA applications called INFOrmation and Resource Management (INFORM) which includes multi-modal sensing architecture, advanced data association algorithms [1], track estimation techniques [13], uncertainty quantification [3], RSO attribute estimation [14] and dynamic resource/catalog management elements [2].

This work is supported through AFOSR award #FA9550-17-1-0088.

An important aspect of space object monitoring is detection and tracking of non-cooperative maneuvering space objects in a data-sparse environment. In this respect, the scope of this paper is to summarize the INOFRM framework components to locate and track a maneuvering satellite with the help of space based sensing satellite.

Although there has been a lot of work in terms of tracking maneuvering ground targets [4,9,10], relatively a little of this work is applicable to non-cooperative space object tracking in a data sparse environment. This is primarily due to the fact that most of these methods utilize different kinematic models for target motion and needs to be updated to include dynamic of space objects due to Earth's gravitational field. Methods like multiple models [9] are not directly applicable to space object tracking as one needs to consider a prohibitively large number of models to accurately represent possible satellite motion dynamics. Furthermore, most of the literature for non-cooperative target tracking assumes that measurements are readily available during the maneuver interval. This makes sense in data-rich applications where measurements are available throughout the entire target trajectory such as ground or air target tracking. Unfortunately, in most satellite tracking applications measurements from ground stations are available only in sparse intervals due to the limited number and coverage of sensors. Generally, an assumption of optimality about the maneuver is made to reconstruct an orbit in data-sparse environment [8,11].

The objective of this paper is to summarize the recently developed framework [6] for locating and tracking a maneuvering satellite in data-sparse environments without imposing assumptions on the target control policy. The DDDAS framework proposed in this paper is composed of several interconnected components, each with an important role in the success of the resulting location and estimation capability. There are three main components that will be discussed: 1) Reachability Set Propagation, 2) Particle Filtering Algorithm, 3) Reachability Set Search Algorithm. The reachability set calculations exploits dynamic model forecasts due to uncertainties in maneuver capabilities to define a search space for sensing station. A feedback loop is employed to define a strategy to collect measurements in a dynamic manner and update this search space based upon sensor observation data. Although this work considers a scenario of tracking a single non-cooperative space object, the presented framework is generic in nature and can be adapted for multiple target tracking.

The structure of the paper is as follows: first, a mathematical description for non-cooperative target tracking is presented followed by a brief description of the developed methodology. The paper concludes with numerical results correspond to tracking a non-cooperative GEO object.

2   Problem Formulation

Assume a mixed continuous-discrete time dynamic system is given by,

$$\dot{\mathbf{x}} = \mathbf{f}(\mathbf{x}, \mathbf{u}, t), \quad \mathbf{y}_k = \mathbf{h}(\mathbf{x}_k, k) + \boldsymbol{\nu}_k \tag{1}$$

where $\mathbf{x} \in \mathrm{R}^n$ is the state vector, $\mathbf{u} \in \mathrm{R}^r$ is the control vector, and $\mathbf{y}_k \in \mathrm{R}^m$ is the discrete-time observation vector. $\boldsymbol{\nu}_k$ represents zero mean Gaussian measurement noise vector with covariance $\mathbf{R}_k$. The objective of the classical tracking problem is to obtain the optimal estimate of $\mathbf{x}$ given the discrete set of measurements up to time t_k, $\boldsymbol{Y}_k = \{y_1, y_2 ... y_k\}$. The problem considered in this paper is an extended version of the generic tracking problem in which the target has made an unknown maneuver $\mathbf{u}_m$ at an unknown time t_m during the interval between discrete measurements. This problem formulation is generic, however, the specific case considered is the problem of tracking a maneuvering target satellite with a space-based observer satellite. The system state for this problem consists of both target state $\mathbf{x}_t$ and observer state $\mathbf{x}_{ob}$

$$\mathbf{x} = \begin{bmatrix} \mathbf{x}_t \ \mathbf{x}_{ob} \end{bmatrix}^T, \quad \mathbf{x}_t = \begin{bmatrix} \mathbf{r}_t \ \mathbf{v}_t \end{bmatrix}^T, \quad \mathbf{x}_{ob} = \begin{bmatrix} \mathbf{r}_{ob} \ \mathbf{v}_{ob} \ \boldsymbol{\Theta} \end{bmatrix}^T \tag{2}$$

where $\mathbf{r}_i$ and $\mathbf{v}_i$ are satellite position and velocity vectors respectively, and $\boldsymbol{\Theta}$ is the observer attitude vector. The dynamic model $\mathbf{f}$ governing the position and velocity of each satellite is the Hill-Clohessey-Wiltshire (HCW) model of relative motion [5], where the initial target state is the reference orbit. Maneuvers in this model are considered to be impulsive $\Delta \mathbf{v}$ velocity changes, and impulsive $\Delta \boldsymbol{\Theta}$ angle changes for observer attitude. It is assumed that the observer satellite $\Delta \mathbf{v}$ and $\Delta \boldsymbol{\Theta}$ maneuvers are deterministic. The unknown variables are target maneuver $\mathbf{u}_m$ and maneuver time t_m which are assigned probability density functions (PDFs) $p(\mathbf{u}_m)$ and $p(t_m)$, respectively. Hence, the objective of the maneuvering target tracking problem is to compute the target state PDF $p(\mathbf{x}_{t,k}|\boldsymbol{Y}_k)$ for $t_k > t_m > t_0$ given the joint input PDF $p(\mathbf{u}_m, t_m)$. The contours of the state PDF provide the search region for the sensor, and enable the design of an observer search algorithm. This search region can then be updated in a dynamic manner as observation data becomes available leading to a DDDAS paradigm.

3 Methodology

This section describes the procedure used to implement the maneuvering target tracking algorithm. In the context of this problem, the target PDF and target reachability set are synonymous and used interchangeably. The mathematical framework used to implement the maneuvering target tracking problem is a modified version of the classical particle filter[12]. Particle filters are widely used for general nonlinear filtering applications, however, they suffer from computational limitations especially in applications with high dimension. To circumvent one of the primary computational burdens of the classical particle filter, this method employs the higher order sensitivity matrix (HOSM) method for reachability set propagation [7]. The procedure for searching the maneuvering target reachability set is summarized in Fig. 1.

The HOSM method is substituted for the state propagation step in the classical particle filter, which reduces the computational burden normally associated

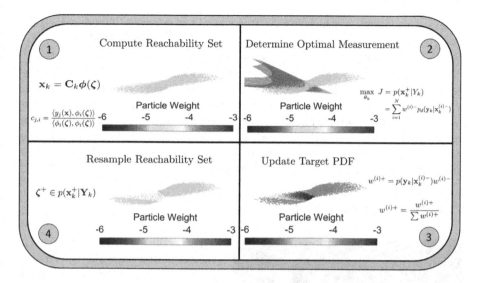

Fig. 1. Reachability set search procedure

with particle propagation by several orders of magnitude. The sensitivity coefficients can be computed as:

$$\mathbf{x}_{k+1} = \int \mathbf{f}(\mathbf{x}, \mathbf{u}, t)dt \approx \mathbf{C}_k\boldsymbol{\phi}(\boldsymbol{\zeta}), \quad c_{j,i} = \frac{\langle x_j, \phi_i \rangle}{\langle \phi_i, \phi_i \rangle} \tag{3}$$

where elements of the matrix $\mathbf{C}$ are sensitivity coefficients, and ϕ is an orthogonal polynomial basis. Computing higher order sensitivity coefficients enables the efficient propagation of the target reachability set. Once the target reachability set is computed, the "optimal" observer control action are computed which maximizes the posterior detection likelihood of the target satellite computed using the particle states $\mathbf{x}^{(i)}$ and weights $w^{(i)}$:

$$\max_{\mathbf{u}_{ob}} J = p(\mathbf{x}^+|Y_k), \quad p(\mathbf{x}^+|Y_k) = \sum_{i=1}^{N} w^{(i)-}p_d(\mathbf{y}_k|\mathbf{x}_k^{(i)-}) \tag{4}$$

where p_d is the likelihood of detecting particle $\mathbf{x}^{(i)}$ from measurement $\mathbf{y}_k$. The next step is to update the target PDF via the particle weights. This step is performed using the classical particle filter weight update formula

$$w^{(i)+} \propto w^{(i)-}p(\mathbf{y}_k|\mathbf{x}_k^{(i)}) \rightarrow w^{(i)+} = \frac{w^{(i)+}}{\sum w^{(i)+}} \tag{5}$$

where $p(\mathbf{y}_k|\mathbf{x}_k^{(i)})$ is the likelihood function. There are two possibilities for the measurement likelihood function: 1) the search likelihood $p_s(\mathbf{y}_k|\mathbf{x}_k^{(i)})$, which is used if the target is not detected from measurement $\mathbf{y}_k$, and 2) the measurement likelihood $p_m(\mathbf{y}_k|\mathbf{x}_k^{(i)})$, which is used if the target is detected. The search likelihood reduces the weight of observed particles based on how probable it is that the observer would have detected the target if the particle was the true target state, i.e., $p_s(\mathbf{y}_k|\mathbf{x}_k^{(i)}) = 1 - p_d(\mathbf{y}_k|\mathbf{x}_k^{(i)-})$. The measurement likelihood describes the likelihood of a particle to be described by the measurement $\mathbf{y}_k$ and is given by Gaussian sensor noise. The final step corresponds to the resampling of the particle filter. This step may be done after every measurement, but to speed our procedure, resampling is only done when the maximum particle weight passes a particular threshold. This avoids the expensive resampling procedure for measurements that do not significantly alter the target PDF.

4   Numerical Simulations

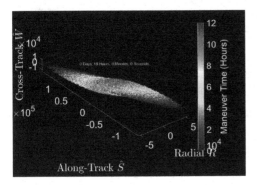

Fig. 2. Computed reachability set for $t = 18$ h.

This section will present numerical simulations for the maneuvering satellite reachability set search problem. The target is in a Geosynchronous Equatorial Orbit (GEO), and is able to make a maneuver of up to 1 (m/s) over the first 12 h of the simulation. The initial target state is assumed to be known deterministically, thus the reachability set is a function of only the unknown maneuver $\mathbf{u}_m$ and maneuver time t_m. The input PDFs $p(\mathbf{u}_m)$ and $p(t_m)$ are defined as spherically uniform with a maximum radius of $1m/s$, and uniform between $[t = 0(h),\ t = 12(h)]$ respectively. The initial semimajor axis of the target spacecraft orbit is $42,241$ (km), and the eccentricity and inclination are both zero. The observer spacecraft starts 100 (km) ahead of the target in the intrack direction and makes a set of deterministically planned maneuvers summarized by Table 1. These maneuvers are pre-planned to enable the observer to search various portions of the reachability set for the target. The true target maneuver time is $t_m = 45$ (min), and the true maneuver is $\mathbf{u}_m^* = \begin{bmatrix} -0.3290\,(\text{m/s}) & -0.7876\,(\text{m/s}) & 0.4890\,(\text{m/s}) \end{bmatrix}^T$.

Table 1. Observer maneuvers

Maneuver #	$\Delta V_x(m/s)$	$\Delta V_y(m/s)$	$\Delta V_z(m/s)$	$t_m(hr)$
1	3.6361	0	0	12
2	−5.4542	0	0	24
3	−7.2722	0	0	36

The total simulation time is 2 days with measurements taken every 10 (mins). The reachability set is computed using 8th order uniform spherical Conjugate Unscented Transform points (CUT) for $\mathbf{u}_m$ [6], and 8th order uniform Gauss-Legendre quadrature points for t_m. Comparison of the CUT approach with conventional quadrature filters such as unscented Kalman filter and cubature Kalman filter is presented in Ref. [3]. A 4th order polynomial basis is used to construct the reachability set. The reachability set after 18 h is illustrated in Fig. 2 where the axes represent the target position in relative coordinates, and the colorbar represents t_m.

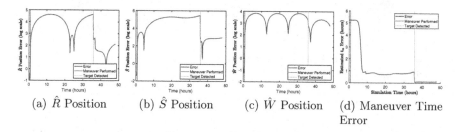

(a) $\hat{R}$ Position   (b) $\hat{S}$ Position   (c) $\hat{W}$ Position   (d) Maneuver Time Error

Fig. 3. GEO test case state estimate error

The observation zone is constrained to a half angle of $\beta = 10°$, and assigned a scale distance of $r_s = 45$ (km). The observation zone detection PDF is given by

$$p_d(\mathbf{x}, \theta_z) = \left(1 - \left(\frac{\theta}{\beta}\right)^4\right) e^{-\left(\frac{|\mathbf{r}|}{r_s}\right)} \tag{6}$$

where θ is the angle between the target position and the observer attitude vector, and $|\mathbf{r}|$ is the target range. The observer measurements consist of range, range-rate, and angles, with noise standard deviations of $\sigma_r = 250$ m, $\sigma_{\dot{r}} = 0.5$ m/s, and $\sigma_\theta = 0.5°$ respectively. Figures 3a–c show the error in position estimate in meters versus simulation time. Notice that at t_m, the error in state estimate starts rapidly growing due to impulsive maneuver $\mathbf{u}_m$. The observer detects the target after 1 day, 11 h, and 40 min. Note in Fig. 3 the drop in target state estimate errors after the first detection. Additionally it is important to take note of the estimated maneuver time plot shown in Fig. 3d. The error in estimated maneuver time is refined throughout the simulation as the observer measures different regions of the reachability set, and finally narrows down on a final estimate once the target has been observed. Figure 4 shows histograms of the filter particles at the end of the simulation which represent the full state PDF. It is apparent that despite only having recorded a handful of measurements towards the end of the simulation, the true target state is captured by the particle filter. The final state histograms in Fig. 4 are strongly non-gaussian due to the nonlinear Bayesian update and resampling step, and it is important to note that the true target estimate is well within the predicted final state PDF. The least accurately captured state is the position in the out of plane $(\hat{W})$ direction. This is likely due to the relative geometry of the observer and the target at the time the target was located. If more measurements were collected, these estimates would likely improve.

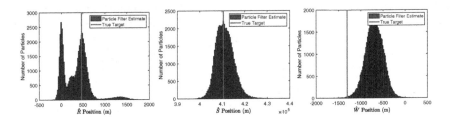

Fig. 4. GEO test case final state distribution

5 Conclusions

This work presents an approach to enable the automated search and estimation of a maneuvering satellite. The proposed approach utilizes the relative motion dynamics between target and sensing satellite to define a reachability set for the maneuvering target based upon provided maneuver magnitude and maneuver time bounds. The computed reachability sets define the search space for the sensing satellite to locate the maneuvering target and a feedback loop is designed to search and update the computed reachability set based upon collected measurement data. This interplay between dynamic models and sensor observations to define the search space to optimally collect measurements and update control input for dynamical model corresponds to a Dynamic Data Driven Application Systems (DDDAS) paradigm and considerably improves the accuracy of conventional Bayesian approaches for tracking a maneuvering satellite. The main contribution of this work stems from the application of novel non-product quadrature method known as the *Conjugate Unscented Transformation* (CUT) to compute the reachability sets in a computationally attractive manner. The proposed approach is validated by considering a scenario of tracking a maneuvering satellite in an Geosynchronous Equatorial Orbit (GEO). The simulation results clearly shows the efficacy of the developed approach in tracking a maneuvering satellite and provides the basis of optimism in its further utility to track multiple maneuvering satellites.

References

1. Adurthi, N., Majji, M., Singla, P.: Quadrature-based nonlinear joint probabilistic data association filter. J. Guid. Control Dyn. **42**(11), 2369–2381 (2019)
2. Adurthi, N., Singla, P., Majji, M.: Mutual information based sensor tasking with applications to space situational awareness. J. Guid. Control Dyn. **43**(4), 767–789 (2020)

3. Adurthi, N., Singla, P., Singh, T.: Conjugate unscented transformation: Applications to estimation and control. J. Dyn. Syst. Meas. Contr. **140**(3), 030907 (2018)
4. Bar-Shalom, Y., Li, X.R., Kirubarajan, T.: Estimation with Applications to Tracking and Navigation: Theory Algorithms and Software. Wiley, New York (2004)
5. Clohessy, W., Wiltshire, R.: Terminal guidance system for satellite rendezvous. J. Aerosp. Sci. **27**(9), 653–658, 674 (1960)
6. Hall, Z., Singla, P.: A particle filtering approach to space-based, maneuvering satellite location and estimation. In: AAS 2020 Astrodynamics Specialist Conference, August 2020
7. Hall, Z., Singla, P.: Higher order polynomial expansion for uncertain lambert problem. In: AAS 2018 Astrodynamics Specialists Conference, January 2018
8. Holzinger, M.J., Scheeres, D.J., Alfriend, K.T.: Object correlation, maneuver detection, and characterization using control distance metrics. J. Guid. Control Dyn. **35**(4), 1312–1325 (2012)
9. Li, X.R., Jilkov, V.P.: Survey of maneuvering target tracking, Part 5: multiple-model methods. IEEE Trans. Aerosp. Electr. Syst. **41**(4), 1255–1321 (2005)
10. Mazor, E., Averbuch, A., Bar-Shalom, Y., Dayan, J.: Interacting multiple model methods in target tracking: a survey. IEEE Trans. Aerosp. Electron. Syst. **34**(1), 103–123 (1998)
11. Shen, D., Jia, B., Chen, G., Pham, K., Blasch, E.: Space based sensor management strategies based on informational uncertainty pursuit-evasion games. In: National Aerospace and Electronics Conference (NAECON) (2015)
12. Simon, D.: Optimal State Estimation: Kalman, H. and Nonlinear Approaches. Wiley, Hoboken (2006)
13. Vishwajeet, K., Singla, P., Jah, M.: Nonlinear uncertainty propagation for perturbed two-body orbits. J. Guid. Control Dyn. **37**(5), 1415–1425 (2014)
14. Wong, X.I., Majji, M., Singla, P.: Photometric stereopsis for 3D reconstruction of space objects. In: Blasch, E., Ravela, S., Aved, A. (eds.) Handbook of Dynamic Data Driven Applications Systems, pp. 253–291. Springer, Cham (2018). https://doi.org/10.1007/978-3-319-95504-9_13

Sparse Regression and Adaptive Feature Generation for the Discovery of Dynamical Systems

Chinmay S. Kulkarni, Abhinav Gupta, and Pierre F. J. Lermusiaux[✉]

Massachusetts Institute of Technology, Cambridge, MA, USA
{chinmayk,guptaa,pierrel}@mit.edu

Abstract. We study the performance of sparse regression methods and propose new techniques to distill the governing equations of nonlinear dynamical systems from data. We start from the recently proposed generic methodology of learning interpretable equation forms from data, followed by performance of least absolute shrinkage and selection operator (LASSO) for this purpose. We first develop an algorithm that uses the dual of LASSO optimization for higher accuracy and stability. We then derive a second algorithm that learns the candidate function library in a dynamic data driven applications systems (DDDAS) manner to distill the governing equations of the dynamical system. This is achieved via sequentially thresholded ridge regression (STRidge) over a orthogonal polynomial space. The performance of the methods is illustrated using the Lorenz 63 system and a marine ecosystem model.

Keywords: Machine learning · DDDAS · Sparse regression · Nonlinear dynamical systems · Dual LASSO · System identification

1 Introduction and Overview

Data today are no longer used mostly to verify models derived from first principles but also to dynamically adapt and learn such models [9]. This is particularly important for non-autonomous nonlinear dynamical systems that describe a multitude of problems from science and engineering. Recent groundbreaking methods leverage the fact that most dynamical equations governing physical systems contain a few terms, making them sparse in high-dimensional nonlinear function space [2,12]. By constructing an appropriate feature library based on the data coordinates, one can apply sparse regression to discover the governing equations of the dynamical system. Few studies however try to improve upon the sparse regression algorithm at the core of the approach. This is exactly the first focus area of the present work. We examine the sparse regression method most commonly employed in this field: Least Absolute Shrinkage and Selection Operator (LASSO) [13]. Although LASSO works well with assured fast convergence rates for uncorrelated features, it converges more slowly for highly correlated features,

© Springer Nature Switzerland AG 2020
F. Darema et al. (Eds.): DDDAS 2020, LNCS 12312, pp. 208–216, 2020.
https://doi.org/10.1007/978-3-030-61725-7_25

and tends to choose a feature at random from each of the correlated groups [7]. To alleviate these difficulties, we propose to solve the dual of LASSO to learn the governing equations. Even in the case of correlated features, the dual LASSO has a unique solution, which allows us to correctly choose the features. The second part of this work deals with the case when the exact function blocks that describe the dynamical system are not present in the feature library. We develop a way to handle such cases by using an appropriate family of orthogonal functional basis to span the feature library combined with an approach to adaptively increase and decrease the dimension of the feature space. This allows us to add new components to the feature space that are orthogonal to the existing features while discarding those that do not have any projection of the dynamical system along them. We employ this algorithm iteratively, while adding or removing appropriate features to dynamically adapt our feature space for the best approximation of the equations from data. These Dynamic Data Driven Applications Systems (DDDAS) [3] approaches are demonstrated on the Lorenz 63 system [11] and a marine ecosystem model [6,8] with a non-polynomial nonlinearity. We show that our dynamic data driven algorithms robustly and accurately learn the presence of active features and of the nonlinearities without requiring any explicit feature information.

1.1 General Methodology

Let us assume that we have n state space parameters $(x_1, \ldots, x_n)$, with measurements for x_i and $\dot{x}_i = dx/dt$ at times $t = 1, \ldots, T$ (denoted by a superscript). If only state observations are available, the rate parameters can be computed using finite difference. This is followed by constructing a nonlinear library of features using the state space parameters. The span of these features now describes the feature space. Typically we would construct this feature space through a class of functions that are dense in the space that our dynamical system lives in. In this work, we assume a polynomial feature library, however the methodology is agnostic towards the choice of functional basis and would apply to any other feature library as well. After constructing the feature library (say X), we formulate the regression problem as $\dot{X} = XW + \varepsilon$, where $\dot{X}_{(t,j)} = \dot{x_j}^t$ and W are the unknown weights, with ε being the noise. Often in dynamical models, not all the features in the library that we consider are required to explain the dynamical model. Thus, as in [2], we utilize sparse regression to select the relevant features. However, unlike the aforementioned work, we dynamically build an suitable feature library which allows us to infer the nonlinear terms in the governing equations effectively, without knowing the type of functional space they live in. We also use the dual of LASSO optimization for higher accuracy and stability. These features, with their corresponding coefficients describe the functional form of the governing equations.

2   Regression Over Fixed Feature Space

In this section, we assume that the feature library is fixed, and that we wish to find either the exact sparse equation form from this library or the closest approximation to the governing equation only from the terms in the library. The highest polynomial degree in the feature space (X) is p. Then, the feature space contains terms of the form $(x_1^t)^{p_1} \ldots (x_i^t)^{p_i} \ldots (x_n^t)^{p_n}$, such that $p_1 + \ldots + p_n \leq p$. The number of terms in the feature library is $m = \binom{n+p}{n} = \frac{(n+p)!}{n!p!}$ (*i.e.* $X \in \mathbb{R}^{T \times m}$). Empirically the number of distinct terms in the governing equations is $\mathcal{O}(n)$. Thus even for small enough p, the terms in the feature library are much more in number than those to be chosen, which justifies sparse regression to select the features. Let us denote the coefficient matrix obtained from the sparse regression by W. The optimization problem with some penalty $(\mathcal{P})$ is:

$$\min_{W} \mathcal{L}(W) = \left[\left(\dot{X} - XW \right)^2 + \mathcal{P}(W) \right]. \qquad (1)$$

To further select the features appropriately, we use our knowledge of the underlying physics of the dynamical system. We select features by looking at their net characteristic magnitude instead of just the regression coefficients. We refer to this as 'scale based thresholding'.

As is well-known, the LASSO penalty is $\mathcal{P}(W) = \lambda ||W||_1$ (hyperparameter λ), which serves as a convex counterpart to the non-convex L_0 norm. The pitfalls of LASSO (even after removing the irrelevant features using the SAFE bounds [15]) are that it requires significant hyperparameter tuning and it is extremely sensitive to λ for correlated features (observed empirically). These motivate us to instead formulate a new approach to solve the sparse regression problem.

To overcome the difficulties in the application of LASSO (along with the SAFE rules), we formulate and solve its dual problem. For the LASSO solution to be unique, the feature matrix must satisfy the irrepresentability condition (IC) and beta-min condition [15]. The feature library violates the IC for highly correlated columns, leading to an unstable feature selection. However, even for highly correlated features, the corresponding dual LASSO solution is always unique [13]. The dual problem is given by Eq. (2), which is strictly convex in θ (implying a unique solution).

$$\max_{\theta} \mathcal{D}(\theta) = ||\dot{X}||_2^2 - ||\theta - \dot{X}||_2^2 \text{ such that } ||X^T \theta||_\infty \leq \lambda. \qquad (2)$$

Let $\hat{W}$ be a solution of Eq. (1) with LASSO penalty and $\hat{\theta}$ be the unique solution to the corresponding dual problem Eq. (2). Then a stationarity condition implies:

$$\hat{\theta} = \dot{X} - X\hat{W}. \qquad (3)$$

Even though LASSO does not have a unique $\hat{W}$, the fitted value $X\hat{W}$ is unique, as the optimization problem Eq. (1) is strongly convex in XW for $\mathcal{P}(W) = \lambda ||W||_1$. We make use of this by first computing a solution to the primal LASSO problem and then computing the unique dual solution by using the primal fitted value and Eq. (3). Once we have the unique dual solution $\hat{\theta}$, we complete the feature selection by using the dual active set, which is same as the primal active set with high probability under the IC [7]. The KKT conditions imply:

$$\hat{\theta}^T X_i = \text{sign}(\hat{W}_i) \text{ if } \hat{W}_i \neq 0 \text{ and } \hat{\theta}^T X_i \in (-1, 1) \text{ if } \hat{W}_i = 0. \tag{4}$$

Equation (4) gives us a direct way to compute the active dual set once we have $\hat{\theta}$. We discard the features for which $\hat{\theta}^T X_i \in (-1, 1)$ and retain the others. This does not give us a good fit of the solution, so to compute the coefficients accurately, we perform ridge regression ($\mathcal{P}(W) = \lambda_2 \|W\|_2^2$ over the active features. We refer to this new algorithm as 'dual LASSO feature selection'.

3   Regression Over a Dynamic Data Driven Feature Space

In this section, we consider cases where the feature library is not known and learned using DDDAS. If we have no prior belief over the form of the equations, we may not be able to construct an efficient feature library. In such situations, learning this library from data might be the most advantageous choice. The naïve approach of adding any new functions to the feature library until convergence can be very expensive and ill conditioned. A more principled and efficient approach is to make the use of orthogonal functions of some parametric family to construct this library, ensuring that the problem is always well conditioned. The drawback in this case is that the regressor may not be sparse over this feature library.

Starting with an empty library, we recursively add a feature to it and compute the corresponding loss function of the resulting fit by using STRidge (as will be described). If the loss function decreases by more than a certain fraction, we keep this feature. Otherwise, we discard it and look at the next orthogonal feature. Once every few addition timesteps, we perform a removal step to discard the feature(s) that do not result in a significant increase in the loss function. This ensures that we do not keep lower order functions that may not be required to describe the equations as higher order functions are added. Our algorithm is inspired by previous greedy feature development algorithms such as FoBa [14]. However, these algorithms require pre-determined full possible feature space, whereas we construct new features on the fly. Once the equations are obtained in terms of these orthogonal polynomials, we distill their sparse forms by using symbolic equation simplification [1].

To compute regressors over the orthogonal feature space, we use sequentially thresholded ridge regression (STRidge), developed by [12]. The idea is simple: we iteratively compute the ridge regression solution with decreasing penalty proportional to the condition number of X, and discard the components using scale based thresholding (Sect. 2). We iterate with ridge regression until there is no change in the feature space. As the feature matrix is orthonormal by construction, the analytical solution is $W = (1 + \lambda)^{-1} X^T \dot{X}$. The overall pseudocode for

learning the governing equations through adaptively growing the feature library
is given by Algorithm 1, and the corresponding results are presented in Sect. 4.

Algorithm 1. Learning Governing Equations through Adaptive Feature Library

---

Require: state parameters: $x = x_i^t, \dot{x} = \dot{x}_i^t$; orthogonal family $F_j(\bullet)$; feature addition
/ removal thresholds: $r_a \ (\leq 1), r_r \ (\geq 1), \lambda_0$; removal step frequency k_r
Initialize: $X = \emptyset, W = \mathbf{0}, t = 0, \mathcal{L} = \infty, k = 0$
while True **do**
    $X_t = [X, F_k(x)]$; solve the STRidge problem: $W_t = \text{STRidge}(\dot{X}, X_t, \lambda_0)$
    Compute the loss $\mathcal{L}_t = \left(\dot{X} - X_t W_t \right)^2$
    if $\mathcal{L}_t \leq r_a \mathcal{L}$ **then** $X = X_t$; $W = W_t$
    if   mod $(k, k_r) == 0$ **then**
        for $i = 1, \ldots, X.$shape[1] **do**
            $X_t = [X[:, 1 : i - 1], X[:, i + 1 : \text{end}]]$; solve: $W_t = \text{STRidge}(\dot{X}, X_t, \lambda_0)$
            Compute the loss $\mathcal{L}_t = \left(\dot{X} - X_t W_t \right)^2$
            if $\mathcal{L}_t \leq r_r \mathcal{L}$ **then** $X = X_t$; $W = W_t$
    $k = k + 1$.
    break if no change in feature space over multiple iterations.
Perform symbolic simplification of $\dot{X} = XW$ to obtain the final form of the equations

---

4   Results

4.1   Lorenz 63 System

For the first applications, our testbed will be the Lorenz 63 system $(n = 3)$
given by Eq. (5), and fixed polynomial feature libraries with $p = 3$, 10 and 20
$(m = 20, 286$ and 1771). The idea behind considering larger orders (p) is that it
highlights the poor performance of LASSO for highly correlated features.

$$\dot{x} = 10(yz - x) \ ; \quad \dot{y} = x(28 - z) \ ; \quad \dot{z} = xy - 2.667z \tag{5}$$

Figure 1a plots the number of non-zero features in the equations for different
p values. LASSO has a much higher number of non-zero terms, and this number
increases significantly with p (and m), indicating instability of the solution. Dual
LASSO feature selection performs very well, and the number of present features
does not change for the most part with p. Figure 1b plots the absolute weights
for the components for the $p = 3$ case for the $\dot{y}$ equation. Dual LASSO feature
selection retrieves the correct features (with accurate weights), while LASSO
detects the correct features but also detects high order features that have low
weights and are highly correlated to each other. This serves as a great validation
of the superiority of dual LASSO feature selection over conventional LASSO
feature selection for model discovery.

(a) 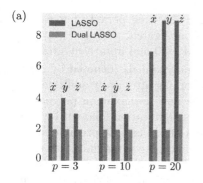   (b)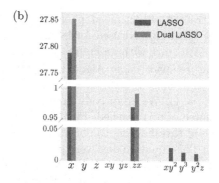

Fig. 1. (a) Number of nonzero terms for $\dot{x}, \dot{y}, \dot{z}$, and (b) absolute weights in the ODE for $\dot{y}$ ($p = 3$) for the Lorenz 63 system.

4.2 Marine Ecosystem Model

To demonstrate the capabilities of adaptive feature library growth algorithm (Sect. 3), we evaluate the learning scheme in a more complicated and realistic scenario. Hence, we now try to learn marine ecosystem models, which contain non-polynomial non-linearities. Realistic ecosystem models are very complex, but in broad-terms they can be seen as flow of food energy from nutrients, to phytoplanktons, to zooplanktons, to fishes, and finally recycling back to nutrients. Due to the lack of governing laws, and empirical nature of the development of these models, there are many different options in-terms of complexity and model parameterizations available, which could be highly nonlinear. But given the regional and seasonal differences at different locations in the world's oceans, one can quickly run out of all the options suggested by different biologists, and there is a need for DDDAS that adapt and learn new models from data [4,5,9,10]. Such models could be further adapted to run 'online', *i.e.* the inferred models can be updated as more data comes in, thereby improving and assimilating the observations on the fly. For the present test case, we consider a 3-component Nutrients-Phytoplankton-Detritus (NPD) model [6], given by,

$$\dot{N} = -\frac{r_{max}NP}{(k_N) + N} + l_N^P P + l_N^D D; \dot{P} = \frac{r_{max}NP}{(k_N) + N} - l_N^P P - l_D^P P; \dot{D} = l_D^P P - l_N^D D \quad (6)$$

where N, P and D are normalized biological concentrations. The involved parameters are the nutrient uptake rate for phytoplanktons, r_{max}, losses by respiration, l_N^P, and mortality l_D^P. Mineralization is simulated by the rate l_N^D. The choice of the parameter values determine the dynamical stability of this system, and it can vary between stable point, spiral to stable point, and stable limit cycle.

The parameter values chosen for the testcase are: $r_{max} = 1\ day^{-1}$, $K_N = 0.3\,\mathrm{mmol\ m^{-3}}$, $l_N^P = 0.50\ day^{-1}$, $l_D^P = 0.05\ day^{-1}$, $l_N^D = 0.06\ day^{-1}$, and $T = 1\ \mathrm{mmol}\ m^{-3}$, which makes the system spiral towards a stable point. Noise free data of the states and derivatives computed using a forward Euler scheme are extracted at a time-step of $\Delta t = 0.01\ day$ for the time period of $t = 0$ to $t = 50\ days$, and used for learning the system from scratch.

We start with an empty feature library and $W = \mathbf{0}$ and iteratively grow the feature space using Algorithm 1 with Legendre polynomials (denoted by $\mathbb{L}_p^{(\bullet)}$), $r_a = 0.85$, $r_r = 1.10$, $\lambda_0 = 1$, and removal step working after every addition step ($k_r = 1$). We adaptively grow the feature space until a maximum polynomial degree of 6 is reached. Finally, we use symbolic simplification followed by scale based thresholding to obtain the governing equations in an interpretable form.

This equation discovery problem presents a challenging paradigm as the exact evolution equations for the N and P states contain a non-polynomial nonlinearity. We expect that our algorithm captures an approximation of this term in the space spanned by (multivariable) polynomials. Equation (7) describes the final active terms of the governing equations obtained after the adaptive growth of the feature space along with their corresponding coefficients.

$$
\frac{dN}{dt} = 27.92\mathbb{L}_1^{(P)} + 0.053\mathbb{L}_1^{(D)} - 199.18\mathbb{L}_1^{(N)}\mathbb{L}_1^{(P)} + 77.13\mathbb{L}_2^{(N)}\mathbb{L}_1^{(P)}
$$
$$
- 194.94\mathbb{L}_3^{(N)}\mathbb{L}_1^{(P)} + 27.90\mathbb{L}_4^{(N)}\mathbb{L}_1^{(P)} + 1.12\mathbb{L}_4^{(P)}\mathbb{L}_2^{(D)} - 51.50\mathbb{L}_5^{(N)}\mathbb{L}_1^{(P)}
$$
$$
\frac{dP}{dt} = -28.65\mathbb{L}_1^{(P)} + 199.18\mathbb{L}_1^{(N)}\mathbb{L}_1^{(P)} - 77.13\mathbb{L}_2^{(N)}\mathbb{L}_1^{(P)} + 196.71\mathbb{L}_3^{(N)}\mathbb{L}_1^{(P)}
$$
$$
- 0.94\mathbb{L}_3^{(N)}\mathbb{L}_3^{(D)} - 27.22\mathbb{L}_4^{(N)}\mathbb{L}_1^{(P)} + 52.12\mathbb{L}_5^{(N)}\mathbb{L}_1^{(P)}
$$
$$
\frac{dD}{dt} = 0.0502\mathbb{L}_1^{(P)} - 0.061\mathbb{L}_1^{(D)} - 0.0003\mathbb{L}_3^{(N)}\mathbb{L}_2^{(D)}
$$

(7)

Amongst the $\binom{9}{3} = 84$ terms, only a few are determined to be active for each of the evolution equations. Once Eq. (7) is simplified using symbolic simplification and scale based thresholding (cutoff 0.1%), we obtain the functional form of the governing equations:

$$
\frac{dN}{dt} = 0.51P - 3.40NP + 11.55N^2P - 36.30N^3P + 124.69N^4P - 382.72N^5P
$$
$$
\frac{dP}{dt} = -0.56P + 3.30NP - 10.78N^2P + 37.76N^3P - 127.16N^4P + 378.60N^5P
$$
$$
\frac{dD}{dt} = 0.0505P - 0.062D - 0.0002N^2D
$$

(8)

We write Eq. (8) in a more concise form as given by Eq. (9). The terms within the parentheses in the first two expressions is the truncated Taylor series for $0.3/(0.3 + N)$ (expanded around $N = 0$, with $\tilde{N} = N/0.3$.) that our algorithm learns. This is the best representation of the non-polynomial nonlinearity in the available subspace. Thus, without any prior information, our adaptive algorithm infers the presence and the best approximation of the present nonlinearity. Unfortunately, our algorithm does not recognize the presence of the $l_N^D D$ term in the equation for dN/dt, but it does capture it in the dD/dt equation. It also incorrectly adds a term ND^2 to the evolution equation of D with a very small coefficient. However, all other active terms are correctly chosen and their corresponding learned coefficients are very close to the actual values from Eq. (6).

This example effectively shows the superiority of our algorithm in identifying the nonlinearities present in the governing equations without any prior information.

$$\frac{dN}{dt} = 0.51P - P\tilde{N}\left(1.02 - 1.04\tilde{N} + 0.98\tilde{N}^2 - 1.01\tilde{N}^3 + 0.93\tilde{N}^4\right)$$

$$\frac{dP}{dt} = -0.56P + P\tilde{N}\left(0.99 - 0.97\tilde{N} + 1.02\tilde{N}^2 - 1.03\tilde{N}^3 + 0.92\tilde{N}^4\right)$$

$$\frac{dD}{dt} = 0.0505P - 0.062D + 0.00067ND^2$$

$$\dot{N} \approx 0.5P - \frac{PN}{0.3 + N}; \dot{P} \approx -0.50P - 0.06P + \frac{PN}{0.3 + N}; \dot{D} \approx 0.0505P - 0.062D$$

(9)

5   Conclusions and Future Work

We investigated the LASSO and developed the dual LASSO feature selection algorithm and dynamic data driven feature learning approaches to solve the problem of discovering governing equations only from state parameter data. After defining the problem and the solution methodology, we addressed the limitations of LASSO in feature selection through a new algorithm, referred to as 'dual LASSO feature selection', that relies on the uniqueness of the dual solution for the active set selection. This was followed by proposing a new methodology to learn the governing equations from scratch by dynamically building the feature library using appropriate orthogonal functional basis. We showcased results of the learning schemes on the classic Lorenz 63 system and also a marine ecosystem model with a non-polynomial nonlinearity. We found that our adaptive subspace algorithm effectively learns a Taylor series approximation of such a nonlinearity, even when no prior information about the presence and the nature of this nonlinearity is provided. Future directions involve extending the ideas of feature library building to the construction of the functions to be added through a mix of a larger family of orthogonal functions. It would be interesting to study the applications of these algorithms in the presence of model and observation noise, and to higher dimensional systems often encountered in science and engineering. Further, using the learned system to guide future observations would also close the loop for the DDDAS paradigm.

Acknowledgments. We are grateful to the Office of Naval Research for support under grants N00014-19-1-2693 (IN-BDA) and N00014-20-1-2023 (MURI ML-SCOPE) to the Massachusetts Institute of Technology.

References

1. Bailey, D.H., Borwein, J.M., Kaiser, A.D.: Automated simplification of large symbolic expressions. J. Symbol. Comput. **60**, 120–136 (2014)
2. Brunton, S.L., Proctor, J.L., Kutz, J.N.: Discovering governing equations from data by sparse identification of nonlinear dynamical systems. PNAS **13**, 3932–3937 (2016)

3. Darema, F.: Dynamic data driven applications systems: a new paradigm for application simulations and measurements. In: Bubak, M., van Albada, G.D., Sloot, P.M.A., Dongarra, J. (eds.) ICCS 2004. LNCS, vol. 3038, pp. 662–669. Springer, Heidelberg (2004). https://doi.org/10.1007/978-3-540-24688-6_86

4. Davis, C.S., Steele, J.H.: Biological/physical modeling of upper ocean processes. Technical report, Woods Hole Oceanographic Institution (1994)

5. Evangelinos, C., Chang, R., Lermusiaux, P.F.J., Patrikalakis, N.M.: Rapid real-time interdisciplinary ocean forecasting using adaptive sampling and adaptive modeling and legacy codes: component encapsulation using XML. In: Sloot, P.M.A., Abramson, D., Bogdanov, A.V., Gorbachev, Y.E., Dongarra, J.J., Zomaya, A.Y. (eds.) ICCS 2003. LNCS, vol. 2660, pp. 375–384. Springer, Heidelberg (2003). https://doi.org/10.1007/3-540-44864-0_39

6. Fennel, W., Neumann, T.: Introduction to the modelling of marine ecosystems. Elsevier (2014)

7. Gauraha, N.: Dual lasso selector. arXiv preprint arXiv:1703.06602 (2017)

8. Gupta, A., Haley, P.J., Subramani, D.N., Lermusiaux, P.F.J.: Fish modeling and Bayesian learning for the Lakshadweep Islands. In: OCEANS 2019 MTS/IEEE SEATTLE. pp. 1–10 (2019)

9. Lermusiaux, P.F.J.: Adaptive modeling, adaptive data assimilation and adaptive sampling. Physica D **230**(1), 172–196 (2007). https://doi.org/10.1016/j.physd.2007.02.014

10. Lermusiaux, P.F.J., et al.: Adaptive coupled physical and biogeochemical ocean predictions: a conceptual basis. In: Bubak, M., van Albada, G.D., Sloot, P.M.A., Dongarra, J. (eds.) ICCS 2004. LNCS, vol. 3038, pp. 685–692. Springer, Heidelberg (2004). https://doi.org/10.1007/978-3-540-24688-6_89

11. Lorenz, E.N.: Deterministic nonperiodic flow. J. Atmos. Sci. **20**(2), 130–141 (1963)

12. Rudy, S.H., Brunton, S.L., Proctor, J.L., Kutz, J.N.: Data-driven discovery of partial differential equations. Sci. Adv. **3**(4), e1602614 (2017)

13. Tibshirani, R.J., et al.: The lasso problem and uniqueness. Electr. J. Stat. **7**, 1456–1490 (2013)

14. Zhang, T.: Adaptive forward-backward greedy algorithm for sparse learning with linear models. In: Advances in Neural Information Processing Systems (2009)

15. Zhao, P., Yu, B.: On model selection consistency of lasso. J. Mach. Learn. Res. **7**, 2541–2563 (2006)

Improving Prediction Confidence in Learning-Enabled Autonomous Systems

Dimitrios Boursinos[✉] and Xenofon Koutsoukos

Vanderbilt University, Nashville, TN, USA
{dimitrios.boursinos,xenofon.koutsoukos}@vanderbilt.edu

Abstract. Autonomous systems use extensively learning-enabled components such as deep neural networks (DNNs) for prediction and decision making. In this paper, we utilize a feedback loop between learning-enabled components used for classification and the sensors of an autonomous system in order to improve the confidence of the predictions. We design a classifier using Inductive Conformal Prediction (ICP) based on a triplet network architecture in order to learn representations that can be used to quantify the similarity between test and training examples. The method allows computing confident set predictions with an error rate predefined using a selected significance level. A feedback loop that queries the sensors for a new input is used to further refine the predictions and increase the classification accuracy. The method is computationally efficient, scalable to high-dimensional inputs, and can be executed in a feedback loop with the system in real-time. The approach is evaluated using a traffic sign recognition dataset and the results show that the error rate is reduced.

Keywords: Learning-enabled components · Prediction confidence · Conformal prediction

1 Introduction

Autonomous systems are equipped with sensors to observe the environment and take control decisions. Such systems can benefit from methods that allow to improve prediction and decision making through a feedback loop that queries the sensor inputs when more information is needed [7]. Such a paradigm has been used in a variety of applications such as multimedia context assessment [2], aerial vehicle tracking [14], automatic target recognition [4], self-aware aerospace vehicles [1], and smart cities [8]. In particular, autonomous systems can utilize perception learning-enabled components (LECs) to observe the environment and make predictions used for decision making and control. LECs such as deep neural

This work is supported in part by AFOSR DDDAS through contract FA9550-18-1-0126 program and DARPA through contract number FA8750-18-C-0089. Any opinions, findings, and conclusions or recommendations expressed are those of the author(s) and do not necessarily reflect the views of the sponsor.

F. Darema et al. (Eds.): DDDAS 2020, LNCS 12312, pp. 217–224, 2020.
https://doi.org/10.1007/978-3-030-61725-7_26

networks (DNNs) can generalize well on test data that come from the same distribution as the training data and their predictions can be trusted. However, during the system operation the input data may be different than the training data resulting to large prediction errors. An approach to address this challenge is to quantify the uncertainty of the prediction and query the sensors for additional inputs in order to improve the confidence of the prediction. The approach must be computationally efficient so it can be executed in real-time for closing the loop with the system.

Computing a confidence measure along with the model's predictions is essential in safety critical applications where we need to take into account the cost of errors and decide about the acceptable error rate. Neural networks for classification typically have a softmax layer to produce probability-like outputs. However, these probabilities cannot be used reliably as they tend to be too high, they are overconfident, even for inputs coming from the training distribution [9]. The softmax probabilities can be calibrated to be closer to the actual probabilities scaling them with factors computed from the training data. Different methods that have been proposed to compute scaling factors include temperature scaling [9], Platt scaling [13], and isotonic regression [16]. Although such methods can compute well-calibrated confidence values, it is not clear how they can be used for querying the sensors for additional inputs. Conformal prediction (CP) is another framework used to compute set predictions with well-calibrated error bounds [3]. The set predictions can be computed efficiently leveraging a calibration data set [11]. However, such approaches do not scale for high-dimensional inputs such as camera images. In our prior work, we have developed methods handling high-dimensional inputs using inductive conformal prediction (ICP) [5,6].

This paper extends our prior work by designing a feedback loop between LECs used for classification and the sensors of an autonomous system in order to improve the confidence of the predictions. We design a classifier using ICP based on a triplet network architecture in order to learn representations that can be used to quantify the similarity between test and training examples. Given a significance level, the method allows computing confident set predictions. A feedback loop that queries the sensors for a new input is used to further refine the predictions and increase the classification accuracy. The method is computationally efficient, scalable to high-dimensional inputs, and can be executed in a feedback loop with the system in real-time. The approach is evaluated using a traffic sign recognition dataset and the results show that the error rate is reduced.

2   Triplet-Based ICP

We consider an autonomous system that takes actions based on its state in the environment as shown in Fig. 1. For example, a self-driving vehicle needs to take control actions based on the traffic signs it encounters. We design a classifier using ICP based on a triplet network architecture in order to learn representations that can be used to quantify the similarity between test and training

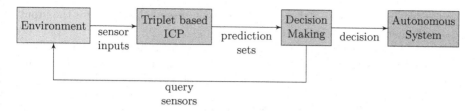

Fig. 1. Feedback loop between the decision-making process and sensing

examples. Given a significance level, the method allows computing confident set predictions. A feedback loop that queries the sensors for a new input is used to further refine the predictions and increase the classification accuracy.

Triplet networks are DNN architectures trained to learn representations of the input data for distance learning [10]. The last layer of a triplet network computes a representation $Net(x)$ of the input x. For training, a triplet network is composed using three copies of the same neural network with shared parameters. It is trained on batches formed with triplets of data points. Each of these triplets has an anchor data point x, a positive data point x^+ that belong to the same class as x and a negative data point x^- of a different class. The objective is to maximize the distance between inputs of different classes $|Net(x) - Net(x^-)|$ and minimize the distance of inputs belonging to the same class $|Net(x) - Net(x^+)|$. To achieve this, training uses the loss function:

$$Loss(x, x^+, x^-) = max(|Net(x) - Net(x^+)| - |Net(x) - Net(x^-)| + \alpha, 0)$$

where α is the margin between positive and negative pairs.

The simplest way to form triplets is to randomly sample anchor data points from the training set and augment them by randomly selecting one training sample with the same label as the anchor and one sample with a different label. However, for many of these (x, x^+, x^-) triplets $|Net(x) - Net(x^-)| >> |Net(x) - Net(x^+)| + \alpha$, which provides very little information for distance learning and leads to slow training and poor performance. The training can be improved by carefully mining the training data [15]. For each training iteration, first, the anchor training samples are randomly selected. For each anchor, the hardest positive sample is chosen, that is a sample from the same class as the anchor that is located the furthest away from the anchor. Then, the triplets are formed by mining all the hard negative samples, that is the samples that satisfy $|Net(x) - Net(x^-)| < |Net(x) - Net(x^+)|$. When the training is completed, only one of the three identical DNN copies is used to map an input x to its embedding representation $Net(x)$.

Consider a training set $\{z_1, \ldots, z_l\}$, where each $z_i \in Z$ is a pair (x_i, y_i) with x_i the feature vector and y_i the label. We also consider a test input x_{l+1} which we wish to classify. The underlying assumption of ICP is that all examples (x_i, y_i), $i = 1, 2, \ldots$ are independent and identically distributed (IID) generated from the same but typically unknown probability distribution. For a chosen classification significance level $\epsilon \in [0,1]$, ICP generates a set of possible labels Γ^ϵ for the input x_{l+1} such that $P(y_{l+1} \notin \Gamma^\epsilon) < \epsilon$.

Central to the framework is the use of *nonconformity measures* (NCM), a metric that indicates how different an example z_{l+1} is from the examples of the training set $z_1, \ldots, z_l$. A NCM that can be computed efficiently in real-time is the *k-Nearest Neighbors* (k-NN) [12] defined in the embedding space generated by the triplet network. The k-NN NCM finds the k most similar examples in the training data and counts how many of those are labeled different than the candidate label y of a test input x. We denote $f : X \to V$ the mapping from the input space X to the embedding space V defined by the triplet's last layer. After the training of the triplet is complete, we compute and store the encodings $v_i = f(x_i)$ for the training data x_i. Given a test example x with encoding $v = f(x)$, we compute the k-nearest neighbors in V and store their labels in a multi-set Ω. The k-NN nonconformity of the test example x with a candidate label y is defined as:

$$\alpha(x, y) = |i \in \Omega : i \neq y|$$

For statistical significance testing, p-values are assigned based on the computed NCM scores using a calibration set of labeled data that are not used for training. The training set $(z_1 \ldots z_l)$ is split into two parts, the *proper training set* $(z_1 \ldots z_m)$ of size $m < l$ that is used for the training of the triplet network and the *calibration set* $(z_{m+1} \ldots z_l)$ of size $l - m$ that is used only for the computation of the p-values. The empirical p-value assigned to a possible label j of an input x is defined as the fraction of nonconformity scores of the calibration data that are equal or larger than the nonconformity score of a test input:

$$p_j(x) = \frac{|\{\alpha \in A : \alpha \geq \alpha(x, j)\}|}{|A|}.$$

The p-values are used to form the sets of candidate labels for a given significance level ϵ. The label j is added to Γ^ϵ if $p_j(x) > \epsilon$.

3   Feedback-Loop for Querying the Sensors

Only the prediction sets Γ^ϵ that have exactly one candidate label can directly be used towards the final decision. When $|\Gamma^\epsilon| \neq 1$ the approach queries the sensors for a new input. Incorrect classifications are more likely to happen during the first time steps of the process as every sensor input offers new information that may lead to a more confident prediction. For example, in the traffic sign recognition task, it is more likely for an incorrect classification to happen when the sign is far away from the vehicle and the image has low resolution as shown in Fig. 2. To avoid such incorrect classifications, in our method the final decision is made only after k consecutive identical predictions. The parameter k represents a trade-off between robustness and decision time, as larger k leads to additional delay but more confident decisions. Further, very low k values may lead to incorrect decisions while very large values may not allow a timely a decision.

$t = 1$ $\qquad\qquad$ $t = 10$ $\qquad\qquad$ $t = 20$ $\qquad\qquad$ $t = 30$

Fig. 2. Traffic sign over time (in frames)

The ICP framework produces well-calibrated prediction sets Γ^ϵ when inputs are IID. Depending on how small the chosen significance level is, Γ^ϵ may include a different number of candidate labels. The classification of an input requires $|\Gamma^\epsilon| = 1$. In our previous work [5,6], we use a labeled validation set to compute the minimum significance level ϵ to reduce the prediction sets with more than one candidate label. However, in dynamic systems, sensor measurements change over time. Each new input in a sequence is related to previous inputs and the inputs are not IID. In this case, even though the calculated significance level ϵ will not lead to $|\Gamma^\epsilon| > 1$, the actual error rate may not be bounded by ϵ.

The main idea is to utilize a feedback-loop in order to lower the error-rate. In order to reduce the incorrect predictions that may occur especially for low quality inputs, we require that $|\Gamma^\epsilon| = 1$ with identical single candidate label for k consecutive sensor measurements. When this condition is satisfied for an input sequence, the prediction can be used for decision making by the autonomous system.

4   Evaluation

Experimental Setup. We apply the proposed method to the German Traffic Sign Recognition Benchmark (GTSRB). A vehicle uses an RGB camera to recognize the traffic signs that are present in its surroundings. The dataset consists of 43 classes of signs and provides videos with 30 frames as well as individual images. The data are collected in various light conditions and include different artifacts like motion blur. The image resolution depends on how far the sign is from the vehicle as shown in Fig. 2. Since the input size depends on the distance between the vehicle and the sign, we convert all inputs to size $96 \times 96 \times 3$. 10% of the available sequences is randomly sampled to form the sequence test set. 10% of the individual frames is randomly sampled to form another test set. All the remaining frames are shuffled and 80% of them are used for training and 20% are used for calibration and validation.

The triplet network is formed using three identical convolutional DNNs with shared parameters. We use a modified version of the VGG-16 architecture using only the first four blocks because of the reduced input size. A dense layer of 128 units is used to generate the embedding representation of the inputs. All the experiments run in a desktop computer equipped with and Intel(R) Core(TM) i9-9900K CPU and 32 GB RAM and a Geforce RTX 2080 GPU with 8 GB memory.

Table 1. Triplet-based classifier performance

Training accuracy	Validation accuracy	IID testing	Sequence testing
0.991	0.987	0.986	0.948

Model Performance. The triplet network can be used for classification of inputs using a k-Nearest Neighbors classifier in the embedding space. We first investigate how well the triplet network classifier is trained looking at the accuracy of the two test sets. One basic hypothesis of machine learning models is that the training and testing data sets should consist of IID samples. This is confirmed in Table 1 where the accuracy for the testing set of IID examples is similar to the training accuracy while the testing accuracy for the set that includes sequences is lower.

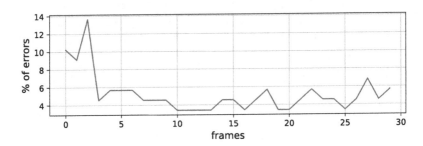

Fig. 3. Average error per frame for all the test sequences

In order to investigate which frames are responsible for the larger error-rate in the sequences we plot the average error-rate per frame for the 30 frames of all the test sequences in Fig. 3. The early frames of each sequence tend to have more incorrect classifications as expected since the sign images have lower resolution.

Table 2. Triplet-based ICP performance for individual frames

	IID Test		Sequences test	
ϵ	Errors	Multiples	Errors	Multiples
0.017	1.7%	0%	5.6%	0%

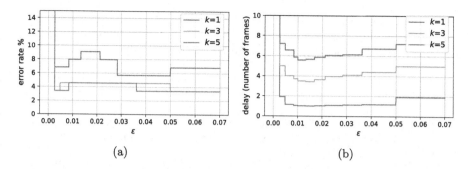

Fig. 4. (a) Error-rate and (b) average number of frames until a decision.

ICP Performance. We apply ICP on single inputs to understand how the classifier performs without the feedback loop. The ICP is evaluated for both test sets in Table 2. An error corresponds to the case when the ground truth for a sensor input is not in the computed prediction set. We compute the smallest significance level ϵ that does not produce sets of multiple classes using the validation set. Similar to the point classifier, the ICP classifier produces well-calibrated predictions only for the IID test inputs.

Improving Prediction Accuracy. We can improve the LEC classification performance using the feedback loop as described in Sect. 3. As we can see in Fig. 3, the first frames of a sign tend to have more incorrect predictions as they have lower resolution and they lack details. Based on the feedback loop, the LEC uses a new input from the camera until the prediction remains the same for k consecutive frames. Experimenting with different values of k, Fig. 4 shows that as k increases, the error-rate decreases for most of the ϵ values but the number of frames required to take a decision increases. When $\epsilon < 0.003$ the classifier enhanced with the feedback loop could not reach a decision. We also evaluate the efficiency of this classifier regarding to the real-time requirements. A decision for each new sensor query takes on average 1 ms, which can be used with typical video frame rates. The memory required to apply the method consists of the memory used to store the representations of the proper training set and the nonconformity scores of the calibration data (45.9 MB) and the memory used to store the triplet network (28.5 MB) for a total of 74.4 MB.

5 Conclusions

The ICP framework can be used to produce prediction sets that include the correct class with a given confidence. When the inputs to the system are sequential and not IID, applying ICP is not straightforward. Motivated by DDDAS, we design a feedback loop for handling sequential inputs by querying the sensors when a confident prediction cannot be made. The evaluation results demonstrate that when the inputs to the autonomous system are not IID, the error-rate cannot be bounded. However, the addition of the feedback loop can lower the error-rate by classifying a number of consecutive inputs until a confident decision can be made. The running time and memory requirements indicate that this approach can be used in real-time applications.

References

1. Allaire, D., et al.: An offline/online DDDAS capability for self-aware aerospace vehicles. Procedia Comput. Sci. **18**, 1959–1968 (2013). 2013 International Conference on Computational Science
2. Aved, A., Blasch, E.: Multi-int query language for DDDAS designs. Procedia Comput. Sci. **51**, 2518–2532 (2015)
3. Balasubramanian, V., Ho, S.S., Vovk, V.: Conformal Prediction for Reliable Machine Learning: Theory, Adaptations and Applications, 1st edn. Morgan Kaufmann Publishers Inc., San Francisco (2014)
4. Blasch, E., Seetharaman, G., Darema, F.: Dynamic data driven applications systems (DDDAS) modeling for automatic target recognition. In: Sadjadi, F.A., Mahalanobis, A. (eds.) Automatic Target Recognition XXIII, International Society for Optics and Photonics, SPIE, vol. 8744, pp. 165–174 (2013)
5. Boursinos, D., Koutsoukos, X.: Assurance monitoring of cyber-physical systems with machine learning components. arXiv preprint arXiv:2001.05014 (2020)
6. Boursinos, D., Koutsoukos, X.: Trusted confidence bounds for learning enabled cyber-physical systems. arXiv preprint arXiv:2003.05107 (2020)
7. Darema, F.: Grid computing and beyond: the context of dynamic data driven applications systems. Proc. IEEE **93**(3), 692–697 (2005)
8. Fujimoto, R.M., et al.: Dynamic data driven application systems for smart cities and urban infrastructures. In: 2016 Winter Simulation Conference (WSC), pp. 1143–1157. IEEE (2016)
9. Guo, C., Pleiss, G., Sun, Y., Weinberger, K.Q.: On calibration of modern neural networks. In: Proceedings of the 34th International Conference on Machine Learning, ICML 2017, vol. 70, pp. 1321–1330. JMLR.org (2017)
10. Hoffer, E., Ailon, N.: Deep metric learning using triplet network. In: Feragen, A., Pelillo, M., Loog, M. (eds.) SIMBAD 2015. LNCS, vol. 9370, pp. 84–92. Springer, Cham (2015). https://doi.org/10.1007/978-3-319-24261-3_7
11. Papadopoulos, H.: Inductive conformal prediction: theory and application to neural networks. In: Tools in artificial intelligence. IntechOpen (2008)
12. Papernot, N., McDaniel, P.: Deep k-nearest neighbors: towards confident, interpretable and robust deep learning. arXiv preprint arXiv:1803.04765 (2018)
13. Platt, J.C.: Probabilistic outputs for support vector machines and comparisons to regularized likelihood methods. In: Advances In Large Margin Classifiers, pp. 61–74. MIT Press (1999)
14. Uzkent, B., Hoffman, M.J., Vodacek, A.: Integrating hyperspectral likelihoods in a multidimensional assignment algorithm for aerial vehicle tracking. IEEE J. Sel. Top. Appl. Earth Obs. Remote Sens. **9**(9), 4325–4333 (2016)
15. Xuan, H., Stylianou, A., Pless, R.: Improved embeddings with easy positive triplet mining. arXiv preprint arXiv:1904.04370 (2019)
16. Zadrozny, B., Elkan, C.: Transforming classifier scores into accurate multiclass probability estimates. In: Proceedings of the Eighth ACM SIGKDD International Conference on Knowledge Discovery and Data Mining, KDD 2002, pp. 694–699. ACM, New York (2002)

Posters Session-1

Physics-Based SAR Modeling and Simulation for Large-Scale Data Generation of Multi-platform Vehicles for Deep Learning-Based ATR

Branndon Jones$^{(\boxtimes)}$, Ali Ahmadibeni, Maxine Beard, and Amir Shirkhodaie

Tennessee State University, Nashville, TN 37209, USA
{bjone161,aahmadib,mbeard}@my.tnstate.edu,
ashirkhodaie@tnstate.edu

Abstract. One critical challenge of Automatic Target Recognition (ATR) systems are that of effective modeling and interpretation of sensory data obtained under constantly changing dynamic environments. In this paper, we address physics-based modeling and simulation of multi-platform vehicles and propose a method for systematic generation of synthetic SAR Imagery for training of Deep Learning (DL) techniques. Starting with computer-aided design (CAD) models of aerial, ground and maritime vehicles, we present a multi-layer method for describing physics-based models of these objects. Next, by considering SAR system constraints and modeling far-field incident and backscattering radiation waves returns, we construct realistic simulated (i.e., synthetic) SAR imagery of the test vehicles and annotate them semantically to aid their DL training. To evaluate and verify the effectiveness of this approach, we compare our synthetically generated SAR imagery against the real SAR images. Several examples of our test scenarios are demonstrated and explained including our post image modulation technique that further enhances realisms of the synthetic SAR images. Finally, we discuss the implication of our technical approach in support of dynamic data-driven applications systems.

Keywords: Deep learning · SAR · ATR · Target detection · Physics-based modeling · Dataset generation

1 Introduction

Automatic Target Recognition (ATR) of objects based on Synthetic Aperture Radar (SAR) is highly in for both military and civilian applications. In particular, SAR offers a unique capability as it is an all-day, all-weather remote sensing system. Due to inherent nature of radar, SAR images often suffer from a low signal-to-noise ratio (SNR) making them difficult visual images to analyze.

For reliable training of SAR image classifiers, there is a need for rich training datasets of target objects with proper annotations. However, such datasets are nonexistent or at

© Springer Nature Switzerland AG 2020
F. Darema et al. (Eds.): DDDAS 2020, LNCS 12312, pp. 227–235, 2020.
https://doi.org/10.1007/978-3-030-61725-7_27

least are not publicly available. Furthermore, generating rich SAR imagery datasets in the real world is also impractical. Providentially, by developing an Electromagnetic (EM) modeling and simulation software conducive to SAR imaging it would be possible to introduce a variety of different target objects of interest in the physics-based virtual environment (VE) and employ a simulated model of a physics-based SAR system to generate corresponding synthetic SAR images of different test vehicles [1–3]. In this paper, we demonstrate how to generate synthetic SAR imagery of test objects in the VE under different operational contexts and produce high-quality simulated SAR imagery ideal for DL systems training and testing that eventually leads to achievement of transfer learning. The proposed approach can also support of training of dynamic data-driven applications systems including data assimilation and adaptive learning.

The organization of this paper is as such. Firstly, we explain our method for preparation of the physics-based modeling of test vehicles prior to generating their simulated SAR images. Secondly, we describe our scheme for systematic simulated SAR imaging of test vehicles from different perspective views. Thirdly, we explain our method for composition of a simulated speckled SAR image via implication of multiplicative additive noise to a synthetically generated reflectivity map of a test vehicle to enhance its SAR signature characteristics close to the actual SAR images. Fourthly, we discuss how this work impacts the DDDAS data-centric real-time training and learning adaptation paradigm. Lastly, we present the conclusion of this work.

2 EM Modeling and Simulation

In this work, we model EM radiation wave rays of an actual SAR system similar to projected and bouncing rays in the Ray Tracing (RT) technique. RT is a popular Computer Graphics technique for rendering 3D graphical scenes with photo-realistic illumination and reflectivity realism. In RT, this is accomplished by tracing the path of multiple light beams originated from a source and propagate them toward a scene systematically. The system keeps track of rays as they hit surfaces and bounce off of them to hit other neighboring surfaces. Similar to RT, we model SAR projected radiation waves as far field incident radiation waves bouncing off of object surfaces in the scene and becoming incident toward the radar antenna due to multiple residual rebounds. Surfaces may be of different material, texture, and curvature, hence they possess different physics properties and interact with the incident radiation wave differently based on principle laws of optics. Some portion of the produced backscattered radiations incident to the radar antenna are returned in a different strength and phase. Depending on the hit surface characteristics (i.e., geometrical formation and physical properties), each radiation wave may result a specular reflection, a refraction, or diffraction. Different combination of such radiation reflection, emission, and absorption could also happen. Using the wave propagation principle, we simulate the aspect of our simulated SAR imaging. In our physics-based simulation, we model environment objects geometrically based on their Computer-Aided Design (CAD) model. Primarily, we convert such a CAD model to a physics-based model in compliance with our EM simulation modeling requirements. Based on wave propagation modeling as explained in [1, 2], we treat our simulated SAR system function similar to a monostatic high-density phased-array radar and form a scaled SAR reflective map corresponding to the EM radiation reflectivity of objects in the far field view of the simulated SAR system.

In our model, the radiation backscattering may take different forms: diffused, reflected, or diffracted. The acute case of specularity reflections are also exclusive and modeled under unique conditions. Furthermore, the bounced-off rays from certain surfaces may hit other neighboring surfaces and creating a double-bounce incidental echo return (e.g., in case of walls), or turn into a resonance (e.g., in case of a hole) under certain frequency wavelength, or simply vanishing into empty space as illustrated in case of a military

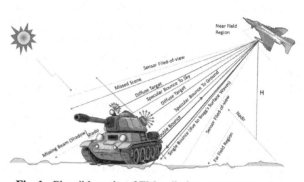

Fig. 1. Plausible paths of EM radiation wave propagation.

tank in Fig. 1. Our model has provisions to deal with such cases as a situation may arises. Our model limits the number of radiation wave bounces to three.

The portion of radiation energy returned back to the antenna is scaled proportional to the cosine angle of incident ray with respect to surface norm. This reflection is further modulated with respect to surface material reflectivity, texture, and, roughness characteristics.

3 IRIS Electromagnetic Modeling and Simulation

In this project, we employed IRIS software. IRIS stands for Integrated Robotics Interface System developed at Tennessee State University, by the third author, [12]. IRIS offers an electromagnetic computation engine, called IRIS-EM. IRIS-EM engine provides an automatic interface for obtaining synthetic SAR images per user defined operating conditions. While generating systematic SAR datasets in the physical environment is tedious, time-consuming, and costly – in simulation, this task can be rather seamlessly performed with confidence and systematically. IRIS offers two integrated interfaces: a virtual environment simulation model, called IRIS-VESM and an intelligent CAD interface, called IRIS-ICAD. The latter interface is used for preparing physics-based object models from standard CAD models. IRIS-EM offers essential utilities for generating synthetic multi-modal sensor imagery (e.g., SAR, ISAR, Pol-SAR, In-SAR, Thermal-IR, LIDAR, RCS, and Doppler SAR) per user specified requirements. Such requirements fall into five categories, (1) sensor operating parameters, (2) imaging formation, (3) remote sensing staging, (4) sensor modality selection, and (5) scanned images annotation and archiving requirements.

These synthetic images are obtained based on physics-based implication of the governing laws and principles of EM, thermodynamics, optics, hydrodynamics, and kinematics (in case of Doppler SAR imaging) [1, 2]. To further improve the realism of such imagery dataset, we add additive multiplication speckled noises (modeled statistically based on publically accessible SAR imagery) and modulate them to represent different operational contexts (e.g., to different atmospheric conditions reasonably meeting a marine environment context). The nature of noises in a physical SAR system is encumbered and come from many sources: antenna transmitter, atmospheric media with varying density and EM absorption rate, object surface curvature irregularities (e.g., textures and roughness), object radar cross section equivalency, antenna receiver, electronics noise, and inherent algorithm processing noise. From a practical standpoint, it is impractical to assume such noises are known ahead of time.

Other peculiarity of SAR images that we produce, is related to modeling of residual specularity reflectivities that is very circumstantial – yet they could happen unexpectedly when the radiation optical circumstance is right and the returned radiation wave is perfectly incident to the radar antenna. Therefore, our entire SAR image synthesis is composed of three main steps: (1) far field EM modeling for test object reflectivity map generation, (2) Augmentation of additive multiplicative speckled noise modulated per type of background environment intended conditioned via considered operating radar parameters, and (3) precise Sparkled effects with varying degrees of implication. Figure 2 demonstrates this process. For each CAD model, we specify eight layers of meta-data including: (1) Geometrical Layer, (2) Material Layer, (3) Physical Layer, (4) EM Layer, (5) Thermal Layer, (6) Optics Layer, (7) Kinematic Layer, and (8) Environment Layer. Details of these layers is described in elsewhere [1] and in brevity of space limitation, we do not discuss them here.

The RT technique is computational extensive. To avoid this overburden, we developed an efficient optimized RT technique that significantly lowers its computational time. Our technique is based on an octree subspace modeling of surface patches representing the body of physics-based objects within the field of view of SAR system.

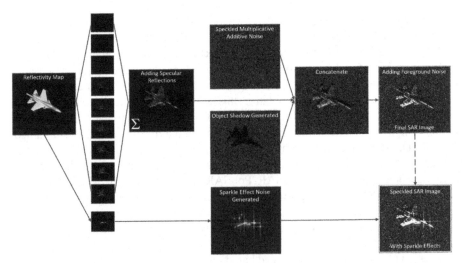

Fig. 2. The IRIS scheme for generating simulated SAR imagery.

For increased efficiency, we initially limit object surfaces falling within the prism of field of view of the SAR system. This step is fast and limits the scope of the RT technique to a subspace of surface scatters. Furthermore, we form a three-level octree structure of observable subspace surfaces for efficient determination of nearby surfaces to a projected ray. Further, we limit our ray tracing extend to three-bounce only within the lowest subspace observable scatters. One problem with this approach is that there would be some surfaces not entirely fitting into their spatially arranged subspace volumes. We mitigate this problem by placing the oversized surfaces into as many subspace volumes that they occupy. This optimization method improves computational aspects of RT technique significantly. With utilization of multi-core GPU-based computers, this computational time burden can be of a lesser concern.

3.1 Radar Imaging Scheme

IRIS-SAR interface implements an automation system that saves significant manual labor and provides consistency in datasets generation. Through this process, the physics-based objects can be allocated to an automation queue and the desired radar configuration (e.g., range, elevation, and rotation angles), and the type of modality for scanning can be specified. The permissible modalities are as follows: Depth Map, Height Map, Reflectivity Map (RM), Specularity Map, Phase Map, Polarimetric Map, RCS Map, and Doppler Map. This interface automatically chooses each object individually, performs the scanning and saves the output images. After the completion of imaging an object, IRIS-EM interface automatically chooses the next object for scanning and saves its generated images in assorted image modalities in multiple folders automatically.

An automated annotation scheme was also developed for proper labeling of scanned imagery and archiving them systematically. This annotation information is crucial for batch processing and training of deep learning image classifiers. Our filename annotation convention consists of the object class ID, object name, scanning modality, object number in queue, scanning range, and azimuth (Rotation) and elevation angles.

3.2 Salient Subspace Reflection Extraction

We initially generate synthetic SAR images based on their reflectivity map representation. The reflectivity map represents the distribution of backscattering of EM waves as they bounce off of the surfaces of the object in the environment. Using a salient subspace reflectivity extraction (SSRE) technique, we identify high reflectivity points of the test vehicles. These salient reflectivity points correspond to surface meshes having geometrical shape factors similar to trihedral, dihedral, plates, cylinders, edges, wedges and fillets that are generally recognized as returning light illumination with high reflectivity strength. The reflectivity map is divided into nine subspaces to form a hierarchical subspace structure of the reflectivity responses. The topmost subspace designates maximum object reflectivity regions. These regions are registered by their center points. The center points are a representative of the saddle-point of high reflectivity material with sharp curvatures, edges wedges and plates whose local norm is perpendicular to an incident ray. These center points also correspond to direct specular noise, i.e. sparkles. The information from the topmost subspace is used in the final synthetic SAR image formation to produce random-scale illumination sparkles. The pertaining point clouds of each intermediate sub-space are aggregated using a Gaussian filter and a mean filter. This process is illustrated in the Fig. 2.

3.3 Noise Augmentation and Shadow Formation

Multiplicative noise is another common characteristic of SAR imagery. For this research, we introduced different SAR noise generator functions for making background and overlap noise effects in our synthetic SAR imagery. We sampled SAR background noise characteristics from MSTAR and Senteniel-1 datasets. Based on this sampling we developed various noise generator functions that are statistically close to those of the two datasets. We parametrically control these noise function generators and thus randomly adapting background noise patterns mimicking those of real SAR images. This approach can be readily adapted for DDDAS paradigm for real timer training and learning.

Sparkle Effect noise is another common characteristic in SAR imaging. This is a result of random distribution of backscatters in each resolution cell with different amplitudes and phases. We developed a generative function to produce SAR sparkles with random size and brightness. These sparkle generated noise patterns are then superimposed at the final stage of the simulated SAR image. This step is demonstrated in the last stage of Fig. 2.

Object shadows are a key characteristic of SAR images, carrying pertaining information about object shape and orientation proportional to radar elevation and azimuth angles. To introduce SAR shadow effect for our test vehicles, we can either compute it or use its original RM to form a shadow template. The former approach creates background formation dependency (e.g., land elevation) - not an ideal case for generalizing deep learning systems training. Consequently, we adopted the second approach. To produce the needed shadow, we shift its shadow template while minimizing its intensity strength and adding it to the generated speckled RM image. Next, we concentrate the final image from the SSRE technique, with SAR shadow image and speckled ocean RM image. This process is illustrated in Fig. 2.

4 Performance Evaluation

To evaluate the quality and realism of our generated synthetic SAR images, we compared our results with actual SAR images of several physical aerial, ground and marine vehicles. Figure 3 presents some samples of the MSTAR dataset and their corresponding simulated SAR image using our technique. Figure 4 presents a sample of four cargo vessels and their corresponding real SAR images are presented on the left-hand side. On the right-hand side, we have presented our synthetically generated SAR images for equivalent size and marine vehicles. Though our marine test objects are not identical to the physical vessels, the synthetic SAR image quality was achieved realistically.

5 DDDAS Implication

Dynamic Data Driven Applications Systems (DDDAS) are distinctive predictive models taking advantage of a *data assimilation feedback loop when discrete sensors data are available*. Using sensor data error, the system attempts to drive the physical system simulation so that the trajectory of the simulation more closely follows the trajectory of the physical system. In parallel, a sensor guidance control loop can be employed to guide the physical sensors to enhance the information content of the collected data. The data assimilation and sensor guidance control feedback loops are computational rather than physical feedback loops. The simulation can guide the observational aspects of the sensor and the collected data, and in turn, improves the accuracy of the physical system simulation. In the control feedback loops, the appropriate machine-learning or deep-learning based algorithmic as well as statistical methods can be incorporated to relate the measurement data with that of the high-dimensional modeling and simulation. To improve situational awareness of ATR systems, the features extracted from an image should be explainable, interpretable, and understandable to the user. As detailed in the DARPA XAI program, it is highly advantageous to create AI models whose learned models and decisions can be trusted by its users [5]. An example of this is extracting features from a target object of interest (TOI) such as turrets/weaponry from tanks, and the number of wheels on trucks [6]. In the battlefield environments, target objects of interest (TOI), may be subject to obscuration, camouflage, and deception. Through a feedback data assimilation, for example, the active sensors can be guided to perform additional exploration to maximize entropy of cues detected and such data can be modeled to create an improved situational awareness of potential TOI. Though, through this work, this aspect of research was not addressed. In our future work, we plan to investigate the data assimilation feedback loops that exploit and explore such sensor control opportunity to improve detectability of TOI despite of their physical SAR signature inconsistencies.

Fig. 3. Comparison of IRIS SRE method vs real SAR images from MSTAR dataset [7]. Top: sample military vehicles. middle: the corresponding vehicles' SAR image from MSTAR dataset. Bottom: simulated SAR image of the same vehicle models using our proposed IRIS-SRE method.

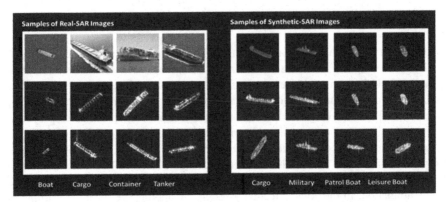

Fig. 4. Comparison of actual physical SAR images of marine vehicles (Right) against, the simulated SAR images of comparable marine vehicle from IRIS-EM simulator (Left).

6 Conclusion

In this paper, we presented a physics-based approach for synthetic generation of SAR like imagery of some test vehicles. The objective has been to generate high fidelity simulated SAR imagery suitable for the training of deep learning algorithms and techniques. The proposed technique the advanced DDDAS requiring large-scale SAR imagery datasets for the machine learning and deep learning system training and learning of ATR systems.

Acknowledgment. This research work is currently sponsored by the Office of Naval Research under research grant account: N00014-18-1-2738. The ONR program manager is Dr. Martin Kruger. The authors also thanks Mr. Antony Smith, director of ONR HBCU Office for the support of this project.

References

1. Ahmadibeni, A., Borooshak L., Shirkhodaie, A.: Aerial and ground vehicles synthetic SAR dataset generation for automatic target recognition. In: SPIE DCS, Algorithms for Synthetic Aperture Radar Imagery XXVII, paper 11393-20, April 2020
2. Jones, B., Ahmadibeni, A., Shirkhodaie, A.: Marine vehicles simulated SAR imagery datasets generation. In: SPIE DCS, paper 11420-24, April 2020
3. Ahmadibeni, A., Borooshak, L., Jones, B., Shirkhodaie, A.: Automatic target recognition of aerial vehicles based on synthetic SAR imagery using hybrid stacked denoising autoencoders. In: SPIE DCS, Algorithms for Synthetic Aperture Radar Imagery XXVII, paper 11393-25, April 2020
4. Shirkhodaie, A.: IRIS – Intelligent Robotics Interface Systems," developed at Tennessee State University, Department of Mechanical and Manufacturing Engineering, (2006). LNCS http://www.springer.com/lncs. Accessed 21 Nov 2016
5. Gunning, D., Aha, D.W.: DARPA's explainable artificial intelligence program. AI Mag., Summer, 44–58 (2019). https://doi.org/10.1609/aimag.v40i2.2850

6. Blasch, E., Majumder, U., Zelnio, E., Velten, V.: Review of recent advances in AI/ML using the MSTAR data. In: Proceedings of the SPIE 11393, Algorithms for Synthetic Aperture Radar Imagery XXVII, 113930C, 19 May 2020. https://doi.org/10.1117/12.2559035
7. Diemunsch, J., Wissinger, J.: Moving and stationary target acquisition and recognition (MSTAR) model-based automatic target recognition: search technology for a robust ATR. In: Zelnio, E.G. (ed.), Proceedings of SPIE – International Society for Optical Engineering, vol. 3370, pp. 481–492, April (1998)

Towards Provably Correct Probabilistic Flight Systems

Elkin Cruz-Camacho$^{(\boxtimes)}$, Saswata Paul$^{(\boxtimes)}$, Fotis Kopsaftopoulos$^{(\boxtimes)}$, and Carlos A. Varela$^{(\boxtimes)}$

Rensselaer Polytechnic Institute, Troy, NY 12180, USA
{cruzce,pauls4,kopsaf}@rpi.edu, cvarela@cs.rpi.edu

Abstract. *Safety envelopes* are meant to determine under which conditions and state space regions a probabilistic property of a data-driven system can be asserted with high confidence. Dynamic data-driven applications systems (DDDAS) can make use of safety envelopes to be cognizant of the formal warranties derived from their models and assumptions. An example of safety envelopes is presented as the intersection of two simpler concepts: *z-predictability* and *τ-confidence*; which correspond to state estimation and classification, respectively. To illustrate safety envelopes, stall detection from signal energy is shown with data gathered by piezo-electric sensors in a composite wing inside a wind tunnel under varying angles of attack and airspeed configuration. A formalization of these safety envelopes is presented in the Agda proof assistant, from which formally proven sentinel code can be generated.

1 Introduction

Aerospace systems will be increasingly autonomous in terms of self-diagnosis, self-healing, and overall self-awareness. They will be capable of sensing, reasoning, and reacting in real-time to their actual operating conditions, allowing for optimal control and decision-making abilities [13]. This will be aided by access to an unprecedented amount of real-time data from onboard sensors which can be interpreted to sense the aeroelastic state, environmental conditions, and structural conditions of aerospace systems [14]. Smart aerospace systems will be capable of detecting aerodynamic conditions – *e.g.*, stall or flutter, using data from piezo-electric and other sensors placed on the wings of an aircraft [12,13]. Dynamic data-driven applications systems (DDDAS) [8] can use this data to create accurate aerodynamic models that can be updated to reflect the real-time aerodynamic performance of such systems [18].

Since the failure of safety-critical aerospace systems can cause harm to human life, the environment, or property [22], it is necessary to verify the correctness of the software used in these systems. Model checking and formal methods can be used for verification of such software [1], *e.g.*, by writing mechanically-verified proofs of correctness. However, formal proofs usually only hold under some conditions which may not necessarily be true during actual operation

© Springer Nature Switzerland AG 2020
F. Darema et al. (Eds.): DDDAS 2020, LNCS 12312, pp. 236–244, 2020.
https://doi.org/10.1007/978-3-030-61725-7_28

[19]. Breese *et al.* [6] have proposed an approach for classifying a system's state space into distinct regions with respect to a formal proof. They introduce *safety envelopes* to represent the subset of the state space where the formal proof of a probabilistic statement holds. The extent of a safety envelope depends on a data-driven model of the system and parameters to quantify the certainty of state estimation. Safety envelopes can only guarantee behavior for stochastic systems that follow the underlying statistical assumptions on the data, *e.g.*, Gaussian distributions. Special runtime programs called *sentinels* can analyze real-time data against a safety envelope and determine whether the system conditions fall within the envelope or not. DDDAS can use safety envelopes formalize data-driven probabilistic guarantees that hold in real-time.

The contributions of this paper are: a definition of safety envelopes as regions delimited by a model and user-definable parameters, an example of a safety envelope that warranties z-predictability and τ-confidence for state estimation and classification respectively (Sect. 2), and the formalization of the safety envelope concepts in Agda [17] and generation of Haskell [16] code from the formal specification (Sect. 3).

2 Signal Energy Safety Envelopes as Parameterized Statements

Safety envelopes are a step forward for provably robust dynamic data-driven applications systems (DDDAS). This section presents a definition for safety envelopes and exemplifies the construction of safety envelopes for the prediction of stall for a self-sensing composite wing given a single energy signal input.

A flight state can be identified as a quadruple $\langle x, \alpha, v, stall \rangle$, where x is the signal energy received from a sensor in a wing, α the angle of attack, v is the airspeed and *stall* is a boolean value that indicates whether the wing is stalled or not. A model M is a $\langle S_M, f_M \rangle$, where S_M is a subset of $\mathbb{R} \times \mathbb{R}$ (all possible airspeeds and angles of attack), and f_M is a map with the signature $S_M \rightarrow \mathcal{N} \times \mathbb{B}$. A map f_M receives a valid input (v, α) and returns a $\langle \mathcal{N}(\mu, \sigma^2), stall \rangle$ where $\mathcal{N}(\mu, \sigma^2)$ is the normal distribution that the energy signal is assumed to follow. This means, a model M is a collection of probability distributions each drawn from a partial flight state denoted by $\langle \alpha, v, stall \rangle$.

A model M is computed from data collected in wind tunnel experiments. The example model considered in this paper has been constructed from the experiments presented by Kopsaftopoulos and Chang in [13].

Definition 1. *Signal Energy Safety Envelope:* *Given a model M and parameters Π, a safety envelope for the signal energy is the region $\xi \subseteq \mathbb{R}$ under which a probabilistic statement[1] P with arguments M and Π holds, i.e., a safety envelope is the region defined by $\xi = \{x \in \mathbb{R} : P(M, \Pi, x) = true\}$, where x is a signal energy measurement.*

---

[1] A probabilistic statement is a statement that includes probabilistic assertions as part of its definition, *e.g.*, the expected value after flipping a fair coin ($0 =$ heads; $1 =$ tails) is $\frac{1}{2}$.

For a simple and slightly contrived example of safety envelopes, suppose that all signal energy measurements follow the normal distribution with parameters $\mathcal{N}(10,1)$ (the model M) and consider the statement "the signal energy measurement falls within the 95.4% prediction interval (PI) around the mean" (the statement P with model M and at least 95.4% PI as Π), then the safety envelope defined by the statement is the region contained inside $[\mu - 2\sigma, \mu + 2\sigma] = [8, 12]$.

2.1   Data Consistency with Model Using z-Predictability

Definition 2. *An energy signal x is z-predictable iff there exist $\langle d_i, b_i \rangle \in Imf_M$ such that $x \in pred\_i(d_i, z)$, where $pred\_i$ is the prediction interval for the z score, i.e., $pred\_i(\mathcal{N}(\mu, \sigma^2), z) = [\mu - z\sigma, \mu + z\sigma]$.*

In statistics z is called the z-score. The main idea of z-predictability is to determine whether a single measurement of signal energy is consistent with the model at hand. For a z score of 3, around 99.7% of the measurements are

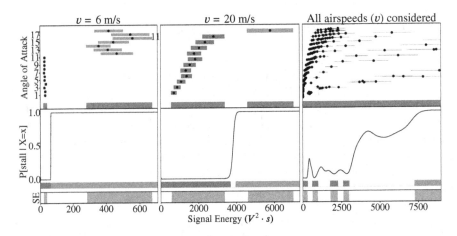

Fig. 1. ROWS: *Top row:* Prediction intervals for each angle of attack. The black dot is the mean, blue indicates no stall, and orange indicates stall. The gray line below is the region of z-predictability—*i.e.*, the region $\{x \in \mathbb{R} : \exists \langle \alpha, v \rangle \in S_M . f_M(\langle \alpha, v \rangle)_1 = d_i \wedge x \in pred\_i(d_i, z)\}$—with $z = 2$. *Middle row:* Probability function $P[\texttt{stall} \mid X = x]$, which indicates the probability of the wing to be in stall given a single measurement of the signal energy. The classification regions for stall and no stall are shown below with confidence of $\tau = 90\%$, *i.e.*, the τ-confident region is the union of both colored regions, blue and red, where blue indicates no-stall and red stall. *Bottom row:* The green region indicates the safety envelopes, the region where a signal energy measurement is both z-predictable and τ-confident. COLUMNS: *Left column:* The model M includes all flight states with an airspeed of 6 m/s. *Center column:* Only flight states with an airspeed of 20 m/s. *Right column:* All flight states recorded, all airspeeds ($v \in \{6, 8, 10, 11, 12, 13, 14, 15, 16, 17, 18, 19, 20, 21, 22\}$m/s) and angles of attack ($\alpha \in [1, 18]$) are considered in the model M. (Color figure online)

z-predictable. A value that falls outside the prediction interval is considered to be not z-predictable and it is treated as a possible error.

From the definition of z-predictability it can be proven that (see Subsect. 3):

Theorem 1. *An energy signal x is z-predictable iff there exist $\langle \alpha, v \rangle \in S_M$ such that $f_M(\langle \alpha, v \rangle)_1 = d_i$ and $x \in pred\_i(d_i, z)$.*

On the top row of Figs. 1 and 2, a region generated by the z predictability can be seen. The z-score in Figs. 1 and 2 is 2 and 4, respectively.

2.2 Stall Detection Using Statistical Inference

This section presents a procedure using statistical inference to classify the stall condition of a wing, then it is shown how this classification can be parameterized to delimit a confidence region of classification.

Definition 3. *Conditional Probability of Stall: Given a model M and a measurement x, the probability of stall is defined as:*

$$P\left[stall \mid X = x\right] = \frac{P[stall]f(x \mid stall)}{f(x)}$$
$$= \frac{\sum_{\langle \alpha, v \rangle \in S_M} (f_s(x)P[\langle \alpha, v \rangle]P[stall \mid \langle \alpha, v \rangle])}{\sum_{\langle \alpha, v \rangle \in S_M} (f_s(x)P[\langle \alpha, v \rangle])} \quad (1)$$

where f_s corresponds to the probability density function for the distribution $d_s = f_M(\langle \alpha, v \rangle)_1$, the conditional probability $P[stall \mid \langle \alpha, v \rangle]$ is either 0 or 1 and determined by $f_M(\langle \alpha, v \rangle)_2$, and the distribution $P[\langle \alpha, v \rangle]$ uniform for all $\langle \alpha, v \rangle \in S_M$ ($P[\langle \alpha, v \rangle] = \frac{1}{|S_M|}$).

The probability of stall can be seen in the middle row of Figs. 1 and 2. The following is the definition of a classification procedure from the conditional probability function:

Definition 4. *Classification Function: Given a model M, an energy signal x can be classified in one of three categories as:*

$$c(M, \tau, x) = \begin{cases} stall & P\left[stall \mid X = x\right] \geq \tau \\ nostall & P\left[\neg stall \mid X = x\right] \geq \tau \\ uncertain & \text{in any other case.} \end{cases}$$

where τ, the threshold, is a real number in the range $(0.5, 1]$ and indicates the level of confidence wanted from the classification (alternatively, $1 - \tau$ indicates the risk that will be accepted for the classification [3]). The signature of c is $M \times \mathbb{R} \times \mathbb{R} \rightarrow \{stall, nostall, uncertain\}$.

The classification region can be seen at the bottom of the middle row in Figs. 1 and 2, for $\tau = 90\%$ and 99.9%, respectively.

Definition 5. *A classification $c(M, \tau, x) = k$ is τ-confident iff $k \neq$ **uncertain**.*

A τ-confident classification is one in which the risk of misclassification is below the threshold τ. Alternatively, τ-confidence can be defined as:

Theorem 2. *A classification k is τ-confident iff $P[k \mid x] \geq \tau$.*

2.3   Safety Envelopes as τ-Confident Classifications on z-Predictable Measurements

Definition 6. *A safety envelope $se(M, z, \tau)$ for stall detection is the region $x \in \mathcal{P}(\mathbb{R})$ with parameters $\Pi = \langle z, \tau \rangle$, where the following probabilistic statement holds: x is z-predictable and $c(M, \tau, x)$ is τ-confident.*

As a corollary from Theorems 1 and 2:

Theorem 3. *An energy signal x belongs to a safety envelope $se(M, z, \tau)$ iff there exist $\langle \alpha, v \rangle \in S_M$ such that $f_M(\langle \alpha, v \rangle)_1 = d_i$ and $x \in pred\_i(d_i, z)$, and the classification $k = c(M, \tau, x)$ has a confidence bigger than τ, i.e., $P[k \mid x] \geq \tau$.*

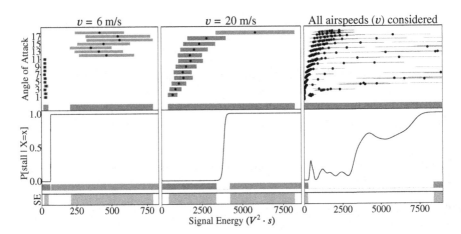

Fig. 2. ROWS and COLUMNS as in Fig. 1 but with parameters $z = 4$ and $\tau = 99.9\%$. Notice that compared with the τ-confident region displayed in Fig. 1 with an airspeed $v = 20\,\text{m/s}$ (red and blue regions in the middle-center plot), the τ-confident region for a value of $\tau = 99.9\%$ is smaller, it has a wider gap, which shows that the higher the τ the smaller the safety envelope will be. Conversely, the more samples admitted as z-consistent, the bigger the safety envelope will be, as it can be seen comparing the gray regions on the top row from Fig. 1. The optimum values for z and τ will depend on the application, but a meaningful range of values for z would be $[2, 6]$ (which correspond to 5% or less data thrown away) and for τ around 95% and upwards. (Color figure online)

The last row of Figs. 1 and 2 shows the safety envelopes derived from three different data-driven models with varying z-scores and τ thresholds. For easily separable stall/no-stall conditions, such as $6\,m/s$, the safety envelope is the same as the region defined by the z-predictability; in other cases, the region defined by the τ-confidence reduces the region described by z-predictability, or viceversa.

Notice that when safety envelopes are applied to a model where all airspeeds and angles of attack have been taken into account, the safety envelopes become significantly smaller. This means that it is not possible to assert with high confidence whether a signal energy entails a stall condition. In Fig. 2 rightmost column, safety envelopes do not include any signal with values from around 200 and until 8000.

3 Formalization and Sentinel Generation

Formally proving properties of DDDAS using a proof assistant is a necessary step to ensure fault-free or near fault-free certified software. Signal energy safety envelopes have been implemented in Agda[2], a formal verification system, in order to prove their properties mechanically. Three procedures have been implemented: computing whether an energy signal input is z-predictable, τ-confident, and whether it falls inside the safety envelope defined by a model M with parameters $\Pi = \langle z, \tau \rangle$. The following is an excerpt of the formalization, where z-predictability is defined:

```
inside : NormalDist → ℝ → ℝ → Bool
inside nd z x = ((μ - z * σ) <ᵇ x) ∧ (x <ᵇ (μ + z * σ))  where open NormalDist nd using (μ; σ)

z-predictable : Model → ℝ → ℝ → ℝ × Bool
z-predictable M z x = ⟨ x , any (λ nd → inside nd z x) (map (proj₁ ∘ proj₂) (Model.fM M)) ⟩
```

The power of formalization comes from the fact that properties can be mechanically proven, $i.e.$, it can be proven that the definition entails the implementation. Such is the case presented in the proof below, where Theorem 1 is formally proven using the proof that the implementation in Agda (above) follows from the Definition 2. In the same manner, Theorems 2 and 3 have been encoded in Agda and proven formally, $i.e.$, in a mechanized manner.

---

[2] Full implementation and proofs can be found at http://wcl.cs.rpi.edu/pilots/fvdddas (repository name: `safety-envelopes-sentinels`, version 0.1.1.0).

```
-- In words: Given a Model `M` and parameter `z`, `x` is z-predictable iff
-- there exists a pair ⟨α,v⟩ (angle of attack and velocity) such that they are
-- associated to a `nd` (Normal Distribution) and `x` falls withing the
-- Predictable Interval
theorem1← : ∀ (M z x)
           → z-predictable M z x ≡ ⟨ x , true ⟩
           → Any (λ{⟨ ⟨α,v⟩ , ⟨ nd , p ⟩ ⟩ → x ∈ pi nd z}) (Model.fM M)
theorem1← M z x res≡x,true = any-map (proj₁ ∘ proj₂) (follows-def← M z x res≡x,true)
theorem1→ : ∀ (M z x)
           → Any (λ{⟨ ⟨α,v⟩ , ⟨ nd , p ⟩ ⟩ → x ∈ pi nd z}) (Model.fM M)
           → z-predictable M z x ≡ ⟨ x , true ⟩
theorem1→ M z x proofAny = follows-def→ M z x (any-map-rev (proj₁ ∘ proj₂) proofAny)
```

A *sentinel* is a binary, a program, whose job is to monitor for the consistency and correctness of the data received and generated in flight. Agda has the capability of generating Haskell code which can be executed and tested. From the formalization shown above, a sentinel has been built such that it monitors when a stream of floating-point numbers is z-predictable. The implementation uses floating-point numbers as an approximation to real numbers.

To write the sentinel, a wrapper was written around the generated Agda code to pass data from the standard input. The resulting binary can process a continuous stream of data and outputs to the standard output a stream of booleans representing the z-predictability. The implementation and proofs occupy a total of 760 lines in Agda and 130 lines of code in Haskell. From the Agda code, a total of 1160 lines of Haskell code were generated.

4   Related Work

HOL and Isabelle are interactive proof assistants with a rich history of proofs from discrete and continuous probability theory [5,9,10,20]. Agda, opposed to HOL and Isabelle, is a programming language and proof assistant built on top of a constructive theory [15]. Copilot [19] and PILOTS [7,11] have presented strategies to find and recover from faulty data-streams due to hardware errors in airplane systems and dynamic data-driven applications systems (DDDAS), respectively. Those systems do not yet incorporate formal verification. Veridrone [21] and other Coq initiatives (*e.g.,* [4]) have incorporated formal verification into working systems to formally prove aircraft safety properties. In this work, an approach to build a formally verified monitor/sentinel from a specification was presented and applied to aircraft safety.

5   Conclusion

An extension and modularization of the concepts put forward by Breese *et al.* [6] was presented. The modularization included the separation of what it means to be consistent, *z-predictability*, and how to quantify confidence in the stall classification of an aircraft, τ-confidence. It was shown that knowing only a single energy signal measurement from a piezo-electric sensor is not enough to confidently determine the stall state of a wing. Knowing the airspeed of the aircraft significantly improves the classification confidence.

A formalization of safety envelopes in Agda was also presented. From it, formally verified Haskell code was generated, wrapped and extended to process a stream of data. Safety envelopes are an important step forward in the direction of formally correct and robust dynamic data-driven applications systems (DDDAS).

Future work includes the definition of safety envelopes for a sequence of signal energy measurements as opposed to single, isolated values, as in *Ahmed et al.* [2]; and the implementation of runnable real number arithmetic as opposed to floating-point arithmetic operations.

Acknowledgment. This research was partially supported by the National Science Foundation (NSF), Grant No. – CNS-1816307, and the Air Force Office of Scientific Research (AFOSR), DDDAS Grant No. – FA9550-19-1-0054.

References

1. Agha, G., Palmskog, K.: A survey of statistical model checking. ACM Trans. Model. Comput. Simul. **28**(1), 6:1–6:39 (2018)
2. Ahmed, S., Amer, A., Varela, C., Kopsaftopoulos, F.: Data-driven state awareness for fly-by-feel aerial vehicles via adaptive time series and gaussian process regression models. In: Dynamic Data-Driven Applications Systems (InfoSymbiotics/DDDAS 2020) (October 2020)
3. Alpaydin, E.: Introduction to Machine Learning, 3rd edn. The MIT Press, Cambridge (2014)
4. Anand, A., Knepper, R.: ROSCoq: robots powered by constructive reals. In: Urban, C., Zhang, X. (eds.) ITP 2015. LNCS, vol. 9236, pp. 34–50. Springer, Cham (2015). https://doi.org/10.1007/978-3-319-22102-1_3
5. Avigad, J., Hölzl, J., Serafin, L.: A formally verified proof of the central limit theorem. J. Autom. Reason. **59**(4), 389–423 (2017)
6. Breese, S., Kopsaftopoulos, F., Varela, C.: Towards proving runtime properties of data-driven systems using safety envelopes. In: The 12th International Workshop on Structural Health Monitoring, Stanford, CA (September 2019)
7. Chen, S., Imai, S., Zhu, W., Varela, C.A.: Towards learning spatio-temporal data stream relationships for failure detection in avionics. In: Blasch, E., Ravela, S., Aved, A. (eds.) Handbook of Dynamic Data Driven Applications Systems, pp. 97–121. Springer, Cham (2018). https://doi.org/10.1007/978-3-319-95504-9_5
8. Darema, F.: Dynamic data driven applications systems: a new paradigm for application simulations and measurements. In: Bubak, M., van Albada, G.D., Sloot, P.M.A., Dongarra, J. (eds.) ICCS 2004. LNCS, vol. 3038, pp. 662–669. Springer, Heidelberg (2004). https://doi.org/10.1007/978-3-540-24688-6_86
9. Hasan, O., Tahar, S.: Probabilistic analysis of wireless systems using theorem proving. Electron. Notes Theor. Comput. Sci. **242**(2), 43–58 (2009)
10. Hurd, J.: Formal verification of probabilistic algorithms. Tech. rep. UCAM-CL-TR-566, University of Cambridge, Computer Laboratory (May 2003)

11. Imai, S., Blasch, E., Galli, A., Zhu, W., Lee, F., Varela, C.A.: Airplane flight safety using error-tolerant data stream processing. IEEE Aerosp. Electron. Syst. Mag. **32**(4), 4–17 (2017)
12. Kopsaftopoulos, F.: Data-driven stochastic identification for fly-by-feel aerospace structures: critical assessment of non-parametric and parametric approaches. In: AIAA Scitech 2019 Forum, p. 1534 (2019)
13. Kopsaftopoulos, F., Chang, F.-K.: A dynamic data-driven stochastic state-awareness framework for the next generation of bio-inspired fly-by-feel aerospace vehicles. In: Blasch, E., Ravela, S., Aved, A. (eds.) Handbook of Dynamic Data Driven Applications Systems, pp. 697–721. Springer, Cham (2018). https://doi.org/10.1007/978-3-319-95504-9_31
14. Kopsaftopoulos, F., Nardari, R., Li, Y.H., Chang, F.K.: Data-driven state awareness for fly-by-feel aerial vehicles: experimental assessment of a non-parametric probabilistic stall detection approach. In: Structural Health Monitoring 2017, pp. 1596–1604. DEStech Publications, Inc. (September 2017)
15. Luo, Z.: Computation and Reasoning: A Type Theory for Computer Science. Oxford University Press Inc., USA (1994)
16. Marlow, S., et al.: Haskell 2010 language report (2010). https://www.haskell.org/onlinereport/haskell2010
17. Norell, U.: Towards a practical programming language based on dependent type theory. Ph.D. thesis, Department of Computer Science and Engineering, Chalmers University of Technology, SE-412 96 Göteborg, Sweden (September 2007)
18. Paul, S., Hole, F., Zytek, A., Varela, C.A.: Flight trajectory planning for fixed wing aircraft in loss of thrust emergencies. In: Dynamic Data-Driven Application Systems (InfoSymbiotics/DDDAS 2017), Cambridge, MA (August 2017)
19. Pike, L., Wegmann, N., Niller, S., Goodloe, A.: Copilot: monitoring embedded systems. Innov. Syst. Softw. Eng. **9**(4), 235–255 (2013)
20. Qasim, M., Hasan, O., Elleuch, M., Tahar, S.: Formalization of normal random variables in HOL. In: Kohlhase, M., Johansson, M., Miller, B., de de Moura, L., Tompa, F. (eds.) CICM 2016. LNCS (LNAI), vol. 9791, pp. 44–59. Springer, Cham (2016). https://doi.org/10.1007/978-3-319-42547-4_4
21. Ricketts, D., Malecha, G., Alvarez, M.M., Gowda, V., Lerner, S.: Towards verification of hybrid systems in a foundational proof assistant. In: 2015 ACM/IEEE International Conference on Formal Methods and Models for Codesign (MEMOCODE), pp. 248–257 (September 2015)
22. Srivatanakul, T.: Security analysis with deviational techniques. Ph.D. thesis, University of York, York, UK (April 2005)

Dynamic Data-Driven Formal Progress Envelopes for Distributed Algorithms

Saswata Paul$^{(\boxtimes)}$, Fotis Kopsaftopoulos, Stacy Patterson, and Carlos A. Varela

Rensselaer Polytechnic Institute, Troy, NY 12180, USA
{pauls4,kopsaf}@rpi.edu, {sep,cvarela}@cs.rpi.edu

Abstract. This work presents *formal progress envelopes* applied to flight systems for distinctly classifying a system's state space into regions where a formal proof of progress for a distributed algorithm holds or does not hold. It also presents an approach for runtime integration of formal methods in the dynamic data-driven applications systems (DDDAS) architecture using *parameterized proofs*. Finally, it showcases the development of reusable parameterized proof libraries for high-level statistical and stochastic reasoning in the Athena proof assistant and demonstrates their use with a progress proof for the Paxos distributed consensus protocol.

1 Introduction

Intelligent aerospace systems of the future will be "smarter" and more self-sufficient in terms of self-diagnosis [5,18], self-healing [16], safe navigation [24], and overall situational awareness. Such enhanced capabilities will stem from access to an unprecedented amount of real-time data collected from onboard sensors and a network of ground-stations, satellites, and aircraft, which we call the *Internet-of-Planes* (IoP). *Dynamic data-driven applications systems* (DDDAS) [6] can use this data for creating low-fidelity models in real-time that can reflect the operating conditions of an aerospace system almost as effectively as a high-fidelity model [23].

Data from the IoP can be used for various *mission-critical* and *safety-critical* applications such as *conflict-aware* [24] and *weather-aware* [7] navigation. Many *distributed consensus algorithms* [19,22] allow participating aircraft to *eventually* reach agreement on data in a decentralized manner. However, the useful lifetimes of navigation and weather data are usually limited, rendering them obsolete after relatively short durations. Guarantees of eventual agreement are, therefore, ill-suited for most data-driven applications in the IoP. Moreover, the asynchronous and stochastic nature of real-life networks makes it impossible to provide deterministic guarantees about the progress of consensus algorithms, as message delays are indistinguishable from failures [8]. Under such circumstances, guarantees of probabilistic progress properties can be provided using statistical techniques. The failure of safety-critical aerospace systems can be catastrophic to life, property, or the environment [26], making it necessary to verify their

© Springer Nature Switzerland AG 2020
F. Darema et al. (Eds.): DDDAS 2020, LNCS 12312, pp. 245–252, 2020.
https://doi.org/10.1007/978-3-030-61725-7_29

correctness guarantees. Formal methods [3] can be used for the mechanical verification of such systems by writing machine-checked correctness proofs.

In this paper, we present the concept of *formal progress envelopes* applied to flight systems for distributed algorithms (Sect. 2) and propose an approach for integrating formal methods in the runtime architecture of DDDAS by using *parameterized proofs* (Sect. 3). We also showcase the development of a proof library in the Athena proof assistant [1] for reasoning about statistical properties of dynamic data-driven systems (Sect. 4) and provide a simple example to demonstrate its application (Sect. 5). We compare related work on runtime and stochastic verification (Sect. 6) and conclude the paper with a discussion about possible future directions of work (Sect. 7).

2   Formal Progress Envelopes

A *formal progress envelope* for a distributed algorithm is a computable subset of the system state space where the formal proof of a progress property holds. It is defined by a set of logical constraints parameterized by the system's operational conditions. Progress, depending on the algorithm, may refer to either termination or the successful completion of a given sequence of message rounds. To illustrate formal progress envelopes, let us consider asynchronous distributed consensus algorithms for use in safety-critical applications. The asynchronous and stochastic nature of real-life distributed systems makes it difficult to deterministically predict the message delay between any two nodes. However, we can statistically analyze the message delays – *e.g.*, if the message delays from a node A to another node B and vice-versa are represented by the continuous random variables X and Y respectively, over a period of time, it is possible to statistically observe the behavior of X and Y as their *probability density functions* (pdf) $f_X(t)$ and $f_Y(t)$. A distributed consensus algorithm may require multiple rounds of messages between two or more nodes for making progress. If in the worst-case scenario, a deterministic number of message rounds are required for reaching consensus, then the total worst-case message delay can be represented by a random variable which is the sum of the random variables representing the delays of each message involved. Since there exist statistical theorems about the nature of random variables (*e.g.*, *Cramér's Decomposition Theorem* [17]) it is possible to provide probabilistic guarantees about the worst-case time of progress – *e.g.*, "*The probability that the worst-case time for consensus will be at most 0.8 s is 98%*". A naive progress envelope for this particular property would be: $\forall D \in \mathbb{D} : D \sim \mathcal{N}(\mu_D, \sigma_D^2)$, where $\mathbb{D}$ is the set of all message delays and $D \sim \mathcal{N}(\mu_D, \sigma_D^2)$ implies that the random variable D is normally distributed.

Since the parameters that define formal progress envelopes can be quantified and measured, the envelopes can be analyzed against real-time data. Special runtime-accessible programs called *sentinels* [4] can analyze real-time data to check if the system state satisfies the progress envelope constraints. To ensure their correctness and effectiveness, sentinels may be generated directly from the formal specifications of the envelopes and some underlying models of uncertainty.

3   Augmenting DDDAS with Formal Methods

Unpredictable operating conditions of dynamic data-driven systems restrict the practicality of pre-developed formal proofs to the pre-deployment stages. It is, therefore, desirable to develop *parameterized proofs* that can be augmented in real-time, making them versatile over dynamic parameters – *e.g.*, instead of stating a static property such as: "*The probability that the round-trip message delay will be at most 0.9 s is* 99%", a parameterized proof would state: "*If the one-way message delays follow normal distributions* $\mathcal{N}(\mu_X, \sigma_X^2)$ *and* $\mathcal{N}(\mu_Y, \sigma_Y^2)$, *then the probability that the round-trip message delay will be at most t seconds is* $F(\mu_X, \sigma_X, \mu_Y, \sigma_Y, t)$", where F is the cumulative distribution function (cdf).

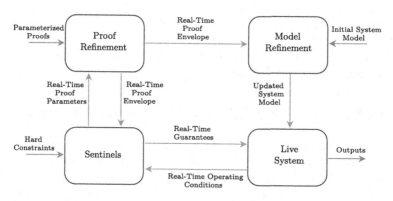

Fig. 1. Integrating formal proofs in the DDDAS architecture.

Formal envelopes, in conjunction with parameterized proofs and runtime sentinels, can be directly incorporated in the DDDAS architecture using a feedback loop (Fig. 1). This involves four logically separate components:

- The *proof refinement* component receives a parameterized proof with a set of initial parameters and real-time inputs from the sentinels. If possible, it refines the proofs with the real-time parameters and provides new envelopes.
- The *model refinement* component receives real-time envelopes from the proof refinement component and an initial system model. It updates the system model according to the latest envelopes.
- The *sentinels* analyze the real-time operating conditions of the system against the latest envelopes. If the conditions do not conform to the envelopes, they send real-time parameters to the proof refinement component. They also inform the live system about guarantees that hold in real-time. Hard constraints dictate when possible guarantees cease to be useful.
- The *live system* runs using the updated system model from the model refinement component.

To illustrate, let us consider an aircraft that is participating in distributed consensus for collaborative flight-planning by implementing the feedback loop in Fig. 1. It may propose a conflict-aware flight-plan p [24] that is due to start after 1 s, as there is an initial proof that traffic aircraft will reach consensus under 1 s with 99.8% probability. During runtime, the sentinels observe that the actual message delays do not conform to the envelope of the initial proof, so they send the actual parameters to the proof refinement component. The proof refinement component generates new proofs which state that consensus under 1 s has a probability of only 60% and consensus under 2 s has a probability of 99.5%. The model refinement component may then update the proposal with another flight-plan p' that is due to start after 2 s.

The above example shows that our approach can be used to dynamically update formal proofs with parameters that reflect the runtime operating conditions of a system. This will allow the development of highly-adaptive dynamic data-driven applications systems that can adapt to formally-verified properties that hold during runtime, thus extending the practicality of formal verification techniques beyond the pre-deployment stages.

4   Proof Library for High-Level Statistical Inference

The nature of foundational verification makes the process of developing mechanically verified formal proofs an arduous task. This is because when developing the proofs of high-level properties in mechanically-verifiable languages, a significant amount of effort needs to be put in for formalizing the lower-level theory. This calls for the development of proof libraries for formal verification languages, which can be reused to prove higher-level properties, similar to code libraries developed for general-purpose programming languages. Mechanically verifying the higher-level statistical properties of stochastic systems requires reasoning about the lower-level mathematical theory of random variables, distributions of random variables, algebra, and probability. We adopt a top-down approach of proof development which allows us to first formalize the high-level properties and then develop the lower-level theory required for fully verifying them. We present two mechanically-verified results that can be used for reasoning about the statistical properties of stochastic systems.

Lemma 1. *Given two normal probability density functions $f_X(x) = \mathcal{N}(\mu_X, \sigma_X^2)$ and $f_Y(y) = \mathcal{N}(\mu_Y, \sigma_Y^2)$, the probability that a random variable following their convolution will take a value of at most r is given by: $\int_{-\infty}^{z} \frac{1}{\sqrt{2\pi}} e^{-x^2/2} dx$ where $z = \frac{r - (\mu_X + \mu_Y)}{\sqrt{2(\sigma_X^2 + \sigma_Y^2)}}$.*

Theorem 1. *If two independent random variables X and Y are normally distributed with probability density functions $f_X(x) = \mathcal{N}(\mu_X, \sigma_X^2)$ and $f_Y(y) = \mathcal{N}(\mu_Y, \sigma_Y^2)$, then the probability that $X + Y$ will take a value of at most r is given by: $\int_{-\infty}^{z} \frac{1}{\sqrt{2\pi}} e^{-x^2/2} dx$ where $z = \frac{r - (\mu_X + \mu_Y)}{\sqrt{2(\sigma_X^2 + \sigma_Y^2)}}$.*

The formal proof of Theorem 1 uses Cramèr's Decomposition Theorem and the following postulates:

Postulate 1. *The standard score of a value v with respect to a normal distribution* $\mathcal{N}(\mu_X, \sigma_X^2)$ *is given by:* $z = \frac{v - \mu_X}{\sigma_X}$

Postulate 2. *Given the standard score z of a value v with respect to a normal distribution* f_X, *the probability that a random variable X following* f_X *will take values of at most v is given by:* $\int_{-\infty}^{z} \frac{1}{\sqrt{2\pi}} e^{-x^2/2} dx$

Postulate 3. *Given two independent random variables X and Y, the pdf of their sum* $X + Y$ *is the convolution of their individual pdfs.*

```
conclude # Lemma 1
(forall X Y T .
  ((and (is_normal X) (is_normal Y))
    ==>
    (= (probability (convolution X Y) T)
       (integral_SND (z_score T (convolution X Y))))))
pick-any x:Dist
pick-any y:Dist
pick-any t:Real
assume (and (is_normal x) (is_normal y))
let{xyNormal := (and (is_normal x) (is_normal y));
  xyCramers := (!uspec (!uspec Cramers_Decomposition_Theorem x) y);
  xPlusyNormal := (!mp xyCramers xyNormal);
  txPlusyProbability := (!uspec (!uspec probability_result t) (convolution x y))}
(!mp txPlusyProbability xPlusyNormal)
```

```
conclude # Theorem 1
(forall x y T .
  (and (is_normal (pdf x)) (is_normal (pdf y)))
    ==>
      (= (probability_randVar (sum x y) T)
         (integral_SND (z_score T (convolution (pdf x) (pdf y))))))
pick-any x:RandVar
pick-any y:RandVar
pick-any T:Real
assume (and (is_normal (pdf x)) (is_normal (pdf y)))
let{xPDF := (pdf x);
  yPDF := (pdf y);
  xyPDFnormal := (and  (is_normal xPDF) (is_normal yPDF) );
  convolutionxyPDF := (convolution xPDF yPDF);
  z := (sum x y);
  xySumRandVars := (!uspec (!uspec sum_randVars x) y);
  zPDF := (pdf z);
  zPDFConvolution := (!chain [(pdf z)
                    = (pdf (sum x y)) [z]
                    = convolutionxyPDF [xySumRandVars]]);
  probthm1 := (!uspec (!uspec (!uspec Probability_Theorem1 xPDF) yPDF) T);
  probthm1result := (!mp probthm1 xyPDFnormal)}
(!chain [(probability_randVar (sum x y) T)
      = (probability (pdf (sum x y) ) T) [probability_randVar_axiom]
      = (probability (pdf z) T)     [z]
      = (probability convolutionxyPDF T) [zPDFConvolution]
      = (probability (convolution xPDF yPDF) T) [convolutionxyPDF]
      = (integral_SND (z_score T (convolution (pdf x) (pdf y)))) [probthm1result]])
```

We have used the Athena proof assistant to formalize and mechanically verify our proofs (shown above). Our work extends the Athena proof library [2] with theory about statistical inference that can be reused for higher-level proofs[1].

---

[1] Available at http://wcl.cs.rpi.edu/pilots/fvdddas.

5   A Sample Application of Our Proof Library

We demonstrate how our extensions to the Athena proof library can be used to provide a mechanically-verified proof of probabilistic progress for a simple implementation of Paxos [20], a consensus algorithm which involves a set of agents called *proposers* that propose values to be chosen and a set of agents called *acceptors* that vote on those values. For our example, we consider a system in which there is one proposer and two acceptors. Paxos assumes an asynchronous, non-Byzantine system model where agents operate at arbitrary speed, may fail and restart, and have stable storage. Messages can be duplicated, lost, and have arbitrary transmission times, but are not corrupted. For the sake of simplicity, we make some additional assumptions – all agents are always available; there is no message loss; it is possible to observe the pdf of the message delay between any pair of agents as a normal distribution; and it is possible to observe the pdf of the processing time of every agent as a normal distribution. Our implementation of Paxos involves two *prepare* messages from the proposer to the acceptors, followed by two *promise* messages from the acceptors to the proposer, and finally, two *accept* messages from the proposer to the acceptors. The agents take some time to process each message. The algorithm makes progress when all messages have been transmitted, received, and processed.

We can define the worst-case scenario as the sequential operation of the protocol where no pair of actions (processing or message transmission) have any overlap in time. The total time for progress will, therefore, be the sum of the total processing time and the total message delay. If the message delays and processing times are represented by the sets of random variables $\mathbb{X} = \{X_1, X_2, X_3, X_4, X_5, X_6\}$ and $\mathbb{Y} = \{Y_1, Y_2, Y_3, Y_4, Y_5, Y_6\}$ respectively, then under our assumptions, Cramer's Decomposition Theorem can be recursively used to prove that $Z = \sum_{i=1}^{6} X_i + \sum_{i=1}^{5} Y_i$ follows a normal distribution $\mathcal{N}(\mu_Z, \sigma_Z)$. Theorem 1 can then be used to prove the following stochastic progress property:

Theorem 2. *The probability that $Z + Y_6$ will take a value of at most c_2 is given by:* $\int_{-\infty}^{z} \frac{1}{\sqrt{2\pi}} e^{-x^2/2} dx$ *where* $z = \frac{c_2 - (\mu_{Y_6} + \mu_Z)}{\sqrt{2(\sigma_{Y_6}^2 + \sigma_Z^2)}}$.

A straightforward progress envelope for Theorem 2 would be the constraint $\forall X \in \mathbb{X} : X \sim \mathcal{N}(\mu_X, \sigma_X^2) \land \forall Y \in \mathbb{Y} : Y \sim \mathcal{N}(\mu_Y, \sigma_Y^2)$.

6   Related Work

Runtime monitoring of formal properties has been previously investigated in [21] and [25]. Formal safety envelopes for stochastic state identification have been proposed in [4]. Formal verification of expectation and variance of discrete random variables and tail distribution bounds have been studied in [12] and [13]. Formalizations of the uniform random variable and continuous probability distributions in the HOL theorem prover[15] have been presented in [11] and [10].

Probabilistic analysis of wireless systems has been studied in [14]. [9] addresses probabilistic theorem proving as the problem of computing the probability of a logical formula given the probabilities of a set of formulas.

The existing work does not focus on augmenting formal proofs with runtime data or creating a dedicated proof library that can be directly reused for higher-level statistical properties of stochastic aerospace systems. We improve upon it by introducing runtime-modifiable formal proof techniques in the DDDAS architecture to allow the development of safety-critical aerospace systems that can dynamically adapt to the formal proofs that hold during runtime.

7 Conclusion

We have presented an approach for integrating formal methods directly in the dynamic data-driven applications systems (DDDAS) architecture that will allow the development of highly-adaptive formally-verified aerospace systems. We have also showcased the development of formal proof libraries in the Athena proof assistant that can be used as reusable building blocks to develop proofs of higher-level probabilistic properties of stochastic systems.

Real-life data is seldom perfect – e.g., normality of sensor data may only be tested up to some significant level and may also be affected by pre-processing. It is also computationally expensive to effectively estimate the tail bounds of distributions in real-time. Future directions of work, therefore, include investigating the development of formally-verified runtime sentinels that can find accurate and meaningful estimates from data and further expansion of our stochastic proof library in Athena by creating parameterized proofs for lower-level theory.

Acknowledgment. This research was partially supported by the National Science Foundation (NSF), Grant No. – CNS-1816307 and the Air Force Office of Scientific Research (AFOSR), DDDAS Grant No. – FA9550-19-1-0054.

References

1. Arkoudas, K.: Athena. http://proofcentral.org/athena
2. Arkoudas, K., Musser, D.: Athena libraries, http://proofcentral.org/athena/lib
3. Arkoudas, K., Musser, D.: Fundamental Proof Methods in Computer Science: A Computer-Based Approach. MIT Press, Cambridge (2017)
4. Breese, S., Kopsaftopoulos, F., Varela, C.: Towards proving runtime properties of data-driven systems using safety envelopes. In: The 12th International Workshop on Structural Health Monitoring, Stanford, CA (September 2019)
5. Chen, S., Imai, S., Zhu, W., Varela, C.A.: Towards learning spatio-temporal data stream relationships for failure detection in avionics. In: Blasch, E., Ravela, S., Aved, A. (eds.) Handbook of Dynamic Data Driven Applications Systems, pp. 97–121. Springer, Cham (2018). https://doi.org/10.1007/978-3-319-95504-9_5
6. Darema, F.: Dynamic data driven applications systems: a new paradigm for application simulations and measurements. In: Bubak, M., van Albada, G.D., Sloot, P.M.A., Dongarra, J. (eds.) ICCS 2004. LNCS, vol. 3038, pp. 662–669. Springer, Heidelberg (2004). https://doi.org/10.1007/978-3-540-24688-6_86

7. DeLaura, R., Robinson, M., Pawlak, M., Evans, J.: Modeling convective weather avoidance in enroute airspace. In: 13th Conference on Aviation, Range, and Aerospace Meteorology, AMS, New Orleans, LA (2008)
8. Fischer, M.J., Lynch, N.A., Paterson, M.S.: Impossibility of distributed consensus with one faulty process. J. ACM (JACM) **32**(2), 374–382 (1985)
9. Gogate, V., Domingos, P.: Probabilistic theorem proving. Commun. ACM **59**(7), 107–115 (2016)
10. Hasan, O., Tahar, S.: Formalization of continuous probability distributions. In: Pfenning, F. (ed.) CADE 2007. LNCS (LNAI), vol. 4603, pp. 3–18. Springer, Heidelberg (2007). https://doi.org/10.1007/978-3-540-73595-3_2
11. Hasan, O., Tahar, S.: Formalization of the standard uniform random variable. Theor. Comput. Sci. **382**, 71–83 (2007)
12. Hasan, O., Tahar, S.: Using theorem proving to verify expectation and variance for discrete random variables. J. Autom. Reason. **41**(3–4), 295–323 (2008)
13. Hasan, O., Tahar, S.: Formal verification of tail distribution bounds in the HOL theorem prover. Math. Methods Appl. Sci. **32**(4), 480–504 (2009)
14. Hasan, O., Tahar, S.: Probabilistic analysis of wireless systems using theorem proving. Electron. Notes Theor. Comput. Sci. **242**(2), 43–58 (2009)
15. Hurd, J.: Formal verification of probabilistic algorithms. Ph.D. thesis, University of Cambridge (2002)
16. Imai, S., Chen, S., Zhu, W., Varela, C.A.: Dynamic data-driven learning for self-healing avionics. Clust. Comput. **22**(1), 2187–2210 (2017). https://doi.org/10.1007/s10586-017-1291-8
17. Jaynes, E.T.: Probability Theory: The Logic of Science. Cambridge University Press, Cambridge (2003)
18. Kopsaftopoulos, F.: Data-driven stochastic identification for fly-by-feel aerospace structures: critical assessment of non-parametric and parametric approaches. In: AIAA Scitech 2019 Forum, pp. 15–34 (2019)
19. Lamport, L.: The part-time parliament. ACM Trans. Comput. Syst. (TOCS) **16**(2), 133–169 (1998)
20. Lamport, L.: Paxos made simple. ACM SIGACT News **32**(4), 18–25 (2001)
21. Mitsch, S., Platzer, A.: Modelplex: verified runtime validation of verified cyber-physical system models. Form. Methods Syst. Des. **49**(1–2), 33–74 (2016)
22. Ongaro, D., Ousterhout, J.: In search of an understandable consensus algorithm. In: 2014 USENIX Annual Technical Conference, pp. 305–319 (2014)
23. Paul, S., Hole, F., Zytek, A., Varela, C.A.: Wind-aware trajectory planning for fixed-wing aircraft in loss of thrust emergencies. In: The 37th AIAA/IEEE Digital Avionics Systems Conference, London, England, pp. 558–567 (September 2018)
24. Paul, S., Patterson, S., Varela, C.A.: Conflict-aware flight planning for avoiding near mid-air collisions. In: The 38th AIAA/IEEE Digital Avionics Systems Conference, San Diego, CA (September 2019)
25. Pike, L., Goodloe, A., Morisset, R., Niller, S.: Copilot: a hard real-time runtime monitor. In: Barringer, H., et al. (eds.) RV 2010. LNCS, vol. 6418, pp. 345–359. Springer, Heidelberg (2010). https://doi.org/10.1007/978-3-642-16612-9_26
26. Sommerville, I.: Software Engineering. Addison-Wesley/Pearson, Boston (2011)

Dynamic Sensor Processing for Securing Unmanned Vehicles

Raul Quinonez[2]([✉]), Luis Salazar[1], Jairo Giraldo[3], and Alvaro A. Cardenas[1][iD]

[1] Computer Science and Engineering Department,
University of California, Santa Cruz, Santa Cruz, CA, USA
{luedsala,alvaro.cardenas}@ucsc.edu
[2] Computer Science Department, University of Texas at Dallas,
Richardson, TX, USA
raul.quinoneztirado@utdallas.edu
[3] Electrical and Computer Engineering Department, University of Utah,
Salt Lake City, UT, USA
jairo.giraldo@utah.edu

Abstract. Unmanned Vehicles (UVs), including aerial, sea, and ground vehicles, include remotely operated vehicles and autonomous vehicles. The use of these vehicles is increasing rapidly, from military operations to the consumer space. UVs assess their environment (or relay it to the remote operator) with a variety of sensors and actuators that allow them to perform specific tasks such as navigating a route, hovering, or avoiding collisions. So far, UVs tend to trust the information provided by their sensors to make navigation decisions without data validation or verification. Therefore, attackers can exploit these limitations by feeding erroneous sensor data to disrupt or take control of the system. In this paper, we leverage the Dynamic Data Driven Application Systems (DDDAS) paradigm to design and implement an architecture for securing unmanned vehicles. We argue that DDDAS principles are a perfect fit to secure feedback-control systems with protections that classical security mechanisms cannot provide. In particular, by using exact models of the vehicle dynamics, we can compare and correlate their expected behavior (given by the models) with the values from data acquisition. If there is a persistent anomaly, we can replace sensor values with models, or fuse other sensors to replace the missing ones, enabling the vehicle to maintain safety in the immediate future.

Keywords: DDDAS · Unmanned vehicles · Security

1 Introduction

Unmanned Vehicles (UVs), including remote and autonomous aerial, ground, sea, and underwater vehicles, are becoming an integral part of our life [9].

This research was partially supported by the Air Force Office of Scientific Research under award number FA9550-17-1-0135.

F. Darema et al. (Eds.): DDDAS 2020, LNCS 12312, pp. 253–261, 2020.
https://doi.org/10.1007/978-3-030-61725-7_30

Unmanned aerial vehicles have applications ranging from agricultural management to aerial mapping and freight transportation [6]. To operate correctly, UVs rely on sensors (transducers that translate a physical signal into an electrical one), and actuators (transducers that deliver a physical effect to the surrounding environment). Currently, most UVs trust sensor data to make navigation and other control decisions, and believe the control command given to actuators is executed faithfully; however, there is a growing threat. While trusting sensor and actuator data without any form of validation has proven to be a valid trade-off in current market solutions, it is not sustainable as UVs become ubiquitous, and sensor attacks continue to mature in their sophistication.

Classical security solutions cannot protect UVs from several types of attacks, including *analog attacks*: for example, soundwaves can affect accelerometers [12] and gyroscopes [11], lasers can affect the camera image processing of drones [4], and lidar sensors in cars [2]. Similarly, attackers can use electromagnetic interference to manipulate rotors in drones [10]. In addition to transduction attacks, UVs are vulnerable to GPS spoofing and data injection attacks through classical security vulnerabilities. GPS spoofing attacks affecting the navigation of more than 24 vessels in the Black Sea have been reported [13] (experts believe these GPS attacks are anti-drone measures), and it is believed, Iran spoofed a military-grade GPS to capture a U.S. Unmanned Aerial Vehicle [8]. Launching a similar UV takeover attack in commercial GPS systems is quite straightforward [5].

Therefore to protect UVs, we need new data-driven algorithms that can detect poisoned data and dynamically reconfigure the system to survive attacks. The Dynamic Data Driven Applications Systems (DDDAS) paradigm [1] is particularly well suited to help us model the problem of detecting data poisoning in control systems. While the Cyber-Physical Systems paradigm is used to refer to the modernization of control systems with embedded controllers, wireless sensors, and computer networks, its definition does not give us any insights on how to leverage this modernization to design better control systems. The DDDAS paradigm, in contrast, encourages us by its definition to think in terms of how to use models of the physical system to guide the data acquisition, how data acquisition can change the operation and simulation of our models, and in ultimately, on how to dynamically reconfigure the control system based on the outputs of computation, model simulations, and sensor inputs.

These unique characteristics of DDDAS are precisely the ones we need to detect and respond to attacks against control systems. In particular, in this paper, we apply our previously proposed DDDAS Anomaly Detection and Response (DDDAS-ADR) architecture [3] to UVs. DDDAS-ADR can simulate the physical system under control (e.g., the dynamics of unmanned vehicles and their expected response to the control commands), and the output of these computations can then lead us to reclassify sensors, actuators, and controllers as more trustworthy or less trustworthy. For example, a sensor reporting readings that do not match the model-predicted computation of the physical system will be deemed less trustworthy. Our DDDAS-ADR algorithm can then dynamically reconfigure the selection of sensors that we trust, use only trustworthy sensors and accurate computer simulations, and create synthetic data to mitigate the lack of missing sensor observations to drive the system to a safe place, even under attack. This paper complements and expands our recent work on SAVIOR [7] by giving more details on our attacks, and adding new examples of our defenses.

2   Motivating Examples: Data Poisoning in UVs

To motivate our defenses against data poisoning in UVs, we now illustrate how different UVs can be attacked and the effects of these attacks. In particular, we consider the Intel Aero Drone, the jMAVSim simulator (which allows developers to run real-world drone controllers such as PX4 in a simulated environment), and an autonomous ground vehicle based on a *Basher RZ-4 1/10 scale rally racer* remote control vehicle. We modified the original car in order to make it autonomous (it can sense its environment with a camera and a lidar and it can then follow a lane and avoid obstacles). A low-level controller translates these commands into signals sent to the actuators. The hardware in which the state observer and the high-level controller run is an Odroid XU4, a single board computer in which the Robot Operating System (ROS) is implemented on top of Linux Ubuntu MATE. Videos for some of these attacks can be found in the following link: https://www.youtube.com/playlist? list=PLxjvyevQzqzxPAQcOjzzo9ZrR3UuyfP6h.

2.1   Attacking MAVLink in Drones

We first consider the MAVLink implementation of the Intel Aero drone, and the jMAVSim. A general connection between a remote controlled drone, where a user has a Radio Controller (RC) that communicates directly with a radio receiver in the drone that is connected to a companion computer and sends commands to the flight controller of the drone. Here, manual commands are received, interpreted, and executed by the flight controller. These commands require user interaction. The second type of input comes from the ground control station. These commands include GPS routing and re-routing, as well as calibration and system information. This communication is on top of the MAVLink protocol that is sent using a TCP or UDP connection. The third type of connection uses the Wi-Fi interface to create an SSL connection with the companion computer on the drone. Here, commands and program execution can be given directly to the drone. These communication channels are represented in the Intel Aero drone (See Fig. 1), which we use in our experiments.

MAVLink message signing is optional and only supported in MAVLink 2.0. Moreover, most communication channels implemented with MAVLink in commercial drones have no encryption or obfuscation, allowing an attacker to sniff the legitimate traffic. If a communication channel between a ground controller

1 byte	:: Packet starter
1 byte	:: Payload length
1 byte	:: Incompatibility flags
1 byte	:: Compatibility flags
1 byte	:: Sequence number
1 byte	:: System ID
1 byte	:: Component ID
1|3 bytes	:: Message ID
0-255 bytes	:: Payload
2 bytes	:: Checksum (X.25 CRC)
0-13 bytes	:: Signature (optional)

Fig. 1. General architecture for the remote operation of drones.

Fig. 2. MAVLink packet format.

and a drone does not implement message signing, a third party can send arbitrary messages to the drone over the same communication channel and the drone would acknowledge such messages as legitimate messages since there is no real authentication mechanism. Attacks through MAVLink will also allow us to inject and overwrite data in the drone, such as IMU or GPS data.

In order to fool the drone to recognize the malicious host as a ground controller, the latter must periodically send a heartbeat message indicating to the drone that the host is both alive and a ground controller. This is achieved by implementing a MAVLink communications channel that connects to the drone's MAVLink router and sends the message with ID 0 (a heartbeat message). The structure of the packets in MAVLink can be seen in Fig. 2.

Values needed for the actual communication between the ground controller and the drone were captured while sniffing the legitimate traffic exchanged between the drone and the legitimate ground station. In particular, the first heartbeat message has an uninitialized *custom_mode* field and sets the *system_status* field to represent the 'MAV_STATE_UINIT' state. This initial message is necessary to allow the drone to register the ground controller as such. Afterwards, the heartbeat messages are sent with a 'custom_mode' set to 0xc0080600 and the *system_status* set to 'MAV_STATE_ACTIVE'. Once the heartbeat messages are sent, the drone acknowledges the host as a ground controller and accepts commands incoming from said host.

We start by testing two attacks; a "disarm" command, which causes the drone to plummet to the ground. This attack was effective in both the Intel Aero and the jMAVSim simulator. We also tested a different attack to cause the drone to change its current course or receive the instruction to go to a particular set of coordinates. For this, a new traffic capture was taken in which the command to

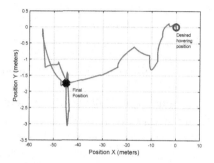

Fig. 3. GPS attack on drone. The red line is what the drone and remote operator believe is happening, while the blue line shows what happened in reality. (Color figure online)

Fig. 4. X-Y position of the quadcopter subject to the attack in the gyroscope. The goal of the controller was to keep the drone hovering but the attack caused an erratic displacement because the controller was trying to compensate the fake change in the roll angle data.

send the instruction to travel to a specific latitude, longitude, and altitude tuple was captured. The attack sends a message to the drone in which the malicious host instructs the drone to go to a specific location. Afterwards, the malicious host monitors the telemetry information broadcasted by the drone to all registered ground stations in order to determine whether the drone is reducing its distance with the desired destination. If a significant increase of distance is detected, the automated attack script sends again the same instruction, forcing the drone to resume the trajectory. Once the drone is within a reasonably close distance from the target location, a 'land' command is sent to the drone. This attack can effectively steal the drone and make it land at the target location by the attacker.

We also launch attacks on the GPS and gyroscope data of the drone and test their results. For the GPS attack, we change mid-flight the GPS coordinates of the drone, making the drone (and the remote operator) believe they are on track to the destination, while in reality, a bias in the coordinates will shift the drone in the opposite direction. Figure 3 illustrates this attack, which manages to steer the drone out of its planned course. Similarly, Fig. 4 shows the effect of attacking the gyroscopes of the drone. While the drone was programmed to hover over a fixed point, the attacks on the gyroscope data force the drone to follow an erratic trajectory, ultimately being displaced from where it was supposed to hover.

2.2   Attacking ROS in the Ground Vehicle

In addition to launching attacks on the drone, we also launched similar attacks on the ground vehicle. The ground vehicle is operated with the Robot Operating System (ROS). The main objective of ROS is to provide a framework with libraries to aid common functionality, hardware abstractions, and communication between processes with low coupling. The communication between processes follows a publish-and-subscribe architecture with a master node acting as an intermediary for initial connection. The master node is aware of all the current nodes and the topics being published and receives query requests from nodes to either publish or subscribe to a given topic. Once a node is launched, it can initiate a request to the master node, which in turn will provide the appropriate information for the nodes to establish the communications channel (TCPROS or UDPROS). This allows the nodes to be independent from each other, and reduces the coupling between modules since they could start, reboot, or finish execution at any time.

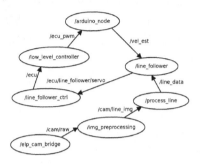

Fig. 5. Line follower node graph in ROS for the ground vehicle showing how data is exchanged between nodes.

Despite the fact that nodes are communicating with each other to establish the exchange of information, nodes are not aware of the veracity of the information or how many nodes are subscribed to publish any given topic. This implies that there can be multiple subscribers for any specific topic and the master node does not enforce any sanity checks on the data. As an example, Fig. 5 depicts the current nodes and topics present when a simple "lane" algorithm is executed. This algorithm takes an image from the camera, processes it, and discerns whether the vehicle should steer in a given direction based on a line drawn on top of a track in which the vehicle is driving.

The line follower algorithm greatly depends on the image published by the camera on the "/cam/raw" topic since it is the main source of data for the decision-making process. Given the fact that there can be multiple nodes publishing the same topic and that there are no sanity checks in place, a malicious node can publish the same camera topic and replay a chosen image at a higher rate than that of the camera, overwriting any legitimate image with a malicious one and compromising the data that would be used by the controller in order to make the steering decisions.

3   Detecting Attacks

Our DDDAS-ADR architecture was previously proposed to detect attacks on industrial control systems [3]. Here we adapt this framework to UVs. In particular, one advantage that we have over general industrial control systems, is that the physical models for drones (quadcopters) and ground vehicles are well-understood. So we just need to learn the specific parameters of the vehicles that we have (we do this with system identification tools) and then use them to predict and simulate the behavior of the physical system, and we then compare these predictions with the information we get from the sensors. In our DDDAS-ADR architecture, we first have data from the sensors (e.g., IMU, GPS, etc.) and then preprocess the data to obtain the variables that are needed for the differential equations of the models of the systems. Because both the models for quadcopters and for ground vehicles are nonlinear, we need to use the Extended Kalman Filter (instead of the Kalman Filter) to predict future measurements. We then compare our predictions with the received information and see if there is any systematic pattern of historical anomalies. We keep track of these historical anomalies with the nonparametric CUmulative SUm (non-parametric CUSUM) algorithm. If the historical anomalies reach a threshold, an alert is raised.

IMUs used in vehicles are composed of a 3-axis accelerometer, 3-axis gyroscope, and 3-axis magnetometer that can be combined to calculate the vehicle attitude (roll ϕ, pitch θ, yaw ψ angles) and attitude rates ($\dot{\phi}, \dot{\theta}, \dot{\psi}$). Also, most AVs have GPS receivers to collect information about the spacial position of the drone (x, y, z). Table 1 shows the raw sensor information on the x, y, and z axis for IMU readings of the accelerometer, gyroscope, and magnetometer with their respective units. Similarly Table 2 illustrates the type of sensor data we have in the car.

Table 1. IMU data from Intel Aero.

IMU variable	Value	Unit
Accelerometer on x-axis	$-.27762287$	m/s^2
Accelerometer on y-axis	$-.18123956$	m/s^2
Accelerometer on z-axis	-9.80503749	m/s^2
Gyroscope on x-axis	$-.01762431$	rad/s
Gyroscope on y-axis	$.01770246$	rad/s
Gyroscope on z-axis	$.00378060$	rad/s
Magnetometer on x-axis	$.15779675$	gauss
Magnetometer on y-axis	$-.89283788$	gauss
Magnetometer on z-axis	1.77371621	gauss

Table 2. Ground vehicle data.

Sensor measurement	Value	Unit
Velocity:	0.027154	m/s
Angle:	-0.061717	rad
Y-position:	0.099662	m
Steering:	-0.114908	rad

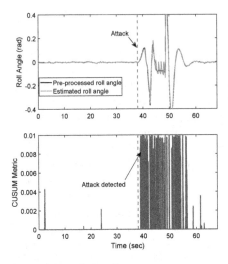

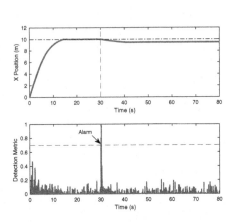

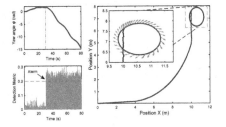

Fig. 6. Attack in the gyroscope sensor that adds a bias of 0.1 rad/s during 3 s to the x-axis.

Fig. 7. GPS bias attack on the car. The bias attack adds a small increment of 0.5 m to the current position.

Our algorithms [7] can detect attacks with high precision and low overhead. Figure 6 shows how due to the fake increase in the roll speed of the drone, the controllers start compensating trying to drive the roll angle to zero, causing a difference in the prediction and triggering an alarm after 1.5 s. Similarly, Fig. 7 illustrates the impact of a GPS bias attack and the detection of the attack in the ground vehicle.

Fig. 8. Attack and detection in ground vehicle.

A second attack to the car induces a time-varying change in the roll angular velocity that increases with a rate of 0.01 rad/s. The attack causes the control to try to compensate causing the vehicle to follow a circular trajectory and never reaching its destination (see Fig. 8). This attack is also easily detected with our proposed detection strategy.

4   Conclusions

The DDDAS paradigm is particularly well-suited to design defenses against data poisoning in control systems. The ability to dynamically reevaluate sensor data trustworthiness based on physical models of the system under control allows us to detect attacks and reconfigure the system to be resilient to these threats. In future work, we will expand our work with sensor fusion to validate and replace sensor data with information from trustworthy sensors.

References

1. Blasch, E., Ravela, S., Aved, A. (eds.): Handbook of Dynamic Data Driven Applications Systems. Springer, Cham (2018). https://doi.org/10.1007/978-3-319-95504-9
2. Cao, Y., et al.: Adversarial sensor attack on LiDAR-based perception in autonomous driving. In: Proceedings of the 26th ACM Conference on Computer and Communications Security (CCS 2019), London, UK (November 2019)
3. Combita, L.F., Giraldo, J.A., Cardenas, A.A., Quijano, N.: DDDAS for attack detection and isolation of control systems. In: Blasch, E., Ravela, S., Aved, A. (eds.) Handbook of Dynamic Data Driven Applications Systems, pp. 407–422. Springer, Cham (2018). https://doi.org/10.1007/978-3-319-95504-9_17
4. Davidson, D., Wu, H., Jellinek, R., Ristenpart, T., Singh, V.: Controlling UAVs with sensor input spoofing attacks. In: Proceedings of the 10th USENIX Conference on Offensive Technologies, WOOT 2016, pp. 221–231. USENIX Association, Berkeley (2016)
5. Humphreys, T.E., Ledvina, B.M., Psiaki, M.L., O'Hanlon, B.W., Kintner, P.M.: Assessing the spoofing threat: development of a portable GPS civilian spoofer. In: Radionavigation Laboratory Conference Proceedings (2008)
6. Jenkins, D., Vasigh, B.: The economic impact of unmanned aircraft systems integration in the United States. In: Association for Unmanned Vehicle Systems International (AUVSI) (2013)
7. Quinonez, R., Giraldo, J., Salazar, L., Bauman, E., Cardenas, A., Lin, Z.: Savior: securing autonomous vehicles with robust physical invariants. In: 2020 USENIX Security Symposium (2020)
8. Rawnsley, A.: Iran's alleged drone hack: tough, but possible. Wired (2011)
9. Seetharaman, G., Lakhotia, A., Blasch, E.P.: Unmanned vehicles come of age: the DARPA grand challenge. Computer **39**(12), 26–29 (2006)
10. Selvaraj, J., Dayanıklı, G.Y., Gaunkar, N.P., Ware, D., Gerdes, R.M., Mina, M., et al.: Electromagnetic induction attacks against embedded systems. In: Asia Conference on Computer and Communications Security (AsiaCCS), pp. 499–510. ACM (2018)
11. Son, Y.M., et al.: Rocking drones with intentional sound noise on gyroscopic sensors. In: 24th USENIX Security Symposium. USENIX Association (2015)
12. Trippel, T., Weisse, O., Xu, W., Honeyman, P., Fu, K.: Walnut: waging doubt on the integrity of mems accelerometers with acoustic injection attacks. In: 2017 IEEE European Symposium on Security and Privacy (EuroS&P), pp. 3–18. IEEE (2017)
13. Weise, E.: Mysterious GPS glitch telling ships they're parked at airport may be anti-drone measure (September 2017)

A Scalable Mixture Model Based Defense Against Data Poisoning Attacks on Classifiers

Xi Li, David J. Miller, Zhen Xiang, and George Kesidis[✉]

School of EECS, The Pennsylvania State University,
University Park, PA 16802, USA
{xzl45,djm25,zux49,gik2}@psu.edu

Abstract. Classifiers, e.g., those based on Naive Bayes, a support vector machine, or even a neural network, are highly susceptible to a data-poisoning attack. The attack objective is to degrade classification accuracy by covertly embedding malicious (labeled) samples into the training set. Such attacks can be mounted by an insider, through an outsourcing process (for data acquisition or training), or conceivably during active learning. In some cases, a very small amount of poisoning can result in dramatic reduction in classification accuracy. Data poisoning attacks are successful mainly because the malicious injected samples significantly skew the data distribution of the corrupted class. Such attack samples are generally data outliers and in principle separable from the clean samples. We propose a generalized, scalable, and dynamic data driven defense system that: 1) uses a mixture model both to well-fit the (potentially multi-modal) data and to give potential to isolate attack samples in a small subset of the mixture components; 2) performs hypothesis testing to decide both which components and which samples within those components are poisoned, with the identified poisoned ones purged from the training set. Our approaches addresses the attack scenario where adversarial samples are an unknown subset embedded in the initial training set, and can be used to perform data sanitization as a precursor to the training of any type of classifier. The promising results for experiments on the TREC05 spam corpus and Amazon reviews polarity dataset demonstrate the effectiveness of our defense strategy.

Keywords: Adversarial learning · Data poisoning attack · Mixture modeling · Parsimonious mixtures · Spam filter · Sentiment analysis

1 Introduction

Machine-learned classifiers can be used to support the cooperation between sensing and high-dimensional analysis in Dynamic Data Driven Applications Systems (DDDAS) [2]. Machine learning systems are vulnerable to inputs crafted

This research is supported in part by an AFOSR DDDAS grant and a Cisco Systems URP gift.

F. Darema et al. (Eds.): DDDAS 2020, LNCS 12312, pp. 262–273, 2020.
https://doi.org/10.1007/978-3-030-61725-7_31

by an adversary. Interest in adversarial learning (AL) has grown dramatically in recent years, focusing on devising attacks against machine learning models and defenses against such attacks. Three important types of AL attacks [10] are: data poisoning (e.g., [3,7,22,23]), test-time evasion (e.g., [1,12,16,19]) and reverse engineering (e.g., [15,20,21]). In this work, we address data poisoning attacks on classifiers, e.g., those based on a support vector machine (SVM), a Bayesian network, or neural network, that seek to degrade classification accuracy. The proposed defense can be widely deployed to sanitize the training set **prior to the initial training process and during dynamic reinforcement learning.**

Data poisoning (DP) is an effective attack to mislead a classifier. DP is able to dramatically degrade accuracy by adding relatively few maliciously crafted data points to a training set. To expand on this point, first note that a DP attack may be done before data collection to form the training set. For the example of a spam filter, emails sent from known malicious Internet Protocol (IP) addresses are regarded as spam, and an attacker may generate and send emails that are more representative of ham via blacklisted IP addresses to pollute the spam training set. For a sentiment analysis problem, an attacker could insert positively labeled samples with words conveying very negative sentiments [14] to misguide the model of positive sentiment. Second, existing classifiers are highly vulnerable to data poisoning attacks. The malicious samples injected by an adversary will skew the data distributions of the corrupted class in a manner confounding the class discriminating features. Once the training set is poisoned with sufficient malicious samples, the overall classification accuracy will be significantly degraded.

Defenses against DP attacks on various systems include [9,13,18]. [18] constructs approximate upper bounds on the loss across a family of DP attacks, for defenders that first perform outlier removal followed by empirical risk minimization. [9] proposes a defender named Curie to protect an SVM from a DP attack. [9] assumes that the malicious data are crafted by maximizing the loss function of an SVM by flipping labels of legitimate samples. Therefore such data are similar to the normal points from the opposite set. If an additional dimension, the class label, is added to the feature space, the attack samples will be separated from the benign ones. [9] is not a generalized defense strategy as its assumption on malicious samples is specific to an SVM. A Reject on Negative Impact (RONI) strategy was proposed in [13] – although this work specifically focuses on spam filtering, it generalizes to defenses of classifiers on any domain. The defender in [13] rejects putative additional training samples if trial-adaptation of the spam model based on use of these samples causes degradation in classification accuracy on a held-out validation set. This strategy makes two strong assumptions: 1) that there is sufficient labeled data to have a held-out validation set; and 2) that the classifier has already been trained on "clean" data, with the attack consisting of additional labeled samples for classifier retraining. [13] is not a practical strategy when the malicious data are embedded within the original training set (with the attack samples an unknown subset). This more difficult scenario is addressed here.

A potential strategy for designing a **generalized** defender against an **embedded** data poisoning attack is to conduct "data sanitization" on the training set, *i.e.*, identifying and removing the attack samples as training set outliers. While such ideas are mentioned in [8] and are related to [11], we are not aware such ideas have been practically, effectively applied. Again, a main reason why the victim classifiers are susceptible to data poisoning attacks is that, under the corrupted class, the training/model estimation is degraded in an unimpeded fashion by the planted malicious "outliers". **Hence, we propose a mixture based outlier detection method, both to well-fit the (potentially multimodal) data and to allow potential concentration and isolation of poisoned samples in a small subset of the mixture components.** The validity of our defense strategy is demonstrated by experimental results on the TREC05 spam corpus and Amazon reviews polarity dataset.

This paper is organized as follows. We first define the threat model of data poisoning attacks in Sect. 2. In Sect. 3, we propose our mixture based defense against data poisoning attacks on generative classifiers. Experimental results are presented in Sect. 4. Finally, we conclude our work and discuss future work in Sect. 5.

2 Threat Model of Data Poisoning Attack

In this section, we build the threat model of data poisoning attacks against statistical classifiers, including the knowledge and objective of attacker and defender, as well as the plausible attack scenarios.

2.1 Notation

We consider a D-dimensional feature space, with a sample represented as a vector $\underline{x} = (x_1, x_2, \ldots, x_D)$, where x_d $(d = 1, \ldots, D)$ can be discrete valued, such as word counts if $\underline{x}$ is text data, following a multinomial distribution, or can be continuous valued, *e.g.*, $\underline{x}$ is generated via a multivariate Gaussian distribution. The dataset is then represented by a fixed (high) dimensional (possibly highly sparse) feature matrix – e.g., many words may have zero occurrences in a given document, in which case the vector will be sparse. Let $\mathcal{X}_p = \{\underline{x}_i^p, i = 1, \ldots, N_p\}$ be a given training set of positive samples used to build a multi-component *positive-class* model. Likewise, let $\mathcal{X}_n = \{\underline{x}_i^n, i = 1, \ldots, N_n\}$ be the negative training set for building a multi-component *negative-class* model. For concreteness, we consider binary classification here. It is possible to extend our work to a multi-class (>2classes) classifier.

2.2 Threat Model

Attacker's Assumption and Goal: We assume that an attacker: 1) has full knowledge of the learning approach and classification framework, *e.g.*, a standard naive Bayes (NB) classifier; 2) does not need access to the clean training set as poisoning is done before data collection to form the training set; 3) only pollutes the negative training set, *e.g.*, polluting spam set of a spam filter by sending ham emails via known blacklisted IP addresses, or poisoning negative set in sentimental analysis on product reviews by verbally recommending a product but giving it a low numerical rating; 4) is unaware of any deployed defense. The **goal** of an attacker is to decrease classification accuracy with as few attack samples as possible.

Defender's Assumption and Goal: The defender presumes that: 1) The positive set is untouched (clean); 2) it is unknown whether the negative set is corrupted and if so, which is the attack subset of samples. The defender **aims to:** 1) identify and remove attack samples, as many as possible, before classifier training/retraining; 2) maintain the classification accuracy as high as that of a classifier trained without data poisoning.

Attack Scenarios: Our approach is applicable to two attack scenarios: 1) classifier retraining and 2) classifier training, where the latter is more challenging. In the retraining scenario, one can initially build clean positive and negative models (those uncorrupted by attack) using $\mathcal{X}_p$ and $\mathcal{X}_n$, respectively. Let us denote a batch of additional samples that are treated as labeled negative by $\tilde{\mathcal{X}}_n = \{\underline{\tilde{x}}_i, i = 1, \ldots, \tilde{N}_n\}$. In the retraining case, the learner pools $\tilde{\mathcal{X}}_n$ with $\mathcal{X}_n$, retraining the negative model using the combined data pool $\mathcal{X}_{nc} = \{\mathcal{X}_n, \tilde{\mathcal{X}}_n\}$. Note that $\tilde{\mathcal{X}}_n$ may consist of legitimate negative samples, attack samples, or some combinations of the two. If one can utilize a separate, uncorrupted, held-out validation set, the approach in [13] can effectively mitigate an attacking $\tilde{\mathcal{X}}_n$. However, consider the other scenario – the training scenario. Unlike retraining, where the subset $\tilde{\mathcal{X}}_n$ is known to the learner, in the training scenario the attack samples are embedded amongst the clean negative samples. The learner does not know whether an attack is present and if so, which is the attack sample subset. Again the learner uses $\mathcal{X}_{nc}$, but in this case to perform the inaugural learning of the negative model, not model retraining. In the sequel, we develop a mixture based defense strategy, which effectively defeats the attack under the more challenging classifier training scenario.

3   Mixture Model Based Defense Against Data Poisoning Attack

3.1   Mixture Modeling

To defend a data poisoning attack, a "data sanitization" strategy will be applied, *i.e.*, identifying and removing attack samples as training set "outliers". Such outliers are conjectured to form disjoint subpopulations from the normal negative samples in the feature space. Mixture modeling is a sound approach for seeking to concentrate (and thus isolate) poisoned samples in a few components, which can assist in accurately identifying and removing them. Accordingly, we build a mixture model based defender to distinguish the distribution of attack samples from benign ones.

The mixture representation of $\underline{x}$ for an M_k-component mixture model is given by (1), where $k \in \{p, nc\}$ represents the positive (p) or possibly contaminated negative class (nc), M_k is the number of components, and $\Theta(M_k) = \{\{\alpha_{j|k}\}, \{\theta_{j|k}\}\}$ denotes the parameters at model order M_k.

$$P[\underline{x}|\Theta(M_k)] = \sum_{j=1}^{M_k} \alpha_{j|k} P[\underline{x}|\theta_{j|k}] \tag{1}$$

Here, $\{\alpha_{j|k}\}$ are component masses which satisfy $0 \leq \alpha_{j|k} \leq 1$ and $\sum_{j=1}^{M_k} \alpha_{j|k} = 1$, and $\theta_{j|k}$ is the set of parameters specifying the joint probability mass function (PMF) for component j under model k. Model order M_k is selected by minimizing the Bayesian Information Criterion (BIC) cost [17], and the model parameters $\Theta(M_k)$ are estimated by the Expectation-Maximization (EM) algorithm [5].

Detection Inference: To significantly mislead a classifier with fewest attack samples, the adversary skews the distribution of the negative samples in a manner confounding the positive and negative discriminating features. Hence, the attack samples should be more representative of positive samples and present **atypicality** with respect to the negative set. Log mixture likelihood, $\log(P[\underline{x}|\Theta(M_k)])$, measures how typical a sample is to class k and therefore is used as the statistic for detection inference. (To avoid underflow, we use log-likelihood rather than likelihood.) Herein, we propose the null hypothesis of our detection inference, that the negative training set is not poisoned, *i.e.*, all negative training samples are generated according to the null distribution. Alternatively, if the data poisoning attack exists, the negative training set is generated by an alternative model, which is a mixture of negative and positive distributions. The test statistic is to check on which side of the positive-negative boundary, $\log(P[\underline{x}|\Theta(M_p)]) = \log(P[\underline{x}|\Theta(M_{nc})])$, a negative sample $\underline{x}$ resides. If $\log(P[\underline{x}|\Theta(M_p)]) > \log(P[\underline{x}|\Theta(M_{nc})])$, then $\underline{x}$ is better explained by the positive model. Thus, we reject the null hypothesis, and the negative training set is deemed contaminated (poisoned). Otherwise, we accept the null hypothesis.

Implementation: We first separately apply mixture modeling to both the positive set $\mathcal{X}_p$ and negative set $\mathcal{X}_{nc}$ to compute the model parameters $\Theta(M_p)$ and $\Theta(M_{nc})$. Then, we do detection inference on negative samples for a given model component. The component label on a negative sample $\underline{x}$,

$$j^* = arg\, max_j P[j|\underline{x}, \Theta(M_{nc})],$$

can be obtained from the E-step of EM-learning, and is fixed during detection.

To weaken the impact brought by the attack components on likelihood evaluation, suspect components in the negative model are pruned one by one. The components are traversed by the component score, which is the average sample log-likelihood under the positive model. For example, the score of component i with samples $X_i \subset \mathcal{X}_{nc}$ (those samples MAP-assigned to component

i) is defined as $\frac{1}{|X_i|}\log(P[X_i|\Theta(M_p)])$. If a negative component is fundamentally formed by attack samples, it gets a higher score as its samples are more positive-representative. Otherwise, it gets a lower score. Then, from the highest to the lowest-scored negative component, we perform the following detection and response:

1. A sample $\underline{x}$ in the current component i is rejected if it is more likely positive than negative with margin of m. Here $m \in [0,1]$ is a hyperparameter for relaxing this decision, because benign samples may be close to the positive-negative boundary. In other words, the suspicious subset

$$\tilde{X}_i = \{\underline{x} \in X_i | \log(P[\underline{x}|\Theta(M_p)]) > m\log(P[\underline{x}|\Theta(M_{nc}-1)])\}$$

is removed from X_i (and also from $\mathcal{X}_{nc}$). To avoid bias if component i is contaminated, the model used to evaluate negative likelihood is the re-weighted mixture excluding component i, i.e.,

$$\Theta(M_{nc}-1) = \{\{\frac{\alpha_{j|nc}}{\sum_{j'\neq i}\alpha_{j'|nc}}\}, \{\theta_{j|nc}\}|\forall j \neq i\}.$$

2. Denoting the surviving samples of component i as $X'_i = X_i \backslash \tilde{X}_i$, the component parameters $\theta_{i|nc} = arg\,max_\theta \log(P[X'_i|\theta])$ are re-estimated, and updated component weights become $\alpha_{j|nc} = |X'_j|/|\mathcal{X}_{nc}|$ for $j = 1...M_{nc}$. Here, $X'_j = X_j$ for the negative components j not yet visited.
3. Evaluate the BIC cost of the current negative mixture, $BIC(\Theta(M_{nc}), \mathcal{X}_{nc})$, and that of the re-weighted negative mixture with component i pruned, $BIC(\Theta(M_{nc}-1), \mathcal{X}_{nc})$.
4. If the BIC cost decreases ($BIC(\Theta(M_{nc}), \mathcal{X}_{nc}) > BIC(\Theta(M_{nc}-1), \mathcal{X}_{nc})$), we prune component i and re-weight the remaining components, i.e., update $\Theta(M_{nc})$ by $\Theta(M_{nc}-1)$ and the optimal model order M_{nc} by $M_{nc}-1$.

As mentioned previously, we use log-likelihood rather than likelihood to avoid underflow. However, underflow still exists if we simply take the log-likelihood of sample $\underline{x}$ as $\log(\sum_{j=1}^{M_k}\alpha_{j|k}P[\underline{x}|\theta_{j|k}])$. Thus, we compute log mixture likelihood by (2), where it is the sum of the expected complete data log likelihood and entropy of soft component assignments ($P[j|\underline{x}, \Theta(M_k)]$) [25]:

$$\log P[\underline{x}|\Theta(M_k)] = \sum_{j=1}^{M_k} P[j|\underline{x}, \Theta(M_k)]\log\left(\alpha_{j|k}P[\underline{x}|\theta_{j|k}]\right)$$

$$-\sum_{j=1}^{M_k} P[j|\underline{x}, \Theta(M_k)]\log\left(P[j|\underline{x}, \Theta(M_k)]\right) \qquad (2)$$

$$\forall \underline{x} \in \mathcal{X}_{nc}, k \in \{p, nc\}$$

3.2 Parsimonious Mixture Model (PMM) Framework

The standard mixture model is not a feasible solution for a high dimensional feature space. It maintains an independent parameter for every feature in each component, which causes the dominance of model complexity in the BIC cost. This leads to gross underestimation of the model order for high D [6], with a standard mixture model choosing a single component for a high dimensional dataset. PMMs [6] solve this fundamental problem by introducing shared parameters which represent feature distributions common to all components. Model complexity is then determined by the number of components and the number of unique parameters in each component. Therefore model complexity does not dominate the BIC cost any more, and it is possible for a PMM to select a proper model order for a high dimensional dataset.

Maximum likelihood estimation of the parsimonious multi-component mixture can be performed via a generalized application of the EM algorithm (GEM) [6]. With the assumption on independence of features conditioned on the component of origin, we rewrite the likelihood under the parsimonious mixture as

$$P[\underline{x}|\Theta(M)] = \sum_{j=1}^{M} \alpha_j \prod_{d=1}^{D} P[x_d|\theta_j]^{v_{jd}} P[x_d|\theta_s]^{(1-v_{jd})} \tag{3}$$

where $\Theta(M) = \{\{\alpha_j\}, \{\theta_j\}, \theta_s, \{v_{jd}\}\}$ is the model parameters at order M: M is the number of components, $\{\alpha_j\}$ are component masses satisfying $0 \leq \alpha_j \leq 1$ and $\sum_{j=1}^{M} \alpha_j = 1$, $P[x_d|\theta_j]$ and $P[x_d|\theta_s]$ are component-specific and shared distributions, respectively, and $v_{jd} \in \{0, 1\}$ is the switch between component-specific and shared distribution for feature d. The model is initialized with $M = M_{\max}$ (chosen to overestimate the true number of clusters), and the component with smallest mass is pruned in each iteration until $M = 1$. For each model order we perform GEM learning to optimize model parameters. The one which yields the least BIC cost is the optimal model order M, and the parameters associated with M are the optimal parameters. For brevity, we omit the detailed EM learning process and derivation of model parameters, which can be found in [6].

Component pruning and component parameter re-estimation in PMMs is similar to the method of the previous subsection. For example, to prune component i, the model order M is decremented to $M - 1$, and

$$\Theta(M) = \{\{\frac{\alpha_j}{\sum_{j' \neq i} \alpha_{j'}}\}, \{\theta_j\}, \theta_s, \{v_{jd}\}|\forall j \neq i\}.$$

For re-estimating parameters of component i by its surviving samples, we only update component-specific parameters $\theta_i = arg\,max_\theta \log(P[X'_i|\theta])$, and the other parameters (θ_s) are untouched. PMMs are used in all our experiments.

4   Experiments

In this section we provide convincing experiments for our proposed defense. We first introduce the datasets and target classifier applied, and then demonstrate the effectiveness of an embedded data poisoning attack – "pure-positive" poisoning attack. Finally we present and analyze the performance of our defender against such adversarial attacks.

4.1   Experiment Setup and Evaluation Criterion

Datasets: The experiments were conducted on two datasets, TREC 2005 spam corpus (TREC05) [4] and Amazon reviews polarity dataset (Amazon Reviews) [24]. We choose these datasets since spam filters and sentimental analysis are common victims of DP attacks. TREC05 includes real ham and spam emails which are labeled based on the sender/receiver relationship. The Amazon Reviews dataset contains product reviews spanning 18 years which are labeled positive/negative sentiment by associated user ratings. For TREC05, the training set contains 8651 ham and 8835 spam emails, and the (exclusive) test set consists of 2861 ham and 2968 spam emails. The dictionary, following case normalization, stop word removal, stemming and low-frequency word filtering, has around 30000 unique words. As for the Amazon Reviews, the training set contains 50000 positive reviews and 50000 negative reviews, and the (exclusive) test set consists of 10000 positive and negative reviews, respectively. The dictionary, following the same text preprocessing procedure, has roughly 11000 distinct features.

Target Classifier: Since standard Naive Bayes is effective in spam filtering and sentimental analysis, we choose it as the target classifier of a data poisoning attack. It distinguishes positive samples from negative ones. In our experiment, positive samples are ham emails (positive reviews) in TREC05 (Amazon Reviews) and, accordingly, negative samples are spam emails (negative reviews).

Attack: As a reasonable and potent embedded data poisoning attack, we launch a "pure-positive" poisoning attack on the target classifier, where real positive samples are added into the negative training set with various attack strengths, *i.e.*, the number of injected positive samples.

Evaluation Criterion: Under both datasets, we first train a benign NB classifier, then poison the negative set with various strengths and validate the impact on test accuracy brought by the "pure-positive" attack. We next deploy our mixture based defender on the corrupted training set and measure its performance by 1) improvement in classification accuracy after retraining, 2) true positive rate (TPR)—the fraction of poisoned samples that are detected, and 3) false positive rate (FPR) – the fraction of non-poisoned samples falsely detected.

4.2   "Pure-Positive" Poisoning Attack

We conduct 6 "pure-positive" poisoning attacks on TREC05 with strength from 1000 to 6000, and on Amazon Reviews with strength from 10000 to 60000, respectively. The resulting test accuracies are plotted in Figs. 1a and 1b as "poisoned NB classifier". Initially, when there is no attack, the benign NB classifier has test accuracy of 0.85 and 0.83 on TREC05 and Amazon Reviews, respectively. On TREC05, as the attack is strengthened to 3000 ham emails, the test accuracy drops rapidly – from 0.85 to 0.67. Similarly, on poisoned Amazon Reviews, the classification accuracy falls continuously (from 0.83 to 0.727) as the number of adversarial reviews is increased to 60000. In both cases, roughly half of the positive test samples are misclassified as negative. Thus, embedding "pure-positive" samples into the negative set is indeed a strong attack on a standard NB classifier.

4.3 Mixture Model Based Defense

Following the detection methodology proposed in the last section, our defender locates and purges all suspicious data in both datasets, with m set to 0.9 on TREC05 and 0.95 on Amazon Reviews. Then the NB classifier is retrained on the purged datasets, and the corresponding performance is shown as the solid line in Fig. 1a and 1b. As expected, the retrained classifier performs well and stable under all attack cases, with accuracy of around 0.89 on TREC05 and 0.83 on Amazon Reviews. The reason why the classifier retrained on purged TREC05 outperforms the one trained on the *clean* dataset is discussed below. Besides, the average true positive rates of the defender in both experiments, 0.946 in TREC05 and 0.898 in Amazon Reviews, are relatively high, which demonstrates the validity of our detection method in practice.

Although our defense strategy succeeds in defending against a data poisoning attack, making the retrained NB classifier achieve high classification accuracy – at least comparable to the benign classifier – the false positive rate is relatively poor – **in the range of 0.12–0.37**. Moreover, as mentioned before, the standard NB retrained on purged TREC05 outperforms the one trained on the clean dataset. Given these observations, for different attack strengths, we train a standard NB classifier on the "clean" datasets where false detected training spam (*i.e.*, samples which have ground truth labels of spam but are detected as ham) are kept, and training ham are untouched. In each case, there are roughly 4000 training spam and 8000 training ham. Not surprisingly, on the same test set, this "benign" classifier only achieves an average test accuracy of 0.72, with the averaging over all considered attack strengths. Nearly half of the test ham are misclassified as spam and 90% of test spam are classified correctly, indicating that the false detected samples (real spam) have similar distributions as ham emails. Otherwise more test data will be classified as ham considering the greater apriori amount of ham than spam. **Hence, our method performs effective defense against "pure-positive" poisoning attacks, as the unsatisfying false positive rate is actually rooted in the inherent impurity of TREC05.**

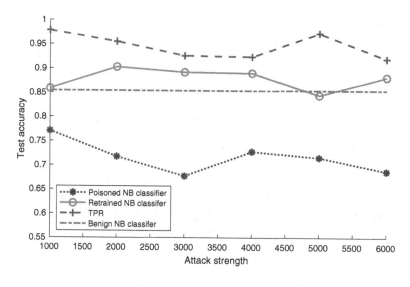

(a)

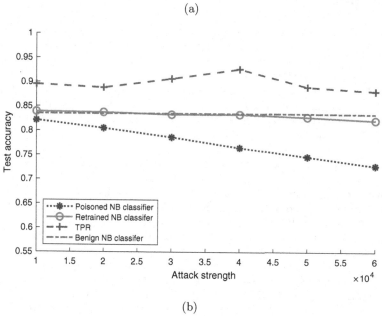

(b)

Fig. 1. Performance of mixture-based defender against "pure-positive" attacks on (a) TREC05 and (b) Amazon Reviews

5 Conclusions and Future Work

In this work, we proposed a mixture model based defense against data poisoning attacks against classifiers where attack samples are an unknown subset embedded in training set. We successfully launched defenses against "pure-positive" attacks on datasets TREC05 and Amazon Reviews. The experiments on two completely different datasets demonstrate the effectiveness of our defender under strong attacks. Consisting with the DDDAS paradigm, our approach is a generalized scalable defense strategy that is applicable to defend against embedded data poisoning attacks on any classifier – it can remove malicious data before they corrupt (discriminative) training of a deep neural network or support vector machine based classifier.

We have considered attacks which corrupt the negative set. Our approach could also be applied if the attack targets positive data, rather than negative data. However, our assumption towards the adversary is strong – we assume the attacker only pollutes one of the training sets, either positive or negative. In general, the attacker may simultaneously poison both positive and negative sets with different strengths. Defending against such attacks is a good subject for future work.

References

1. Biggio, B., et al.: Evasion attacks against machine learning at test time. In: Blockeel, H., Kersting, K., Nijssen, S., Železný, F. (eds.) ECML PKDD 2013. LNCS (LNAI), vol. 8190, pp. 387–402. Springer, Heidelberg (2013). https://doi.org/10.1007/978-3-642-40994-3_25

2. Blasch, E., Ravela, S., Aved, A.: Handbook of Dynamic Data Driven Applications Systems. Springer, Cham (2018). https://doi.org/10.1007/978-3-319-95504-9

3. Chen, X., Liu, C., Li, B., Lu, K., Song, D.: Targeted backdoor attacks on deep learning systems using data poisoning. Arxiv (2017). http://arxiv.org/abs/1712.05526

4. Cormack, G.V., Lynam, T.R.: TREC 2005 spam public corpora (2005). https://plg.uwaterloo.ca/~gvcormac/trecspamtrack05

5. Dempster, A.P., Laird, N.M., Rubin, D.B.: Maximum likelihood from incomplete data via the EM algorithm. J. Roy. Stat. Soc. Ser. B (Methodol.) **39**, 1–22 (1977)

6. Graham, M.W., Miller, D.J.: Unsupervised learning of parsimonious mixtures on large spaces with integrated feature and component selection. IEEE Trans. Sig. Process. **54**, 1289–1303 (2006)

7. Gu, T., Liu, K., Dolan-Gavitt, B., Garg, S.: Badnets: evaluating backdooring attacks on deep neural networks. IEEE Access **7**, 47230–47244 (2019)

8. Huang, L., Joseph, A.D., Nelson, B., Rubinstein, B.I.P., Tygar, J.D.: Adversarial machine learning. In: Proceedings of the 4th ACM Workshop on Security and Artificial Intelligence (2011)

9. Laishram, R., Phoha, V.V.: Curie: a method for protecting SVM classifier from poisoning attack. Arxiv (2016). http://arxiv.org/abs/1606.01584

10. Miller, D.J., Xiang, Z., Kesidis, G.: Adversarial learning targeting deep neural network classification: a comprehensive review of defenses against attacks. Proc. IEEE **108**(3), 402–433 (2020)

11. Miller, D.J., Browning, J.: A mixture model and EM-based algorithm for class discovery, robust classification, and outlier rejection in mixed labeled/unlabeled data sets. IEEE Trans. Pattern Anal. Mach. Intell. **25**, 1468–1483 (2003)

12. Miller, D.J., Wang, Y., Kesidis, G.: When not to classify: anomaly detection of attacks (ADA) on DNN classifiers at test time. Neural Comput. **31**, 1624–1670 (2019)
13. Nelson, B., et al.: Misleading learners: co-opting your spam filter. In: Tsai, J.J., Philip, S.Y. (eds.) Machine Learning in Cyber Trust, pp. 17–51. Springer, Boston (2009). https://doi.org/10.1007/978-0-387-88735-7_2
14. Newell, A., Potharaju, R., Xiang, L., Nita-Rotaru, C.: On the practicality of integrity attacks on document-level sentiment analysis. In: Proceedings of the 2014 Workshop on Artificial Intelligent and Security Workshop, AISec (2014)
15. Oh, S.J., Augustin, M., Fritz, M., Schiele, B.: Towards reverse-engineering black-box neural networks. In: 6th International Conference on Learning Representations, ICLR (2018)
16. Papernot, N., McDaniel, P.D., Jha, S., Fredrikson, M., Celik, Z.B., Swami, A.: The limitations of deep learning in adversarial settings. In: IEEE European Symposium on Security and Privacy, EuroS&P (2016)
17. Schwarz, G.: Estimating the dimension of a model. Ann. Stat. **6**, 461–464 (1978)
18. Steinhardt, J., Koh, P.W., Liang, P.: Certified defenses for data poisoning attacks. In: Conference on Neural Information Processing Systems (2017)
19. Szegedy, C., et al.: Intriguing properties of neural networks. In: 2nd International Conference on Learning Representations, ICLR (2014)
20. Tramèr, F., Zhang, F., Juels, A., Reiter, M.K., Ristenpart, T.: Stealing machine learning models via prediction APIs. In: 25th USENIX Security Symposium, USENIX (2016)
21. Wang, Y., Miller, D.J., Kesidis, G.: When not to classify: detection of reverse engineering attacks on DNN image classifiers. In: IEEE International Conference on Acoustics, Speech and Signal Processing, ICASSP (2019)
22. Xiang, Z., Miller, D.J., Kesidis, G.: A benchmark study of backdoor data poisoning defenses for deep neural network classifiers and a novel defense. In: 29th IEEE International Workshop on Machine Learning for Signal Processing, MLSP (2019)
23. Xiao, H., Biggio, B., Nelson, B., Xiao, H., Eckert, C., Roli, F.: Support vector machines under adversarial label contamination. Neurocomputing **160**, 53–62 (2015)
24. Zhang, X., Zhao, J., LeCun, Y.: Character-level convolutional networks for text classification. In: Proceedings of the 28th International Conference on Neural Information Processing Systems (2015)
25. Zhao, Q., Miller, D.J.: Mixture modeling with pairwise, instance-level class constraints. Neural Comput. **17**, 2482–2507 (2005)

Resilient Machine Learning (rML) Ensemble Against Adversarial Machine Learning Attacks

Likai Yao[1]($\boxtimes$), Cihan Tunc[1,2], Pratik Satam[1], and Salim Hariri[1]

[1] NSF Center for Cloud and Autonomic Computing, University of Arizona, Tucson, USA
{lyao0,cihantunc,pratiksatam,hariri}@email.arizona.edu
[2] Department of Computer Science and Engineering, The University of North Texas, Denton, Texas, USA

Abstract. Machine Learning (ML) algorithms have been widely used in many critical applications, including Dynamic Data Driven Applications Systems (DDDAS) applications, automated financial trading applications, autonomous vehicles, and intrusion detection systems for the decision-making process of users or automated systems. However, malicious adversaries have strong interests in manipulation the operations of machine learning algorithms to achieve their objectives in gaining financially, injecting injury or disasters. Adversaries against ML can be classified based on their capabilities and goals into two types: Adversary who has full knowledge of the ML models and parameters (white-box scenario) and one that does not have any knowledge and use guessing techniques to figure out the ML model and its parameters (black-box scenario). In both scenarios, the adversaries will attempt to maliciously manipulate model either during training or testing. Defending against these attacks can be successful by following three methods: 1) making the ML model robust to adversary, 2) validating and verifying input, or 3) changing ML architecture. In this paper, we present a resilient machine learning (rML) ensemble against adversarial attacks by dynamically changing the ML architecture and the ML models to be used such that the adversaries have no knowledge about the current ML model being used and consequently stop their attempt to manipulate the ML operations at testing phase. We evaluate the effectiveness of our rML ensemble using the benchmarking, zero-query dataset "DAmageNet" that contains both clean and adversarial image samples. We use three main neural networks in our ensemble that includes VGG16, ResNet-50, and ResNet-101. The experimental results show that our rML can tolerate the adversarial samples and achieve high classification accuracy with small execution time degradation.

Keywords: Resiliency · Adversarial machine learning · Dynamic data driven applications systems · Moving target defense · Resilient decision support

1 Introduction

The recent advances in big data, and machine learning (ML) algorithms have led the proliferation of data-driven intelligent applications in many areas including speech recognition, recommender systems, computer gaming, market analysis, medical health-care,

© Springer Nature Switzerland AG 2020
F. Darema et al. (Eds.): DDDAS 2020, LNCS 12312, pp. 274–282, 2020.
https://doi.org/10.1007/978-3-030-61725-7_32

computer vision, financial trading applications, autonomous vehicles as well as intrusion detection and prevention systems and Dynamic Data Driven Applications Systems (DDDAS). Many ML algorithms, including deep neural networks (DNN) and support vector machines (SVM) have been integrated in these applications to improve analysis performance and prediction.

Due to the wide-spread usage of ML in critical decision processes applications (e.g., mission critical applications), there is an exponential growth in cyberattacks to maliciously manipulate the ML algorithms and consequently influence their decision process in favoring of the attackers [1–4]. Adversaries against ML can be classified based on their capabilities and goals into two types: Adversary who has full knowledge of the ML models and parameters (white-box scenario) and one that does not have any knowledge and use guessing techniques to figure out the ML model and its parameters (black-box scenario). In both scenarios, the adversaries will attempt to maliciously manipulate the ML model either during training or testing phases. Furthermore, adversarial attacks can be built either to poison systems either during offline training period or during the continuous training periods with or just by exploiting the vulnerabilities of an existing trained system using black-box method [5]. For example, Microsoft's Twitter chatbot Tay was poisoned with by the malicious users, which ended up racist and sexist tweets in less than 24 h after it was opened to public for learning [6]. Also, the adversarial input can be maliciously built to misguide the medical health-care systems. Similarly, autonomous vehicles that heavily rely on the ML algorithms, they can be receiving malicious adversarial inputs by the attackers, which are not detectable by the human eyes, and hence can lead to severe accidents. Such examples can be even extended to the ML-based mission-critical applications that if their ML algorithms are compromised, the impact can be severely impact life and the mission success.

There have been several studies on how to create an adversarial input to misguide the ML algorithms [3] and on how to harden the ML algorithms by correct feature extraction and detection of the malicious inputs [16]. Furthermore, adversarial learning attacks can be built to affect other ML algorithms even though they have different structures/architectures, which is called adversarial sample transferability [7]. In general, the current defense mechanisms cannot effectively prevent the malicious adversarial learning techniques.

In this paper, we present a resilient ML (rML) ensemble architecture that can overcome the limitations of the current defense mechanisms by tolerating the adversarial learning attacks. Our rML is based on Moving Target Defense (MTD) and autonomic computing that aim at dynamically changing the ML algorithms used to drive the decision processes of mission critical applications (e.g., DDDAS). In this approach, even if the attacker succeeds in maliciously impacting the ML decision process, it will be guaranteed to fail in the other types of ML algorithms and hence, the rML will continue to operate normally in spite of the adversarial learning attacks. To validate and evaluate the performance of our approach, we use three as a convolutional neural network (CNN) in our ensemble; i.e., VGG16, ResNet-50 (50 layers deep CNN), and ResNet-101 (101 layers deep CNN).

The rest of the paper is organized as follows: In Sect. 2, we present the related work in ML usage in DDDAS and adversarial machine learning attacks. Next, Sect. 3

describes our approach to provide a resilient machine learning ensemble (rML). In Sect. 4, we demonstrate our implementation, experimental performance and results. Finally, in Sect. 5, we present our paper summary and concluding remarks.

2 Related Work

Adversarial ML has been demonstrated in many domains; including subverting fraud detection, bypassing content filters or malware detection, misleading autonomous navigation systems [7]. Therefore, to provide the required background in this section, we summarize the use of ML in the domain of DDDAS and adversarial ML attacks.

2.1 DDDAS and Machine Learning

The DDDAS paradigm was first introduced by Darema et al. as a dynamic feedback control loop of the instrumentation data and models in a way that measurement data are dynamically incorporated into an executing model to improve or accelerate the model accuracy [8–12]. In this regard, DDDAS uses the controlled measurement data to update models. Hence, DDDAS has been bringing together both practitioners and theorists in mathematics, statistics, engineering, and computer sciences, as well as well as designers. It has been demonstrated that DDDAS has been successfully applied in many problems of mathematics, statistics, engineering, and sciences [9].

It has been expected that DDDAS-inspired methods would greatly benefit from the recent advances in ML [9]. Since the sensor measurements from the real world is enormous, there is a need to apply data normalization, sampling alignment, and data mining. Hence, the researchers in [13] have focused on a joint nonlinear manifold learning approach to incorporate ML and model-based simulation propagators for DDDAS. Having sensor faults in a real-life is another challenge in DDDAS. It has been proposed to use ML to estimate parameterized models of aircraft sensor data relationships and statistically determine aircraft operating modes [14].

2.2 Adversarial ML Attacks

For adversarial ML attacks, there are two types of expected attacks: (1) White-box-attacks assuming that the adversary knows the model or the learning dataset. In the white-box-attacks, the adversary would have information about all the parameters including features and the learning algorithm settings. It is assumed that the attacker can get such an information either during the training time or by learning the ML decision through obtaining sufficient information. (2) Black-box-attacks where the attacker does not have any precise information about the model or the algorithm.

It has been shown that DNNs is susceptible to adversarial manipulation [15]. Papernot et al. trained a local DNN using crafted inputs and output labels generated by the target "victim" DNN even though the adversary has limited information about the architecture or parameters – they only had information about the inputs and outputs and the ML is based on DNN [7]. In [16], the authors develop black box attacks that exploit on broad classes of ML, which is considered as the transferability of the ML attacks and they explore DNNs, logistic regression (LR), support vector machine (SVMs), decision trees (DT), nearest neighbors (kNN), and ensembles. The authors in [17] study SVM security to well-crafted, adversarial label noise attacks where the attacker aims to maximize the SVM's classification error by flipping labels in the training data.

The authors from different studies [3, 18] presented that the cross-model transferability of adversarial data points between DNNs – in this case, an efficient attack can be launched through the use of surrogate models even through their training or neural network architectures are different. As a solution against the adversarial attacks, authors demonstrate the effectiveness of injecting adversarial examples into the training set (i.e., adversarial training) to increase robustness against adversarial attacks [4, 19].

3 Resilient Machine Learning Ensemble (rML)

In order to avoid the adversarial attacks, in this study we present an MTD based resilient ML approach that dynamically changes the ensemble architecture to make adversarial learning attacks unsuccessful in affecting the ML-based decision processes. In what follows, we present the architecture of rML and its implementation.

3.1 Resilient DDDAS Development Environment

Our resilient DDDAS development environment architecture is presented in Fig. 1, which includes three layers: composition of the environment, DDDAS design, and the resilient DDDAS that consists of different services namely commands services, information repository services, data analytics, etc. and middleware service. During the design time, using Service Oriented Architecture (SOA) paradigm [12], the requirements and decisions of different plans are organized by composing the selected services. During the runtime, these services would operate to provide the required capabilities to provide a feedback back to the composition and design layers to apply the dynamic feedback control. As the ML algorithms are commonly used, we create data analytics services in a resilient way to prevent the success of the adversarial attacks.

An adversarial learning attack changes the input provided to a ML algorithm in a way that with small perturbation invisible to the eyes, the input can change the label of the prediction. Most of the defense solutions focus on input verification, feature extraction and selection methods to enhance the security of ML algorithms, which are tedious and require time to adapt and change the existing ML algorithms. In our approach, we take a significantly different approach that assumes attackers will succeed and our goal is to tolerate their attacks, as it was done in fault tolerance computing. Therefore, we develop a resilient machine learning ensemble (rML) that utilizes moving target defense (MTD) technique. Using MTD, our rML approach changes the diversified ML algorithms to implement used in the decision mechanism at runtime. By using different ML algorithms, but they are equally functional, the adversarial input, which can severely impact the function of on one ML algorithms, but it will not be able to misguide the other types of ML algorithms. The rML architecture is shown in Fig. 2 where a user can describe the DDDAS application at the design level using an application workflow editor. The input uploaded to the system may be a regular input or an adversarial input aiming at misguiding the decision process mechanism; in this architecture as an example, a fish picture is provided, which is in reality adversarial input because the targeted ML fails to detect it as a fish due to invisible changes in the picture. The rML controller pulls the required ML models and algorithms from the rML repository and creates the environment for the resilient decision mechanism. Each of the ML models evaluate the input from the user and provides a prediction. Next, a voting mechanism is applied to determine if there is any different output from the ML models and the majority of the decisions is accepted as the true output. For the acceptance test, we apply Boyer-Moore majority vote algorithm [21].

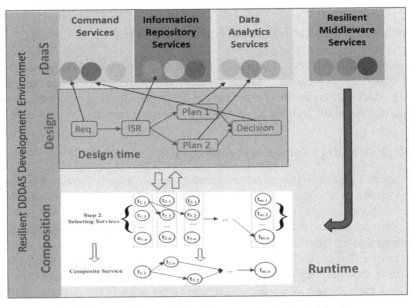

Fig. 1. Resilient DDDAS development environment architecture

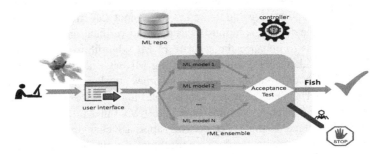

Fig. 2. resilient machine learning ensemble (rML) architecture

4 Implementation and Experimental Results

To demonstrate the applicability and performance of our approach, as an input we have chosen ImageNet and DAmageNet – ImageNet is an ongoing research effort to provide easily accessible image database [19] and DAmageNet is the first universal adversarial dataset that beats many models trained in ImageNet [20]. For the benchmarking images, we use class label that demonstrates the type of the focus of the image (for example, for class 0 the focus is a fish) and sample ID showing the image number. Therefore, for a clean image, the output of the ML would give the correct class number; however, for the adversarial ones, the ML output is an incorrect class.

For the ML algorithms and models, we have chosen multiple DNNs such as VGG16, ResNet-50, and ResNet-101, which are pre-trained on ImageNet. For the experimentation, we have used 253 images. In Table 1, we demonstrate the example behavior of each algorithm, including rML, in terms of what class ID is given as an input and what class ID the algorithm predicts – the inputs are randomly chosen in this set of examples and it does not try to demonstrate the effectiveness of any ML over others. If the input was not adversarial, the outputs would be the same class ID with the input class ID. Hence, the bold and italic-font results are used to demonstrate the incorrect output due to the adversarial input specifically designed for that ML. From the demonstrated results, it is clear that by leveraging MTD for rML, we can obtain high performance in the prediction accuracy without the need to change the existing algorithms and methodologies.

Table 1. Example of class identification for adversarial images.

Class ID	Sample Id	VGG16	ResNet50	ResNet101	rML
0	59	*389*	0	**0**	0
5	114	5	5	*3*	5
35	1	35	*37*	35	35
36	1	36	36	*938*	36
46	46	46	46	*39*	46
68	90	68	68	**66**	68

In our implementation, we are running each ML algorithm using one virtual machine (VM) on a private cloud. For the image transfer and controller commands, we have chosen Apache Kafka (open-source stream-processing software). Since the images (both clean and adversarial) are not big in size, the operations of Kafka do not introduce any considerable overhead to the system and also in terms of execution time.

We further evaluated our approach in terms of the execution time overhead. Figure 3 shows the execution time for VGG16, ResNet-50, ResNet-101, and rML for both clean images and adversarial images. The experiments were run using 253 images from ImageNet and from DAmageNet (adversarial versions of the ImageNet dataset) and the mean execution time together with the standard deviation are shown in Fig. 3 in y-axis.

We observe the expected execution time of the individual ML models would be less than the rML and the classification time for the clean images and adversarial images are almost the same. This also conveys us the message that we cannot understand if the input is adversarial malicious input due to the execution time difference. Checking the ML models individually, we can observe that the VGG16 execution time is the smallest, which follows ResNet-50 and then ResNet-101. This is also expected since ResNet-50 has 50 layers and ResNet-101 has 101 layers that require more computation compared to the VGG16. The execution of the proposed rML is very similar to ResNet-101 since the execution time overhead introduced by the acceptance test is almost negligible. We also introduce the error bar based on the standard deviation, which is around 2% only. In summary, the overhead of rML compared to the ResNet-101 is 5% in the mean execution time.

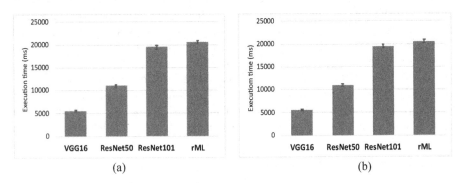

(a)   (b)

Fig. 3. Execution time comparison for (a) clean images and (b) adversarial images

4.1 Conclusion

Machine Learning (ML) has been widely used in many critical applications, including Dynamic Data Driven Applications Systems (DDDAS) applications. Therefore, there is a strong interest in adversaries and their ability impact the ML algorithm used to implement the decision processes. In this paper, we present a resilient ML (rML) ensemble to tolerate adversarial learning attacks that utilizes moving target defense (MTD) to dynamically change the ML models so that the adversaries have no knowledge about the currently ML models being used and consequently fail the exploitation. We evaluated the effectiveness of our rML ensemble using the benchmarking, zero-query dataset "DAmageNet" that contains both clean and adversarial image samples. We used three main neural networks in our ensemble that includes VGG16, ResNet-50, and ResNet-101. The experimental results show that our rML can tolerate the adversarial samples and achieve high classification accuracy with small execution time degradation.

Acknowledgements. This work is partly supported by the Air Force Office of Scientific Research (AFOSR) Dynamic Data-Driven Application Systems (DDDAS) award number FA9550-18-1-0427, National Science Foundation (NSF) research projects NSF-1624668 and NSF-1849113,

(NSF) DUE-1303362 (Scholarship-for-Service), and National Institute of Standards and Technology (NIST) 70NANB18H263, and Department of Energy/National Nuclear Security Administration under Award Number(s) DE-NA0003946.

References

1. Dalvi, N., Domingos, P., Sanghai, S., Verma, D.: Adversarial classification. In: Proceedings of the tenth ACM SIGKDD International Conference on Knowledge Discovery and Data Mining, pp. 99–108 (2004)
2. Biggio, B., et al.: Evasion attacks against machine learning at test time. In: Joint European Conference on Machine Learning and Knowledge Discovery in Databases (2013)
3. Goodfellow, I.J., Shlens, J., Szegedy, C.: Explaining and harnessing adversarial examples. arXiv preprint arXiv:1412.6572 (2014)
4. Goodfellow, I., et al.: Generative adversarial nets. In: Advances in Neural Information Processing Systems, pp. 2672–2680 (2014)
5. Biggio, B., Roli, F.: Wild patterns: ten years after the rise of adversarial machine learning. Pattern Recogn. **84**, 317–331 (2018)
6. Lee, P.: Learning from Tay's introduction. Official Microsoft Blog (2016). https://blogs.microsoft.com/blog/2016/03/25/learning-tays-introduction/. Accessed 27 July 2020
7. Papernot, N., McDaniel, P., Goodfellow, I., Jha, S., et al.: Practical black-box attacks against deep learning systems using adversarial examples. arXiv:1602.02697 (2016)
8. Darema, F.: Grid computing and beyond: the context of dynamic data driven applications systems. Proc. IEEE **93**(3), 692–697 (2005)
9. Blasch, E.: DDDAS advantages from high-dimensional simulation. In: 2018 IEEE Winter Simulation Conference (WSC), pp. 1418–1429 (2018)
10. Blasch, E., Al-Nashif, Y., Hariri, S.: Static versus dynamic data information fusion analysis using DDDAS for cyber security trust. Procedia Comput. Sci. **29** (2014)
11. Ditzler, G., Hariri, S., Akoglu, A.: High performance machine learning (HPML) framework to support DDDAS decision support systems: design overview. In: IEEE 2nd International Workshops on Foundations and Applications of Self* Systems (FAS* W) pp. 360–362 (2017)
12. Badr, Y., Hariri, S., Youssif, A.N., Blasch, E.: Resilient and trustworthy dynamic data-driven application systems (DDDAS) services for crisis management environments. Procedia Comput. Sci. **51**, 2623–2637 (2015)
13. Blasch, E., e al.: DDDAS-based Joint Nonlinear Manifold Learning for Target Localization. Structural Health Monitoring (2017)
14. Chen, S., Imai, S., Zhu, W., Varela, C.A.: Towards learning spatio-temporal data stream relationships for failure detection in avionics. In: Blasch, E., Ravela, S., Aved, A. (eds.) Handbook of Dynamic Data Driven Applications Systems, pp. 97–121. Springer, Cham (2018). https://doi.org/10.1007/978-3-319-95504-9_5
15. Nguyen, A., Yosinski, J., Clune, J.: Deep neural networks are easily fooled: high confidence predictions for unrecognizable images. In: Proceedings of the IEEE Conference on Computer Vision and Pattern Recognition, pp. 427–436 (2015)
16. Katzir, Z., Elovici, Y.: Quantifying the resilience of machine learning classifiers used for cyber security. Expert Syst. Appl. **92**, 419–429 (2018)
17. Biggio, B., Nelson, B., Laskov, P.: Support vector machines under adversarial label noise. In: Asian Conference on Machine Learning, pp. 97–112 (2011)
18. Rosenberg, I., Shabtai, A., Rokach, L., Elovici, Y.: Generic black-box end-to-end attack against RNNs and other api calls based malware classifiers. arXiv:1707.05970 (2017)

19. Russakovsky, O., et al.: Imagenet large scale visual recognition challenge. Int. J. Comput. Vision **115**(3), 211–252 (2015)
20. Chen, S., Huang, X., He, Z., Sun, C.: DAmageNet: A Universal Adversarial Dataset. arXiv: 1912.07160 (2019)
21. Boyer, R.S., Moore, J.S.: MJRTY—a fast majority vote algorithm. In: Boyer, R.S. (ed.) Automated Reasoning, pp. 105–117. Springer, Dordrecht (1991). https://doi.org/10.1007/978-94-011-3488-0_5

Data-Based Defense-in-Depth of Critical Systems

Styliani Pantopoulou[✉], Pola Lydia Lagari[✉], Clive H. Townsend[✉], and Lefteri H. Tsoukalas[✉]

Purdue University, West Lafayette, IN 47906, USA
{spantopo,plagari,clive,tsoukala}@purdue.edu

Abstract. Cyber Physical Systems (CPS) are attracting intense research interest due to the explosive availability of data and connectivity. The Dynamic Data Driven Applications Systems (DDDAS) paradigm provides a suitable framework for solutions to the risks of connectivity through big data and machine learning. Computational and measurement data come together to produce integrative yet discriminating features and patterns amenable to machine learning and Artificial Intelligence (AI) decision approaches and thus DDDAS and CPSs bridge the physical with the cyber world in numerous applications principally anchored in unique physics.

DDDAS is of great value in prioritizing and categorizing data in accordance with system dynamics. The physical aspect of CPSs is considered as an advantage, as the inherited inertia of systems like these affords additional time for processing and protective activities. This characteristic proves helpful towards intrusion detection and projection of failures as well as buttressing the system with defense-in-depth capabilities demonstrated through effectively achieving Byzantine Fault Tolerance.

Keywords: Cyber Physical Systems · DDDAS · Critical systems · Data management · Attack detection

1 Introduction

Cyber Physical Systems (CPS) have been placed in the center of research interest throughout the years. This comes naturally as one contemplates the multifaceted nature of CPSs, namely the seamless combination of physical and computational components. It is moreover crucial to consider the immense capabilities of CPSs regarding data abundance and abilities to connect with other systems. The Dynamic Data Driven Applications Systems (DDDAS) paradigm can prove helpful towards mitigating the risks that arise from the connectivity aspect. Artificial Intelligence (AI) and Machine Learning (ML) approaches render the CPSs and DDDAS capable of conjoining the physical and the cyber world in several applications governed by unique physics.

Digitalization has been of immense importance in industrial systems as it offers many advantages compared to the classical, analog systems. The use of digital components

© Springer Nature Switzerland AG 2020
F. Darema et al. (Eds.): DDDAS 2020, LNCS 12312, pp. 283–290, 2020.
https://doi.org/10.1007/978-3-030-61725-7_33

promises a plethora of advantages including, but not limited to, the reduction of complexity, faster processing of incoming data, more accurate monitoring of system parameters and improved maintenance practices. These features, combined with the incorporation of other technologies, such as Bluetooth or WiFi, render the systems capable of operating under a variety of circumstances with enhanced reliability and reduced cost.

Despite numerous advantages, digitalization produces a broad spectrum of challenges ranging from data corruption to cyber intrusion and compromised controllers and effectors. The every growing data volumes produced by a system become even more multitudinous and multi-faceted, resulting in difficulties with further processing, resulting in new vulnerabilities to the system's integrity and safety.

The DDDAS paradigm can prove extremely helpful towards a procedure of data assortment and classification. This comes in accordance with system dynamics, varying time-scales and unique windows that may open and close in ways that match idiosyncratic system phases corresponding to different transients. The challenge of defense-in-depth based on observable system dynamics with machine learning to identify origin and estimate ability of tracking every type of incoming data is shown to be effectively addressed through DDDAS. The inherited property of inertia in CPSs is a valuable advantage, as this allows time for system protecting activities. Consequently, the system is reinforced towards potential cyber threats and gets fortified by achieving Byzantine Fault Tolerance.

The paper is organized as follows: Sect. 2 presents a review of related work on the topic of CPS control and cybersecurity. Section 3 is focused on the methodology followed towards developing a framework for detecting and eliminating attack strategies using the DDDAS paradigm in a nuclear power plant (NPP) as an example. Finally, the paper's conclusions are presented in Sect. 4.

2   Related Work

Plenty of research exists facing the problem of CPS safety and security. A paper by Ahmad et al. [1] focuses on various threats that CPSs face, regarding both control security and information security. These involve the physical exploitation of a system, the injection of false data, the estimation of a system's model and the connectivity to the internet. Furthermore, a report of immense importance regarding the cyber-attack on the Ukrainian power grid in 2015 [2] notes the multi-faceted form of an attack. In that case, the attackers performed a long-term exploration of the system; consequently, they were able to get familiar with the environment and execute the attack. Some examples of this system's vulnerabilities were the abundance of online information and the absence of two-factor authentication protocols.

Redundancy and diversity are considered among the recent popular trends towards mitigating cyber-attacks. More specifically, the concept of Artificial Fault Tolerance (AFT), namely the modification of identical system components [3] with the purpose of different response to non-normal inputs [4], is proved to be more effective, as it can even perform well for detecting a cyber-attack. Some of the methods used for that purpose are discussed in a paper by Rowe et al. [5]. These include binary transformations, network diversity transformations or diversity in network protocols. A special case, that of the Byzantine Fault Tolerance (BFT) algorithm, is examined in a paper by the Office of

Naval Research (ONR) [6]. In this work, the inherited inertia of a CPS is exploited. BFT is a combination of AFT as well as delayed input sharing, with the purpose of alleviating attack schemes.

Classical control methods often accompany the approaches discussed above. In a study by Ashaari et al. [7], a state space model of a pressurized water reactor (PWR) was designed to control the core, and further simulation showed the connection between temperature and power of the plant. In another work [8], a mix of statistics and fuzzy logic was used to identify NPP transients.

The DDDAS paradigm is furthermore strongly connected with the sector of cyber-security. In a related paper, Blasch et al. [9] explore a method that offers increased levels of security during dynamically changing attack detections. Another work [10] focuses on security in Cloud Computing by implementing a resilient DDDAS architecture. This includes, among others, replication, software encryption and diversity. Finally, Tucker et al. [11] investigate whether cybersecurity is capable of tampering with the functionality and usefulness of a DDDAS, which in this study is represented by a social media model.

3 Methodology

3.1 System Modeling

Several studies have dealt with the problem of critical systems modeling with the purpose of achieving their control. More specifically, when these systems fall into the category of CPSs, one has to approach this matter by regarding their physical aspect. Systems like these are governed by laws of physics; consequently, equations that describe their operation for varying time instances should be used. State space equations, i.e., equations that describe a system's state as a function of time, are widely used for that reason. In this work the system under review is a NPP, which various researchers have studied by using the basic point kinetic equations [12, 13]:

$$\frac{dn(t)}{dt} = \frac{\rho(t) - \beta}{\Lambda} \cdot n(t) + \lambda \cdot c(t) \tag{1}$$

$$\frac{dc(t)}{dt} = \frac{\beta}{\Lambda} \cdot n(t) - \lambda \cdot c(t) \tag{2}$$

Here, n refers to the neutron density, c represents the neutron precursor density and ρ is the reactivity of the plant. The constants β and λ are characteristic of the specific reactor under review, namely the Purdue University Reactor-1 (PUR-1), while Λ results from the Monte-Carlo Neutron Transport (MCNP) code. A related work studying and modeling the reactor core [13] further proposes the use of a differential equation connecting reactivity with the control rod speed z. In this equation, G stands for the rod reactivity worth:

$$\frac{\partial \rho(t)}{\partial t} = G(t, T, B, \ldots) \cdot z(t, T, B, \ldots) \tag{3}$$

The translation of the preceding equations to a state space system representation, as shown below, reveals the system's inputs and outputs. Control rod speed z acts as the input, the neutron density n is the system output, and finally n, c and ρ are variables pertinent to the reactor's state. Control of the variable that defines rod speed results in obtaining the reactor's neutron density for each time instance.

$$\begin{bmatrix} \dot{n} \\ \dot{c} \\ \dot{\rho} \end{bmatrix} = \begin{bmatrix} \frac{-\beta}{\Lambda} & \lambda & \frac{n_0}{\Lambda} \\ \frac{\beta}{\Lambda} & -\lambda & 0 \\ 0 & 0 & 0 \end{bmatrix} \cdot \begin{bmatrix} n \\ c \\ \rho \end{bmatrix} + \begin{bmatrix} 0 \\ 0 \\ G \end{bmatrix} \cdot z \tag{4}$$

$$n = \begin{bmatrix} 1 & 0 & 0 \end{bmatrix} \cdot \begin{bmatrix} n \\ c \\ \rho \end{bmatrix} \tag{5}$$

3.2 Mitigation of a Cyber-Attack

Following the representation of this critical system in the control space, a protection architecture against cyber-attacks has to be implemented. Figure 1 depicts a block diagram describing the relationship between the reactor system (plant) and the protection architecture. The fundamental key to the realization of the protection system is a specific version of the BFT algorithm presented in [6]. This approach makes use of several important concepts discussed above, such as redundancy and diversity, which are properties fully based on the DDDAS paradigm.

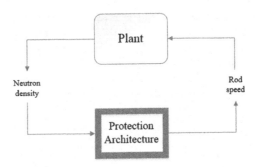

Fig. 1. Connection of protection system and plant.

To begin with, this architecture makes use of the plant's original controllers, namely the Programmable Logic Controllers (PLCs), which are able to operate as simple Proportional – Integral – Derivative (PID) controllers for the purpose of this work. Three identical controllers are used in this case. A schematic of the complete system is shown in Fig. 2. The error term, required as an input for the PID controllers, is derived by a DDDAS-based component, which produces an estimation of the plant output (measurement), based on previous ones, and then subtracts it from the actual incoming value. The dynamic perspective in this part of the system is crucial, as it provides the controllers with a constantly updating setpoint, based on the trends and transients followed by the CPS.

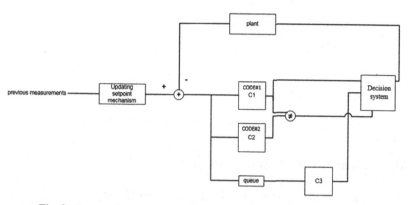

Fig. 2. Proposed protection architecture with DDDAS-based features.

As can be seen in Fig. 2, the error term resulting from the updating setpoint component of the system is forwarded as an input to two controllers that share the same hardware structure, C1 and C2, as well as to a delay queue connected to the third controller, C3. The existence of the delay queue is a characteristic of this specific BFT algorithm, and ensures continuous operation, as explained later in the text. The existing redundancy of the controllers is only meaningful when combined with the principal of Artificial Diversity. The identical nature of the controllers is not able to offer results in attack detection by itself.

There needs to be a process of distinction for the two controllers first. Usually, diversity in PLCs can be achieved by performing alterations in the controller software. These slight changes do not have an impact on the final result in normal operation; however, since the CPS behaves according to physical laws, any sensor measurement that has been tempered with will cause at least one of the controllers to stop operating. The crucial point where a decision system offers an answer regarding the existence - or not - of an attack is one more major DDDAS feature. Its precision and level of confidence regarding attack detection renders it a crucial step of the signal processing in this system. There are two distinct cases for the operation of the overall system from this point forward. Both cases are depicted in Fig. 3. In the incident when the outputs of the first two controllers match, the input is considered safe and this output is pushed forward, so as to be used by the plant. In the case when at least one of the two controllers stops operating, the system recognizes an attack; these two controller outputs are blocked, and the delay queue is flushed. Simultaneously, the output of the third controller can be used from the plant. This output has been stored from a previous operation cycle. The inherited inertia of the CPS allows for restoration of the controllers after an attack.

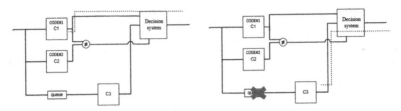

Fig. 3. Demonstration of the system dynamics.

4 Algorithm and Preliminary Results

This section presents the algorithm followed in more detail and provides some preliminary results regarding the continuous operation of the system. Table 1 explains how one cycle of operations is performed from the point of acquiring a plant measurement $x(n)$ until getting the next one, $x(n+1)$. Variables *out1*, *out2* denote the outputs of controllers C1, C2 respectively.

Table 1. Description of followed procedure

Algorithm
1. Get measurement $x(n)$ from plant
2. $x(n-k) \cdot h(n-k) + x(n-k+1) \cdot h(n-k+1) + \ldots + x(n-1) \cdot h(n-1) = x(n-k+1)$ … $x(n-1) \cdot h(n-k) + x(n-2) \cdot h(n-k+1) + \ldots + x(n-k) \cdot h(n-1) = x(n)$
3. $\hat{x}(n) = h(1) \cdot x(n-1) + \ldots + h(k) \cdot x(n-k)$
4. Controllers C1 and C2 get error signal $\hat{x}(n) \text{-} x(n)$
5. C1 runs PLC_code1, C2 runs PLC_code2
6. Comparator checks $\lvert out1\text{-}out2 \rvert$
7. If $\lvert out1\text{-}out2 \rvert \leq$ noise threshold $\rightarrow$ *Mux_control_signal* = 0   Else *Mux_control_signal=1*
8. Contents of queue erased and not added to previous_measurements vector
9. C1, C2 get restarted
10. $x(n+1)$ calculated from state space equations

Figure 4 shows the response of the decision system, i.e., of a multiplexer. For this first stage of implementation, plant measurements are considered as following the normal distribution [8], with specific mean and standard deviation values. It is evident that, when the two controller outputs differ more than a threshold imposed by the allowed noise in the system, the multiplexer control signal changes, allowing C3 to forward its output to the plant.

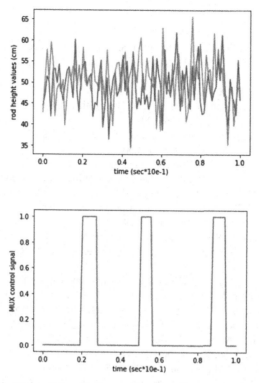

Fig. 4. Change in multiplexer output after discrepancy detection.

5   Conclusions and Future Work

All in all, this work emphasizes the importance and connection of the DDDAS paradigm with critical systems. CPSs are mostly benefited from this combination, due to their physical nature and the abundance of data being produced. Especially in this case, a NPP can be transformed into a trustworthy, digital system. However, implementations like this should be performed with caution, as no system is completely reliable under all conditions. A second layer of protection or suitable operators' training would aid towards avoiding dangerous situations. Moreover, more complex attack schemes have to be tested in order to ensure the system's integrity and security under a greater variety of circumstances.

Acknowledgement. This work is supported in part by ONR under Grant No N00014-18-1-2278, the US Department of Energy under Grant No. 2014-0501-03 and a GS-Gives grant to AI Systems Lab (AISL).

References

1. Ahmad, I., Zarrar, M.K., Saeed, T., Rehman, S.: Security aspects of cyber physical systems. In: 1st International Conference on Computer Applications & Information Security (ICCAIS) (2018)
2. E-ISAC: Analysis of the Cyber Attack on the Ukrainian Power Grid, Washington, DC (2016)
3. Shoker, A.: Exploiting universal redundancy. In: 15th IEEE International Symposium on Network Computing and Applications (2016)
4. Cox, B., et al.: N-Variant systems: a secretless framework for security through diversity. In: Security 2006: 15th USENIX Security Symposium (2006)
5. Rowe, J., Levitt, K., Demir, T., Erbacher, R.: Artificial diversity as maneuvers in a control theoretic moving target defense. In: National Symposium on Moving Target Research (2012)
6. Mertoguno, J.S., Craven, R.M., Mickelson, M.S., Koller D.P.: A physics-based strategy for cyber resilience of CPS. SPIE 11009. In: Autonomous Systems: Sensors, Processing, and Security for Vehicles and Infrastructure (2019)
7. Ashaari, A., Ahmad, T., Shamsuddin, M., Wan Mohamad, W.M., Abdullah, M.: State space modeling of reactor core in a pressurized water reactor. In: AIP Conference Proceedings (2014)
8. Wang, X., Tsoukalas, L., Wei, T., Reifman, J.: An innovative fuzzy-logic-based methodology for trend identification. Nuclear Technol. **135**(1), 67–84 (2001)
9. Blasch, E., Al-Nashif, Y., Hariri, S.: Static versus dynamic data information fusion analysis using DDDAS for cyber security trust. Procedia Comput. Sci. **29**, 1299–1313 (2014)
10. Dsouza, G., Hariri, S., Al-Nashif, Y., Rodriguez, G.: Resilient dynamic data driven application systems (rDDDAS). Procedia Comput. Sci. **18**, 1929–1938 (2013)
11. Tucker, C.S., Burrows, M., Lesniak, K., Klein, S.: Cybersecurity policies and their impact on dynamic data driven application systems. In: 2017 IEEE 2nd International Workshops on Foundations and Applications of Self* Systems (FAS*W), pp. 363–365 (2017)
12. Wang, G., Wu, J., Zeng, B., Xu, Z., Wu, W., Ma, X.: State-space model predictive control method for core power control in pressurized water reactor nuclear power stations. Nucl. Eng. Technol. **49**(1) (2016)
13. Ansarifar, G.R., Rafiei, M.: Second-order sliding-mode control for a pressurized water nuclear reactor considering the xenon concentration feedback. Nucl. Eng. Technol. **47**, 94–101 (2015)

Posters Session-2

Physics-Driven Machine Learning for Time-Optimal Path Planning in Stochastic Dynamic Flows

Rohit Chowdhury and Deepak N. Subramani[(✉)]

Department of Computational and Data Sciences, Indian Institute of Science,
Bangalore, India
{rohitchowdhury,deepakns}@iisc.ac.in

Abstract. Optimal path planning of autonomous marine agents is important to minimize operational costs of ocean observation systems. Within the context of DDDAS, we present a Reinforcement Learning (RL) framework for computing a dynamically adaptable policy that minimizes expected travel time of autonomous vehicles between two points in stochastic dynamic flows. To forecast the stochastic dynamic environment, we utilize the reduced order data-driven dynamically orthogonal (DO) equations. For planning, a novel physics-driven online Q-learning is developed. First, the distribution of exact time optimal paths predicted by stochastic DO Hamilton-Jacobi level set partial differential equations are utilized to initialize the action value function (Q-value) in a transfer learning approach. Next, the flow data collected by onboard sensors are utilized in a feedback loop to adaptively refine the optimal policy. For the adaptation, a simple Bayesian estimate of the environment is performed (the DDDAS data assimilation loop) and the inferred environment is used to update the Q-values in an $\epsilon-$greedy exploration approach (the RL step). To validate our Q-learning solution, we compare it with a fully offline, dynamic programming solution of the Markov Decision Problem corresponding to the RL framework. For this, novel numerical schemes to efficiently utilize the DO forecasts are derived and computationally efficient GPU-implementation is completed. We showcase the new RL algorithm and elucidate its computational advantages by planning paths in a stochastic quasi-geostrophic double gyre circulation.

Keywords: Path planning · Q-learning · Markov Decision Process · Dynamically orthogonal equations · Transfer Learning

1 Introduction

Autonomous marine agents that explore and collect data in stochastic dynamic ocean environments play a crucial role in ocean science and engineering missions.

Partially supported by Prime Minister's Research Fellowship to RC, IISc Start-up, DST Inspire and Arcot Ramachandran Young Investigator grants to DNS.

F. Darema et al. (Eds.): DDDAS 2020, LNCS 12312, pp. 293–301, 2020.
https://doi.org/10.1007/978-3-030-61725-7_34

Optimal path planning of these missions is essential to minimize operational costs and maximize utility, within the constraints of their limited capabilities (e.g., battery, maneuverability). Planning involves predicting and using paths for these agents such that travel time or energy consumption is minimized, utility of data collected is maximized and safety is always ensured. The size and speed of autonomous marine vehicles are such that the ocean flow plays a major role in their navigation by strong advection which could be intelligently used to plan optimal paths [13]. Notably, the challenges of predicting optimal paths are compounded when the environmental flow is stochastic and dynamic, necessitating a DDDAS approach for solution [1,5]. Here, planning requires all the ingredients of DDDAS, i.e., a combination of rigorous theoretical decision-making frameworks, environmental modeling with uncertainty quantification, data assimilation and practical algorithms with computationally efficient implementations [2,4].

In the recent years, several approaches have been proposed for optimal path planning, however, the stochastic dynamic environment results in several classical techniques to be infeasible, and Monte Carlo methods [18] and Markov Decision Process [9] to be computationally expensive. Efficient level-set methods that solve the exact Hamilton Jacobi (HJ) Partial Differential Equations (PDE) have been successful for optimal path planning [10]. Nevertheless, choosing one path from the probabilistic distribution is challenging and an expensive offline risk-optimal framework was proposed [16]. Very recently, online machine learning approaches such as Gaussian process regression [6] and Reinforcement Learning (RL) [7,8,12,19,21] have gained popularity due to their appealing theory and suitability for on-board routing. However, limited underwater applications are reported [20], but with prohibitive computational costs for realistic applications.

In the present paper, we develop a computationally efficient online path planning algorithm that utilizes the framework of RL together with a transfer learning from the HJ-PDEs and data assimilation. In what follows, we first formally state our problem. Next, we describe our modeling framework (Sect. 2). Thereafter, we describe our proposed RL algorithm (Sect. 3), and apply it in a canonical stochastic flow scenario to elucidate the advantages (Sect. 4).

1.1   Problem Statement

Consider a spatio-temporal domain $(\mathbf{x}, t) : \mathbb{R}^n \times [0, \infty)$ shown in Fig. 1A. Let us denote $\mathbf{x} \in \mathbb{R}^n$ for space and $t \in [0, \infty)$ for time. Here, $n = 2, 3$ for 2-D and 3-D space respectively. Let the domain have a stochastic, dynamic flow $\mathbf{v}(\mathbf{x}, t; \omega)$ where ω is a sample of the random velocity field with an associated probability distribution function. Consider an autonomous agent P with a maximum speed $F(t)$ that must travel from $\mathbf{x}_s$ to $\mathbf{x}_f$ starting at time $t = 0$ in the minimum expected travel time. What is the optimum path or policy that P must follow?

We discretize the domain to a spatio-temporal grid world (Fig. 1B), where each discreet state s, visualized as a cell, is indexed by both space and time. The random velocity at a discreet state is $\mathbf{v}(s; \omega)$. At each state s, P can take an action a. Our problem is to find the optimum deterministic policy $\pi^*(s)$ of actions that P must follow so as to minimize the expected travel time. As the optimality is in terms of the expectation under uncertainty, we also require that the optimal policy π^* can be updated efficiently with new experiences of the stochastic environment. This final requirement is crucial and informs our data-driven solution methodology as we see in the coming sections.

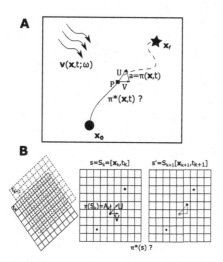

Fig. 1. (A) *Schematic of the path planning problem in continuous state-space.* The autonomous agent P undertakes a mission from $\mathbf{x}_0$ to $\mathbf{x}_f$ in a domain under the influence of a stochastic dynamic flow field $\mathbf{v}(\mathbf{x}, t; \omega)$. P experiences an instantaneous velocity V and takes an action $a = \pi(\mathbf{x}, t)$ according to a deterministic policy. The effective path taken by P is the vector sum $\mathbf{U} = \mathbf{V} + a$. We seek the optimal policy $\pi^*(\mathbf{x}, t)$ that minimizes the expected travel time of this mission. **(B)** *Schematic of the problem in discrete state-space.* The domain is discretized into a spatio-temporal grid world (left panel). Middle and right panels show two time-steps of the grid world. $s = [x_k, t_k]$ is a state at which P experiences V and takes an action $A = \pi(S_k)$ and ends up in $s' = S_{k+1}[\mathbf{x}_{k+1}, t_{k+1}]$. We seek the optimal adaptive policy $\pi^*(s)$.

2 Modelling Framework

Data-Driven Probabilistic Environment Modeling. To forecast the environmental flow $\mathbf{v}(\mathbf{x}, t; \omega)$ needed to plan optimal paths, we employ the Dynamically Orthogonal (DO) barotropic Quasi-Geostrophic (QG) stochastic equations for canonical flows [10,14,15]. Following ref. [15], the stochastic barotropic QG dynamics, may be written as conservation of mass, momentum and energy in the Langevin form. Using the DO expansion, we decompose the stochastic dynamic velocity field and obtain equations for its DO mean, DO modes and DO coefficients (not shown here, see [15]). Here, the uncertainty of the stochastic dynamical system is carried in a data-driven adaptive dynamic subspace spanned by the DO modes. Critically, compared to a Monte Carlo approach, computational advantage of solving the DO equations is usually 2–4 orders of magnitude. With new data, an assimilation may be performed in the adaptive subspace (or full space as the case may be), to obtain a posterior velocity distribution. Of course, for realistic applications, an ocean modeling system with deterministic and probabilistic equations must be employed (e.g., [13]).

Reinforcement Learning. To tackle our problem statement (Sect. 1.1), we propose to employ a MDP framework in the discreet grid world (Fig. 1B). In this framework, at every time-step k, the agent P can take an action $a = A_k$ from a state $s = S_k$ to receive a reward $r = R_{k+1}$ and reach a state $s' = S_{k+1}$. The state $S_k = [\mathbf{x}_k, t_k]$ is the rectangular cell with area defined by the diagonally opposite coordinates $(x_k - \Delta x/2, y_k - \Delta y/2)$ and $(x_k + \Delta x/2, y_k + \Delta y/2)$ at time t_k. The actions available for P is to choose the heading $\hat{h} = \cos\theta\hat{e}_x + \sin\theta\hat{e}_y$, where $\hat{e}_x, \hat{e}_y$ are unit vectors along $x-$ and $y-$ axes, and θ is the direction of heading. We discretize $\theta = [0, 360°]$ to obtain the action space $\mathcal{A} = \{\theta_i\}$, and $A_k = \theta_k$, one of the θ_i. In the presence of an uncertain velocity field $\mathbf{v}(\mathbf{x}, t; \omega)$, the state s' is reached by the effect of $(\mathbf{v} + F\hat{h})dt$ on the spatial coordinates and dt on the temporal coordinate. Discreetly, $S_{k+1} = S_k + \Delta t[(\mathbf{v}(S_k; \omega) + F(\cos\theta_k\hat{e}_x + \sin\theta_k\hat{e}_y)), 1]$ for every realization of the uncertain environment ω. The immediate reward for this action is $R_k = -\Delta t$. The goal of the agent is to take a sequence of actions so as to maximize the long term return, i.e., the expected value of total rewards, thereby minimizing the expected travel time. We define the total rewards G_k at the time-step k by the recursive relation $G_k = \sum_{k'=0}^{K} \gamma^{k'} R_{k+k'+1} = R_{k+1} + \gamma G_{k+1}$, where k' is the index of summation, K is the index of the last step in the finite planning horizon, and γ is the discounting factor which quantifies the importance of future rewards. We define an *action-value function* $q_\pi(s, a) = \mathbb{E}[G_k | S_k = s, A_k = a]$ that quantifies the value of taking action a in state s under a policy π. An optimal policy π^* is one which has a better action-value function than all other policies for every state-action pair, i.e., $q_{\pi^*}(s, a) \geq q_\pi(s, a) \forall (s, a)$. Such an optimal policy has the optimal action-value function $q_*(s, a) = \max_\pi q_\pi(x, a)$. Hence, if we have an estimate $Q(S, A)$ of all the action-value functions, then we can compute the optimal policy as the argument that maximizes our estimate of Q, i.e., $\pi^*(s) = \arg\max_\pi Q(S, A)$.

The above framework is similar to a classic MDP setting, which requires knowledge of the state transition probabilities $p(s, s')$ and the reward for every state-action pair $r(s, a)$. However, in the RL framework that we use in the present work, an explicit representation of the probabilities and rewards are not required, and these can be learned with experience, i.e., from data of actual rewards obtained for any action for a large sample size. Specifically, we employ an off-policy Temporal Difference (TD) control algorithm called Q-learning to learn the action-value function and compute the optimal policy [17].

In Q-learning, the $Q(s, a)$ is learned and updated from experience as

$$Q(S_k, A_k) \leftarrow Q(S_k, A_k) + \alpha[R_{k+1} + \gamma \max_a Q(S_{k+1}, a) - Q(S_k, A_k)]. \quad (1)$$

During the learning phase, an ϵ-greedy approach is used to select an action based on the policy according to the $Q(S_k, A_k)$ that has been learned so far. To initialize the learning, any random initial $Q(S, A)$ could be utilized, but convergence is slow and that forms a key challenge in the use of Q-learning algorithms. In our experience, even modest spatio-temporal domain sizes take unacceptably long iterations to converge. In literature, only small domain sizes are considered for RL (e.g., [19,20]). We want to consider realistic domain sizes with spatio-temporal states of dimensions $O(10^6)$ and higher. To speed up computation, we employ transfer learning [3,11] from solutions of stochastic PDEs for exact time-optimal path planning .

Stochastic PDEs for Exact Time-Optimal Path Planning. For the problem setup in Fig. 1A, the stochastic reachability front, i.e., the set of all points that can be reached by P starting from $\mathbf{x}_0$ at $t = 0$ (i.e., reachability front) is governed by the DO stochastic scalar Hamilton-Jacobi (HJ) level-set S-PDE [15]. The first time the reachability front reaches $\mathbf{x}_f$ is the optimal travel time $T(\mathbf{x}_f; \omega)$ and the optimal path $\mathbf{X}_P(\mathbf{x}_0, t; \omega)$ can be computed for every ω by solving the particle backtracking equation. This distribution of exact time-optimal paths for every ω provides the ideal data-set for us to learn Q-values in our RL framework using a transfer learning approach.

Dynamic Programming. To solve the MDP equivalent to the RL framework, a completely offline Dynamic Programming algorithm may be used to validate the Q-learning solution. However, the MDP formulation requires a full transition probability matrix that is very expensive to evaluate, and we have implemented a GPU algorithm for computational efficiency.

3   Physics-Driven Model-Based Q-Learning

We combine the different modelling frameworks to develop a novel online algorithm to compute adaptive, near time-optimal policies for an autonomous agent. Our dynamic data-driven method and has two phases, and *(i)* Transfer learning of initial policy, *(ii)* Dynamic data-driven policy update.

Phase 1: Transfer Learning of Initial Policy. Initialization of the action value function $Q(S, A)$ is important for the Q-learning algorithm to converge to an optimal target policy as it learns from experience. In traditional Q-Learning [17], the update 1 is made using data (s, a, r, s') generated by following a behaviour policy (usually $\epsilon-$greedy exploration-exploitation strategy) in multiple realizations of the environment in simulation. As can be expected, the aforementioned algorithm is computationally expensive due to unfruitful exploration. To avoid this, we use the solution of the optimal planning S-PDE to initialize our Q(S, A). First, from the DO solution of the environment S-PDE and time-optimal S-PDE, $n_{r,\mathbf{v}}$ realizations of the flow and corresponding time-optimal paths (specified as a sequence of waypoints) are reconstructed. These paths are used to learn the initial $Q(S, A)$ and near-optimal policy π^1. To train the agent in this transfer learning, we do the following. First, the agent is placed in a particular realization of the stochastic velocity field. Then, it is made to perform a sequence of actions so as to follow the HJ-PDE time-optimal trajectory for that realization, and the experience tuples (s, a, r, s') at each time step along the way for all realizations is utilized to update $Q(S, A)$. This completes the phase 1 of learning and we have a near-optimal policy transferred from the PDE solution to the RL framework.

Phase 2: Dynamic Data-Driven Policy Update. When the agent is placed in the mission environment, it goes from s to s' by taking the optimum action a based on π^1 learnt in phase 1. Information from the agent's movement data is used as feedback in the DDDAS paradigm to dynamically update $Q(S, A)$ values. First, a simple Bayesian estimation of the mission environment is done using the training realizations used in phase 1 as prior and the data from the mission environment observed so far. Using the posterior forecasts of the environment, a future "roll-out simulation" is performed adopting an ϵ−greedy algorithm to update the Q(S, A) values and thus the optimal policy. Using only the phase 1, or simply the solution of the time-optimal SPDE is only an open-loop control, and the phase 2 that we introduce completes the most important closed loop feedback of the DDDAS paradigm.

4   Applications

We apply our algorithm to plan paths in one illustrative canonical stochastic Quasi-Geostrophic double gyre flow scenario that idealizes a wind-driven flow in a basin. This testcase is a continuation of our previous development enabling

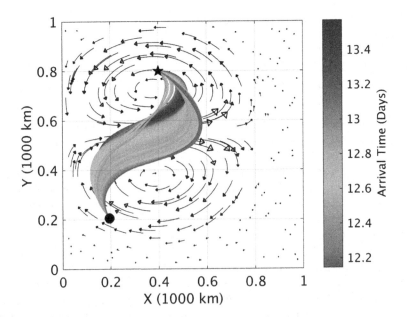

Fig. 2. *Stochastic Quasi-Gesotrophic Double Gyre.* The goal is to travel from the circular marker to the star marker in the presence of a stochastic dynamic flow. The data-set of 5000 time-optimal paths corresponding to the flow realizations, each colored by its arrival time is shown. Background vectors are a particular flow realization at the initial time, shown to illustrate the type of flow encountered. Further details of set-up and flow in [16]. (Color figure online)

comparisons. Specifically, the set-up and data of the stochastic flow and time-optimal paths utilized for the Q-learning in the present paper (Fig. 2) are from ref. [16]. Hereafter, we show only what is required for the RL task and elucidate the advantages of our new algorithm.

As shown in Fig. 2, the mission is to travel from start (circular marker) to target (star marker) in a square domain with an extent of 1000 km ×1000 km. A west to east wind blowing over the basin with uncertain initial conditions generates a stochastic flow field. For RL, the domain is discretized to a spatio-temporal grid of size $100 \times 100 \times 60$, with a spatial resolution of $\Delta x = \Delta y = 10$ km and a temporal resolution of $\Delta t = 0.24$ days. The speed of P is $40\,\mathrm{cm/s}$ and the action space of the agent P, i.e., the heading angle, is discretized with a resolution of $22.5°$ and is $\mathcal{A} = \{0, 22.5, 45, \cdots, 337.5\}$. From the DO environmental forecasts, we obtain 5000 realizations and from the DO level-set S-PDE solution we get the corresponding time-optimal paths. 4000 realizations are used for transfer learning and 1000 realizations are used for testing the learnt policy.

First, the phase 1 of the Q-learning algorithm (Sect. 3) is applied to compute the optimal policy from the 4000 training realizations. Next, for each of the 1000 test realizations, an $\epsilon-$greedy exploration is performed with the posterior realizations estimated from the 4000 prior realizations and likelihood of data from the mission environment. Depending on the capability of the autonomous agent, the estimation and update of the policy can be sparse and we note that our scheme is versatile to accommodate that requirement (not shown here). To validate the solution from the Q-learning, we do a completely offline Dynamic Programming (DP) solution of the MDP corresponding to the time-optimal planning problem. The paths obtained by following the policy computed from the Q-learning are shown in Fig. 3A, those from the DP in Fig. 3B. Both policies result in almost similar paths with comparable expected arrival time and probability of failing to reach the target (Fig. 3C). The key advantage of our Q-learning is in the computational time required. For the present test case, building the transition probability for DP on a modern GPU requires 48 min and DP solution takes 42 min on a 6-core CPU with all threads utilized. On the other hand, for our Q-learning (done on CPU with only 1 thread), it takes 8.4 min to obtain the paths from the DO level-set equations, 1.5 min to complete the phase 1 of Q-learning and 1.5 min for the data-driven update of Q(S, A). Compared to the DP and risk-optimal framework of [16], QL can dynamically update the optimal policy with new experiences at a fraction of the computational cost. Moreover, compared to the risk optimal framework, the failure rate is substantially reduced.

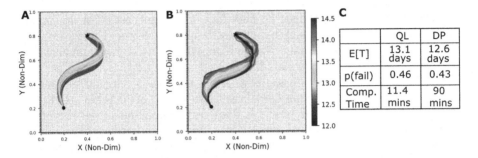

Fig. 3. (A) 1000 mission paths obtained by using the policy learnt from our Q-learning (QL) algorithm. **(B)** Paths obtained by using the policy computed from Dynamic Programming (DP). **(C)** E[T] is the expected travel time, p(fail) is the probability that applying the computed policy results in mission failure and Comp. Time is the total time required to compute the optimal policy.

5   Conclusions and Future Work

We developed and demonstrated a novel computationally efficient Q-learning algorithm that learns the time-optimal policy for an autonomous agent in a stochastic dynamic environment. First, the policy is learnt from the solution of optimal path planning stochastic partial differential equations using a transfer learning approach, and then dynamically updated with data in our Reinforcement Learning framework, closing the control feedback loop. The results show that using the DDDAS paradigm of data-driven policy update in our RL algorithm is a more efficient learning scheme at a fraction of the computational cost required for dynamic programming. We note that a relatively simple policy update scheme is presented here to introduce the idea of utilizing physics based S-PDE solutions to train an RL agent. It is a prelude to more advanced DDDAS within the science of autonomy. In the future, further improvements could be made to the algorithm in the present paper by formulating other assimilation schemes for dynamic update. Moreover, realistic applications and evaluation of the proposed algorithm may be undertaken.

References

1. Blasch, E.: DDDAS advantages from high-dimensional simulation. In: 2018 Winter Simulation Conference (WSC), pp. 1418–1429. IEEE (2018)
2. Blasch, E., Bernstein, D., Rangaswamy, M.: Introduction to dynamic data driven applications systems. In: Blasch, E., Ravela, S., Aved, A. (eds.) Handbook of Dynamic Data Driven Applications Systems, pp. 1–25. Springer, Cham (2018). https://doi.org/10.1007/978-3-319-95504-9_1
3. Celiberto Jr., L.A., Matsuura, J.P., De Màntaras, R.L., Bianchi, R.A.: Using transfer learning to speed-up reinforcement learning: a cased-based approach. In: Latin American Robotics Symposium and Intelligent Robotics Meeting, pp. 55–60 (2010)

4. Cooper, B.S., Cowlagi, R.V.: Dynamic sensor-actor interactions for path-planning in a threat field. In: Blasch, E., Ravela, S., Aved, A. (eds.) Handbook of Dynamic Data Driven Applications Systems, pp. 445–464. Springer, Cham (2018). https://doi.org/10.1007/978-3-319-95504-9_19
5. Darema, F.: Dynamic data driven applications systems: a new paradigm for application simulations and measurements. In: Bubak, M., van Albada, G.D., Sloot, P.M.A., Dongarra, J. (eds.) ICCS 2004. LNCS, vol. 3038, pp. 662–669. Springer, Heidelberg (2004). https://doi.org/10.1007/978-3-540-24688-6_86
6. Denniston, C., Krogstad, T.R., Kemna, S., Sukhatme, G.S.: On-line AUV survey planning for finding safe vessel paths through hazardous environments* (2018)
7. Finn, C., Levine, S., Abbeel, P.: Guided cost learning: deep inverse optimal control via policy optimization. In: ICML, pp. 49–58 (2016)
8. Kober, J., Bagnell, J.A., Peters, J.: Reinforcement learning in robotics: a survey. Int. J. Robot. Res. **32**(11), 1238–1274 (2013)
9. Kularatne, D., Hajieghrary, H., Hsieh, M.A.: Optimal path planning in time-varying flows with forecasting uncertainties. In: 2018 IEEE ICRA, pp. 1–8 (2018)
10. Lolla, T., Lermusiaux, P.F.J., Ueckermann, M.P., Haley Jr., P.J.: Time-optimal path planning in dynamic flows using level set equations: Theory and schemes. Ocean Dyn. **64**(10), 1373–1397 (2014)
11. Murphy, K.P.: Machine Learning: A Probabilistic P. MIT Press, Cambridge (2012)
12. Singh, V., Willcox, K.E.: Methodology for path planning with dynamic data-driven flight capability estimation. AIAA J. **55**(8), 2727–2738 (2017)
13. Subramani, D.N., Haley Jr., P.J., Lermusiaux, P.F.J.: Energy-optimal path planning in the coastal ocean. JGR: Oceans **122**, 3981–4003 (2017)
14. Subramani, D.N., Lermusiaux, P.F.J.: Energy-optimal path planning by stochastic dynamically orthogonal level-set optimization. Ocean Model. **100**, 57–77 (2016)
15. Subramani, D.N., Wei, Q.J., Lermusiaux, P.F.J.: Stochastic time-optimal path-planning in uncertain, strong, and dynamic flows. CMAME **333**, 218–237 (2018)
16. Subramani, D.N., Lermusiaux, P.F.J.: Risk-optimal path planning in stochastic dynamic environments. CMAME **353**, 391–415 (2019)
17. Sutton, R.S., Barto, A.G.: Reinforcement Learning: An Introduction. MIT Press, Cambridge (2018)
18. Wang, T., Le Maître, O.P., Hoteit, I., Knio, O.M.: Path planning in uncertain flow fields using ensemble method. Ocean Dyn. **66**(10), 1231–1251 (2016). https://doi.org/10.1007/s10236-016-0979-2
19. Yijing, Z., Zheng, Z., Xiaoyi, Z., Yang, L.: Q learning algorithm based UAV path learning and obstacle avoidance approach. In: 36th CCC, pp. 3397–3402 (2017)
20. Yoo, B., Kim, J.: Path optimization for marine vehicles in ocean currents using reinforcement learning. J. Mar. Sci. Technol. **21**(2), 334–343 (2015). https://doi.org/10.1007/s00773-015-0355-9
21. Zhang, B., Mao, Z., Liu, W., Liu, J.: Geometric reinforcement learning for path planning of UAVS. J. Intell. Robot. Syst. **77**(2), 391–409 (2015)

Discovering Laws from Observations: A Data-Driven Approach

Chenzhong Yin, Gaurav Gupta, and Paul Bogdan$^{(\boxtimes)}$

University of Southern California, Los Angeles, CA 90089, USA
{chenzhoy,ggaurav,pbogdan}@usc.edu

Abstract. A variety of complex patterns displayed by animal physiology, microbial communities, biological systems, or even artificial networks such as neural networks can be modeled by mathematical techniques which use non-linear, non-stationary, non-Markovian (i.e., long-range dependence) properties, to name a few. To identify the non-stationary changes over time, the models utilizing partial differential equations (PDEs) work well which track minute changes as well as the driving force. Further, the fractional PDEs have the flexibility of modeling long-range dependence across a sample trajectory. The scale-invariance in the magnitudes, as well as long-range dependence across time in a diffusion process, is captured by having fractional operators for both space and time. In this work, we propose to utilize the fractional PDEs to model sample trajectories and provide an estimation of the associated process with fewer samples. The space-time fractional diffusion process is generalized with the diffusion coefficient as well as drift (or advection) terms, which are domain-specific and tunable. Instead of usual methods to model dynamics of the system, the proposed techniques aim at modeling the minute changes in the dynamical system along with scale-invariance properties as well as long temporal dependence. With the essence of Dynamic Data-Driven Applications Systems (DDDAS), we let the data decide which model to use. We estimate all the parameters of the involved generalized fractional PDE by solving optimization problems minimizing error between empirical and theoretical fractional moments. To demonstrate the effectiveness of the proposed algorithm in retrieving the parameters, we perform an extensive set of simulations with various parameters' combinations.

Keywords: Fractional diffusion · Cyber-physical systems · Stochastic modeling · Optimization · Partial differential equations

1 Introduction

In the big data era, machine learning (ML) and artificial intelligence (AI) play a prominent role in boosting numerous scientific areas [1,8,9]. Furthermore, ML and AI have been recently explored into radiological examination to detect the early sign of diseases [15]. In fact, in most of the scenarios, ML is used to analyze

© Springer Nature Switzerland AG 2020
F. Darema et al. (Eds.): DDDAS 2020, LNCS 12312, pp. 302–310, 2020.
https://doi.org/10.1007/978-3-030-61725-7_35

static data by identifying the statistical interdependence between components of a system of interest. Contrary, there is little to say about analyzing dynamical processes from big data and uncertainty quantification for large-scale complex systems. A plethora of complex systems from biology, neuroscience, aerospace or finance has numerous hidden interactions driving the time evolution, which cannot be analyzed using regular ML approaches. Specifically, ML has a limiting ability in deciphering the driving space-time physical laws and governing equations from multi-modal heterogeneous and noisy time series data associated with complex system exhibiting multiscale and multi-physics spatiotemporal evolution.

In this vein, we think that the analysis of spatiotemporal kinetics via a novel AI architecture will offer new horizons to researchers for better understanding of complex systems/phenomena. Developing new AI approaches that deal with complex space-time evolution will provide new opportunities for the data-driven discovery of potentially new physical phenomena and new physics laws/rules. Consequently, unraveling new laws will enhance the detection of causal interdependence. Besides, knowing the non-trivial space-time evolution of a given system is a key step for boosting its causal predictive capabilities even if the data is incomplete since the laws governing the evolution are learned. For the aforementioned reasons/problems, understanding complex spatiotemporal dynamics through classical ML techniques seems to be unfeasible.

Starting from spatiotemporal data, we aim to develop new AI architectures that enable us to discover new physical phenomena and new physics laws/rules that govern complex dynamics in different fields (e.g., neuroscience, physics, biology, aerospace). The multiscale and multi-physics spatiotemporal characteristics that occur in the data from physics, biology, chemistry, neuroscience, aerospace and even geology, are usually encoded through (fractional or integer order) partial differential equations (PDEs) with possibly uncertain parameters [5,13]. These PDEs are usually derived from physical principles conservation laws on energy, momentum, or electric charge (e.g., diffusion equation, Maxwell's equations, Navier-Stokes equations, Schrodinger equations). Next, even with a fixed structure of the PDE, the derivative orders can have significant effect on the data. For example, with one set of values we have Brownian motion, while with another we have a completely different diffusion process. In this work, we let the data decide which model fits best with minimal parameters. Indeed, this is the setting of Dynamic Data-Driven Applications Systems (DDDAS) where the model and data are in cooperation to have better prediction. Finally, the key challenge is how to retrieve the space-time dynamic that drives a dynamical process hence we identify the PDE that governs its evolution. Consequently, one may ask the following fundamental questions: Can we learn a PDE model from given time series measurements and perform accurate, efficient and robust predictions using this learned model?

2 Data-Driven Approach for Analyzing Anomalous Diffusion

2.1 Space-Time Fractional Diffusion Equation

The previous works has proved that the space-time fractional diffusion equation has been presented as a mathematical model which could efficiently analyze anomalous diffusion [6,7,11,12,14]. As a whole, in this paper, we defined the space-time fractional diffusion equation in (1) which comprise fractional Riesz-Feller derivative of the order $0 < \alpha \leq 2$ and the order 1 which represents the space variations, or sometimes referred as advection term, and a fractional Caputo derivative of the order $0 < \beta \leq 1$ which measures the time variations. The space-time fractional diffusion equation is defined as

$$_t\mathcal{D}_*^\beta u(x,t) = D \times {}_x\mathcal{D}_\theta^\alpha u(x,t) + \mathcal{D}'u(x,t), \tag{1}$$

where $_t\mathcal{D}_*^\beta$, $_x\mathcal{D}_\theta^\alpha$, and $\mathcal{D}'$ are the Caputo time-fractional derivative of the order β [2], fractional Riesz-Feller derivative of order α with skewness θ [3], and ordinary derivative of order 1. The θ represents the skewness element in the space derivative of the fractional diffusion equation which has this constraint: $|\theta| \leq min\{\alpha, 2 - \alpha\}$. The parameter D represents the generalized diffusion coefficient.

In this section, our goal is to use a time-series trajectories dataset that encodes the fluctuation of particles that exhibits anomalous diffusion which is based on the Eq. (1) to restore the fractional diffusion equation that generates the previous time-series dataset. It's worth noting that the dataset doesn't include the prior knowledge or records about the parameters of the fractional diffusion equation. For this purpose, we constructed a mathematical model which defines the parameter and mathematical expression as a regression problem that can be expressed as a least squares problem where the minimization implied the theoretical and the empirical statistical moments. Via performing the regression on statistical moments, we could achieve the closed form mathematical expressions from the fractional diffusion equation in Eq. (1). The time empirical moments is shown below used in rest of the paper are stated as

$$M_t^\delta = \frac{1}{N}\sum |X_n(t)|^\delta, \quad S_t^\delta = \frac{1}{N}\sum X_n(t)^{\langle\delta\rangle}, \tag{2}$$

where $X_n(t)$ denotes the time-series data, n has the constraint of $1 \leq n \leq N$ (N denotes the total number of trajectories), $X^{\langle\delta\rangle}$ denotes the signed absolute δ power of X, or $X^{\langle\delta\rangle} = |X|^\delta sign(X)$.

2.2 Fractional Derivatives

In this section, first we present the definitions and preliminaries required to derive the main estimation algorithm utilizing the time-series data.

Riesz-Feller Space Fractional Derivative. For a well-behaved function $f(x)$, the Riesz-Feller space-fractional derivative of order α with skewness θ can be defined as:

$$\begin{cases} \mathcal{F}\{_x\mathcal{D}_\theta^\alpha\} = \psi_\alpha^\theta(k)f(k), & \psi_\alpha^\theta(k) = -|k|^\alpha e^{i\,\mathrm{sign}(k)\theta\pi/2} \\ 0 < \alpha \leq 2, & |\theta| \leq \min\{\alpha, 2-\alpha\}, \end{cases} \tag{3}$$

where the $\psi_\alpha^\theta(k)$ is the logarithm of the characteristic function of a general Levy strictly stable distribution with the stability α and skewness θ, and $\mathcal{F}$ denotes the Fourier transform.

The Caputo Fractional Derivation. For a well-behaved function $f(t)$, the Caputo time-fractional derivative of order β is defined as:

$$_t\mathcal{D}_*^\beta f(t) = \begin{cases} \frac{1}{\Gamma(1-\beta)} \int_0^t \frac{f^{(1)}(\tau)}{(t-\tau)^\beta}d\tau, & 0 < \beta < 1 \\ \frac{d}{dt}f(t), & \beta = 1 \end{cases}. \tag{4}$$

Fractional Order Absolute Moment. By utilizing the method in [10,16], the fractional order absolute moment of order δ for the Eq. (1) is obtained using the following result.

Proposition 1. *The time-dependent signed absolute moment of the order δ with $0 < \delta < \alpha$ is written as follows*

$$E[|X(t)|^\delta] = \frac{1}{\alpha}\frac{-\Gamma(1+\delta)}{\pi}\sin\left(\frac{\delta\pi}{2}\right)$$
$$\times \sum_{j=0}^\infty \frac{\Gamma(m)\Gamma(n+1)}{\Gamma(j+1)\Gamma(1+\beta n)}2(-1)^j \cos\left(\frac{\theta\pi m}{2}\right)t^{\beta(j+\frac{\delta-j}{\alpha})}D^{\frac{\delta-j}{\alpha}}, \tag{5}$$

where $n_j = j + \frac{\delta-j}{\alpha}$ and $m_j = \frac{-\delta+j}{\alpha}$.

Signed Fractional Order Moment. The signed fractional order moment of order δ is presented in the following result.

Proposition 2. *The time-dependent signed absolute moment of the order δ with $0 < \delta < \alpha$ is written as follows*

$$E[X(t)^{\langle\delta\rangle}] = -\frac{1}{\alpha}\frac{-\Gamma(1+\delta)}{\pi}\cos\left(\frac{\delta\pi}{2}\right)$$
$$\times \sum_{j=0}^\infty \frac{\Gamma(m)\Gamma(n+1)}{\Gamma(j+1)\Gamma(1+\beta n)}2(-1)^j \sin\left(\frac{\theta\pi m}{2}\right)t^{\beta(j+\frac{\delta-j}{\alpha})}D^{\frac{\delta-j}{\alpha}},$$

$$\tag{6}$$

where $n_j = j + \frac{\delta-j}{\alpha}$ and $m_j = \frac{-\delta+j}{\alpha}$.

Algorithm 1. Fractional Diffusion with drift: Parameters Estimation

---

Input: Time-series data $\{X_n(t_l); 1 \leq n \leq N, 1 \leq l \leq L\}$, order δ, $\Delta = \{\delta_1, \delta_2, \cdots, \delta_K\}$
Output: Parameters: α, β, θ and D

1: **for** $l = 1, 2, \cdots, L$ **do**
2:     Calculate the empirical absolute and signed moments $M_{t_l}^{\delta}$ and $S_{t_l}^{\delta}$ ▷ Eq.2
3: **end for**
4: $\left(\frac{\beta}{\alpha}\right) \leftarrow \frac{m_1}{\delta}$, m_1 being slope of linear regression $\log(t)$ vs $\log(M_t^{\delta})$
5: Get the estimate $\widehat{\left(\frac{\theta}{\alpha}\right)}$ ▷ Eq.11
6: **for** $k = 1, 2, \cdots, K$ **do**
7:     Calculate the empirical absolute moments $M_{t_l}^{\delta_k}$, $\forall l$ ▷ Eq.2
8:     $m_2 \leftarrow$ slope of linear regression $t^{\delta_k\left(\widehat{\frac{\beta}{\alpha}}\right)}$ vs $M_t^{\delta_k}$ with zero intercept
9:     $V_k \leftarrow m_2 \cdot \dfrac{\Gamma\left(1 + \delta_k\left(\widehat{\frac{\beta}{\alpha}}\right)\right)\Gamma(1 - \delta_k)\cos\left(\frac{\pi\delta_k}{2}\right)}{\cos\left(\frac{\pi\delta_k}{2}\left(\widehat{\frac{\theta}{\alpha}}\right)\right)}$ ▷ Eq.13
10: **end for**
11: Find $\hat{\alpha}, \widehat{D} \leftarrow \underset{\alpha,D}{\mathrm{argmin}} \sum\limits_{k=1}^{K} \left| D^{\frac{\delta_k}{\alpha}} \times \frac{\pi}{\sin(\frac{\delta_k\pi}{\alpha})} - V_k \right|^2$: non-linear regression over space
    (sinc inversion)
12: Calculate $\hat{\beta}, \hat{\theta}$.

2.3 Parameter Estimation

For the time-series dataset which has N independent trajectories with unknown parameters, we aim to estimate the α, β, θ, and D of the Eq. (1) via exploring the theoretical and the empirical expressions. Here, we use the method given by [16]. Since the theoretical moments in Proposition 1 and 2 involve infinite series making it infeasible to directly implement in the regression problem. Therefore, we resort to the first term in the expansion. The method is outlined in the Algorithm 1. The algorithm regresses over time and space to find the parameters. Thus these two equations can be rewritten as:

$$E[|X(t)|^{\delta}] \approx \frac{\Gamma(1 - \frac{\delta}{\alpha})\Gamma(\frac{\delta}{\alpha})\cos(\frac{\theta\pi\delta}{2\alpha})}{\Gamma(1 - \delta)\Gamma(1 + \beta\frac{\delta}{\alpha})\cos(\frac{\delta\pi}{2})} t^{\beta\frac{\delta}{\alpha}} D^{\frac{\delta}{\alpha}}, \tag{7}$$

$$E[X(t)^{\langle\delta\rangle}] \approx \frac{\Gamma(1 - \frac{\delta}{\alpha})\Gamma(\frac{\delta}{\alpha})\sin(\frac{\theta\pi\delta}{2\alpha})}{\Gamma(1 - \delta)\Gamma(1 + \beta\frac{\delta}{\alpha})\sin(\frac{\delta\pi}{2})} t^{\beta\frac{\delta}{\alpha}} D^{\frac{\delta}{\alpha}}. \tag{8}$$

The log of absolute moments in Eq. (7) is defined as:

$$\log(E[|X(t)|^{\delta}]) = \delta\frac{\beta}{\alpha}\log(t) + V, \tag{9}$$

where V is a constant and independent with t. The theoretical moments in the left hand side of Eq. (9) can be replaced by the empirical moments in Eq. (2) and thus, the $\frac{\beta}{\alpha}$ can be evaluated by the linear regression of $\log(t_l)$ and $\log(M_{t_l}^{\delta})$ where l is the index of points. Next, by observing the Eq. (7) and (8), we calculate the ratio between the absolute moments and signed fractional order moment as follow:

$$\frac{\overline{M_{t_l}^{\delta}}}{S_{t_l}^{\delta}} = \frac{E[X(t)^{\langle\delta\rangle}]}{E[|X(t)|^{\delta}]} = -\frac{\tan(\frac{\pi\delta\theta}{2\alpha})}{\tan(\frac{\pi\delta}{2})}, \tag{10}$$

where the $\frac{\overline{M_{t_l}^{\delta}}}{S_{t_l}^{\delta}}$ is the average ratio between $M_{t_l}^{\delta}$ and $S_{t_l}^{\delta}$. Therefore, the ratio $\frac{\theta}{\alpha}$ can be calculated by inverting the tangent functions. From the Eq. 3, the parameter θ is constrained with $|\theta| \leq min(\alpha, 2 - \alpha)$, thus, the ratio of $|\frac{\theta}{\alpha}|$ must less than or equal to 1. Thus, the ratio of $\frac{\theta}{\alpha}$ is defined as:

$$\frac{\theta}{\alpha} = -\frac{2}{\pi\delta} \arctan(\tan(\frac{\pi\delta}{2})(\frac{\overline{S_{t_l}^{\delta}}}{M_{t_l}^{\delta}})). \tag{11}$$

Table 1. The results for fractional diffusion parameter estimation with the first 9 epochs (The mean represents the average values for all 20 epochs)

	Epoch									Mean
	1	2	3	4	5	6	7	8	9	
Test set (α)	0.511	0.511	0.511	0.510	0.511	0.511	0.511	0.511	0.512	0.511
Valid set (α)	0.505	0.507	0.506	0.508	0.505	0.507	0.507	0.506	0.505	0.507
Test set (β)	0.011	0.011	0.011	0.011	0.011	0.010	0.012	0.011	0.010	0.011
Valid set (β)	0.009	0.010	0.010	0.011	0.010	0.010	0.010	0.097	0.011	0.010
Test set (θ)	0.488	0.493	0.489	0.489	0.489	0.490	0.489	0.488	0.488	0.489
Valid set (θ)	0.495	0.493	0.494	0.492	0.495	0.493	0.493	0.494	0.495	0.494
Test set (D)	1.000	1.000	1.000	1.000	1.000	1.000	1.000	1.000	1.000	1.000
Valid set (D)	1.000	1.000	1.000	1.000	1.000	1.000	1.000	1.000	1.000	1.000

To achieve the precision of the prediction, the θ can be replaced by a set of moment exponents $\triangle = \{\delta_1, \delta_2, ..., \delta_K\}$. We use the Eq. 10 to obtain a series of $\widehat{(\frac{\theta}{\alpha})}_K$ and the optimal estimation result can be expressed by $\widehat{(\frac{\theta}{\alpha})} = \frac{1}{K}\sum_{k=0}^{K}(\frac{\theta}{\alpha})_K$. Afterwards, the absolute moments in Eq. 7 can be rewritten as:

$$\frac{E[|X(t)|^{\delta}]}{t^{\beta\frac{\delta}{\alpha}}} = D^{\frac{\delta}{\alpha}} \times \frac{\pi}{\sin(\frac{\pi\delta}{\alpha})} \times \frac{\cos(\frac{\theta\pi\delta}{2\alpha})}{\Gamma(1-\delta)\Gamma(1+\beta\frac{\delta}{\alpha})\cos(\frac{\delta\pi}{2})}. \tag{12}$$

Thus, the δ can be replaced by δ_k where $\delta_k \in \triangle$ and the Eq. (11) can be rewritten as:

$$V_k = \frac{\Gamma(1-\delta_k)\Gamma(1+\beta\frac{\delta_k}{\alpha})\cos(\frac{\delta_k\pi}{2})}{\cos(\frac{\theta\pi\delta_k}{2\alpha})} \times \frac{E[|X(t)|^{\delta_k}]}{t^{\beta\frac{\delta_k}{\alpha}}} = D^{\frac{\delta_k}{\alpha}} \times \frac{\pi}{\sin(\frac{\pi\delta_k}{\alpha})}. \tag{13}$$

To estimate the α and θ in Eq. 13, we utilize non-linear least squares method. Upon estimating the α, the parameters β and θ can be well estimated by the ratios of $\frac{\beta}{\alpha}$ and $\frac{\theta}{\alpha}$ which are presented in Eqs. (9) and (10).

3   Experiments

Simulations: We simulate the trajectories in this section, and then provide a proof of concept by running the provided estimation algorithm. The trajectories are generated using the similar procedure as outlined in [16] with an additional term of order 1 derivative representing the advection term as shown in Eq. (1). In Fig. 1, we run several experiments over various choice of the parameters α, β, θ. We show the estimated value of the parameters by varying the number of trajectories under consideration. The solid line denote mean and shaded area denote

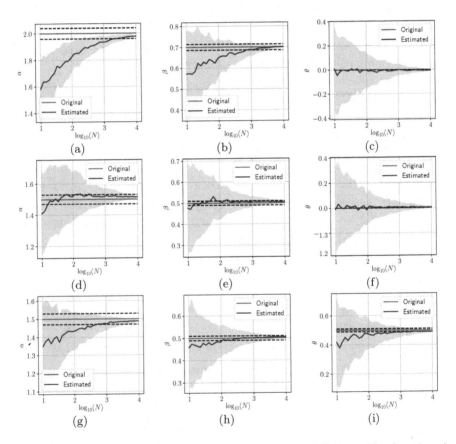

Fig. 1. Estimating parameters of the space-time fractional diffusion with advection via the Algorithm 1 while varying the number of trajectories. The dotted line indicate 2% error tube around the original parameter value in the red: (**1a, 1b, 1c**) ($\alpha = 2, \beta = 0.7, \theta = 0$), (**1d, 1e, 1f**) ($\alpha = 1.5, \beta = 0.5, \theta = 0$), (**1g, 1h, 1i**) ($\alpha = 1.5, \beta = 0.5, \theta = 0.5$). (Color figure online)

standard deviation across 200 random experiments. We observe that with around 1000 trajectories we reach with 2% error margin, and hence the Taylor approximation with only one term works well. However, a better accuracy could be achieved by using more terms in (5), (6) which we leave for future.

Real-World Data: In this experiment, we validate our algorithm using the real-world time-series data from [4]. This dataset is a spike train generated from Drosophila brain neuron. This spike train is separated into 500 independent time series with same length, where 400 of them are combined as the test set and 100 of them are merged as the validation set. We shuffle these time series, randomly create the test and validation set, and use the Algorithm 1 to retrieve the parameters (α, β, θ, and D) on both sets for 20 times. The Table 1 expresses estimation results of the first 9 epochs and the mean values denote the results for all 20 epochs.

4 Conclusion

In this work, along the principles of DDDAS, we have presented an approach in which we let the data decide to choose from among a wide variety of governing equations. Such applications can benefit DDDAS, for example, incorporating them in the feedback loops to improve performance/speed. We have used fractional diffusion with advection/drift term along with range of fractional orders. The estimation algorithm involve regression over theoretical and empirical moments. Using synthetic data, we have first shown the effectiveness of the proposed approach. Next, we have shown the application of the proposed model on the real-world data of Drosophila insect.

Future work along this direction can include an advection coefficient for better generalization. In this work, to avoid computational complexity, we have only taken the first term in the resulting Taylor expansion but more could be taken.

References

1. Alber, M., et al.: Integrating machine learning and multiscale modeling-perspectives, challenges, and opportunities in the biological, biomedical, and behavioral sciences. NPJ Digit. Med. **2**(1), 1–11 (2019)
2. Caputo, M.: Linear models of dissipation whose Q is almost frequency independent-II. Geophys. J. Int. **13**(5), 529–539 (1967)
3. Feller, W.: On a generalization of Marcel Riesz'potentials and the semi-groups generated by them. Gleerup (1962)
4. Fisher, Y.E., Lu, J., D'Alessandro, I., Wilson, R.I.: Sensorimotor experience remaps visual input to a heading-direction network. Nature **576**(7785), 121–125 (2019)
5. Fox, C., Nicholls, G.: Statistical estimation of the parameters of a PDE. Can. Appl. Math. Quater **10**, 277–810 (2001)
6. Gorenflo, R., Mainardi, F.: Parametric subordination in fractional diffusion processes. arXiv preprint arXiv:1210.8414 (2012)
7. Gorenflo, R., et al.: Mapping between solutions of fractional diffusion-wave equations. Fract. Calc. Appl. Anal. **3**(1), 75–86 (2000)

8. Gruson, D., Helleputte, T., Rousseau, P., Gruson, D.: Data science, artificial intelligence, and machine learning: opportunities for laboratory medicine and the value of positive regulation. Clin. Biochem. **69**, 1–7 (2019)

9. He, J., et al.: The practical implementation of artificial intelligence technologies in medicine. Nat. Med. **25**(1), 30–36 (2019)

10. Kuruoglu, E.E.: Density parameter estimation of skewed/spl alpha/-stable distributions. IEEE Trans. Signal Process. **49**(10), 2192–2201 (2001)

11. Mainardi, F., Luchko, Y., Pagnini, G.: The fundamental solution of the space-time fractional diffusion equation. arXiv preprint cond-mat/0702419 (2007)

12. Metzler, R., Klafter, J.: The random walk's guide to anomalous diffusion: a fractional dynamics approach. Phys. Rep. **339**(1), 1–77 (2000)

13. Müller, T.G., et al.: Fitting parameters in partial differential equations from partially observed noisy data. Phys. D: Nonlinear Phenom. **171**(1–2), 1–7 (2002)

14. Saichev, A.I., et al.: Fractional kinetic equations: solutions and applications. Chaos: Interdiscip. J. Nonlinear Sci. **7**(4), 753–764 (1997)

15. Yang, J., Feng, X., Laine, A., Angelini, E.: Characterizing Alzheimer's disease with image and genetic biomarkers using supervised topic models. IEEE J. Biomed. Health Inform. **24**, 1180–1187 (2019)

16. Znaidi, M.R., Gupta, G., Asgari, K., Bogdan, P.: Identifying arguments of space-time fractional diffusion: data-driven approach. Front. Appl. Math. Stat. **6**, 14 (2020)

An On-Demand Weather Avoidance System for Small Aircraft Flight Path Routing

Eric Lyons[1]([☒]) [iD], David Westbrook[1]([☒]), Andrew Grote[1]([☒]),
George Papadimitriou[2]([☒]) [iD], Komal Thareja[3]([☒]) [iD], Cong Wang[3]([☒]) [iD],
Michael Zink[1]([☒]), Ewa Deelman[2]([☒]) [iD], Anirban Mandal[3]([☒]) [iD],
and Paul Ruth[3]([☒]) [iD]

[1] University of Massachusetts Amherst, Amherst, MA 01003, USA
elyons@engin.umass.edu, westy@cs.umass.edu, agrote@umass.edu,
zink@ecs.umass.edu
[2] Information Sciences Institute, University of Southern California,
Marina Del Rey, CA 90292, USA
{georgepap,deelman}@isi.edu
[3] Renaissance Computing Institute (RENCI), University of North Carolina
at Chapel Hill, Chapel Hill, NC 27517, USA
{kthare10,cwang,anirban,pruth}@renci.org

Abstract. Convective weather events pose a challenge to the burgeoning low altitude aviation industry. Small aircraft are sensitive to winds and precipitation, but the uncertainty associated with forecasting and the frequency with which impactful weather occurs require an active detect and response system. In this paper, we propose a dynamic, data-driven decision support system, with components of forecasting, realtime sensor observations, and route planning. We demonstrate our technology in the Dallas/Fort Worth metroplex, a large urban area with frequent thunderstorms which hosts the CASA Doppler radar network.

The high temporal and spatial resolution data provided by this network allows us to quickly and accurately identify ongoing meteorological hazards for flight planning purposes. Rapidly updating short term (0–90 min) forecast data are generated with features extracted as obstacles to avoid. A flight path generator submits requests for path routing which include randomized start and end locations and times, weather tolerance parameters, and buffer zones. A customized obstacle course is created and used as the basis for routing. Weather processing workflows are instantiated with Mobius, a multicloud provisioning system. The Pegasus Workflow Management System orchestrates processing via scalable workload distribution to compute resources. Sensor data is transmitted and processed in real time, and routes are periodically calculated for proposed flights. A Google Maps front-end interface displays the weather features and flight paths. Herein, we focus on the overall system design,

Supported by the National Science Foundation (Awards #: 1826997, 2018074, and 1700967) and the North Central Texas Council of Governments.

F. Darema et al. (Eds.): DDDAS 2020, LNCS 12312, pp. 311–319, 2020.
https://doi.org/10.1007/978-3-030-61725-7_36

with particular emphasis on the dynamic flexibility and interoperability that our architecture allows.

Keywords: Cloud computing · UAS · UAM · Doppler radar · Flight planning · DDDAS

1   Introduction

The Urban Air Mobility (UAM) concept is rapidly advancing and could be a trillion dollar industry by 2040 [1]. Small aircraft are sensitive to weather conditions however, and the detection and avoidance of threatening meteorological features is a key safety consideration [2]. Weight restrictions may preclude on-board remote sensing equipment needed for proactive response. If industry operations are to expand beyond benign weather days, risk information will have to be provided before and during flights. As tolerances vary not just across aircraft types, but also rapidly changing aircraft states, the underlying Dynamic Data Driven Applications Systems (DDDAS) must be customized and adjustable on the fly. In this paper, we propose and implement such a system using live Doppler radar observations, deriving meteorological products and forecasts, and extracting areas of relevance on a per flight basis, based on declared risk parameters. We use a flight path simulator to inject proposed routes and a diverse and randomized set of weather requirements. We have developed a flight path routing algorithm to navigate obstacle courses, consisting of dynamic weather risk areas and static areas such as no fly zones. We also present an implementation of this system, which makes use of compute clouds and private, high-speed networks.

2   Background

Our work makes use of technologies and concepts that the team has developed over the course of many years.

CASA. Doppler radar is a key technology for the detection and quantification of precipitation. Since 2013, the graduated NSF Engineering Research Center for Collaborative and Adaptive Sensing of the Atmosphere (CASA), has installed and operated a network of seven high resolution, X-band Doppler weather radars in the Dallas/Fort Worth (DFW) metroplex in North Texas [3]. These rapidly updating radars focus scans on the lowest portion of the atmosphere, providing observations near the ground where they are most relevant to people and low flying aircraft. Our DDDAS system leverages live CASA radar data for situational awareness.

DyNamo. is an NSF Campus Cyberinfrastructure (CC*) integration project for creating a dynamic, network-centric platform for data-driven science. By coupling existing toolsets, the workflow management software suite Pegasus [4] and the high throughput computing framework HTCondor [5], and by developing the multi-cloud provisioning and monitoring tool Mobius [6], DyNamo has enabled new weather risk extraction workflows for CASA that were not previously possible [6]. Mobius allows provisioning virtual machine (VM) pools from multiple national-scale infrastructures like ExoGENI [7], and Chameleon [8], connecting them to the CASA data repository with private layer2 networks, and modulating provisioned bandwidths using virtual Software Defined Exchanges (SDX) [9]. DyNamo allows us to efficiently scale our flight path routing system as the number of flights increases and the weather deteriorates.

3   Dynamic Data Driven System for Urban Air Mobility and Weather

In our system (Fig. 1), routes are determined based on atmospheric observations, which are represented as dynamic weather risk obstacles. Such obstacles are created by workflows that operate on sensor data (radars and other weather sensors) and stored in the Obstacle database (Sect. 3.2). The Flight database (Sect. 3.1) contains information about planned or current flights. Pathing requests are submitted into DyNamo's workflow management system for resource acquisition and load balancing.

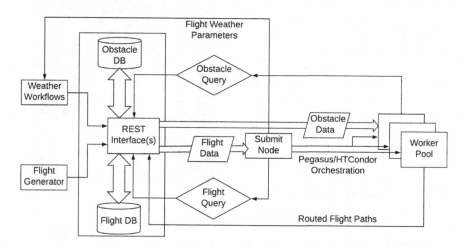

Fig. 1. Overall system architecture.

3.1   Flight Handling

Flight Database Interface. We implemented a Java based controller with a secure http based REST interface to a MySQL database. REST architectures with well defined API endpoints for information exchange are ubiquitous in the industry and reduce barriers to adoption. Flight descriptions are encoded as geoJSON [10], which combines the flexible and easily parsed JSON format, with well defined spatial GIS descriptors for location information. GeoJSON is natively supported by Google Maps which is our basis for flight and weather visualization. Flight information includes names, start and end points, waypoints (optionally), start time, weather parameter sets, and aircraft location if the flight is in progress. Our path routing function appends optimized path recommendations and the weather obstacle course on which the optimized path was generated back to the flight properties.

Flight Request Simulator. To evaluate our system, we have implemented a flight request simulator that mimics predefined flight requests. For demonstration purposes, we picked two random hospital locations in the DFW metroplex as start and end points, along with a randomized subset of discretized weather parameters for avoidance purposes.

3.2   Obstacle Handling

Obstacle Database Interface. Similar to the flight database interface, a Java based secure https REST interface has been created to receive and query geoJSON features representing areas of weather risk with certain representative characteristics. These can include magnitude or intensity thresholds, valid times ranging from the recent past into the future, or simple binary indicators such as the presence of hail. Static areas such as restricted airspaces around airports are also contained in the obstacle database. Areas of risk can be defined as closed concave polygons extracted from gridded datasets with contouring algorithms or simple point measurements.

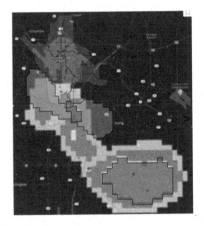

Fig. 2. Contours from CASA Wind (red) and CASA Hail (orange) products. Underlying raster image of CASA winds shown for reference. Static DFW airport contour also on display (clear) representing restricted air space. (Color figure online)

Meteorological Products. Numerous meteorological feature detection algorithms contribute to populating the obstacle database (Table 1) and represent the primary variability of our DDDAS. Many are derived from the CASA radar data, but not exclusively. Each feature type has its own associated DyNamo workflow for product creation and/or extraction.[1]

Table 1. Weather products used to populate obstacle database.

Product	Description
Rainfall rates	Dual polarized radar data is converted to gridded quantitative precipitation estimates to determine rainfall rates [11]
Observed winds	Radar velocity data is blended together to produce gridded estimates of the maximum observed wind speeds [6]
Reflectivity nowcast	Multi-radar reflectivity data is merged into an advection model producing Nowcast data, a predictive grid of Reflectivity valid 0–30 min into the future [12]
Reflectivity forecast	Radar and other sensor data is fed into a full atmospheric data assimilation model called ARPS [13], producing a forecast from 30–90 min into the future, including resolving convective initiation
Hail detection	Multi-radar data are merged together and binary areas indicating the presence of hail are derived [14]
Lightning Detection	The Earth Networks lightning detection network [15] reports the location of cloud to ground lightning strikes
NDFD winds	The National Digital Forecast Database [16] produces a forecast of gridded 10 m winds
METARs	METeorological Aerodrome Reports are point based observations from weather stations located at airports across the region [17]. They report temperature, wind, atmospheric pressure, and cloud cover information

Contouring. Feature extraction from gridded meteorological products relies heavily on contouring. Contour levels are determined dynamically by the superset of weather parameters from all flights in the database. For obstacle avoidance, we seek closed, ordered, concave polygons that can be treated as discrete objects. We have developed a C++ contouring class, implementing the Marching Squares algorithm [18] for generating isolines, and a stitching function to connect these together [19]. The results are encoded as geoJSON polygon features and posted into the obstacle database. Figure 2 depicts overlapping weather contours from the wind and hail workflows.

3.3 Flight Path Planning

Custom Querying. Once a minute our main control process queries the contents of the flight database, and creates a Pegasus job file for each active flight for

---

[1] Further details on workflows for weather product generation can be found in [6].

route planning. These jobs are submitted to the HTCondor master node, which distributes them to the pool of available cloud worker nodes. Workers extract the time and weather parameters from the geoJSON properties of the flight and generate a set of queries to the obstacle database for the weather feature data of relevance, gradually constructing a full obstacle course. Queries include weather feature type, threshold magnitude, and radius for avoidance. Finally, static areas to avoid are added to the obstacle course.

Obstacle Buffering and Merging. Due to the fast developing nature of convective weather, forecast uncertainty, imperfect sensors and detection algorithms, processing latencies, and changing physical characteristics of different aircraft, we apply a convolution filtering algorithm for obstacle buffering on a per hazard basis, based on a flight's declared radius of avoidance for that hazard type. Additionally, given the spatial correlations of various weather hazards, a substantial amount of overlap often exists among the weather feature obstacles. We therefore apply a concave polygon merging technique. A fine mesh grid is drawn across a bounding box containing the entire obstacle set. Then for each grid cell, we check whether it is inside or outside any of the obstacles, creating binary grid of inside/outside, and reapply the contouring algorithm described above to create a merged obstacle course.

Graphing and Path Routing. Whereas ground traffic routing algorithms typically make use of roadway intersections as graph vertices, free air space provides infinite potential vertices, bound only by minimum incrementation. Therefore to simplify a search we make two assumptions:

(i) the optimal path from start to end is a straight line if no obstacles exist along the straight line path, and

(ii) if the straight line path intercepts an obstacle, the optimal path will include one or more convex hull points of the associated concave polygon obstacle.

With these in mind, the algorithm begins stepping small, fixed distances from the start point toward the end point, with each step checking for line intersection with an obstacle. Should one be encountered, we calculate the convex hull of that concave polygon using the Graham algorithm [20]. Then, from each of the convex points we recurse the algorithm to splay to the start and end points, repeating the splaying process with every new obstacle encountered. Splay paths can traverse along a vertex of the obstacle from which the convex hull point is associated, but cannot cross a vertex thereof, else it is eliminated from the graph. Ultimately, our graph is assembled consisting of all the splayed paths and the vertices of the concave buffered polygons themselves. Once the graph is created, we have implemented the A* ("A star") algorithm to evaluate it and return the shortest path among those defined in the graph [21]. Thereafter, a second optimization function is applied, necessary to shorten any concave traversals. For every waypoint in the route, we evaluate if a straight line path can be traveled to waypoints later in the route without crossing a polyline segment from polygons in our obstacle course, starting from the end working backward. If no obstacles are encountered, we remove all route segments in between. If a valid flight path is found, the newly proposed route is written back into the flight database along with the obstacle course used to create it. Figure 3 depicts unique obstacle sets and two routed paths.

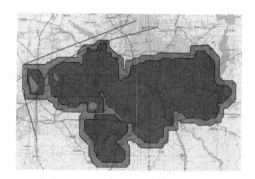

Fig. 3. Two path routed flights are shown as pink lines. Weather obstacles are depicted as green (10 min CASA reflectivity nowcast) and orange (CASA observed hail) polygons. Two sets of black polygons represent customized buffer zones, based on per flight parameters. Flights also avoid DFW airport boundary (not shown). (Color figure online)

3.4   Multi-cloud Resource Management

Our on-demand data-driven system is realized as a series of scientific workflows associated with weather obstacle generation and flight path routing. A dedicated server located at the University of North Texas in Denton, TX serves as a weather data portal/repository and control interface. It uses Mobius [6] to provision the most resource intensive workflows on Chameleon when extra processing power is needed, whereas ExoGENI nodes are used for the bulk of the processing and can be rapidly instantiated. Mobius allows us to connect to ExoGENI and Chameleon with layer2 networks and modulate bandwidth to individual workflows with SDX, prioritizing those associated with weather parameters of ongoing flights and thus extending the DDDAS concept to the networking layer.

Figure 4 depicts data flows for weather processing workflows created by Mobius.

4   Conclusions

In this paper, we have described
the framework of a complete,
functioning DDDAS, operating
with live sensor and model
data that can be instantiated
on demand. Weather geofence
extraction occurs as a function of the declared tolerances
of individual flight requests.
The underlying compute and
networking adapts to weather
related load and flight monitoring needs in an automated
fashion by modulating available
bandwidth to weather workflows with SDX and distribut-
ing processing to pools of
worker nodes with Pegasus and
HTCondor. Flight planning is
therefore unique and customiz-
able for a given aircraft or air-

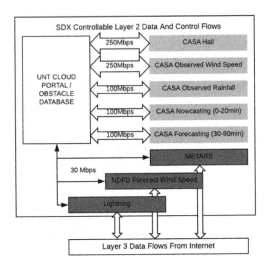

Fig. 4. Weather workflows are provisioned with
layer2 networks and bandwidth modulated by virtual SDX. CASA based workflows shown in green,
other sensors shown in red. (Color figure online)

craft class, with feedback into the underlying data generation. We believe this to
be an effective design that accounts for the necessary considerations associated
with a complex, multi-faceted system in a resource constrained environment.
In future work we intend to formally evaluate the performance of the various
subsystems.

References

1. Are Flying Cars Preparing to Take Off? (2019). https://www.morganstanley.com/
   ideas/autonomous-aircraft
2. Nasa Urban Air Mobility. https://www.nasa.gov/sites/default/files/atoms/files/
   uam-market-study-executive-summary-v2.pdf
3. McLaughlin, D.J., Chandrasekar, V.: Short wavelength technology and the potential for distributed networks of small radar systems. In: 2009 IEEE Radar Conference, pp. 1–3 (2009)
4. Deelman, E., et al.: Pegasus, a workflow management system for science automation. Future Gener. Comput. Syst. **46**, 17–35 (2015)
5. Epema, D., et al.: A worldwide flock of condors: load sharing among workstation
   clusters. Future Gener. Comput. Syst. **12**(1), 53–65 (1996)
6. Lyons, E., et al.: Toward a dynamic network-centric distributed cloud platform
   for scientific workflows: a case study for adaptive weather sensing. In: 2019 15th
   International Conference on eScience (eScience), pp. 67–76 (2019)

7. Baldin, I., et al.: ExoGENI: a multi-domain infrastructure-as-a-service testbed. In: McGeer, R., Berman, M., Elliott, C., Ricci, R. (eds.) The GENI Book, pp. 279–315. Springer, Cham (2016). https://doi.org/10.1007/978-3-319-33769-2_13
8. Keahey, K., et al.: Chameleon: a scalable production testbed for computer science research. In: Contemporary High Performance Computing, pp. 123–148 (2019)
9. Mandal, A., et al.: Toward prioritization of data flows for scientific workflows using virtual software defined exchanges. In: 2017 IEEE 13th International Conference on e-Science (e-Science), pp. 566–575 (2017)
10. The Geojson Format. https://tools.ietf.org/html/rfc7946
11. Chen, H., Chandrasekar, V.: The quantitative precipitation estimation system for Dallas Fort Worth (DFW) urban remote sensing network. J. Hydrol. **531**, 259–271 (2015)
12. Ruzanski, E., et al.: The CASA nowcasting system. J. Atmos. Ocean. Technol. **28**(5), 640–655 (2011)
13. Xue, M., et al.: The advanced regional prediction system (ARPS), storm-scale numerical weather prediction and data assimilation. Meteorol. Atmos. Phys. **82**(1–4), 139–170 (2003)
14. Chandrasekar, V., et al.: DFW urban radar network observations of floods, tornadoes and hail storms. In: 2018 IEEE Radar Conference (RadarConf18), pp. 0765–0770 (2018)
15. Bui, V., et al.: A performance study of earth networks total lighting network (ENTLN) and worldwide lightning location network (WWLLN). In: 2015 International Conference on Computational Science and Computational Intelligence (CSCI), pp. 386–391 (2015)
16. National Weather Service - Wind Speed Forecasts. http://www.weather.gov/ndfd/
17. Federal Aviation Administration: METAR/TAF. https://www.aviationweather.gov/metar
18. Maple, C.: Geometric design and space planning using the marching squares and marching cube algorithms. In: 2003 International Conference on Geometric Modeling and Graphics, 2003, Proceedings, pp. 90–95 (2003)
19. D3-Contour. https://github.com/d3/d3-contour
20. Graham, R.L.: An efficient algorithm for determining the convex hull of a finite planar set. Inf. Process. Lett. **1**, 132–133 (1972)
21. Hart, P., et al.: A formal basis for the heuristic determination of minimum cost paths. IEEE Trans. Syst. Sci. Cybern. SSC **4**(2), 100–107 (1968)

Dynamic, Data-Driven Hyperspectral Image Classification on Resource-Constrained Platforms

Lei Pan[1]($\boxtimes$), Rijun Liao[2], Zhu Li[2], and Shuvra S. Bhattacharyya[1]

[1] ECE Department and UMIACS, University of Maryland, College Park, MD, USA
{lpan1,ssb}@umd.edu
[2] CSEE Department, University of Missouri-Kansas City, Kansas City, MO, USA
rijun.liao@mail.umkc.edu, lizhu@umkc.edu

Abstract. Hyperspectral image processing has attracted increasing research interest in recent years, due in part to the high spectral resolution of hyperspectral images together with the emergence of deep neural networks (DNNs) as a promising class of methods for analysis of hyperspectral images. An important challenge in realizing the full potential of hyperspectral imaging technology is the problem of deploying image analysis capabilities on resource-constrained platforms, such as unmanned aerial vehicles (UAVs) and mobile computing platforms. In this paper, we develop a novel approach for designing DNNs for hyperspectral image processing that are targeted to resource-constrained platforms. Our approach involves optimizing the design of a single DNN for operation across a variable number of spectral bands. DNNs that are developed in this way can then be adapted dynamically based on the availability of resources and real-time performance constraints. The proposed approach supports the DDDAS paradigm as an integrated part of the design and training process to enable dynamic-data driven adaptation of the DNN structure—that is, the set of computational modules and connections that are active when the DNN operates. We demonstrate the effectiveness of the proposed class of adaptive and scalable DNNs through experiments using publicly available remote sensing datasets.

Keywords: Adaptive systems · Deep neural networks · Embedded signal processing · Hyperspectral image classification

1 Introduction

Hyperspectral image processing (HSIP) applications are becoming increasingly common in important application areas such as surveillance, medical diagnostics, forensics, and remote sensing. The utility of HSIP in these fields stems from the high levels of spectral diversity and spectral resolution that hyperspectral images provide compared to conventional image acquisition approaches (e.g., see [13]).

This research was supported in part by the Air Force Office of Scientific Research under the DDIP Program.

© Springer Nature Switzerland AG 2020
F. Darema et al. (Eds.): DDDAS 2020, LNCS 12312, pp. 320–327, 2020.
https://doi.org/10.1007/978-3-030-61725-7_37

An HSIP application of fundamental importance is the problem of *image classification*, which involves mapping each pixel into a set of pre-determined classes. In recent years, deep neural networks (DNNs) have been shown to be useful for accurate image classification in HSIP applications [8]. However, the computational complexity of DNNs together with the large amounts of data involved in HSIP applications makes the deployment of DNNs in resource-constrained scenarios a challenging problem.

The capability for data-driven, real-time processing of hyperspectral image classification on resource-constrained platforms opens up the potential for many novel applications. In this paper, we introduce a novel framework for hyperspectral image classification that integrates adaptive DNN-based image analysis with real-time, resource-constrained processing.

Our approach involves optimizing the design of a single DNN for operation across a variable number of spectral bands. DNNs that are developed in this way can then be adapted dynamically based on the availability of resources and time-varying constraints on real-time performance. The proposed approach allows the deployed DNN configuration to be varied at run time to maximize hyperspectral image analysis accuracy subject to operational requirements that may vary dynamically, and may be unknown at design time. We demonstrate the effectiveness of the proposed class of adaptive and scalable DNNs through experiments using publicly available remote sensing datasets.

This work helps to advance the application of Dynamic Data Driven Applications Systems (DDDAS) by providing new methods for encapsulating a range of HSIP configurations, with alternative trade-offs between complexity and image analysis accuracy, within a single DNN model. The single model can be deployed onto a resource constrained platform and used to adapt system operation based on dynamically changing operational requirements—e.g., based on changes in urgency due to information extracted from recently-acquired imaging data.

2 Related Work

Hyperspectral image classification (HIC) is an important application in HSIP. It is applied, for example, in the area of remote sensing, where different types of land features need to be recognized and categorized. Most studies on HIC focus on maximizing classification accuracy. A common theme in recent works on HIC is the application of DNNs. Many of these recent works have reported very high accuracy when applying DNNs to HIC problems in remote sensing (e.g., see [3, 4, 9, 11]). However, these works often focus on accuracy without taking into account stringent resource constraints or real-time performance.

On the other hand, a number of studies have investigated real-time HIC. For example, Madroñal et al. developed a real-time HIC implementation on a high-performance computing platform called the Massively Parallel Processor Array (MPPA) [12]. Their approach utilized support vector machine (SVM) methods for the classification process. Wu et al. proposed an approach called logistic regression via variable splitting and augmented Lagrangian (LORSAL) for GPU-based, real-time HIC [15]. Sharma et al. proposed a real-time DNN-based approach for face recognition from hyperspectral images [14].

Compared to the related work summarized above, the HIC method presented in this paper is novel in its joint support for resource-constrained deployment, and scalable execution. Moreover our framework is based on DNN techniques, which have potential for very high accuracy HIC. Here, by *scalable*, we mean that trade-offs among accuracy, resource requirements, and real-time performance can be adapted flexibly and efficiently at run-time to match the configuration of the system to time-varying operational requirements.

3   Approach

The proposed system for HIC is designed to adaptively configure system complexity to maximize classification accuracy subject to constraints on real-time performance. The system is designed using a convolutional neural network (CNN) structure that accepts as input a variable number of hyperspectral input channels from among the complete set of channels S that is available from a given hyperspectral sensing subsystem. The elements of S are provided as input to the HIC system as an ordered list of channels $S = \{C_1, C_2, ..., C_m\}$, where m is the total number of available channels. The variable number of channels to use at run-time is selected from a set of predefined options $\Omega = \{n_1, n_2, ..., n_k\}$, where $k \in \{1, 2, ..., m\}$, and $1 \leq n_1 < n_2 < ... < n_k \leq m$. In our experiments, we use $k = 4$, $n_1 = 30$, $n_2 = 60$, $n_3 = 90$, and $n_4 = m$.

At run-time (during inference), an integer-valued input $n_c \in \Omega$ is provided to the HIC system to indicate which band-subset option is selected for image classification. The value of n_c gives the number of input channels that is to be used to classify image pixels; the value of n_c can be varied dynamically by the system in which the CNN is embedded. More specifically, the set of channels used for classification is $\kappa = \{C_i \mid 1 \leq i \leq n_c\}$.

By definition of κ, the ordering $C_1, C_2, ..., C_m$ can be viewed as a priority list with lower-index channels having higher priority for inclusion in the inference process compared to higher-index channels. The priority list can be constructed using arbitrary methods for prioritizing hyperspectral imaging channels; in the experiments developed in this paper, we apply the prioritization methods developed by Li et al. The prioritization methods were developed initially for multispectral video [7], and then extended to hyperspectral video [5].

We refer to our proposed approach as Variable Band Image Classification (VBIC). Our development of VBIC builds upon LDspectral, which was originally developed as a software tool for design optimization of dynamic, data-driven multispectral image processing systems [6], and has been extended more recently with support for hyperspectral image processing [5]. LDspectral in turn applies Lightweight Dataflow (LD), which is a compact set of application programming interfaces and associated libraries for dataflow-based design and implementation of embedded signal and information processing systems [10].

The CNN architecture for VBIC is illustrated in Fig. 1. The network is based on an HIC network proposed in [4]. In this work, we adapt the network of [4] to incorporate the novel capability of being able to operate on a variable number of spectral bands. We would like to emphasize that the adaptation approach that we develop in this paper is not specific to the network of [4]. Instead, our approach can be viewed as a general methodology for adapting fixed-band-set CNNs for HIC into variable-band-subset form.

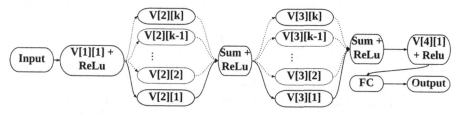

Fig. 1. An illustration of the CNN architecture for VBIC.

In Fig. 1, each block whose label starts with "V" represents a convolutional block. More precisely, each $V[a][b]$ represents the bth convolutional unit in convolutional layer a. Each of the $(2k + 2)$ convolutional blocks in the network performs a 3-D convolution. Each block labeled ReLu is a rectified linear unit, each Sum block performs the addition of results from the previous network stage, and the FC block is a fully connected layer. The dotted edges in Fig. 1 (e.g., the edge from the first ReLu block to $V[2][2]$) are connections that may or may not be active at run-time depending on how many bands the network is configured to execute (i.e., depending on the value of n_c) at that time. We refer to these connections as *dynamic connections*.

We refer to the subsystem consisting of $V[2][1], V[2][2],...,V[2][k]$ as the *first stacked layer*, and similarly, we refer to the subsystem consisting of $V[3][1], V[3][2],...,V[3][k]$ as the *second stacked layer*. For integers $x \in \{2,3\}$, and $y \in [1,k]$, we use a minor abuse of notation to denote the set of convolutional blocks $\{V[x][1], V[x][2],...,V[x][y]\}$ by $V[x][1 : y]$.

The input to the VBIC network is a three-dimensional tensor $T(p)$ with size $M \times M \times n_c$. The tensor $T(p)$ is used to classify a single image pixel p from a given hyperspectral image frame H. The tensor is referred to as the *patch* associated with p. The parameter M is an odd integer that is fixed at design time, and is less than (typically much less than) the number of rows and number of columns in a single hyperspectral image frame. In our experiments, we use $M = 7$. The patch associated with p consists of all of the n_c selected spectral bands for pixel p and its neighbors within the $M \times M$ window within H that is centered at p. If p is at or sufficiently close to the boundary of H, the patch is zero-padded to produce a tensor of the required size $M \times M \times n_c$. A complete image frame H is classified by iteratively invoking the VBIC network on $T(p)$ for all pixels p in H. The output of the VBIC network for a given tensor $T(p)$ is a classification label for p together with a probability value, which indicates the level of confidence in the classification result.

Unique features of VBIC include: (1) n_c, the size of the third dimension of $T(p)$, can be varied dynamically, and (2) the network is trained deliberately to handle such a variable number of spectral bands in the classifier input.

Algorithm 1 provides a pseudocode sketch of the training process for VBIC. The function *initialTraining* takes as arguments an untrained VBIC network Γ with the structure illustrated in Fig. 1, a positive integer n, a labeled training dataset T, and a number of epochs E for training. The function configures Γ by deactivating all of the dynamic connections so that the only blocks V [2][1] and V [3][1] are active in the two stacked layers. The remaining stacked layer blocks are ignored in the training process for this function. The resulting configuration of Γ is then trained for E epochs using T. Only the first n channels (the highest priority n channels) of T are used in the training process.

The function *furtherTraining* takes as arguments a partially-trained VBIC network Γ that has been produced by the previous iteration of the overall VBIC training process. The function arguments also include an integer $i \in [2,k]$, an integer $n \in [1,m]$ (recall that m is the total number of available hyperspectral channels), and as used in function *initialTraining*, a training dataset and number of epochs specification.

The function *furtherTraining* configures Γ by activating the stacked layer blocks V [2][1 : i] and V [3][1 : i] while deactivating all of the other stacked layer blocks. The function activates only those dynamic connections that are incident to activated blocks. In the resulting network, the stacked layer blocks V [2][1 : $i - 1$] and V [3][1 : $i - 1$] have weights that have been trained from preceding iterations of the enclosing training process. These existing weights are "frozen" along with the existing (pre-trained) weights of V [4][1]. Thus, the training process of function *furtherTraining* is configured to train only the weights of V [1][1], V [2][i], V [3][i], and the fully connected layer FC. Based on this configuration of frozen and non-frozen (to-be-trained) weights, the function carries out a training process with the given number of epochs and given training dataset. Only the first n channels of T (as specified by the third function argument) are used in the training process. The network Γ—in particular, its set of trained weights—is updated as a side effect of this function.

An important aspect of Algorithm 1 is the freezing of weights in stacked layer blocks V [2][1 : $i - 1$] and V [3][1 : $i - 1$] in each iteration $i = 2,3,...$ of the for loop, as enforced by function *furtherTraining*. This enables evolution of a single network that is capable of handling all of the pre-defined band subset options. Encapsulation of all of the options within a single DNN model is especially important in resource-constrained deployment scenarios, where there may be insufficient storage space available for multiple DNN models.

As the band subset option index j increases from 1 to k, the system accuracy can be expected to increase, while the processing complexity (and hence the execution time and energy consumption) also increases. The novel approach to designing and training the VBIC system provides systematic optimization of this trade-off between image classification accuracy and processing complexity, and encapsulation of the result compactly within a single DNN model.

Algorithm 1 A pseudocode sketch of the training process for VBIC.

Input Γ: A DNN network of the form illustrated in Fig. 1.
Input k: The number of band-subset options.
Input $\Omega = \{n_1, n_2, ..., n_k\}$: the number of bands in each band-subset option. parameter E: the number of training epochs in each training iteration.
Input T: the labeled hyperspectral image dataset that is to be used for training.
Input$\{C_1, C_2, ..., C_m\}$: the priority list of spectral bands.
Result : the weights of the network Γ are trained as a side effect of this function.

1: procedure VBIC-training
2:     $channelCount = n_1$
3:     $initialTraining(\Gamma, channelCount, T, E)$
4:     for $i = 2, 3, ..., k$ do
5:         $channelCount = channelCount + n_i$
6:         $furtherTraining(\Gamma, i, channelCount, T, E)$

---

4 Experiments

We demonstrate the proposed VBIC approach through experiments on an Android mobile phone (OnePlus 7 pro), which we use as a platform for prototyping resource-constrained image processing applications. In the experiments, we provide hyperspectral image input to the platform through flash storage. The platform is equipped with an 8-core Qualcomm Snapdragon 855 CPU, 12 GB of RAM, and 256 GB storage.

We evaluate our VBIC-based Android implementation using two commonly used datasets in remote sensing: Indian Pines and Pavia University. The Indian Pines dataset has 145×145 pixels and 224 spectral bands with wavelengths ranging from 400–2500 nm(nm) [1]. The pixels are categorized into 16 classes. The Pavia University dataset has 610×610 pixels classified into 9 classes, and 103 spectral bands with spectral coverage spanning 430–860 nm.

The training process for VBIC (Algorithm 1) is implemented using PyTorch. Network training is performed using patch size parameter $M = 7$ (see Sect. 3), batch size of 40, learning rate of 0.1, weight decay of 0.01 for all layers, and number of epochs $E = 100$. The training algorithm employed is AdaGrad [2]. Each of the two datasets investigated is partitioned into a training set and testing set. Each training and testing set contains 80% and 20% of the pixels of the associated dataset, respectively. Moreover, the partitioning is performed so that for each pixel class, 80% of the pixels in that class are in the training set and the other 20% are in the testing set. As stated in Sect. 3, we use $k = 4$, $n_1 = 30$, $n_2 = 60$, $n_3 = 90$, and $n_4 = m$ in our experiments.

Table 1 shows the model size and overall accuracy (testing accuracy across all pixel classes) for the VBIC system under the four different values for $n_c \in \Omega$. Here, by the *model size*, we mean the number of trainable parameters that is required in the network (excluding any parameters associated with non-activated blocks). Note that only the model size associated with n_4 is relevant in assessing the overall model size since all of the models are supported in the VBIC system. However, the model sizes for different values of n_c provide insight into the underlying range of trade-offs provided between model complexity and accuracy.

Table 1. Model size and accuracy.

n_c	Pavia University dataset		Indian Pines dataset	
	Model size	Overall accuracy (%)	Model size	Overall accuracy (%)
30	18,042	88.01	27,009	76.98
60	45,210	93.64	72,097	92.83
90	73,402	95.58	118,209	95.66
Maximum	89,306	95.55	284,897	96.88

The row labeled "Maximum" represents $n_c = m$, where $m = 224$ and $m = 103$ for the Indian Pines and Pavia University datasets, respectively.

We also measure the processing throughput and peak memory consumption (peak mem) of the VBIC system as it performs classification. The results are shown in Table 2. Each throughput value given in the table is derived by averaging over 20 repetitions of an experiment with the associated dataset and n_c value. The standard deviations computed for these 20 trials are listed in the column labeled "Std dev". The units for throughput are pixel classifications per second (PC/s).

Table 2. Processing throughput and peak memory consumption.

n_c	Pavia University dataset			Indian Pines dataset		
	Throughput (PC/s)	Std dev (PC/s)	Peak mem (MB)	Throughput (PC/s)	Std dev (PC/s)	Peak mem (MB)
30	722.14	7.36	219	702.22	64.87	181
60	430.48	7.57	238	399.76	6.77	198
90	206.38	2.47	291	197.16	1.58	254
Maximum	140.58	0.96	374	98.04	2.09	338

Together, the results in Tables 1 and 2 demonstrate the effectiveness of the VBIC approach in practical classification scenarios. The results provide an example of the novel range of performance/accuracy trade-offs that can be deployed using VBIC. Moreover, the results demonstrate that large increases in throughput can be achieved with relatively small reduction in accuracy.

5 Conclusion

In this paper, we have developed a framework for hyperspectral image classification called Variable Band Image Classification (VBIC). VBIC integrates adaptive DNN-based image analysis with real-time, resource-constrained processing. The framework provides novel DDDAS capabilities by enabling dynamic self-adaptation of the deployed

DNN configuration to maximize hyperspectral image analysis accuracy subject to operational requirements that may vary dynamically. We have demonstrated the utility of VBIC through an implementation on an Android platform, and experiments using two relevant datasets. Useful directions for future work include exploration of VBIC implementations on embedded GPUs and neural network accelerators, and investigation of systematic methods for selecting the set of options for band subset sizes.

References

1. Baumgardner, M.F., Biehl, L.L., Landgrebe, D.A.: 220 band AVIRIS hyperspectral image data set: June 12, 1992 Indian Pine Test Site 3. https://purr.purdue.edu/publications/1947/1 (2015)
2. Duchi, J., Hazan, E., Singer, Y.: Adaptive subgradient methods for online learning and stochastic optimization. J. Mach. Learn. Res 12(Jul), 2121–2159 (2011)
3. Hamida, A.B., Benoit, A., Lambert, P., Amar, C.B.: 3-D deep learning approach for remote sensing image classification. IEEE Trans. Geosci. Remote Sens. 56(8), 4420–4434 (2018)
4. He, M., Li, B., Chen, H.: Multi-scale 3D deep convolutional neural network for hyperspectral image classification. In: Proceedings of the International Conference on Image Processing, pp. 3904–3908 (2017)
5. Li, H., et al.: Hyperspectral video processing on resource-constrained platforms. In: Proceedings of the Workshop on Hyperspectral Image and Signal Processing (2019)
6. Li, H., et al.: Dynamic, data-driven processing of multispectral video streams. IEEE Aerosp. Electron. Syst. Mag. 32(7), 50–57 (2017)
7. Li, H., et al.: Design of a dynamic data-driven system for multispectral video processing. In: Blasch, E.P., Ravela, S., Aved, A.J. (eds.) Handbook of Dynamic Data Driven Applications Systems, pp. 529–545. Springer (2018)
8. Li, S., Song, W., Fang, L., Chen, Y., Ghamisi, P., Benediktsson, J.A.: Deep learning for hyperspectral image classification: An overview. IEEE Trans. Geosci. Remote Sens. 57(9), 6690–6709 (2019)
9. Li, Y., Zhang, H., Shen, Q.: Spectral–spatial classification of hyperspectral imagery with 3D convolutional neural network. Remote Sens. 9(1), 1–21 (2017)
10. Lin, S., Liu, Y., Lee, K., Li, L., Plishker, W., Bhattacharyya, S.S.: The DSPCAD framework for modeling and synthesis of signal processing systems. In: Ha, S., Teich, J. (eds.) Handbook of Hardware/Software Codesign, pp. 1–35. Springer (2017)
11. Luo, Y., Zou, J., Yao, C., Zhao, X., Li, T., Bai, G.: HSI-CNN: A novel convolution neural network for hyperspectral image. In: Proceedings of the International Conference on Audio, Language and Image Processing, pp. 464–469 (2018)
12. Madroñal, D., et al.: SVM-based real-time hyperspectral image classifier on a manycore architecture. J. Syst. Architect. 80, 30–40 (2017)
13. Patrick, J., Brant, R., Blasch, E.: Hyperspectral imagery throughput and fusion evaluation over compression and interpolation. In: Proceedings of the International Conference on Information Fusion, pp. 1–8 (2008)
14. Sharma, V., Diba, A., Tuytelaars, T., Van Gool, L.: Hyperspectral CNN for image classification & band selection, with application to face recognition. Tech. Rep. KUL/ESAT/PSI/1604, KU Leuven (2016)
15. Wu, Z., Wang, Q., Plaza, A., Li, J., Sun, L., Wei, Z.: Real-time implementation of the sparse multinomial logistic regression for hyperspectral image classification on GPUs. IEEE Geosci. Remote Sens. Lett. 12(7), 1456–1460 (2015)

Semi-supervised Visual Tracking Based on Variational Siamese Network

Liang Xu and Ruixin Niu[✉]

Virginia Commonwealth University, Richmond, VA 23284, USA
{xul4,rniu}@vcu.edu

Abstract. For object tracking in a visual dynamic data-driven application systems (DDDAS) framework, visual appearance features can be extracted by the convolutional neural network, which has been shown to provide a robust feature representation. In this paper, a new semi-supervised learning framework, variational Siamese neural network, is developed for visual tracking by combining a Siamese network with a variational autoencoder, which supports both supervised and unsupervised training. The learned features are represented as Gaussian distributions in feature space, and the object is represented as a distribution in image space. The similarity between objects' features is measured by an information theoretic distance. The tracking algorithm is based on the detection network's detections to update the object state estimate. Experiment results show that the proposed visual tracking framework outperforms existing state of the art visual tracking approaches.

Keywords: Object tracking · Siamese network · Semi-supervised learning.

1 Introduction

Visual tracking involves state estimation of objects based on dynamic video data, which serves as a critical component of a visual dynamic data-driven application systems (DDDAS) framework, and is imperative in various visual DDDAS applications, such as camera surveillance and environment monitoring. Further, without assuming a certain model for the video data, deep learning based visual tracking is naturally a data-driven approach. In visual tracking, learning the visual appearance features of an object and searching it in the given image feature space have been investigated recently for detection and tracking of visual objects [2,10,15]. The features can be manually selected or extracted by learning algorithms from labeled training dataset. Furthermore, features extracted by the convolutional neural network (CNN) have been shown to represent the object in semantic feature space with robust representation [10].

This work was supported in part by the AFOSR Dynamic Data and Information Processing Portfolio under Grant FA9550-18-1-0362.

F. Darema et al. (Eds.): DDDAS 2020, LNCS 12312, pp. 328–336, 2020.
https://doi.org/10.1007/978-3-030-61725-7_38

In this paper, we develop a new semi-supervised learning framework, the variational Siamese network, by combining the traditional Siamese neural network with a variational autoencoder (VAE). A detector is developed based on this semi-supervised learning framework using both labeled and unlabeled training data. Its first step is to learn the robust feature representation by using an unsupervised deep generative model (VAE). The second step is to use a labeled video sequence to train a visual object detector. The learned features are represented by Gaussian distributions in feature space instead of discrete points as in the traditional methods. The semantic similarity between the object feature and search image feature is measured by using an information theoretic distance metric. Further, we propose to model objects as distributions instead of bounding boxes, which allows measuring the distance continuously. We integrate Kalman filter with our detector, which is used to estimate the object state. To the best of our knowledge, this is the first work where the VAE is used for semi-supervised learning for visual tracking.

2   Related Work

This paper involves three aspects of visual tracking: Siamese network based visual tracking, variational autoencoder, and visual object representation.

Siamese Network Based Visual Tracking. The advantages of Siamese network based tracking include end-to-end training, no need for online training, and high efficiency, attracting a lot attention recently [1,10]. SiamFC [1] adopts the Siamese network as a feature extractor and introduces the correlation layer to combine feature maps. However, these previous methods are based on measuring the distance between two vector feature points and supervised learning only.

Variational Autoencoder. VAE [7] has been used as a generative model in machine learning field recently. For example, VAE has been used to generate more training samples for visual tracking [16] and extract robust features for object segmentation [12], respectively. Different from [12,16], in our work, we use the encoder part of the VAE to extract features for object representation in a visual tracking Siamese network. Rather than representing features with fixed points in a fixed dimensional space, an alternative is to represent them with Gaussian distributions. The distribution's variance can represent the ambiguity, which is a desirable property for modeling the feature representation of an image. Also, the variance can help the learning algorithm to smoothly "fill" the semantic space with continuous representation to generalize better. The distribution features can be learned with deep learning based VAE [7].

Visual Object Representation. One of the basic components in object tracking is to represent the object in space and time. In the case of 2D image, the axis-aligned bounding box representation is widely used to identify an object with its approximate location and size [1]. Because the limitation of subtraction of the object from the background, mask representation becomes popular, such as Siamese-Mask [15]. The mask is a dense representation of the object, which needs much more parameters than other representations. Recently, representation of the object as a Gaussian distribution has been proposed [4], in which the mean represents the object location and the covariance matrix represents the object's shape and orientation in a continuous 2D image space.

3   Methodology

Tracking visual objects based on the initial frame can be accomplished by similarity learning between the objects and the current image frame. Here we propose a framework to learn the similarity between an exemplar image z and a candidate image x' with the same size, and return a similarity score. Here x' is a sub-image from a larger search image x. We can detect the object in x by testing all the possible locations, and find the highest similarity score. We denote $f_\theta(z, x)$ as the similarity score between two input images z and x, which can be constructed by the fully convolutional variational Siamese network.

3.1   Fully Convolutional Variational Siamese Network

We adopt the fully convolutional Siamese network as the base learning structure, which has been successfully applied in tracking scenarios [1,5,8,15]. Instead of cutting a sub-image from the search space and translating it to the feature space, the fully convolutional network can translate the original search space to a more dense grid in a single evaluation. Also, the fully CNN commutes with translation, and based on its output, one can identify the object location in the original image space. The Siamese network has a powerful framework to compare the difference between two unstructured sources. In this paper, we develop a new semi-supervised learning framework by combining VAE and Siamese network, with feature outputs as Gaussian distributions.

As shown in Fig. 1, function $q_\theta(\cdot|x)$ is a fully convolutional network given image x, and the similarity between the two images is typically calculated by the Siamese architecture in feature space. q_θ transforms the two images to the feature space, represented as Gaussian distributions, with parameters μ and Σ.

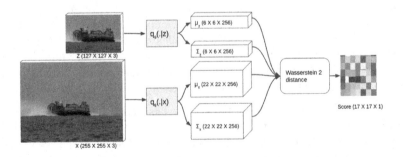

Fig. 1. Fully convolutional variational Siamese network architecture. z: exemplar image; x: search space. Images are from [6].

3.2   Object as Distribution

The object is typically represented by a bounding box in most tracking applications. However, there are several disadvantages with this representation: it is difficult to measure the difference between the proposal bounding box and true label bounding box with different shapes, sizes, and locations; the bounding box provides a binary decision for each pixel with sharp boundaries. In this paper, we propose to use a normal distribution to parameterize a visual 2D object:

$$Z_i = \mathcal{N}(\mu_i, \Sigma_i) \tag{1}$$

where $\mu_i = [x_i \ y_i]^T$, $\Sigma_i = diag(\sigma_{x_i}^2, \ \sigma_{y_i}^2)$, and $x_i, y_i, \sigma_{x_i}, \sigma_{y_i}$ are means and standard derivations. Since most of the labels are axis-aligned, we do not model the correlation between x_i and y_i.

3.3   Wasserstein Distance Between Two Gaussian Distributions

We adopt an information theoretic distance measure in this paper, which is different from the previous work [1]. The object in the feature space is represented by a Gaussian distribution, which allows us to smoothly measure the semantic similarity based on Wasserstein distance [3]. The computation of Wasserstein 2 (W_2^2) is efficient for two Gaussian distributions in $\mathbb{R}^h$.

$$W_2^2(p_1, p_2) = \sum_{i=1}^{h} (\mu_1^i - \mu_2^i)^2 + (\sigma_1^i - \sigma_2^i)^2 \tag{2}$$

3.4   Variational Autoencoder for Semi-supervised Training

Our learning framework consists of two steps, generative and discriminative models. The first step is using the unlabeled data for unsupervised learning. The second step is to use the labeled data for learning the similarity between exemplar image and search image, and detect the object.

As shown in Fig. 2, the generative learning can be carried out by a VAE based on variational inference. In this case, we can use the output from the variational fully convolutional network as input to reconstruct the input or the next few frames of the input images. The intermediate variable $s \sim \mathcal{N}(\mu_z, \Sigma_z)$ is the latent variable, which is also the feature extracted by using the network. The unsupervised learning can help the network to find a good feature extractor, and warm up the next task. The deep neural network is usually difficult to train and it is often stuck in a saddle point. By using both unsupervised and supervised learning, we can achieve better training result, as shown later in the paper.

The parameters of our encoder-decoder architecture are learned by minimizing the following regularized loss based on variational inference and stochastic gradient descent, which is a sigmoid annealing scheme.

$$-L_{\theta,\phi}(z|z') = -E_{q_\theta(s|z)}(\log p_\phi(z'|s')) + \lambda KL(q_\theta(s|z)||\mathcal{N}(0, I)) \tag{3}$$

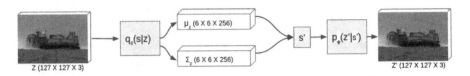

Fig. 2. Unsupervised learning via VAE. Function q_θ: encoder; function p_φ: decoder. Both of them are fully convolutional neural networks. s' is a sample drawn from the distribution.

The first term encourages the sampled latent space to encode the necessary information to reconstruct the input image, which is called the evidence lower bound (ELBO). The second term, a regularization term, enforces the latent variable to match the standard normal $\mathcal{N}(0, I)$, and to fill the semantic space with a positive definite Σ_z.

The second step of the learning framework is supervised learning based on the labeled tracking datasets. The score map is the final output of the network, and the value should between 0 and 1, the higher the more similar. The distance metric in Sect. 3.3 is from 0 to ∞, the lower the similar. The distance can be transformed by $1 - tanh(x)$ with output from 0 to 1. We call this map O. Ground truth score can be calculated similarly. The value also needs to be rescaled by $1 - tanh(x)$, and this map is T. Our loss can be calculated as follows:

$$Loss = \sum_w^{width} \sum_h^{hight} \left(O^{h,w} - T^{h,w}\right)^2 \tag{4}$$

4   Experiments

4.1   Implementation Details

Network Architecture: We use AlexNet [9] with slight modifications to output mean and variance. The detailed parameters are listed in Table 1. There are 5 convolutional layers and the last layer has 2 groups of convolutional filters, which outputs the means and variances. A max pooling layer is employed after each of the first two convolutional layers. A ReLU layer follows each convolutional layer except for conv_5_mean.

Training: For unsupervised training we use the dataset Got-10k [6], which has a large number of visual objects. During unsupervised training, only the objects are fed into the architecture presented in Fig. 2. The input image and the output image could be the same or could be T time steps away. So this step can be trained for static images, or for the object in the video.

Tracking: We use a Kalman filter as the tracking algorithm. The object state is defined as $\mathbf{x} = [x, y, \dot{x}, \dot{y}, \sigma_x, \sigma_y]^T$, consisting of the position and velocity along each direction, and standard deviations of the object distributions in image space.

Table 1. Architecture of variational convolutional embedding function.

Convolutional Kernel					Features map size	
Layer	Kernel	Chan. map	Stride	Chans	Exemplar	Search Img
Input				×3	127 × 127	255 × 255
conv_1	11 × 11	96 × 3	2	×96	59 × 59	123 × 123
pool_1	3 × 3		2	×96	29 × 29	61 × 61
conv_2	5 × 5	256 × 48	1	×256	25 × 25	57 × 57
pool_2	3 × 3		2	×256	12 × 12	28 × 28
conv_3	3 × 3	384 × 256	1	×192	10 × 10	26 × 26
conv_4	3 × 3	384 × 192	1	×192	8 × 8	24 × 24
conv_5_mean	3 × 3	256 × 192	1	×128	6 × 6	22 × 22
conv_5_var	3 × 3	256 × 192	1	×128	6 × 6	22 × 22

4.2 Evaluation for Visual Object Tracking

Here two tracking challenge datasets are used for evaluations: VOT-2016 [5] and VOT-2018 [8]. We compare the proposed tracking approach against some state-of-the-art approaches, using the official VOT toolkit, and the expected average overlap (EAO), a measure that considers both accuracy and robustness of a tracker. The EAO measures the expected non-reset overlap of a tracker run on a short term sequence. The accuracy is the average overlap during successful tracking periods and the robustness measures how many times the tracker drifts from the target and has to be reset [8]. From Table 2, it is clear that our tracker outperforms the state-of-the-art trackers. Also, its speed is fast and allows real time applications. One tracking example is shown in Fig. 3. As we can see, our proposed approach can track the moving ball and its size and shape accurately.

Table 2. Comparison with the state-of-the-art tracking approaches. The arrow indicates that the larger/smaller the better.

	Ours	SiamRPN [10]	SCRDCF [13]	STRCF [11]	LSART [14]	ECO [2]
EAO↑	0.339	0.244	0.263	**0.345**	0.323	0.280
Accuracy↑	**0.526**	0.490	0.466	0.523	0.495	0.484
Robustness↓	**0.213**	0.460	0.318	0.215	0.218	0.276
Speed↑	50	**200**	48.9	2.9	1.7	3.7

4.3 With or Without Unsupervised Learning

The VAE can help us with the training of the detector. In Fig. 4, the supervised learning progress is shown for two different frameworks, with and without the

t=93   t=95   t=98   t=101

Fig. 3. Football tracking [8]. Red box: true label; green ellipse: our tracker output with 95% confidence region.

unsupervised learning step respectively. It is clear that on the average, the one with unsupervised learning has a lower loss function, demonstrating the advantage of the proposed semi-supervised learning framework.

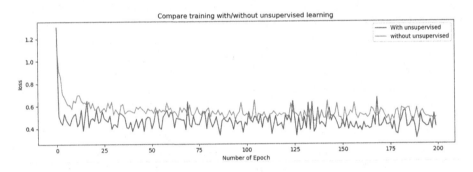

Fig. 4. The training progress with or without unsupervised learning.

In Table 3, the accuracy and robustness of the tracking results with and without unsupervised learning are compared using dataset VOT2016. It is clear that the approach with unsupervised learning outperforms the one without.

Table 3. Training results with/without unsupervised learning.

	With Unsupervised	Without Unsupervised
Accuracy↑	**0.520**	0.498
Robustness↓	**0.220**	0.221

5   Conclusion

For object tracking in a visual DDDAS framework, we departed from the traditional fully convolutional Siamese network, and developed a variational Siamese
network which trains feature embedding through both supervised and unsupervised learning. The embedded features are represented by multivariate Gaussian
distributions in a feature space, and the distance between two objects' features
is measured by an information theoretic metric (Wasserstein distance). To the
best of our knowledge, this is the first work where variational encoder is used
for semi-supervised learning for visual tracking. Numerical experiments showed
that the proposed visual tracking approach outperforms existing state of the art
tracking approaches.

References

1. Bertinetto, L., Valmadre, J., Henriques, J.F., Vedaldi, A., Torr, P.H.S.: Fully-
   convolutional siamese networks for object tracking. In: Hua, G., Jégou, H. (eds.)
   ECCV 2016. LNCS, vol. 9914, pp. 850–865. Springer, Cham (2016). https://doi.
   org/10.1007/978-3-319-48881-3_56
2. Danelljan, M., Bhat, G., Shahbaz Khan, F., Felsberg, M.: Eco: efficient convolution
   operators for tracking. In: Proceedings of the IEEE Conference on Computer Vision
   and Pattern Recognition, pp. 6638–6646 (2017)
3. Deudon, M.: Learning semantic similarity in a continuous space. In: Advances in
   Neural Information Processing Systems. pp. 986–997 (2018)
4. Ding, L., Fridman, L.: Object as distribution. arXiv preprint http://arxiv.org/abs/
   1907.12929, arXiv:1907.12929 (2019)
5. Hadfield, S., Bowden, R., Lebeda, K.: The visual object tracking vot2016 challenge
   results. Lecture Notes in Computer Science **9914**, 777–823 (2016)
6. Huang, L., Zhao, X., Huang, K.: Got-10k: A large high-diversity benchmark for
   generic object tracking in the wild. IEEE Transactions on Pattern Analysis and
   Machine Intelligence (2019)
7. Kingma, D.P., Welling, M.: Auto-encoding variational bayes. arXiv preprint
   http://arxiv.org/abs/1312.6114, arXiv:1312.6114 (2013)
8. Kristan, M., et al.: The sixth visual object tracking vot2018 challenge results. In:
   Proceedings of the European Conference on Computer Vision (ECCV) (2018)
9. Krizhevsky, A., Sutskever, I., Hinton, G.E.: Imagenet classification with deep convolutional neural networks. In: Advances in Neural Information Processing Systems, pp. 1097–1105 (2012)
10. Li, B., Yan, J., Wu, W., Zhu, Z., Hu, X.: High performance visual tracking with
    siamese region proposal network. In: Proceedings of the IEEE Conference on Com-
    puter Vision and Pattern Recognition, pp. 8971–8980 (2018)
11. Li, F., Tian, C., Zuo, W., Zhang, L., Yang, M.H.: Learning spatial-temporal regu-
    larized correlation filters for visual tracking. In: Proceedings of the IEEE Confer-
    ence on Computer Vision and Pattern Recognition, pp. 4904–4913 (2018)
12. Lin, C.C., Hung, Y., Feris, R., He, L.: Video instance segmentation tracking with a
    modified vae architecture. In: Proceedings of the IEEE/CVF Conference on Com-
    puter Vision and Pattern Recognition, pp. 13147–13157 (2020)

13. Lukezic, A., Vojir, T., Cehovin Zajc, L., Matas, J., Kristan, M.: Discriminative correlation filter with channel and spatial reliability. In: Proceedings of the IEEE Conference on Computer Vision and Pattern Recognition, pp. 6309–6318 (2017)
14. Sun, C., Wang, D., Lu, H., Yang, M.H.: Learning spatial-aware regressions for visual tracking. In: Proceedings of the IEEE Conference on Computer Vision and Pattern Recognition, pp. 8962–8970 (2018)
15. Wang, Q., Zhang, L., Bertinetto, L., Hu, W., Torr, P.H.: Fast online object tracking and segmentation: a unifying approach. In: Proceedings of the IEEE Conference on Computer Vision and Pattern Recognition (2019)
16. Wang, X., Li, C., Luo, B., Tang, J.: Sint++: robust visual tracking via adversarial positive instance generation. In: Proceedings of the IEEE Conference on Computer Vision and Pattern Recognition, pp. 4864–4873 (2018)

Occlusion Detection for Dynamic Adaptation

Zachary Mulhollan[(✉)], Aneesh Rangnekar, Anthony Vodacek,
and Matthew J. Hoffman

Rochester Institute of Technology, Rochester, NY, USA
{zjm1400,mjhsma}@rit.edu, aneesh.rangnekar@mail.rit.edu,
vodacek@cis.rit.edu

Abstract. Occlusion is a common issue for object detection and tracking applications using a remote sensor platform, especially in complex
urban environments where occlusions from buildings, bridges, and trees
are frequent events. While occlusions are unavoidable, the events can be
predicted to occur before the object of interest is obscured if there is
prior knowledge of the observed environment. To aid in object detection
and tracking tasks, we create an environment to map terrain and find
obscured regions in the scene which helps with re-detecting objects once
they are no longer obscured. We propose a dynamic data driven applications systems (DDDAS) framework for detecting occluded regions in an
imaged scene by integrating streams of real data with a physics-based
simulation model that updates based on the most recent images.

Keywords: Occlusion detection · Remote sensing · Dynamic
adaptation

1 Introduction

We utilize prior knowledge from open source resources to detect occlusions within
a given scene, allowing us initialize a simulation of the scene before we collect
real data samples and update the scene. We use OpenStreetMap (OSM) [9] for
scene initialization to obtain geo-rectified terrain of a given real world location with dense OSM tags. These tags can be mapped into 3D modeling and
rendering software (for example, Blender). The 3D environment is then used
to synthetically image the scene with the Digital Imaging and Remote Sensing
Image Generation (DIRSIG) model [2,3,13], where common land cover materials such as concrete, grass, and asphalt can be assigned to have hyperspectral
reflectance spectra. DIRSIG is a versatile too. that it can produce simulations of
many image modalities such as RGB, multispectral, and hyperspectral through
the visible and infrared spectrum.

OSM provides a priori information about ground surface regions within the
scene that cannot be imaged directly from a remote imaging platform's specified

© Springer Nature Switzerland AG 2020
F. Darema et al. (Eds.): DDDAS 2020, LNCS 12312, pp. 337–344, 2020.
https://doi.org/10.1007/978-3-030-61725-7_39

Fig. 1. Example of a DIRSIG scene using OSM terrain (left), and addition of trees (right) to the scene to occlude the ground terrain. Green represents ground vegetation and grey/white is paved roads. (Color figure online)

position. For example, an airborne camera viewing a road network from a non-nadir viewing angle may not have direct line of sight on the road if nearby buildings and vegetation are obscuring the road. If road material spectra (asphalt, concrete) are not detected in a region where OSM claims a road exists, we infer the ground terrain in that region is occluded by an object that interrupts the airborne cameras line of sight, as shown in Fig. 1.

Our initial estimate of a simulated region using OSM contains information on a limited set of surface terrain materials such as asphalt and grass, which can then be confirmed or rejected with real image observations (Fig. 2). In a DDDAS sense the executing application is DIRSIG and new imagery are used to modify the DIRSIG inputs to modify the scene. We use the OSM information for constructing a scene and modify the scene with objects, like trees, to occlude the ground (Fig. 1). The proposed process will aid in object tracking systems from remote imagery, where objects moving in and out of occluded regions in a scene limits tracking performance. This paper considers the occlusion challenge in the task of detecting and tracking vehicles from a remote imaging perspective and uses scene simulation to overcome some of the challenge.

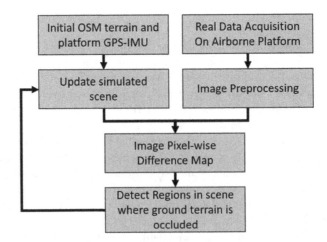

Fig. 2. Proposed framework for scene occlusion identification, with focus on roads and objects that may occlude the road network.

2 Related Work

Hang *et al.* used attention-aided CNN's (spectral and spatial sub-networks) for hypersepctral image classification of urban environments using the HyRANK dataset [5]. For moving object detection in aerial imagery, Palaniappan *et al.* utilizes background subtraction and depth mapping of tall structures that may occlude moving objects to reduce false positives due to parallax [10].

Since there are no publicly available video-rate hyperspectral datasets, simulated hyperspectral imagery is a viable method for constructing a hyperspectral dataset with a high framerate. There are handful of software approaches capable of creating hyperspectral imagery, such as: DIRSIG [2,3], MCScene [12], CHIMES [15], and CameoSim [7]. We use DIRSIG to generate our simulated hyperspcetral imagery because it is a physics based renderer with an established history of publications, and it can accurately model radiation propagation through atmospheric modeling with MODTRAN [1].

Han *et al.* used DIRSIG to adjust atmospheric and environmental conditions for physics based data augmentation of simulated remote sensing imagery to train CNN's in vehicle detection [4]. Uzkent *et al.* modeled vehicle motion through a DIRSIG urban scene at various observation altitudes for object detection and tracking [14]. Kemker *et al.* used a DIRSIG desert scene to increase performance for semantic segmentation applications [6]. AeroRIT annotated all pixels in a hyperspectral aerial flight line over a college campus, initiating a baseline for use in hyperspectral semantic segmentation[11]. Mulhollan *et al.* collected the hyperspectral paint signature of over 450 vehicles using a calibrated drone mounted hyperspectral sensor, to aid in creating simulated hyperspectral imagery with a wide variety of vehicle reflectances [8].

3 On-the-Fly Adaptations

Detecting and tracking a target vehicle with hyperspectral imaging through congested streets in an urban environment is a complex task. To aid in the task, we propose to utilize a-priori knowledge of the scene along with raw imagery to obtain additional geometric information from a 3-D perspective (**Solution 1: Dynamic Metadata Integration**). Metadata resources such as OpenStreetMap provide us with geo-rectified road layouts and land cover materials, which can assist in detecting occluded regions and provide probable locations for an occluded vehicle to reappear. The OpenStreetMap geographical land cover information initializes our scene, and the simulated model of the scene will update in regions of the scene where incoming real data are significantly different than the existing simulated model. Other sources of information such as the position and orientation of the imaging platform, position of the sun in the sky, and updated weather reports, all provide valuable information in predicting the expected spectral signature of the vehicle of interest.

3.1   Tackling Atmospheric Changes

A persistent bottleneck in object detection and tracking is the public availability of hypersepctral data. Hyperspectral cameras that can collect data at approximate video frame rates are rare and obtaining hyperspectral images from an airborne platform is costly and limited to flights in optimal weather conditions. Using physics based simulated imagery is a pragmatic method of acquiring a large hyperspectral video dataset of vehicles travelling through an urban environment. We use DIRSIG to generate our simulated hyperspectral imagery. This can alleviate data limitations and 1) provide pixel-wise ground truth data of all contents in the scene, 2) control for biases that often persist in real image data (such as weather condition and object orientation), and 3) provide a capability to create a scene with multiple imaging modalities. A simulated dataset also provides an automated emthod to tag environment based events such as the vehicle being occluded, shadowed, or contain glint, which we expect will make vehicle detection and tracking performance less dependent on atmospheric and environmental conditions.

Figure 3 demonstrates the need to dynamically adjust the expected spectral signature of the vehicle as the scene changes over time. We observe a target vehicle in simulated hyperspectral imagery under two different weather conditions and five different airborne platform observation angles. Sunny afternoon observations of the light blue vehicle's spectral radiance are shown in orange, and same vehicle's spectral radiance observed in partly cloudy weather is shown in blue. The large difference in the signal amplitude demonstrates the dependence of target appearance on the illumination conditions (weather) and the angle at which the target is observed. Thus, it is important to update the expected target vehicle spectral radiance based on a-priori knowledge of the scene to improve performance of hyperspectral vehicle detection (**Solution 2:** Dynamic Signal Adaptation).

3.2   Dynamic Scene Reconstruction

Instead of an exhaustive training approach where a large hyperspectral dataset is collected of hundreds of vehicles from countless illumination conditions, observation angles, and occlusion events, we propose a DDDAS framework that utilizes physics based simulated hyperspectral imagery to predict how a target vehicle would appear to a real airborne imaging platform. We demonstrate that a physics based approach to hyperspectral vehicle detection can reliably locate a vehicle in complex urban environments, where illumination changes and occlusion events can often occur.

For occlusion detection, we first use OSM and the IMU-GPS positioning data of the aerial hyperspectral imaging platform to create a bare physics based simulated scene, where only on the ground materials such as grass, roads, walkways, and building footprints are geo-spatially placed based on OSM tagging. We simulate our image to look as if there were no vehicles or vertical occluding objects such as trees or buildings present in the scene. We ignore the land topography

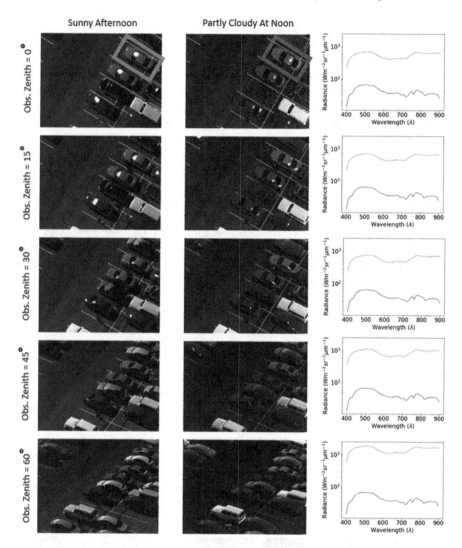

Fig. 3. Demonstration of a vehicle's spectral radiance dependence on atmospheric/weather conditions and image observation angle. It is also shown that expected glint on the vehicle can be modeled with accurate simulations of atmospheric conditions and observation angle.

and use a planar surface to represent the ground for simplicity, but provisions are available to account for major changes in the topography.

In the real world, our airborne imaging platform collects a hyperspectral image of the scene, which may include any number of vehicles and occluding objects that are currently not populated in our physics based model. We update the position and orientation of our simulated platform to best match with the latest position of the real image platform when the last frame was captured. We also process the data to geo-rectify the image and convert the pixel values from digital counts to physical units such as spectral radiance (**Solution 3:** Dynamic Scene Renderings).

To convert the data to physical units, we perform a lab calibration of the sensor to measure its spectral responsivity curve. The spectral responsivity curve paired with updated capture parameters on the airborne platform such as integration time, dwell time, and dark current provide enough information to calculate sensor reaching radiance

$$L_\lambda = (DC_i - DC_{dark}) \cdot \frac{E_\lambda}{DC} \cdot \frac{1}{\pi}, \tag{1}$$

Where L_λ is spectral radiance at the sensor, $\frac{E_\lambda}{DC}$ is the spectral irradiance per digital count obtained through a lab measurement of the sensor's responsivity curve, and DC_i and DC_{dark} are digital counts with incident light and dark current respectively.spectral calibration of the sensor and converting image data to physical units such as spectral radiance allows us to compare our simulated physics based image with the imagery captured with a real hyperspectral sensor.

4   Results

To detect and track a vehicle using its spectral radiance in a scene containing occulsions, we use a DDDAS framework to predict occluded regions in the scene and update where and how we expect the target vehicle to look based on our knowledge of the scene. Predicting occluded regions in a scene is an iterative process as more data are collected. We provide a visualization of how the simulated model of the scene can update through new observations by using a simulation as an example. In Fig. 4 we show the ground truth change detection from the initial OSM landcover simulation alongside a supervised classifier spectral angle mapping image for change detection. The spectral classes used are asphalt and vegetation with the spectral data of these classes sourced from real hyperspectral imagery acquired from the same geometric location of the simulated scene.

Fig. 4. Simulated DIRSIG scene with trees (left) and an occlusion and shadow mask ground truth image (center) showing all occluded and shadowed pixels in the scene in white, with spectral angle classification used to detect change between OSM terrain and the simulated image.

To evaluate object detection and tracking performance in dynamic adapting environment that is full of occlusions, we construct a simulated dataset that contains labeled ground truth information such as the paint color, vehicle make and model, the location of the vehicle using bounding boxes, and also we tag if the vehicle is occluded or visible for each image frame. This simulated dataset is useful to reinforce the logic of occluded objects such as vehicles because it provides examples of vehicles that exist but are not currently visible due to occlusion. We can utilize this simulated dataset along with our existing knowledge of the scene (road networks and occluded regions) to learn where to look in the image to redetect an occluded object, and with a DDDAS feedback loop can guide the airborne platform to a new location in the sky where it has a higher probability of detecting the object unoccluded.

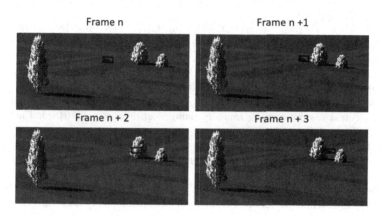

Fig. 5. Ground truth bounding boxes of a target vehicle moving through a simulated scene with occlusions caused by trees. This provides ground truth location of vehicles that are not directly observable due to line of sight obscurations.

5 Conclusion

We use a DDDAS approach to dynamically update a physics based hyperspectral simulated scene to the presence of occluded regions as new image information and metadata are provided. Detecting occluded regions in a scene aids object tracking and detection applications in complex urban environments, where moving objects vacillate between being obscured and visible. For hyperspectral detection of vehicles, we use simulated imagery to predict the expected signature of the vehicle's surface with atmospheric modeling and known geometric position of the imaging platform. We also construct a labeled simulated hyperspectral dataset with bounding boxes around each vehicle present in the scene, including ground truth location of vehicles that are occluded and undetectable in the raw imagery. This dataset will be used to train dynamically adapting detection algorithms to make vehicle detection and tracking applications more robust to occlusions, and in DDDAS framework can reposition an airborne sensor to a line of sight where the target vehicle is no longer occluded.

References

1. Berk, A., Conforti, P., Kennett, R., Perkins, T., Hawes, F., Bosch, J.: MODTRAN®6: A major upgrade of the MODTRAN®radiative transfer code, pp. 1–4, March 2014. https://doi.org/10.1109/WHISPERS.2014.8077573
2. Goodenough, A.A., Brown, S.D.: Dirsig 5: core design and implementation. In: Algorithms and Technologies for Multispectral, Hyperspectral, and Ultraspectral Imagery XVIII. vol. 8390, p. 83900H. International Society for Optics and Photonics (2012)
3. Goodenough, A.A., Brown, S.D.: Dirsig5: next-generation remote sensing data and image simulation framework. IEEE J. Sel. Top. Appl. Earth Obs. Remote Sens. 10(11), 4818–4833 (2017)
4. Han, S., et al.: Efficient generation of image chips for training deep learning algorithms. In: Automatic Target Recognition XXVII. vol. 10202, p. 1020203. International Society for Optics and Photonics (2017)
5. Hang, R., Li, Z., Liu, Q., Ghamisi, P., Bhattacharyya, S.S.: Hyperspectral image classification with attention aided CNNs (2020)
6. Kemker, R., Salvaggio, C., Kanan, C.: Algorithms for semantic segmentation of multispectral remote sensing imagery using deep learning. ISPRS J. Photogram. Remote Sens. 145, 60–77 (2018)
7. Moorhead, I.R., et al.: CAMEO-SIM: a physics-based broadband scene simulation tool for assessment of camouflage, concealment, and deception methodologies. Opt. Eng. 40, 1896–1905 (2001)
8. Mulhollan, Z., Rangnekar, A., Bauch, T., Hoffman, M.J., Vodacek, A.: Calibrated vehicle paint signatures for simulating hyperspectral imagery and Video Processing (2020). arXiv: Image
9. OpenStreetMap contributors: Planet dump retrieved from (2017) https://planet.osm.org. https://www.openstreetmap.org
10. Palaniappan, K., et al.: Moving object detection for vehicle tracking in wide area motion imagery using 4d filtering. In: 2016 23rd International Conference on Pattern Recognition (ICPR), pp. 2830–2835 (2016)
11. Rangnekar, A., Mokashi, N., Ientilucci, E., Kanan, C., Hoffman, M.J.: Aerorit: a new scene for hyperspectral image analysis (2019). arXiv preprint arXiv:1912.08178
12. Richtsmeier, S.C., Berk, A., Bernstein, L.S., Adler-Golden, S.M.: A 3-dimensional radiative-transfer hyperspectral image simulator for algorithm validation (2001)
13. Schott, J.R., Brown, S.D., Raqueno, R.V., Gross, H.N., Robinson, G.: An advanced synthetic image generation model and its application to multi/hyperspectral algorithm development. Can. J. Remote Sens. 25(2), 99–111 (1999)
14. Uzkent, B., Rangnekar, A., Hoffman, M.J.: Tracking in aerial hyperspectral videos using deep kernelized correlation filters. IEEE Trans. Geosci. Remote Sens. 57(1), 449–461 (2018)
15. Zahidi, U.A., Yuen, P.W., Piper, J., Godfree, P.S.: An end-to-end hyperspectral scene simulator with alternate adjacency effect models and its comparison with CameoSim. Remote Sens. 12(1), 74 (2020)

PNEUMON: A DDDAS Framework to Detect Fatigue and Dyspnea in COPD

Varun Kanal[1(✉)], Andrew Miller[1], Diego Vester[1], Jackson Liller[1],
Maria Kyrarini[1], Glenn Wylie[2], Michael J. Falvo[3], and Fillia Makedon[1]

[1] Computer Science and Engineering Department,
University of Texas at Arlington, Arlington, TX 76019, USA
{varun.kanal,andrew.miller2,diego.guerrerovester,
jackson.liller}@mavs.uta.edu,
{maria.kyrarini,makedon}@uta.edu
[2] Rocco Ortenzio Neuroimaging Center,
Kessler Foundation, West Orange, NJ 07052, USA
gwylie@kesslerfoundation.org
[3] War Related Illness and Injury Study Center Veterans Affairs,
East Orange 07018, USA
michael.falvo@va.gov

Abstract. Chronic Obstructive Pulmonary Disease (COPD) is one of
the major pulmonary diseases and a leading cause of morbidity and mortality worldwide. Although there is no cure for COPD, it can be managed
by medication and rehabilitation. Therefore, it is important to monitor
the progression of the disease. In this paper, we propose a framework
to detect and study the symptoms of COPD using multiple physiological sensors. We focus on two main symptoms dyspnea and fatigue. As
there are two types of fatigue physical and cognitive, their detection and
sensor fusion pose a challenge. To address this, we employ the Dynamic
Data-Driven Application System (DDDAS) paradigm that enables us to
collect and analyze data in real-time.

Keywords: COPD · Sensors · Physiological signals · Fatigue · Human
modeling

1 Introduction

Climate changes, increasing pollution, and various biological factors have
adversely impacted human respiratory health and made it even more important to find efficient ways of detecting, monitoring, and treating this condition.
Among respiratory diseases, Chronic Obstructive Pulmonary Disease (COPD)
is one of the most prevalent, affecting 16 million people in the USA [3]. The
symptoms of COPD can be as common as a cough or as severe as wheezing.
COPD consists of two diseases, emphysema, and chronic bronchitis [14]. While
the disease is not curable, its symptoms can be controlled with early diagnosis

© Springer Nature Switzerland AG 2020
F. Darema et al. (Eds.): DDDAS 2020, LNCS 12312, pp. 345–352, 2020.
https://doi.org/10.1007/978-3-030-61725-7_40

and appropriate tracking. Most of the time, the symptoms are misdiagnosed as "smoker's cough".

One important symptom of COPD is dyspnea. Dyspnea can be described as a subjective experience of breathing discomfort [20]. It has been found that including dyspnea in the test for mortality for people suffering from COPD provides better insights into the 5-year survival rate than objective measures of lung function [16]. Dyspnea is such an ingrained symptom of COPD that the anxiety of an impending dyspnea episode has been suggested to be a biomarker for dyspnea events [5].

An important aspect of activities of daily living (ADL) is fatigue. Fatigue is often a result of excessive physical or mental exertion [13]. Among other factors, fatigue plays a vital role in the quality of life in patients with COPD [8]. It has been found that using fatigue as a biomarker in COPD gives a strong indication of hospitalization risk [17]. Fatigue can be broadly classified into two types, physical and cognitive. Historically, these two have been studied independently, but in the real world, these two may co-occur and it is an open problem as to how they impact human performance, separately or jointly. Therefore, it is important to study the effect of both types of fatigue on the body and the interaction between the two under COPD, as the disease severity changes.

Studies have been done into COPD by monitoring patient's respiratory function through their inhalation and exhalation. Some studies have analyzed chemical information of the exhaled breath. Gas arrays [9] and systems with a pattern recognition algorithm like E-Nose [7] have been studied for this application. While these methods have their advantages, a prominent limitation is that they are sensitive to factors such as humidity and temperature. E-Nose requires that the subjects refrain from eating and drinking for at least 12 h before the experiment. An approach that was well received by elderly subjects was remote inhaler monitors [21]. Increased albuterol use captured by the sensor was associated with self-reported episodes of moderate-to-severe exacerbation. The use of computer vision in the monitoring of the most important physiological parameters allows the patient to move more freely without concern for external perturbations. The disadvantages that exist would be a heightened risk of signal noise, loss of subtle physiological data, and discontinuous data sets from the subject's movement [6].

Studies into recording breathing activity using wearable sensors have also been done. Pandian et al. [18] presented a comprehensive wearable smart vest designed to help with the overall assessment of the wearer's health. The vest analyzed multi-sensory data and found a varying degree of success concerning medical accuracy. Another way of measuring respiratory activity using capacitive sensors was presented by Naranjo-Hernández et al. [15]. The results from the study provided preliminary validation for this type of wearable respiratory rate monitoring system. Perriot et al. [19] presents a network of collaborative wearable sensors, for monitoring respiratory events through the daily activities and clinical evaluations of COPD patients.

In this paper, we propose PNEUMON (Greek for lung), a novel computational system to detect the dyspnea, cognitive, and physical fatigue in patients with COPD. This will then be used to study the relationship between cognitive and physical fatigue under acute dyspnea condition. To this end, the framework would need to perform the following three functions, (1) detect physical fatigue, (2) detect cognitive fatigue, and (3) detect dyspnea. PNEUMON relies on the data being extracted by multiple physiological sensors. Some sensors are common for all the detection tasks, while other sensors are unique to a particular detection task. This creates a challenge to model such a dynamic human-centric system. The system needs to adapt based on human activity/behavioral data changes over time. It also needs to account for the variation of the types and the level of fatigue while being able to predict and minimize the occurrence of dyspnea events.

The Dynamic Data-Driven Applications Systems (DDDAS) paradigm is employed as it is perfectly suited to handle such challenges [25]. Using the DDDAS paradigm this framework performs the three detection tasks by analyzing each grouping of sensors and providing personalized feedback to the user. The novelty of this system is that it is a unified system that detects dyspnea, physical, and cognitive fatigue while providing the ability to study the relationship between them.

2   Sensor Suit

The PNEUMON system relies on data collected from multiple sensors. For this, we designed a sensor suit (Fig. 1) that provides a unified approach to sensor management. This suit allows the user to wear the sensors without performing individual sensor placement. The suit is a compression-type shirt within which the sensors are embedded. This suit is designed such that the sensors can be easily removed thus making it possible to wash and maintain the shirt and upgrade if needed. The sensors used in the shirt are a part of the toolkit manufactured by Plux [2]. From this toolkit Electrocardiogram (ECG), Electromyogram (EMG), Electrodermal Activity (EDA), breathing band, and oximeter were embedded in the shirt. This toolkit also comes with a base station to provide a bridge between the sensors and the data collection unit. In this setup, EMG will be attached to the quadriceps femoris muscle in the leg. The suit is also integrated with a microphone array that collects breathing sounds from the lungs. The microphone array consists of four Adafruit 1713 Microphones [12] that are connected to an Arduino Nano 3.3 microcontroller [1] that has the role of a base station. Along with the integrated sensors, the setup also contains an Electroencephalogram (EEG) sensor manufactured by MUSE [4] is used during the assessment of cognitive fatigue.

3   The PNEUMON Framework

The PNEUMON system detects dyspnea, physical, and cognitive fatigue. Using this information the relationship between dyspnea and the two fatigues will be studied. As explained before, fatigue is an important symptom of COPD.

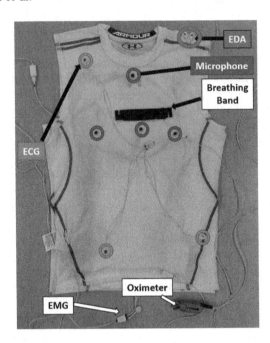

Fig. 1. The prototype of the Sensor Suit (Inside Out View): Sensors are embedded in the shirt which will be in contact with the user's torso

Therefore, the study of this relationship is important as this may give us insight into the progression of the disease and to monitor treatment response. Figure 2 shows the system architecture that uses the DDDAS paradigm [11]. Physiological signals like ECG, EDA, breathing patterns, peripheral oxygen saturation (SpO_2), breathing sounds, EEG, and EMG signals are collected. Although most sensors are common for all detection tasks, some may not be applicable for individual tasks. For example, EMG is not applicable while detecting cognitive fatigue.

The user is also given feedback about their physiological states such as their current heart rate and breathing rate. These constraints create a problem for sensor fusion and processing. The DDDAS paradigm is used to solve this problem as the paradigm allows us to dynamically assess the user's state in terms of the three conditions and improve the measurement process.

From the available sensors (Sect. 2) all except EMG are processed to detect cognitive fatigue, all except EEG are analyzed to detect physical fatigue and all except EMG and EEG are analyzed to detect dyspnea. EEG, EMG, EDA, and ECG provide information on the physiological functioning of the brain, muscle, sympathetic nerve activity, and heart, respectively. SpO_2 gives information about the oxygen level in the blood, therefore, indicating the oxygen saturation in the body. Breathing signals and sounds indicate the mechanical changes in the breathing pattern. Processing of EEG signals during a cognitively difficult task is particularly important as it gives direct information on the changes in brain activity due to the increase in cognitive load [10].

The acquired signals will be processed, and signal features will be extracted from them. Subsequently, the features are passed to a machine learning algorithm that will provide information on dyspnea and both the fatigues using the appropriate set of sensors. For each detection task, some features may be more important than others. For example, while all collected signals for the detection of dyspnea gives information on the presence of dyspnea, features extracted from breathing patterns, and breathing sounds are more important than other signals as they provide direct information about mechanical changes in the lung function. The other signals, however, provide information about the effect of dyspnea on the other systems of the body. To account for this, features extracted from the three signals are given more weight in the machine learning algorithm than the features extracted from the others. This will ensure better detection accuracy even if there is some ambiguity in the less important signals. Along with this, the framework will also gather contextual information like the nature of the current task to identify if conditions for a particular detection task is met. This allows us to adapt the model in real-time using the DDDAS paradigm.

The framework contains a front-end user interface to relay information on the current physiological state of the user as feedback. This interface also provides the user with the means to control the system. The user interface will display data from the sensors and allow test data to be saved and loaded for further analysis. There will be indicators showing which sensors are currently receiving data and indicators showing when cognitive fatigue, physical fatigue, or a dyspnea event has occurred.

The normalized extracted features (see Sect. 4) will be stored in the vector x_i, where $i = 1, \ldots, 7$ represent the features extracted from the EDA, ECG, SpO$_2$, breathing signal, sounds, EEG, and EMG, respectively. Here, w_i represents the weights for the features. Equation (1) presents the detection of Dyspnea D and f_D is a machine learning algorithm that will use as inputs the weighted features. Similarly, Eq. (2) presents the detection of physical fatigue P with f_p as the algorithm, and Eq. (3) presents the detection of cognitive fatigue C with f_c as the algorithm.

$$D = f_d(w_i \times x_i) \ \ where \ \ i \neq 6,7, \ w_4, w_5 > w_1, w_2, w_3 \ and \ \Sigma w_i = 1 \quad (1)$$

$$P = f_p(w_i \times x_i) \ \ where \ \ i \neq 6, \ w_1, w_2, w_7 > w_3, w_4, w_5 \ and \ \Sigma w_i = 1 \quad (2)$$

$$C = f_c(w_i \times x_i) \ \ where \ \ i \neq 7, \ w_6 > w_1, w_2, w_3, w_4, w_5 \ and \ \Sigma w_i = 1 \quad (3)$$

4   Experimental Protocol

To validate the framework, a pilot study will be conducted with healthy participants. This study is designed to induce dyspnea events and study the effect of dyspnea events on fatigue. The study will be conducted on 50 participants which will have the necessary approval by the Institutional Review Board (IRB). The participants will be separated into two groups, healthy individuals and individuals suffering from COPD.

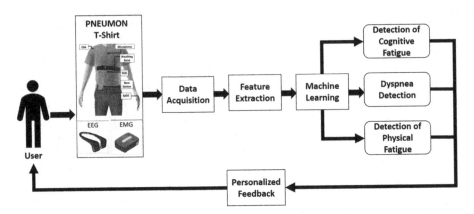

Fig. 2. PNEUMON system: Detects Dyspnea, Physical and Cognitive Fatigue. Provides personalized feedback on the current physiological state.

The pilot study, which will be conducted to validate the proposed framework, consists of four phases. In the first phase, the participants will be asked to perform a cognitively simple task after being fitted with the sensors. This will be the baseline against which the other cognitive phases are compared. Prior to this phase, baseline data will be collected by asking the participant to relax for a minute. This baseline will be used to normalize the signal parameters.

In the second phase, dyspnea and physical fatigue are induced by asking the participant to walk on a treadmill. The participant will be first asked to walk for 3 min at a rate of 1.7 mph and 10% incline (inclination level). Next, they will walk for 3 min at a rate of 2.5 mph and 12% incline. After this, the participant will be asked to stand and recover while data for the recovery period is recorded.

In the third phase, the participant will be asked to perform a cognitively challenging task which will induce cognitive fatigue. In this study, cognitive fatigue will be induced using the N-Back task. In an N-Back task, letters will be presented to the participant in a sequence. If the current letter matches the letter shown N steps back, then the participant will have to perform the instructed task (press a designated button). The N-Back task has been shown to induce cognitive load and cognitive fatigue [22–24]. In phase one, the participant is asked to perform a 0-Back task where the participant will press the button as soon as the target letter is presented. In phase three, they will perform a 2-Back task where the participant will perform the action if the current letter is the same as the letter showed 2 steps back.

In the fourth phase, the participant will be asked to repeat the 0-Back task. This will be used to study the overall effect of physical and cognitive fatigue on the participant. Between each phase, the participant will be asked to fill out a survey designed to extract their subjective level of fatigue.

5   Conclusion

This paper introduced a framework to detect dyspnea, physical, and cognitive fatigue. This framework employed the DDDAS paradigm to handle data fusion and modeling complexity. This, therefore, provides an "All-in-one" system to study the relationship between physical and cognitive fatigue under the dyspnea condition. We have also presented a unified sensor hardware and an experimental procedure as a use-case for this framework.

In the future, we will conduct user studies to build a working prototype of the framework and evaluate it with COPD patients.

References

1. Arduinonano. https://www.arduino.cc/en/Guide/ArduinoNano
2. biosignalsplux. https://plux.info/12-biosignalsplux
3. Fighting for Air: Veterans Face Higher Risk for Developing Lung Diseases. https://www.cdc.gov/copd/index.html
4. Meditation Made Easy, June 2020. https://choosemuse.com/
5. Bailey, P.H.: The dyspnea-anxiety-dyspnea cycle - COPD patients' stories of breathlessness: "it's scary/when you can't breathe". Qual. Health Res. **14**(6), 760–778 (2004)
6. Ballal, T., et al.: A pilot study of the nocturnal respiration rates in COPD patients in the home environment using a non-contact biomotion sensor. Physiol. Meas. **35**(12), 2513–2527 (2014)
7. Bofan, M., et al.: Within-day and between-day repeatability of measurements with an electronic nose in patients with COPD. J. Breath Res. **7**(1), 017103 (2013)
8. Breslin, E., et al.: Perception of fatigue and quality of life in patients with COPD. Chest **114**(4), 958–964 (1998)
9. Capuano, R., et al.: COPD diagnosis by a gas sensor array. Proc. Eng. **5**, 484–487 (2010)
10. Chuckravanen, D.: Approximate entropy as a measure of cognitive fatigue: an EEG pilot study. Int. J. Emerg. Trends Sci. Technol. **1**(7), 1036–1042 (2014)
11. Darema, F.: Dynamic data driven applications systems: a new paradigm for application simulations and measurements. In: Bubak, M., van Albada, G.D., Sloot, P.M.A., Dongarra, J. (eds.) ICCS 2004. LNCS, vol. 3038, pp. 662–669. Springer, Heidelberg (2004). https://doi.org/10.1007/978-3-540-24688-6_86
12. Adafruit Industries: Electret microphone amplifier - MAX9814 with auto gain control. https://www.adafruit.com/product/1713
13. Jensen, S., Given, B.A.: Fatigue affecting family caregivers of cancer patients. Cancer Nurs. **14**(4), 181–187 (1991)
14. Mannino, D.M., Homa, D.M., Akinbami, L.J., Ford, E.S., Redd, S.C.: Chronic obstructive pulmonary disease surveillance-United States, 1971–2000. Respir. Care **47**(10), 1184–1199 (2002)
15. Naranjo-Hernández, D., et al.: Smart vest for respiratory rate monitoring of COPD patients based on non-contact capacitive sensing. Sensors (Switzerland) **18**(7), 2144 (2018)
16. Nishimura, K., Izumi, T., Tsukino, M., Oga, T.: Dyspnea is a better predictor of 5-year survival than airway obstruction in patients with COPD. Chest **121**(5), 1434–1440 (2002)

17. Paddison, J.S., Effing, T.W., Quinn, S., Frith, P.A.: Fatigue in COPD: association with functional status and hospitalisations. Eur. Respir. J. **41**(3), 565–570 (2013)
18. Pandian, P., et al.: Smart vest: wearable multi-parameter remote physiological monitoring system. Med. Eng. Phys. **30**(4), 466–477 (2008). http://www.sciencedirect.com/science/article/pii/S1350453307000975
19. Perriot, B., Argod, J., Pepin, J.L., Noury, N.: A network of collaborative sensors for the monitoring of COPD patients in their daily life. In: 2013 IEEE 15th International Conference on e-Health Networking, Applications and Services, Healthcom 2013 (Healthcom), pp. 299–302 (2013)
20. Society, A.T., et al.: Dyspnea: mechanisms, assessment, and management: a consensus statement. Am. J. Respir. Crit. Care Med. **159**, 321–340 (1999)
21. Sumino, K., et al.: Use of a remote inhaler monitoring device to measure change in inhaler use with chronic obstructive pulmonary disease exacerbations. J. Aerosol. Med. Pulm.y Drug Deliv. **31**(3), 191–198 (2018)
22. Wylie, G., Dobryakova, E., DeLuca, J., Chiaravalloti, N., Essad, K., Genova, H.: Cognitive fatigue in individuals with traumatic brain injury is associated with caudate activation. Sci. Rep. **7**(1), 1–12 (2017)
23. Wylie, G., et al.: Fatigue in gulf war illness is associated with tonically high activation in the executive control network. NeuroImage: Clin. **21**, 101641 (2019)
24. Wylie, G., Genova, H., DeLuca, J., Dobryakova, E.: The relationship between outcome prediction and cognitive fatigue: a convergence of paradigms. Cogn. Affect. Behav. Neurosci. **17**(4), 838–849 (2017). https://doi.org/10.3758/s13415-017-0515-y
25. Yeong, H.C., Beeson, R., Namachchivaya, N.S., Perkowski, N., Sauer, P.W.: Dynamic data-driven adaptive observations in data assimilation. In: Handbook of Dynamic Data Driven Applications Systems, p. 47 (2018)

Panels

Impact of DDDAS/InfoSymbiotics in the Industrial Sector

Daniel Abramovitch[1], Sandeep Gogineni[2], Cory Kays[3(✉)], Chung-Sheng Li[4],
Jose Moreira[5], Chitra Sivanandam[6], and Nurali Virani[7]

[1] Agilent Technologies, Santa Clara, CA 95051, USA
[2] Information Systems Laboratories, La Jolla, CA 92037, USA
[3] Cornerstone Research, San Francisco, CA 94111, USA
kaysca@crgrp.com
[4] PriceWaterhouseCooper, New York 10017, USA
[5] IBM, TJWatson Research, Yorktown Heights, NY 10598, USA
[6] Science Applications International Corporation (SAIC), Reston, VA 20190, USA
[7] GE, Boston, MA 02210, USA

Abstract. This panel convenes representatives from several industries in the information technology, aerospace, power, manufacturing and finance sectors, who will address how advances in modeling and prediction methods, and decision support for complex systems, as well as the underlying information technology infrastructures, can advance the capabilities in their respective sectors. Part of the discussion will include research and technology development within their own organizations as well as the broader academic and research laboratories communities, and potential for collaborative and synergistic advances across the industry, academe, and federal sectors can enhance the opportunities for advances and capabilities sought.

Keywords: Industry panel · Modeling · Prediction

© Springer Nature Switzerland AG 2020
F. Darema et al. (Eds.): DDDAS 2020, LNCS 12312, p. 355, 2020.
https://doi.org/10.1007/978-3-030-61725-7_41

AI/ML Applications for Aerospace and Defense

Kishore K. Reddy[1], Amit Surana[1], Paul Kodzwa[1]([✉]), Shane Zable[2],
Richard LaRowe[3], Eric Brewer[4], and Steven Burd[5]

[1] Raytheon Technologies Research Center, East Hartford, CT 06108, USA
{kishore.reddy,paul.kodzwa}@rtx.com
[2] Raytheon Intelligence and Space, Arlington, VA 22209, USA
[3] Raytheon Missile and Defense, Tucson, AZ 85756, USA
[4] Collins Aerospace, Cedar Rapids, IA 52498, USA
[5] Pratt and Whitney, East Hartford, CT 06108, USA

Abstract. The vast majority of leading executives with aerospace and defense industries expect artificial intelligence (AI) technologies to influence every part of their operations over the next decade. Security leaders have recognized that the human cognitive band-width is emerging as the most severe constraint for data utilization. For this reason, governments need big data, AI and machine learning (ML) to give its analysts the edge in real-time response. Similarly, commercial aerospace is actively seeking AI "killer apps" to revolutionize operations through reducing fuel consumption, accelerating pilot training, innovative product designs and better customer service. For ex-ample, as a leading aerospace and defense corporation, Raytheon Technologies (RTX) is actively exploring the transformative capabilities of AI and ML. This panel discussion will present examples and experiences across all RTX business units.

Keywords: Artificial intelligence · Machine learning · Revolutionizing aerospace and defense

© Springer Nature Switzerland AG 2020
F. Darema et al. (Eds.): DDDAS 2020, LNCS 12312, p. 356, 2020.
https://doi.org/10.1007/978-3-030-61725-7_42

Future Direction of DDDAS/InfoSymbiotics and Collaborations with Related Initiatives

Erik Blasch[1]([✉]), Robert Bohn[2], Jahla Gato[3], Edward McLarney[4], Jasmin Ratchford[5], and Sonia Sachs[6]

[1] Air Force Office of Scientific Research, Arlington, VA 22203, USA
[2] National Institute of Standards and Technology, Gaithersburg, MD 20878, USA
[3] Australian Space Agency, Adelaide SA5000, Australia
[4] National Aeronautics and Space Administration, Hampton, VA 23666, USA
[5] Department of Homeland Security, Washington, DC 20002, USA
[6] Department of Energy, Washington, DC 20585, USA

Abstract. This panel brings together representatives from several funding agencies, who will address programmatic activities within their respective missions, which can support research and technology development in areas addressed in DDDAS2020 as well as those employing the DDDAS paradigm. Also, the panel will address potential for collaborations and synergism across agencies to support of basic and applied research and technology development in critical areas identified at the DDDAS2020 conference. Utilizing knowledge of recent trends, the panel will discuss programmatic changes, development efforts, and research opportunities across the federal sector, industry and academe, in the US and internationally.

Keywords: Programmatic activities · Technology development · Collaborations

Correction to: Dynamic Data Driven Applications Systems

Frederica Darema⊙, Erik Blasch⊙, Sai Ravela⊙, and Alex Aved⊙

Correction to:
F. Darema et al. (Eds.): *Dynamic Data Driven Application Systems*, **LNCS 12312,**
https://doi.org/10.1007/978-3-030-61725-7

The book was inadvertently published with a typo in the main title on the cover and in the frontmatter as "Dynamic Data Driven Application Systems" whereas it should be "Dynamic Data Driven Applications Systems". The main title has been corrected in the book.

The updated version of the book can be found at
https://doi.org/10.1007/978-3-030-61725-7

© Springer Nature Switzerland AG 2020
F. Darema et al. (Eds.): DDDAS 2020, LNCS 12312, p. C1, 2020.
https://doi.org/10.1007/978-3-030-61725-7_44

Author Index

Printed in the United States
By Bookmasters